MAYA® PLUGIN POWER

MARK JENNINGS SMITH

Charles River Media
A part of Course Technology, Cengage Learning

COURSE TECHNOLOGY
CENGAGE Learning™

Australia, Brazil, Japan, Korea, Mexico, Singapore, Spain, United Kingdom, United States

COURSE TECHNOLOGY
CENGAGE Learning

Maya® Plugin Power

Mark Jennings Smith

Publisher and General Manager, Course Technology PTR: Stacy L. Hiquet

Associate Director of Marketing: Sarah Panella

Manager of Editorial Services: Heather Talbot

Marketing Manager: Jordan Casey

Executive Editor: Kevin Harreld

Project Editor: Marta Justak

Technical Reviewer: Les Pardew

CRM Editorial Services Coordinator: Jen Blaney

Copy Editor: Ruth Saavedra

Interior Layout: Jill Flores

Cover Designer: Tyler Creative Services

DVD-ROM Producer: Brandon Penticuff

Indexer: Valerie Haynes Perry

Proofreader: Sue Boshers

Library of Congress Control Number: 2007939359

ISBN-13: 978-1-58450-530-3

ISBN-10: 1-58450-530-3

Course Technology
25 Thomson Place
Boston, MA 02210
USA

Cengage Learning is a leading provider of customized learning solutions with office locations around the globe, including Singapore, the United Kingdom, Australia, Mexico, Brazil, and Japan. Locate your local office at: **international.cengage.com/region**

Cengage Learning products are represented in Canada by Nelson Education, Ltd.

For your lifelong learning solutions, visit **courseptr.com**

Visit our corporate website at **cengage.com**

Printed in the United States of America
1 2 3 4 5 6 7 11 10 09 08

DEDICATION

This book is dedicated to Robin Daphne Rhein. While attempting to avoid the usual cliché, this book would literally, in every sense of the word, not have been possible, without the doubtless and bottomless support and love of Robin Rhein. I am passionately indebted and beholden for her constant, unwavering, and enthusiastic presence.

ACKNOWLEDGMENTS

A book such as this would never rest upon a shelf without the help and support of many people. There are a few people that deserve my deepest gratitude.

I am completely indebted to my project manager, Marta Justak. Marta's cool head, compassion, understanding, professionalism, and seemingly limitless patience made a huge and invaluable difference in the completion of this book.

A book project is sometimes fraught with unknowns. My genuine appreciation must also go to Jennifer Blaney at Cengage Learning for her steely, unending patience and for quelling those unknowns. Thanks also must go to Ruth Saavedra for her copyediting skills and removing my clumsiness. Thanks as well go to Jenifer Niles for seeing value in the subject matter. I am equally grateful to Les Pardew for his technical expertise and Brandon Penticuff for his work on the DVD.

Additionally, a small group of people worked diligently behind the scenes to help with this endeavor. I may never have met them, but like silent and stealthy elves I am conscious of their hard work and vital importance to this book. I am grateful for their unrequited assistance.

There were also several people who contributed guidance, words, know-how, mojo, life experience, imagery, and software support to this effort. My thanks go out to Gerard Banel at Syflex, Renee Lamri and Chris Ford at Disney/Pixar, Lou Badju and Patrik Martin at Craft Animations, André Kutscherauer for an image that is very apropos, Maureen Squillace at Animal Logic, Bob Bennett at Luxology, Jim Battersby at Blast Code, Nicole van der Burg at Next Limit, Matthias Richter at ticket01, Janet Podell and Raf Anzovin at Anzovin Studio, Joe Alter, Ty Shelton, Marco Chiaravalloti, and Pino Mellace. Sincere gratitude must also go to Perry Harovas at Flashpoint Academy.

I desire to thank my dearest parents, Allen and Patricia Smith, for their huge influence, support, small bags of change, and my introduction to PONG. Thanks also go to Michael and Michelle Smith for their constant and timely safety net, Scott and Patricia Sweigart for Ryan, and Mrs. Mary Kane for the peaceful respite on Mulholland Drive where I renewed my interest in this project.

Finally, my requisite gramercy goes to Mr. Tibidy for his serenity, my doctors on the hill, and to my evil twin for whom I am always on the fence.

ABOUT THE AUTHOR

Mark Jennings Smith is a seasoned artist, animator, and writer residing in Beverly Hills, CA. Mark has been fascinated by CG since 1972, when at age 10 a chance encounter with the first coin-op PONG changed his life. He has contributed to several books and magazines in the 3D area, including a chapter in *Maya: Secrets of the Pros*. He also created cover art for the book and a variety of other titles in the 3D arena. He served as the technical editor for *Mastering Maya Complete 2*, and has taught visual FX and computer animation using Autodesk Maya at New York University. He has consulted and beta-tested dozens of software packages.

His interest in the entertainment field led Mark to establish Digital Drama with partner Perry Harovas in 1994, which focused on computer-generated imagery, animation, digital painting, and special digital visual effects. Digital Drama designed the digital film effects and animation for companies such as Universal Pictures, Trimark Pictures, Fox Home Entertainment, HBO, SHOWTIME, and even Roger Corman himself.

Mark is an accomplished ice carver and garde manger. He has been inspired by the work of William Latham, Yoichiro Kawagichi, Karl Sims, Edward Gorey, Roman Dirge, Jhonen Vasquez, and the Quay brothers. He has lived and worked in New York, Los Angeles, San Diego, and Las Vegas.

Mark can be reached at the book's Web site at www.bigheadedkitty.com. He is currently directing his creative energy toward his first novel, and after a long hiatus, he is looking for work. Maybe he'll direct.

CONTENTS

INTRODUCTION

There is no excellent beauty that hath not some strangeness in the proportion.
Sir Francis Bacon (1561–1626), "Of Beauty"

Those of us in the graphic arts have really cool occupations. We get to be creative every single day. Whether you are in 3D animation, visual effects, gaming, print, or visualization, there never seems to be a lack of creative challenges. That's good. It exercises the brain. It might be hard for the people outside of the profession to be excited about the things that pique our interest. We look at everything with a skewed and oddly appreciative view. We are not necessarily more or less thoughtful of our surroundings than anyone else. We merely dissect the beauty before us for the purposes of recreating it some day. Beauty is in the eye of the beholder, and in our profession, everything has its own splendor. The viscous act of creating muddy footprints across a dusty terrazzo floor, the speedy vibrations and the opaque structure of an insect's wing, or the way a tortoise shell comb passes through wet and dry fur, take on strange and worthy meaning to us.

We are sitting on technologically fertile times. The muscle of today's computers and the software that runs within them is unprecedented. These technologies are a far cry from the days of the postage-stamp-size pixel and weeklong renders. Oddly, this great power only helps slightly. It leads us to tackle more complex problems and create more stunning visuals. It's a vicious cycle, conceived by the left brain to taunt the right. Over the last 30 years in computer graphics, there has always been a looming wish list of goals to surmount. Realistic hair, flowing cloth, the human body in general, fluid dynamics, and real-world lighting are all problems that have seemingly been conquered. One by one, these milestones have been passed by. It's been done with greater speed than we could have ever imagined.

Represented within these pages is a collective set of viable solutions to some of the computer graphics problems we have faced. With good tools at our disposal, we are left to re-create for others, our strangely accurate observations of the world. Nuance is the essence of good animation and visual FX. This nuance comes in the form of light, color texture, motion, and the barely perceptible.

This book was written as an introduction to new tools for your Maya work. My hope is that you will find the possibilities that can help you visualize your own excellent beauty.

CHAPTER

1

INTRODUCTION

In This Chapter

- Extensibility
- What Are Plugins and Why Use Them?
- Why a Plugins Book?
- How Do I Use This Book?
- Installing a Plugin

Next Limit's Maxwell Render creates fantastic photo-realistic renderings by the correct simulation of light. This image, called "Selfillumination," is courtesy of Andre Kutscherauer (http://www.ak3d.de).

EXTENSIBILITY

Maya is an amazing and deep program, the origins of which are steeped in a deep lineage of sources. The very best of technologies was combined from the ground up to bring us, arguably, the best visual effects software around. Whether for creating animation for cartoons or high-end gaming or producing fantastical visuals for film, Maya is the most popular "go to" software package in the industry. It has been said that conservatively 300 man-years of programming went into making Maya what it is today. For all the robust functionality within Maya that allows the end users to visit their imagination, there always seems to be a need for just a little more. How many times have you said to yourself, "I wish there was a way to...," or "Wouldn't it be neat if..." and then set about trying to utilize Maya's tools to accomplish that task. There isn't always time available to find a solution to a problem or invent a work-around. Sometimes it seems as though 10,000 man-years of coding would be unable to satiate the creative needs of the Maya community.

From the first drawing boards of Maya's design, it was wisely decided that it would be "open" to being infinitely user configurable and malleable. This meant freedom for the artist, in a myriad of ways. A technical director (TD) could limit what his production team of artists were focused on by changing the interface to suit the workflow, or even fashioning a new and useful tool that could be integrated within Maya. The marketing prior to the release of Maya 1.0 was all about "extensibility" or, in other words, the ability to be modified by changing or adding features. Maya is open to change, whether you want to organize your own custom "favorite tools" shelf or code your own integrated utility program. The creators fashioned a program that, through the OpenMaya C++ API, Maya's embedded scripting language (MEL) and ultra-configurable user interface (UI), placed all the power in the hands of the users (see Figure 1.1).

FIGURE 1.1 Craft Directors Tools allow the user unprecedented control over a variety of crafts.

What Are Plugins and Why Use Them?

As noted, there are never going to be enough programming hours to keep the imaginative needs of the Maya creative community sated. Maya, like most popular graphics applications in use today, has seen the development of a "third-party" support industry, which has emerged to fill some of the perceived creative voids, as well as introduce new ideas, concepts, and technological solutions to today's visual effects production industry. There is more than one way to "bind and skin a cat," so to speak, and that's where the plugin comes into play. Plugins are meant to be extensions to the host program. The term *plugin* means the ability to "plug into" the main program to provide new and additional functionality to it. This isn't a new concept. Some companies have made their fortunes writing plugins to enhance or append the feature set of other broader programs. Adobe Photoshop is an amazing program in and of itself, which becomes immeasurably more visionary when supported by the army of third-party plugins available for it. This holds true for Maya as well. Maya is much richer when given alternative choices in renderers such as Maxwell Render, as seen in the opening chapter image. Maya is introduced to unique ways to capture motion for wheeled vehicles, cameras, and tanks, as with the Craft Animation series of plugins pictured in Figure 1.1. Maya can even explore the abstract and generate plant life with Xfrog, as seen in Figure 1.2.

FIGURE 1.2 Xfrog 4.3 brings photo-realistic plant and abstract modeling to Maya.

In the creative visual media business of animation, film, television, and design, time is money. The cost of adding a plugin to your studio's pipeline may be the difference between making that project deadline and failing miserably. The incorporation of that third-party plugin might be the fertile solution and saving grace that solves a dilemma or provides that much needed "look" to your work. Maya provides an exhaustive toolset that invites the user to apply creative solutions to production challenges and get the job done. Third-party companies have often built a much "better mousetrap," saving you valuable time and money. The range, depth, and usefulness of a particular plugin can run the gamut from the simple to the complex. The cost of implementing a plugin into the production pipeline may run from free to thousands of dollars, but it may be a cost you can't live without.

WHY A PLUGINS BOOK?

There is a small library of Maya books in the marketplace, but none really addresses the exciting area of third-party plugins. Until now, it has been a woefully neglected category. Here are the main goals of this book.

1. Have fun.
2. Promote ideas and solutions through simple tutorials.
3. Introduce technology that is rarely covered or investigated in Maya publications.
4. Provide supplemental sources for consideration beyond this book.

With all Maya's power, there is a world of additional energy waiting to be "plugged in." Some plugins look to enhance the tools that Maya provides, while others offer complete alternative solutions (dare it be said, better solutions) to Maya's core functions. Certain native operations within various Maya versions are actually implemented as plugin technology in and of themselves. These portions of the program such as Maya Live, Maya Cloth, Maya Fur, and mental ray, among others, are actually part of the core Maya program yet are incorporated as plugins.

This book looks at third-party solutions that are not part of any Autodesk release of Maya. We'll start off this exploration by learning about Syflex, an alternative to Maya Cloth in Chapter 2. We will also be looking at the dynamics of 3D Maya demolition. Megaton and Kiloton from Blast Code, discussed in Chapter 8, is an amazing solution for everything from breaking a glass window pane to blasting a car to bits, as seen in Figure 1.3. It's all very realistic. In Chapter 7 we will delve into software helpers for controlling craft such as missiles, four-wheel vehicles, and helicopters while delivering new and amazing ways of using cameras to shoot these scenes.

Although Maya Unlimited comes with a hair solution, we will explore a very cool plugin from Joe Alter in Chapter 3, which far exceeds the capabilities of Maya Fur pictured in Figure 1.4, and we'll look at novel approaches to solving that fuzzy tribble or bigfoot project. Chapter 5 will take a dip into the frothy, gooey, and wet world of fluid dynamics with Next Limit's RealFlow, seen in Figure 1.5, considered to be some of the best software available for sloshing in a muddy swamp, sailing in turbulent seas, making faucets drip, or even coating a cell phone in chocolate.

FIGURE 1.3 Blast Code's Megaton and Kiloton can bring the power of destruction to Maya.
Image courtesy of Blast Code Software

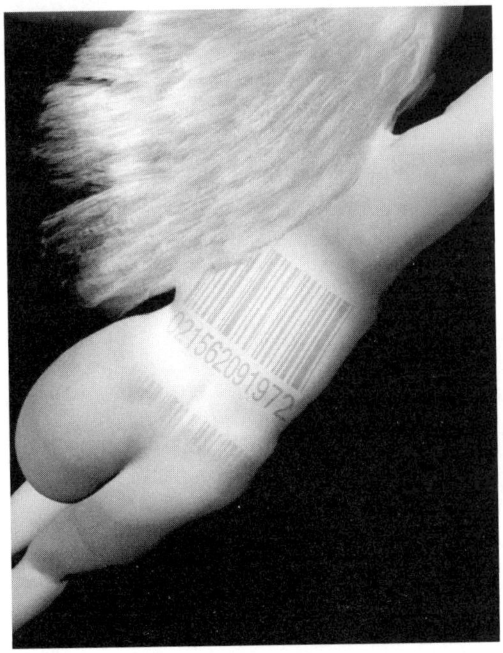

FIGURE 1.4 Joe Alter's Shave and a Haircut adds a new level to computer-generated hair and fur.
Image courtesy of Next Limit Technologies

FIGURE 1.5 Next Limit's RealFlow 4.1 advances Maya with liquids, viscous materials, and more.

We will skim briefly through the precise, strikingly photo-realistic, and deliberately stylized worlds of the alternative renderers available for Maya in Chapter 4. Our investigation in Chapter 10 will lead us to several stand-alone programs and the possibility of implementing them into the Maya workflow. Ultimately, it is best to view this book as a catalyst for stimulating those creative juices. In the process we will discover a variety of very interesting technologies, witness some stimulating samples, and plant a seed for the next time you are seeking a creative solution.

How Do I Use This Book?

This book will by no means be able to cover all the plugins and alternative solutions available, but we hope it will present a wide palette. It is assumed that you have a working knowledge of basic Maya workflow. This book will expose you to concepts through plugins, overviews, and some very simple tutorials. We will be covering some rather complicated concepts, but the complexity will be tamed through an uncomplicated and lighthearted approach. We will not be diving to the extreme depths of any one plugin. Consider this book as a thought-filled briefing, arming you with some food for thought and exciting your imagination. There were several challenges to writing a book about Maya plugins.

What Programs and Plugins to Cover

We decided that covering plugins and programs that provided answers to some very specific requirements in animation and visual effects was best. The diversity of choices ranged from producing computer-generated (CG) water to desktop hand-held motion capture. As the job market grows, there is particular interest in specialized niche artists, who are expert in a particular software package, such as those presented in this book. Appendix A lists a myriad of commercially available plugins for Maya. While not 100 percent comprehensive, the list does feature, with all due diligence, the bulk of known Maya plugin software, past and present. We limited the book to software plugins that are commercially available. This is by no means an indication of the quality of freeware or shareware plugins and scripts that are available. Some of the most unique, innovative, and helpful tools are written and released by the users who know Maya the best. Please check out Appendix A at the end of the book for a variety of sources for these materials.

Versions of the Software Versus the Version of Maya on Which It Runs

It became clear that keeping up with the latest version of the plugin and the latest version of Maya it works with can be tedious. Appendix B addresses each plugin and which versions of Maya they will run on, along with which operating software versions are applicable. Additionally, links and contacts are provided for the latest information available. In deference to completeness, Appendix B lists versions of software that are obsolete or not supported on later versions of Maya but still may prove invaluable to productions that have older seats of Maya in-house. Let's face it—not everyone is working with the current release of Maya or feels the need to disturb a working production pipeline.

Why Does This Book Include Discussions of Some Stand-Alone Software?

While Maya may be the primary 3D software in a production's pipeline, some applications may prove invaluable when used in conjunction with the Maya workflow. We chose to highlight them briefly and expose users to these applications, which might otherwise escape their notice.

While we hope that you read each chapter, this book takes a nonlinear look at a variety of disciplines. Some chapters teach through tutorials while others are used to inform. Each chapter is self-contained and does not build upon the knowledge gained from previous chapters. You won't be confused if you jump from chapter to chapter. This book has been written with the Windows XP version of Maya 8.5 and Maya 2008 running on Microsoft Vista.

Installing a Plugin

Installing a plugin is a pretty standard thing. It is as easy as executing the installer program. Sometimes an installation will ask for the path of Maya's plugin directory.

Most times the standard install of Maya will have the plugin directory in a path similar to the following. This is dependent on where Maya is installed and what version of Maya you are using.

- C:\Program Files\Alias\Maya7.0\bin\plug-ins
- C:\Program Files\Autodesk\Maya8.5\bin\plug-ins

After installation, make sure that the plugin is loaded and recognized by Maya. This can be done by going to the top of the screen in the Maya menus and selecting Window > Setting/Preferences > Plug-in Manager. Make sure that the Loaded box is selected next to the plugin of choice. In the example shown in Figure 1.6, both the Loaded and Auto Load boxes are checked for the selection of the Craft Maya Adapter.mll plugin in the Plugin Manager. This is the listing of the Craft Animation Tools plugin. The Auto Load box should be checked, or you will have to reload the plugin each time you restart Maya.

Each trial plugin will need some sort of demo authorization to use it. These methods will vary and can be found within the plugin documentation.

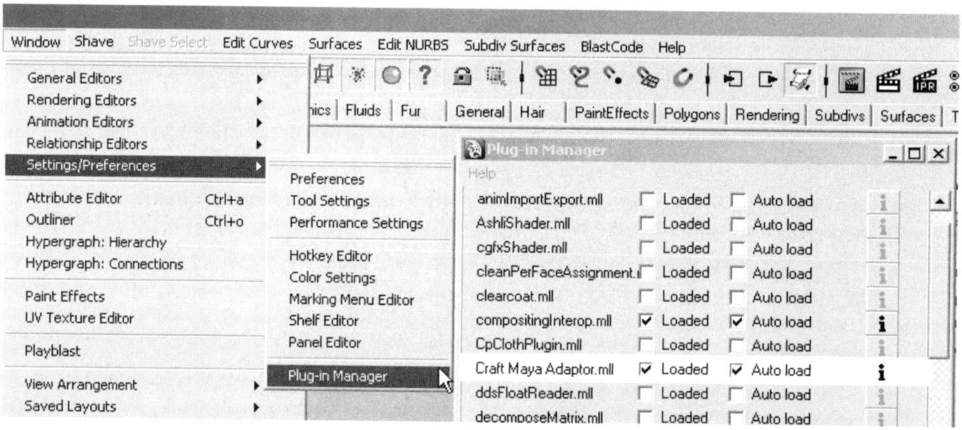

FIGURE 1.6 Check the Plugin Manager to verify that a plugin is loaded for use.

The DVD-ROM

ON THE DVD

The DVD-ROM included with this book has Maya scene files, images, and some animation on it. Look for the DVD-ROM icon within the text that lets you know when there is something available on the DVD. Demo versions are not included on the DVD-ROM. We decided that because the plugins covered in this book run on various operating systems and Maya versions, and because that software is often updated, it was far easier to get the trial plugin via the Web. Appendix A has links to get you to the plugins of your choice.

There is a world of fantastic software out there promising to take your work in Maya to new heights. Let's jump right in.

CHAPTER

2

CLOTH SIMULATION AND MODELING

In This Chapter

- Introduction
- The Quick and Easy Cape
- Object Collision
- 3D Mesh Objects as Cloth Objects
- A Simple Garment

Syflex handles cloth animation with ease. This image is a still from an animation of the curtains being drawn during a storm.

Introduction

In a virtual kingdom, in a virtual land, if the emperor demanded a new set of threads, Maya is able to help. Well, actually that would depend on the version of Maya you are working with. There are two basic flavors of Maya. Autodesk Maya Complete is a robust package, to say the least, whereas Maya Unlimited has all the bells and whistles found in Maya Complete while providing professional artists and animators with extra visual effects magic such as Maya Live, Maya Fluid Effects, Maya Hair, Maya Fur, and, of course, Maya Cloth. If Maya Unlimited is not in your bag of tricks, then the emperor may very well go unclothed.

Thankfully, there is a much better solution on the horizon. Syflex (pronounced sahy-fleks) is a cloth simulator that has been used in Hollywood film because of its amazing power and flexibility. Syflex's origins can be traced to cloth simulation engines originally written for *Final Fantasy: The Spirits Within* and *The Animatrix*. Since that time, Syflex was developed and has lent powerful cloth-generating muscle to dozens of high-profile films. Syflex has become the preferred choice for digital cloth simulation in the industry. It has quickly overshadowed Maya Unlimited cloth's solution because of its power, speed, flexibility (pardon the pun), and ease of use. Syflex is capable of creating very realistic cloth animations. It computes the motion of the cloth by applying forces, constraints, and collisions. The process of animating a cloth is fairly simple.

- Convert a polygonal mesh to a cloth.
- Apply gravity, damping, and other appropriate forces
- Consider collisions with the cloth and other objects.
- Then just let the simulator smoothly compute the animation.

Syflex doesn't require you to be a rocket scientist to use it. Unlike other cloth generating solutions, Syflex doesn't use the sewing archetype. There is no need to sew or stitch together parts of a garment to create a whole article of clothing. Syflex does not work with NURBS, but rather with any polygonal object. This allows tremendous flexibility and begs to be used for effects beyond textile applications. All the functionality in Syflex is flawlessly incorporated into the Maya workflow in its own menu. It is surprising how quickly impressive-looking simulations can be achieved. Syflex is one of those programs that takes the tragically complex and makes it look simple. Although the underlying concepts can be daunting, the actual process of animating a flowing cape or a spinning skirt is rather simple. If you have installed Syflex, let's get started with a very simple and informative example of how rapidly you can accomplish some very impressive results.

The Quick and Easy Cape

Boot up your copy of Maya, and we can begin. It's assumed that you have installed your copy of Syflex. The plugin is very well integrated into the Maya workflow, so it appears as normal as any other set of functions and menus. It appears as a separate

Syflex menu at the top of the screen near the Help Menu, with the rest of Maya's menu selections. It should look similar to Figure 2.1.

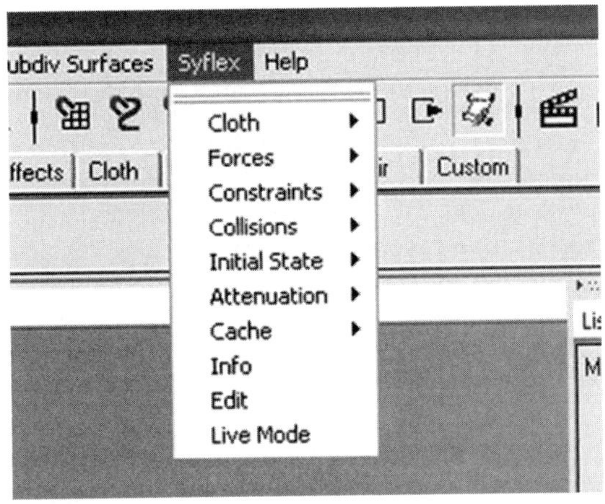

FIGURE 2.1 The opened Syflex menu as it appears in Maya's menu bar.

Let's begin. We will create a cape for a fictional hero named Tartan Man. Create a polygon plane to serve as our cape. Go to Create > Polygon Primitives > Plane and select the options box. Create a plane with the following parameters, as shown in Figure 2.2.

- Width = 30.0
- Height = 20.0
- Subdivisions Along Width = 30
- Subdivisions Along Height = 20
- Axis = Y

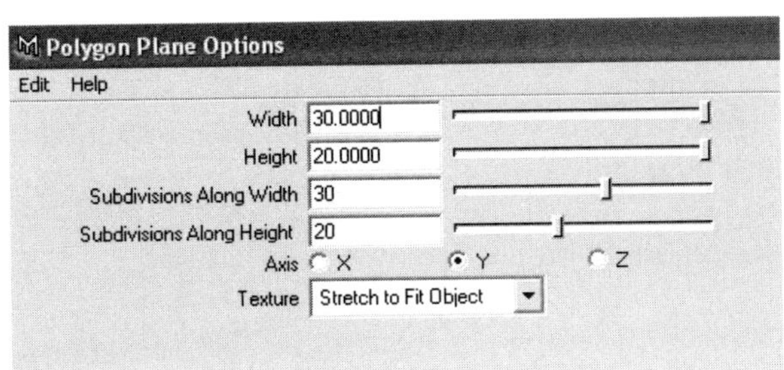

FIGURE 2.2 The proper parameters for the polygon plane to become a cape.

QUADS VERSUS TRIANGLES

Syflex deals with polygon meshes only. It prefers to use quads over triangles, so for the best performance, try modeling with quads whenever possible. This tends to produce a better result. If you need triangles, a quad-based model can be converted to triangles by using Maya's Triangulation tool. This can be found in the Polygons Menu set. Highlight the mesh you want to convert, go to the top of the screen amidst the Maya menus, and select Mesh > Triangulate. Maya can also convert a quad mesh to triangles. This is a bit more difficult of a calculation, but Maya will do its best. To convert the triangle mesh to quads, highlight the mesh and select Mesh > Quadrangulate. This tool has an option box where you can tweak the results for the best conversion.

ON THE DVD

Label the polygon plane Tartan_Cape and give it a lovely texture. For our example, the cape has a blinn shader with a tartan pattern jpeg as a texture map. You can find the texture file tartan_plaid on the companion DVD in the Chapter 2 folder. A shader really isn't necessary, but it does create a better-looking render. It's up to you. Place a point light in your scene and place it above the cape. Your work area should look similar to Figure 2.3.

At this point, it really isn't much of a cape, so let's change that. Our next step is to create a cloth from our new mesh. With Tartan_Cape selected, go to the Syflex menu and choose Syflex > Cloth > Create Cloth. The cape mesh is now defined as a Syflex cloth object capable of amazing cloth-like behavior. If you look at your nodes through the Hypergraph or Outliner window, you will see two Syflex cloth nodes named syCloth1Trs and syCloth1ShapeTrf, which we shall rename syTartan_Cape and syTartan_Cape_Shape, respectively (see Figure 2.4).

The cape has to be constrained in some way, or else it will blow away, as we begin applying dynamic forces to it. In Syflex there are several ways to constrain an object or parts of that object. Imagine taking your beach towel and shaking the sand off it by grasping two of the corners. We will apply that approach to our cape but constrain the entire width edge of it, not just the corners. Select the syTartan_Cape_Shape node and press F8 to select vertices. Select a single row of vertices on one short end of the cape mesh. It should look like Figure 2.5

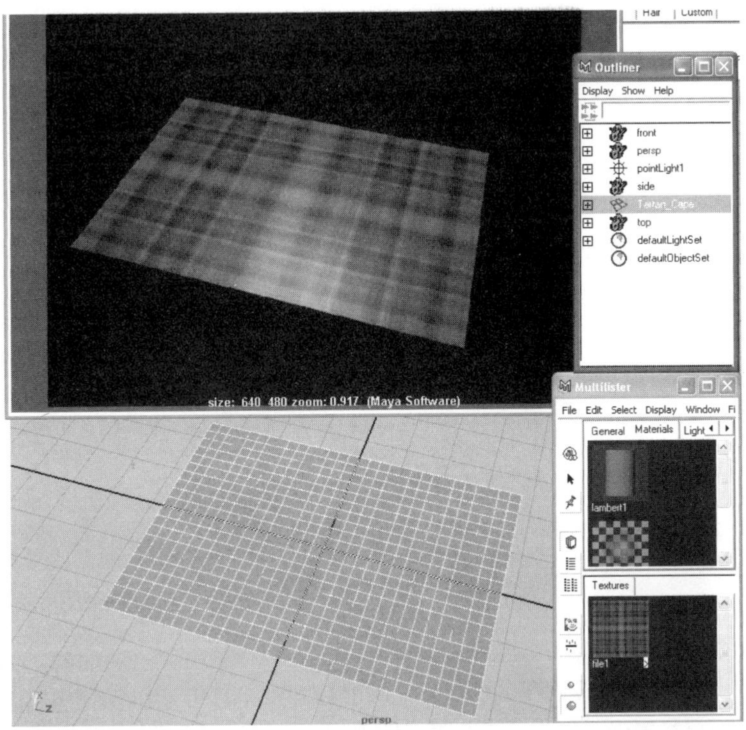

FIGURE 2.3 A quick render of Tartan Man's cape with texture applied.

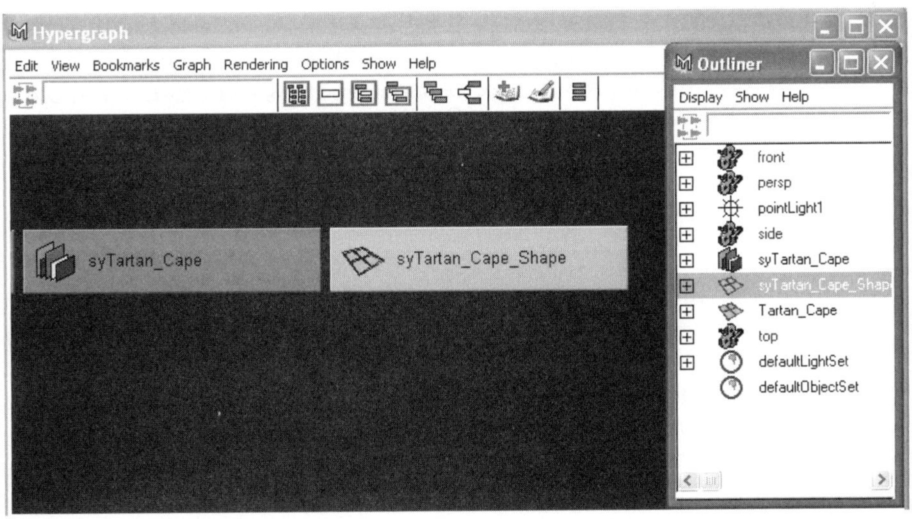

FIGURE 2.4 The new renamed nodes as they now appear in the Hypergraph and Outliner windows.

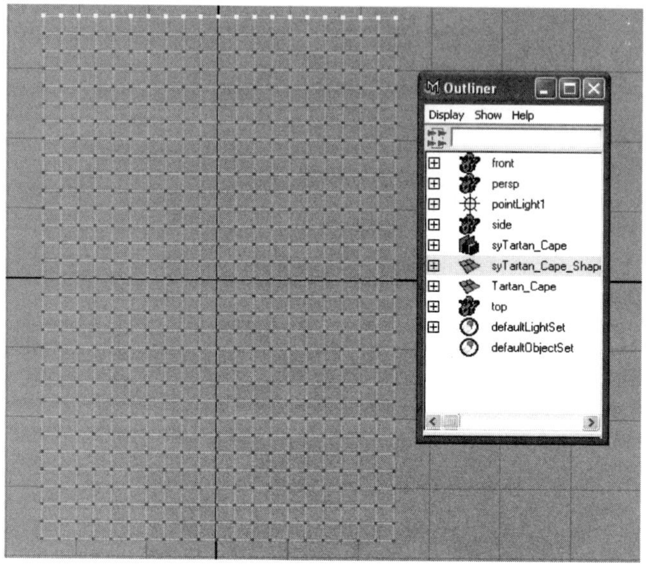

FIGURE 2.5 The cape selected in the Outliner and one row of vertices highlighted.

With the single row of vertices selected, go to the Syflex menu and choose Syflex > Constraints > Nail. With that accomplished, the end of the cape is effectively unmovable by the forces we shall apply to it. The effect of the nail constraint becomes apparent when the cloth is moved. Let's apply a force to the cloth. Select the syTartan_Cape node and then choose Syflex > Forces > Create Gravity. Two new nodes representing the nail constraint and gravity force are in the Outliner window or Hypergraph window. The syGravity1Trs and syNailTrs can remain named as such. Select syTartan_Cape and open the Channel Box. These parameters define the cloth and how it behaves. Input the values listed below, as shown in Figure 2.6.

- Active = on
- Start Frame = 1
- Precision = .001
- Sub Sampling = 0
- Mass Density = .2
- Stretch Stiff = .01
- Shear Stiff = .02
- Bend Stiff = .01
- Stretch Damp = .01
- Shear Damp = .0001
- Bend Damp = .0001

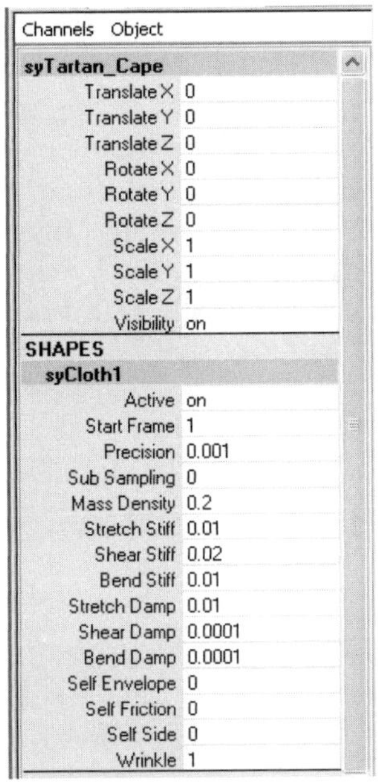

FIGURE 2.6 The proper parameter values for the cloth simulation.

In the Timeslider, give yourself 600 frames and play our dynamic cloth simulation back. If all has gone well, we should have built our first successful cloth animation (see Figure 2.7).

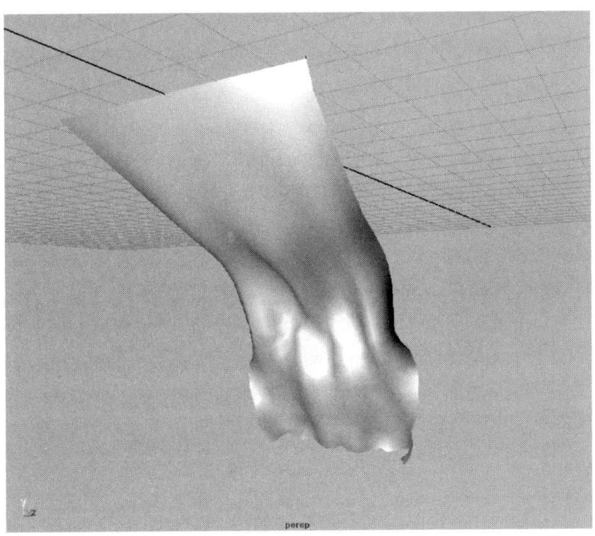

FIGURE 2.7 Smooth shaded render of the near real-time cloth animation.

Depending upon your system configuration, the animation should run very smoothly. It's amazing to see such complex calculations running at near real time. Obviously, the more complex the simulation becomes, the slower the simulation will run. It is surprising how fast Syflex is, even after adding object collision, self-collision, and other dynamic forces. As our animation runs, the cloth seems to stretch as it complies with gravity. We can remedy this by tweaking the parameters of the cloth. In the Channel Box, change the Stretch Stiff parameter from .001 to .3 and rerun the simulation. Now our cape still falls, but it no longer stretches unrealistically.

Cloth by Any Other Name

Cloth is a rather broad term that includes materials such as rubber, leather, and even hair. By tweaking the values, you can get the cloth mesh to act and react as hundreds of real-world materials would.

A Very Sensitive Matter

Syflex is very sensitive to minute parameter changes. Using the Channel Box and bumping the precision up may be in order. This can be accomplished in the Channel Box menu. Select Channels > Settings > Change Precision and set the decimal place value to 4. It's also recommended that you use Maya's default environment of centimeters as the linear working units.

A cape is a far more impressive status symbol when it is flowing in the wind. This can be accomplished by applying a wind force to the cape. With syTartan_Cape highlighted, add a dynamic wind force as we did with the gravity. Syflex > Forces > Create Wind adds a new node that will affect our cape. Don't run the simulation just yet. The wind parameters must be adjusted first. In the Channel Box for the syWind1Trs node, change the parameters to match those in Figure 2.8 and then run the simulation again. Remember to give yourself 600 or so frames to watch it play out properly.

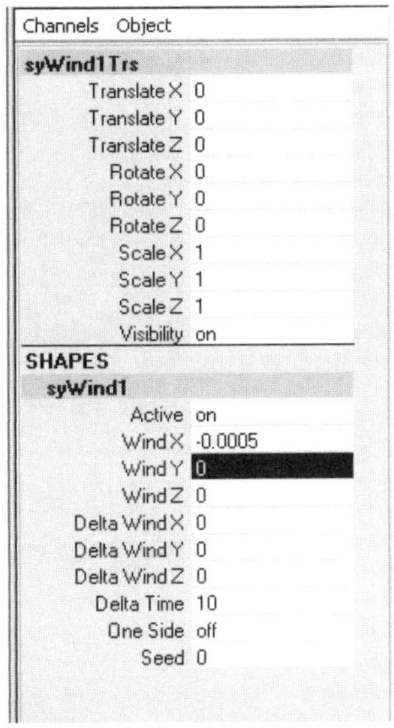

FIGURE 2.8 The proper initial settings for the wind force.

Fantastic! If all is correct, a rendered frame should look similar to Figure 2.9.

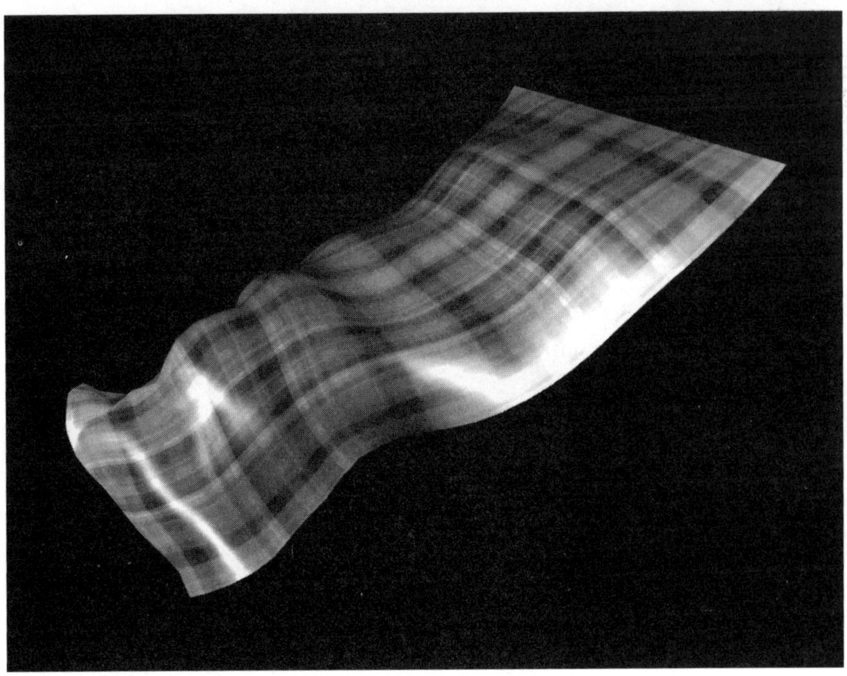

FIGURE 2.9 A rendered frame after applying a wind force.

Notice that the cloth no longer sways back and forth between a negative X and positive X direction. With the wind forcibly blowing in the negative X direction, it maintains an uplifting pressure on the cloth, keeping it from flowing backward. Other forces can be applied to a cloth object. A turbulence force lends a bit of instability to an animation. When used properly, turbulence can shake things up and create a more random realistic look. Our cape could use some turbulent influence for a more realistic appearance. Let's add a turbulent force to the cape. As has been the case, make syTartan_Cape active by selecting it and go to the Syflex menu. Select Syflex > Forces > Create Turbulence and input the numbers shown in Figure 2.10.

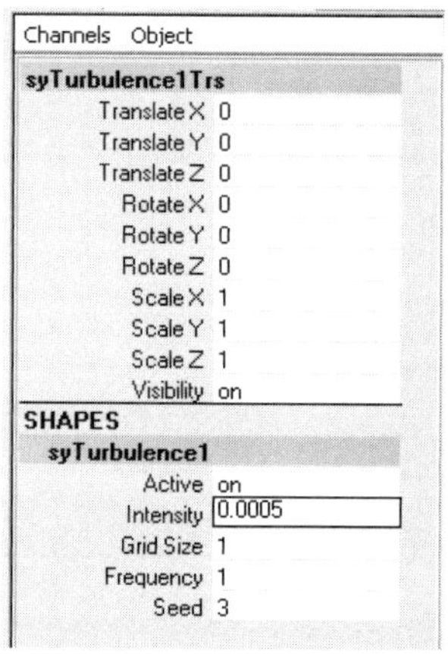

FIGURE 2.10 The proper parameters for the added turbulence node.

Once that's complete, run the simulation again. You should immediately notice in the first few frames that the once smooth cloth is now slightly disturbed. Previously, as gravity overtook the cloth, it fell in a very smooth, uniform manner. That's unrealistic, but a hint of turbulence does the trick as shown in Figure 2.11.

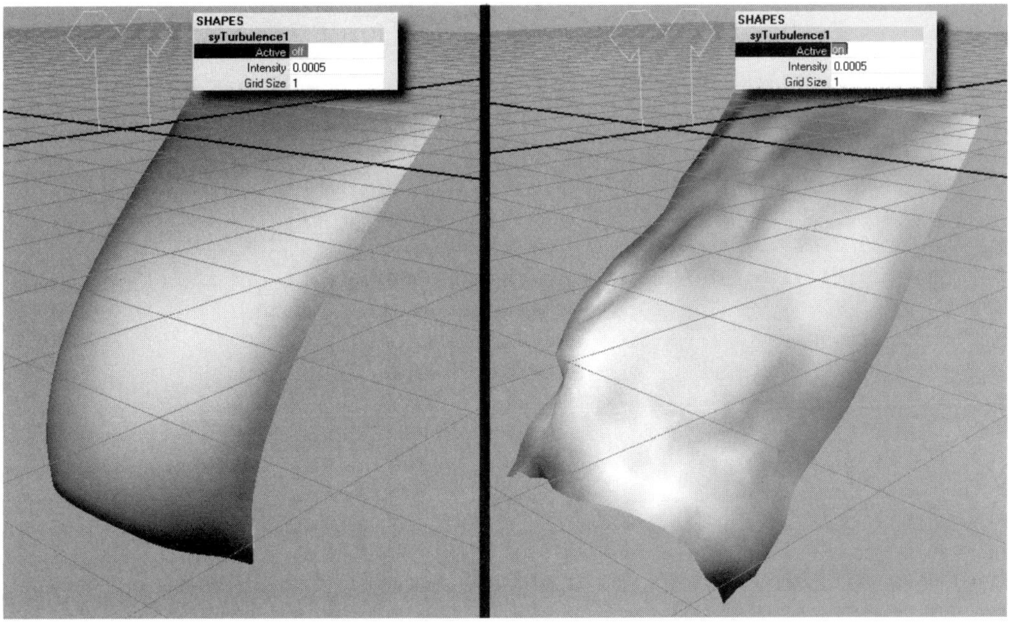

FIGURE 2.11 Our cape before and after turbulence is applied.

THE CRASH CART

Syflex is a very stable program and doesn't crash very much. It does, however, freeze from time to time. This occurs if one or more of the parameters is sorely out of bounds when running a simulation. This is usually represented on the screen as a severely mangled model. Usually, pressing and holding the Esc key gets you out of it. Rewind the simulation to the beginning and try adjusting the set of parameters. It's always a good idea to change only one setting at a time. Doing this allows you to easily find the offending parameter. Just remember to back up your scene files regularly, at various stages along the way and with different names.

A damping force can be used to slow down the movement of a simulation by dissipating energy. It takes the edge off the motion of the cloth animation. The default values are a good starting point for adding a damping force. Start slowly, moving the values higher from there. It may be helpful to think of a cowboy riding a bucking bronco. With no damping force, the cowboy is in for a wild ride. Place that same rider under water, and the ride is more manageable. (Pardon the pun, but it does help with remembering what damping does.) Let's place a damping force on our cape. Again, selecting the syTartan_Cape, go to the Syflex menu. Select Syflex > Forces > Create Damp. The proper parameters are shown in Figure 2.12.

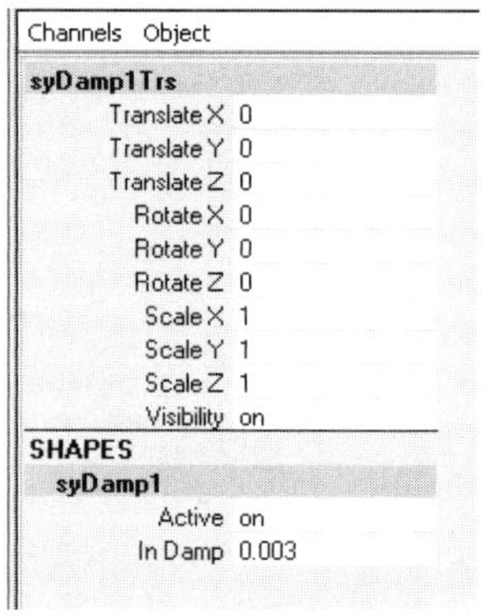

FIGURE 2.12 The proper parameters for the damping node.

Now turn turbulence off. Select the syTurbulence1Trs node and set the Active parameter to 0. This makes it easier to see the effect of damping (see Figure 2.13).

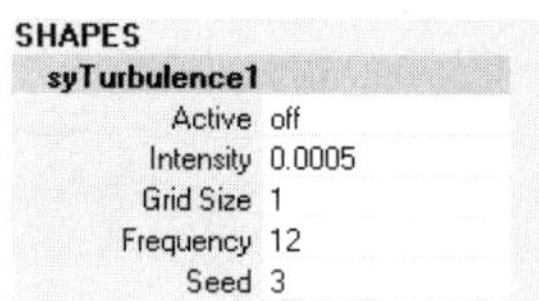

FIGURE 2.13 The setting for turning turbulence off.

In Figure 12.14, we can clearly see the effect that damping has on the simulation.

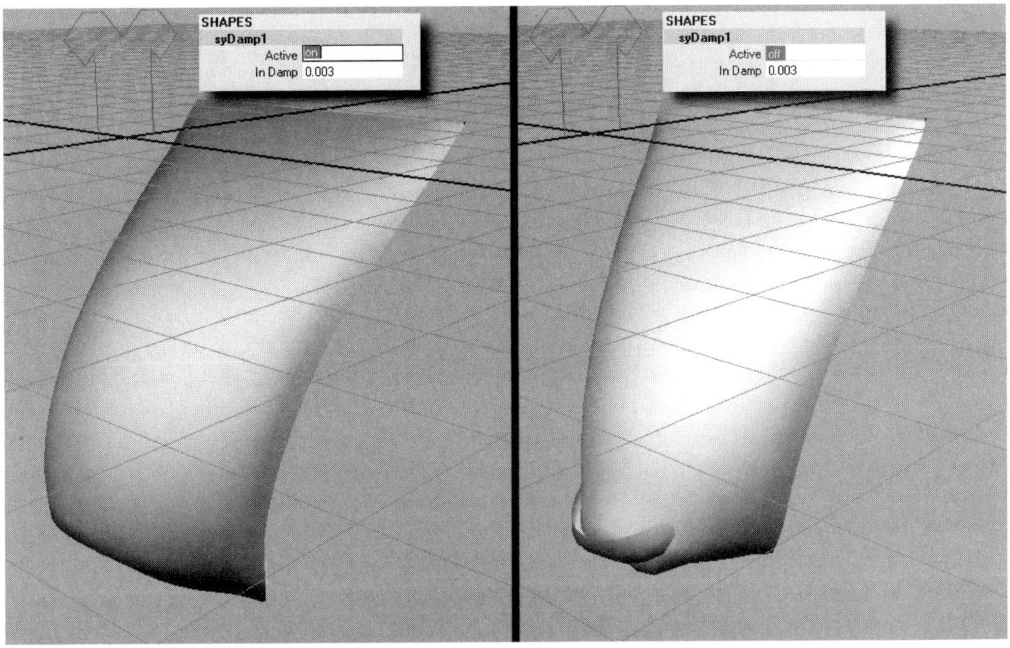

FIGURE 2.14 Frame 109 before and after damping is applied. Turbulence has been turned off.

ONES AND ZEROS

As you can see in Figure 2.13, the Active parameter is currently off. This parameter is a binary choice. It is either on or off. To change the setting, use a 1 to indicate on and a 0 to indicate off. Maya then denotes the proper term in the value's place. You could also type "on" or "off" as the Active value.

A Damp Cloth

Damping is an important force. It can often temper another force. At times it may not be needed. Experimenting with damping on and off, along with minute changes in the damping and turbulence values, will sometimes yield surprising and better results. The perfect combination of turbulence and damping will eventually lead to the cloth action that you are looking for. Remember that these values are sensitive to minute changes in value. Take note of the combinations of turbulence and damping that are most appealing and appropriate. It is sometimes difficult to tell how a force will affect the cloth.

Start with a turbulent force without damping and adjust the values of that force. Note how small parameter changes affect the cloth simulation. Try turbulence with and without damping turned on and off. You will begin to see how damping affects the turbulence. In concert, these two can produce a great flowing cloth effect. It is often a good idea to save a scene file with a base turbulence and damping value. Adjustments made to this base scene will help keep you from getting lost.

ON THE DVD

Congratulations! You have completed your first Syflex simulation. In short order and with little difficulty, the results can be phenomenal. The final scene labeled scene_2_Cape_final can be found on the companion DVD in the Chapter 2 folder. Also included is scene_2_Cape_test, which has a few minor modifications to it. Comparing this bonus scene to our final scene shows how constraints can mold the look and animation of the cloth. This bonus scene adds two separate and additional nail constraints. By scaling and translating these additional constraints, the cape looks more form fitting for someone's neck and shoulders. The bonus scene also adds a Self Envelope parameter on the syTartan_Cape node, which allows the cape to stay clear of intersecting its own geometry. Figure 2.15 shows the reconfiguration of the nail constraint in the bonus scene. Figure 2.16 shows how the bonus scene looks as a final render.

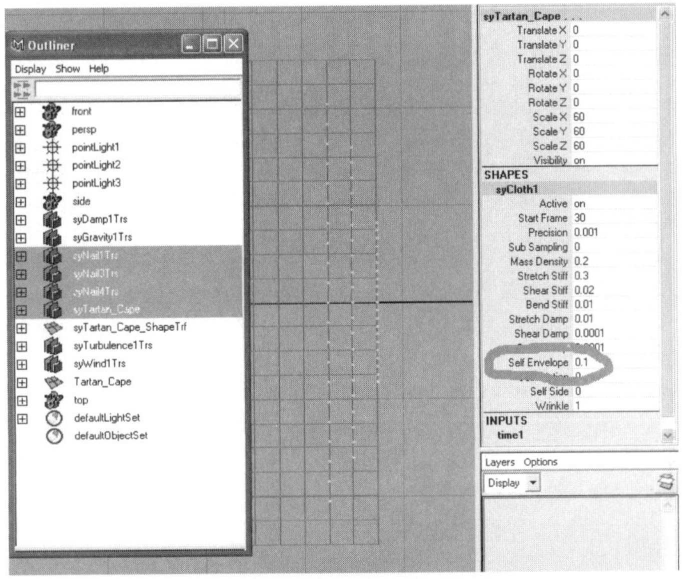

FIGURE 2.15 Bonus scene with constraints and Self Envelope adjustment.

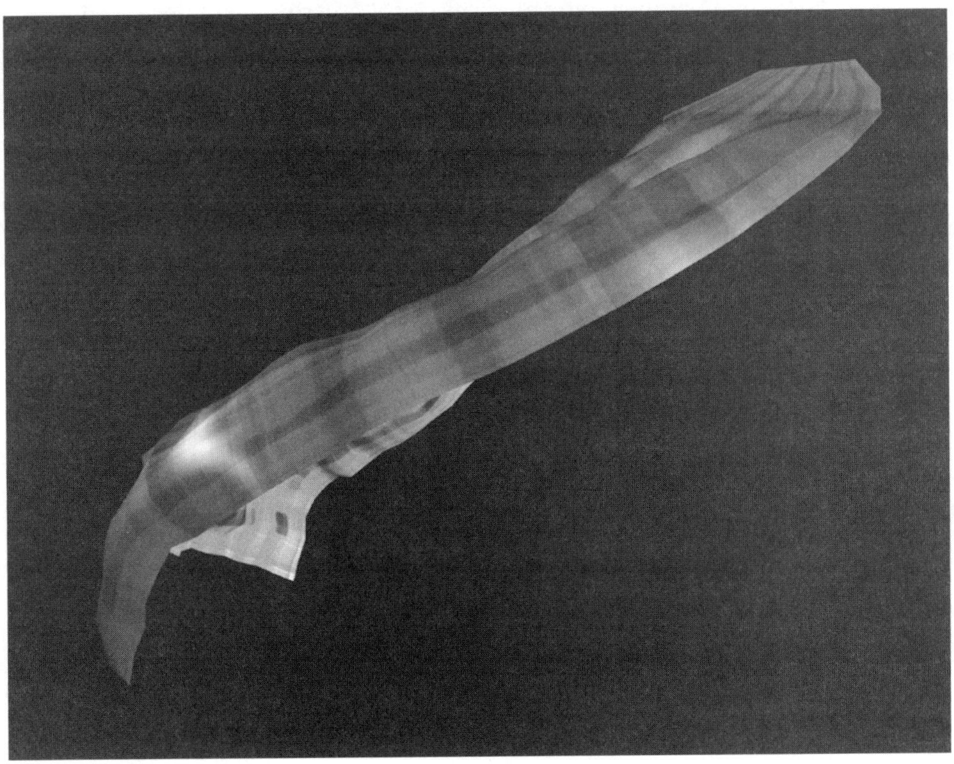

FIGURE 2.16 Bonus scene looks cinched and differs from our final scene.

OBJECT COLLISION

ON THE DVD

As referenced in Figure 2.15, cloth objects can be modified to avoid self-collisions. The Self Envelope parameter is a measurable distance value that detects vertices and establishes proximity. The Self Envelope value creates a sort of force field around the cloth. The Self Envelope value determines the distance this force field is from the cloth surface. The animated actions of the cloth surface will avoid intersecting surfaces by keeping potential intersections at a distance set in the Self Envelope. A cloth's own surface cannot get any closer than the threshold value. Look at it as giving the object some "personal space." Load scene_2_self_envelope on the companion DVD and run the simulation. The camera is positioned such that the self-intersection is unacceptable and unrealistic for any self-respecting hero's cape. This is a problem easily managed in Syflex. Dynamic simulation is not 100 percent predictable. If the dynamic simulation should cause the syTartan_Cape to collide with itself, the geometry will intersect and pass through itself. This is an unrealistic and unwanted behavior. To remedy this problem, the Self Envelope value of cloth node syTartan_Cape must be set to a value higher than 0. Setting the value of Self Envelope to increments starting at .1 should eventually keep the cloth node from intersecting with itself. This is a value to be tried and tested until you get animation that is satisfactory. This is an aesthetic decision, and it depends on what you are trying to achieve.

The many adjustable values in cloth's Attributes editor provide endless possibilities for achieving the proper look and feel. If your cloth object is not required to come dangerously close to folding in on itself, then fine-tuning other values such as Bend, Stretch, Shear, or Damping may solve the problem. Any opportunity to eliminate computationally heavy tasks is time saved. Figure 2.17 shows the cape intersecting itself in two distinct views, with the Self Envelope set to 0. Tweaking the envelope to a value of 1 is shown in Figure 2.18. This value is admittedly higher than it needs to be. A value of .1 or .2 should do the trick as well.

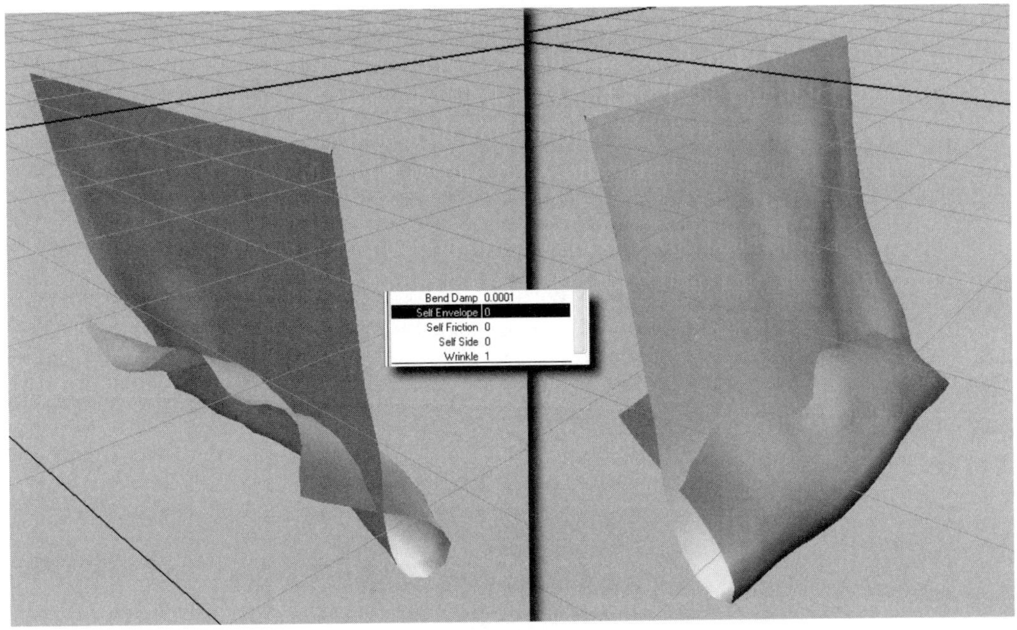

FIGURE 2.17 Unsightly geometry collision with no Self Envelope, as viewed from both sides.

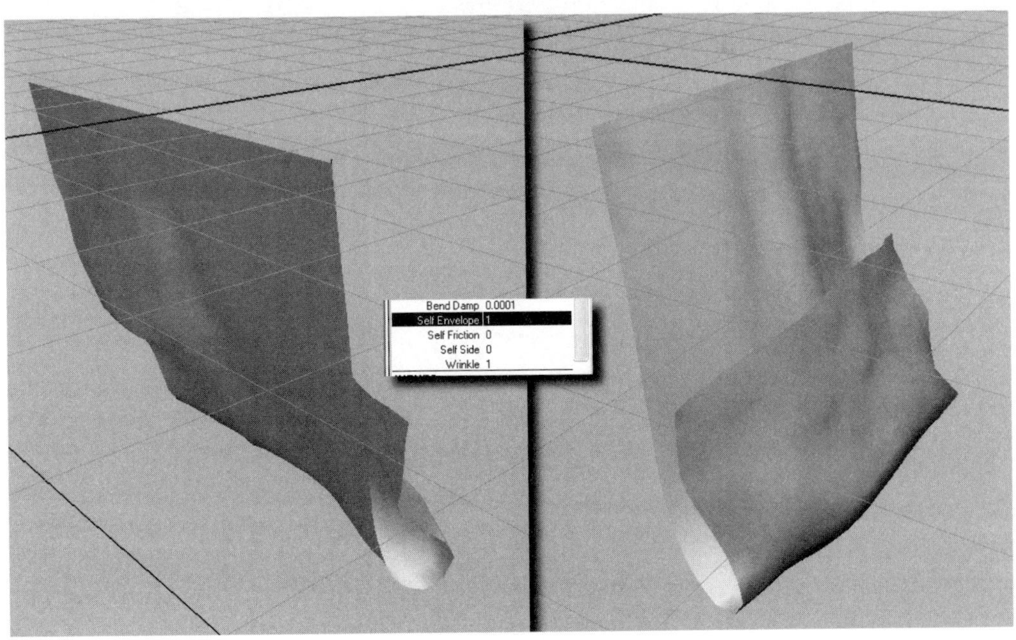

FIGURE 2.18 Outcome of a Self Envelope value of 1.0, as viewed from both sides of cloth object.

ON THE DVD

The collision solver is quite fast and does a good job for almost all applications. Let's do a small tutorial on how Syflex handles another collision situation. Load the Maya binary wavy_plane found on the companion DVD located in the Chapter 2 folder. The scene contains a simple NURBS to polygon conversion using quads and a few lights. Follow these steps:

1. Create a polygon plane for this scene with parameters shown in Figure 2.19 and rename it Wavy_Cloth.
2. Place it above the wavy_plane object, as shown in Figure 2.20.
3. At this point, you want to make the newly created polygon plane into a Syflex cloth object by going to the Syflex menu and selecting Syflex > Cloth > Create Cloth.
4. Change the name of the resulting node from syCloth1ShapeTrf to syWavy_Cloth1ShapeTrf and the cloth node from syCloth1Trs to syWavy_Cloth1Trs.

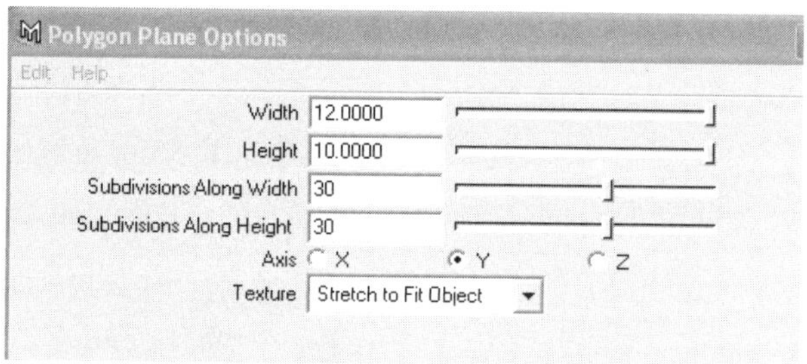

FIGURE 2.19 Proper parameters for your new cloth object.

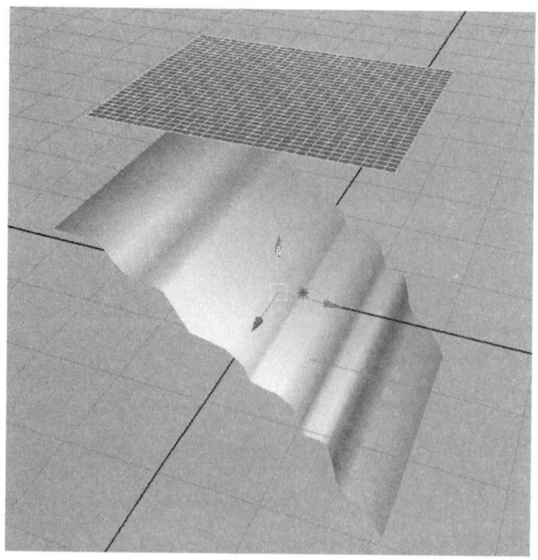

FIGURE 2.20 The properly positioned cloth object and wavy plane.

5. As you may recall, for the cloth object to fall and collide with the wavy plane, you need two more elements. You must first assign gravity to the cloth. Select the syWavy_Cloth1Trs node and go to the Syflex menu. Select Syflex > Forces > Create Gravity.

As in the earlier tutorial, we have now assigned gravity to the cloth. Running the simulation at this point makes the cloth object fall and pass right through the wavy_plane object. We must assign a collider node to the cloth and indicate what we want it to collide with. The collider node tells Syflex that it should consider a selected mesh and object as a dynamic entity. The two objects will react to each other with collision detection. This will make the clothing form fit a body and act as clothing would to the body's movements.

1. As in previous tutorials, select both the wavy_plane object and the syWavy_Cloth1Trs node. After both are highlighted, go to the Syflex menu once again and select Syflex > Collisions > Create Collider.
2. This has now established a collision link between the wavy_plane object and syWavy_Cloth1Trs node. Run the simulation again. This time the cloth should collide and slide right off the wavy_object, as shown in Figure 2.21.

The collision is far from pretty, so it must now be fine-tuned to yield a more realistic and appealing look.

Color and Contrast

It is always helpful to assign a different shader color to the cloth object from that with which it will collide. Choosing a contrasting color makes it easier to see where the geometry collisions are failing. This makes it easy on the eyes when adjusting and rerunning the simulation to fine-tune the collision.

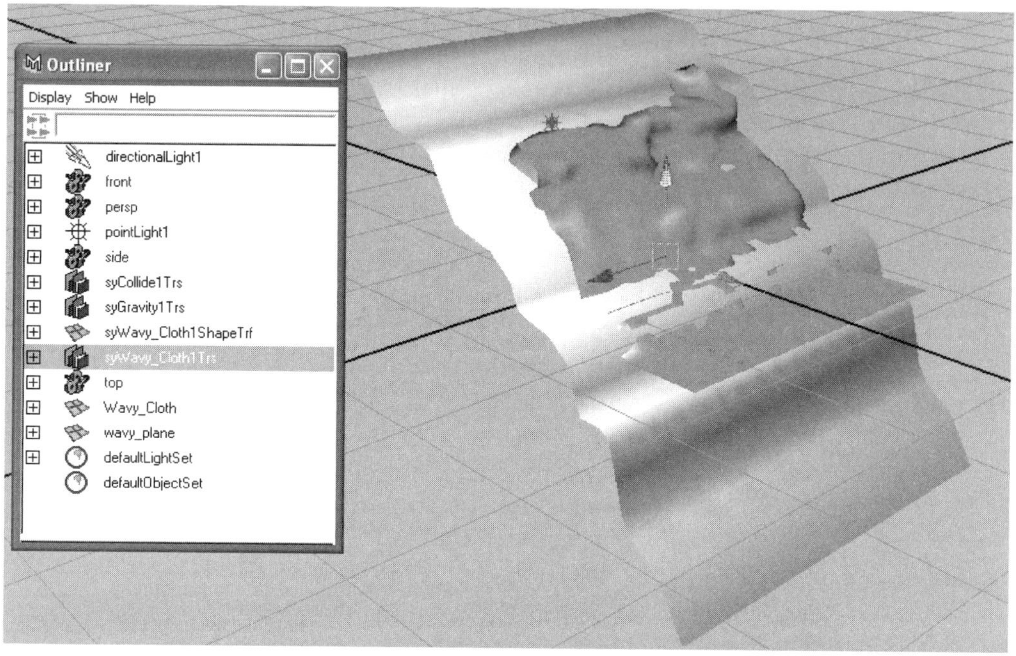

FIGURE 2.21 Collision of the cloth upon the wavy_plane object produces mixed results.

The next consideration in our simulation is adjusting the collision itself. Select the syCollide1Trs node and adjust the parameters to those in Figure 2.22. Run the simulation again. This time the results are more realistic, and there is only a hint of inter-geometry penetration (see Figure 2.23).

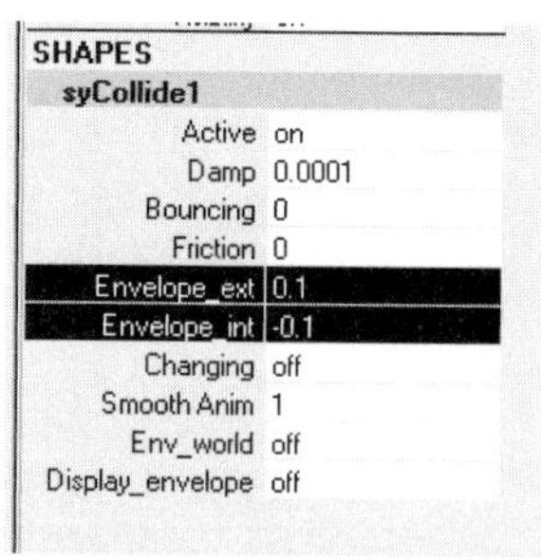

FIGURE 2.22 Envelope parameters produce a much better result.

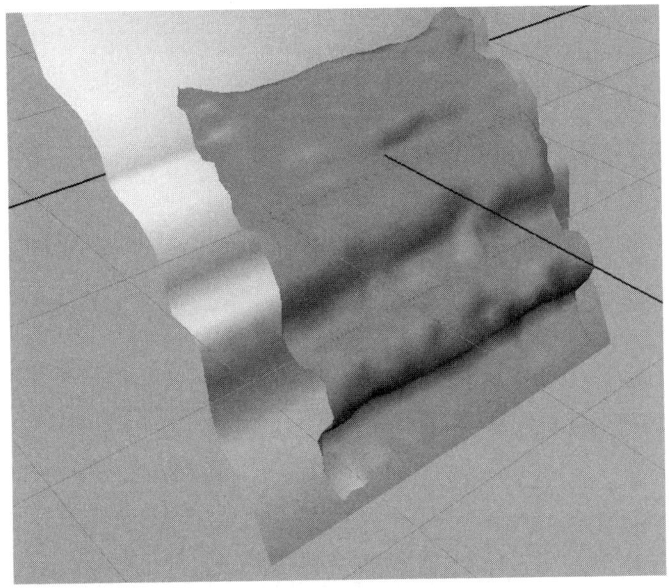

FIGURE 2.23 Envelope changes make for a better-looking collision.

The only parameters that changed from the default are the Envelope parameters. These parameters determine the size of invisible fingers enveloping the collider, or in this case the wavy_plane. This can be seen by toggling the Display_envelope menu selection, in the syCollide1Trs node, to a value of 1, and toggling the envelope to visible. Figure 2.24 shows the syCollide1Trs node with the Display_envelope visible. The purposely exaggerated values make it easier to visualize the uplifting support the fingers provide. As you can see, the higher the value, the farther the cloth is from touching the wavy_plane surface. The values in Figure 2.22 are close, but they can be made even closer.

FIGURE 2.24 Tiny fingers protrude like surface normals defining the distance from the collision envelope

Through tweaking individual cloth, collider, and other properties, the desired look emerges. The cloth animation still seems a little rough. We want the cloth to hug the wavy_plane object. Right now it seems like a roller coaster out of control. Figure 2.25 shows a direct side view as the cloth slips over the surface. To correct this problem, a damping force is in order.

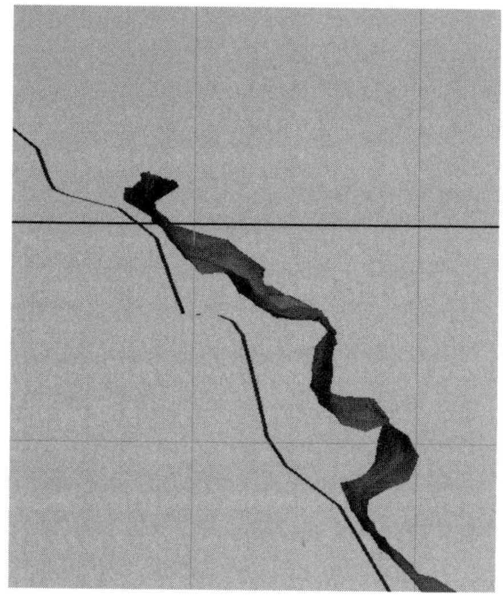

FIGURE 2.25 Frame 73 of the simulation prior to adding the damping force.

Add a damping force to the syWavy_Cloth1Trs object with the same procedure we have used to apply gravity and collision. Select Syflex > Forces > Create Damp. There are other damping parameters within individual nodes, but they are localized. The new damp node dampens globally. The parameters for the damping node are shown in Figure 2.26, and the resulting effect is shown in Figure 2.27. It's a marked difference and makes for a smoother animation.

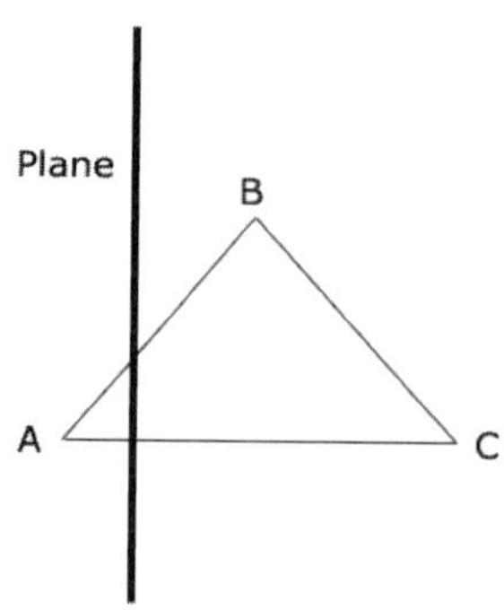

FIGURE 2.26 The setting for the damping force.

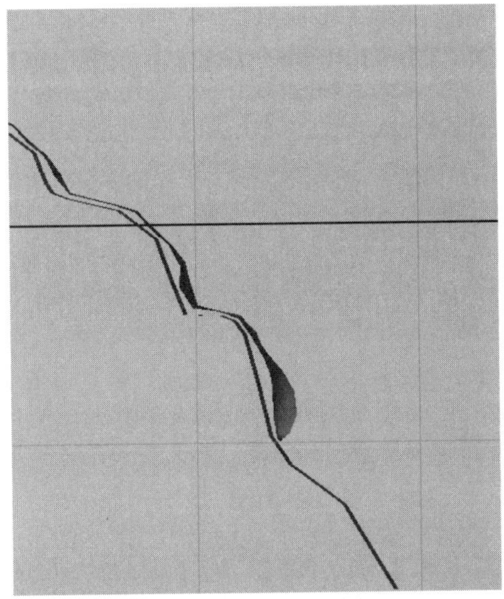

FIGURE 2.27 Frame 73 of simulation after applying the damping force.

AN INTERVIEW WITH GERARD BANEL PRESIDENT OF SYFLEX

I had the opportunity to chat with Gerard Banel, president of Syflex, about Syflex and its impact on the industry. He was kind enough to share some of his insights with me. Among the short list of films that Syflex has left its mark on are Fantastic Four: The Silver Surfer, Charlotte's Web, Spider-Man 3, Shrek, TMNT, 300, Happy Feet, Everyone's Hero, X-Men 3, Pirates of the Caribbean, Poseidon, Renaissance, Stay Alive, V for Vendetta, Aeon Flux, Harry Potter, The Legend of Zorro, Nanny McPhee, Brothers Grimm, Charlie and the Chocolate Factory, Batman Begins, The Adventures of Sharkboy and Lavagirl in 3D, Kingdom of Heaven, Elektra, King Kong, *and* The Lord of the Rings. *A more comprehensive look at the phenomenal studios and artists using Syflex can be found at http://www.syflex.biz/gallery.html.*

How did you get your start in CG or a little company history?
I started working on CG at the age of 13, and haven't stopped since then.

What was the genesis of your software?
I did some research on cloth simulation back in 1997-98, for real-time clothing of 3D characters. In 1999 I joined Square USA, where I wrote the cloth simulation software that was used in *Final Fantasy: The Spirits Within*. Afterward, I wrote my third cloth simulation software and started Syflex.

continued

What types of companies would benefit from your software?
Any company working on movies with CG characters, either full CG or doubles.

Who uses your software?
Our list of clients consists of a wide range of creative companies and individuals, from big-name studios, to smaller special effects houses, and independent animators.

Where can the use of your software be seen?
In many movies, television, and commercials.

What was the most unusual, creative, or inventive use of your code?
Syflex has been used for many non-cloth effects, like ropes, water, clouds, and even saliva!

Where do you see CG lacking right now?
CG is still too complex. It is reserved for a minority of very experienced and talented individuals. There are many plugins out there that complement CG authoring software in order to make them easier to use. We need now a better integration of all these tools.

What's down the road for your company or software?
We are working in many directions: more speed for real-time applications, better integration with other animation tools, and to extend the range of effects needing simulation.

3D Mesh Objects as Cloth Objects

ON THE DVD

A powerful feature within Syflex is the ability to use almost any polygonal object as a cloth-like entity. This opens up an interesting new way of thinking about object interaction and what those objects could be composed of. Let's create a rubber ball using Syflex and have it interact with another object in the scene. Load the scene file bounce.mb. You can find this file on the companion DVD in the Chapter 2 folder. Your scene should look like Figure 2.28.

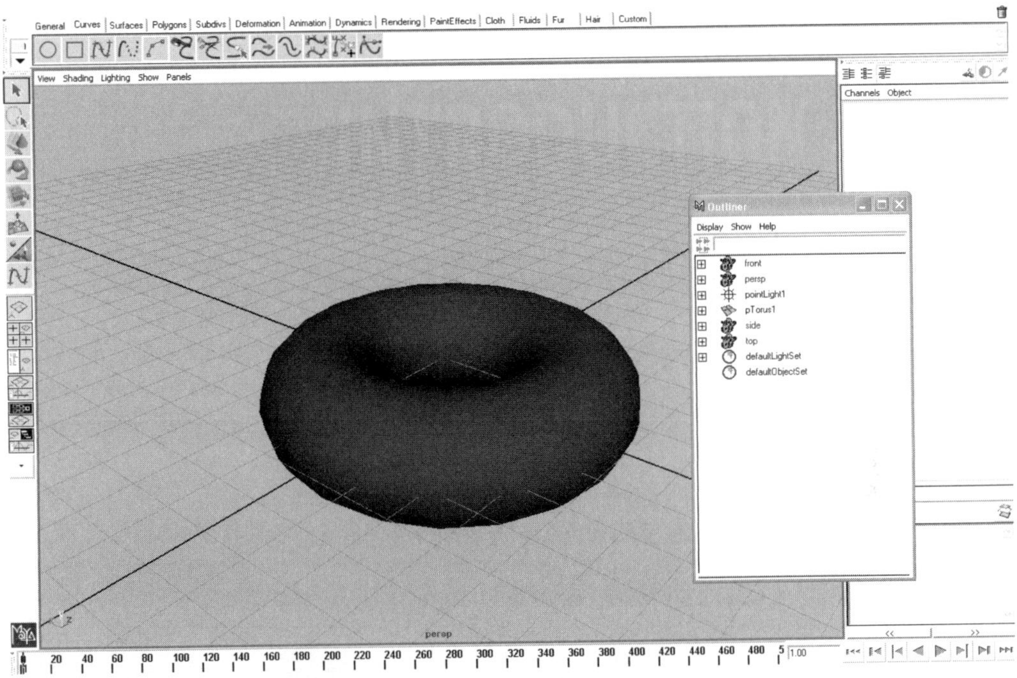

FIGURE 2.28 The bounce.mb scene as it appears loaded into Maya.

1. Create a polygon sphere, in the Y dimension, with a radius of 2.0, and 20 subdivisions along the height and around the axis. Name it squishy_ball, and position it 16 units in the Y direction and scale it to a value of 2.7 in XYZ. These values are shown in Figure 2.29.
2. Next, we will make squishy_ball into a cloth object. As before, select Syflex > Cloth > Create Cloth and change the name of syCloth1Trs to sySquishy_BallTrs and syCloth1ShapeTrf to sySquishy_BallShapeTrf. Let those default cloth values stand for the moment.
3. We want the ball to bounce; therefore, it must fall. Select the cloth node sySquishy_BallTrs and add gravity to it by selecting Syflex > Forces > Create Gravity.
4. Last, the ball must collide with something in order for it to bounce. Select both the Torus1 object and our new cloth node, sySquishy_BallTrs, and then Select Syflex >Collisions > Create Collision.
5. Apply a red blinn shader to the ball. There is one that was loaded in the scene. Run the simulation now.

The results are not generally what is expected. It should be a simple dynamic bounce. By now, you should be familiar with the Syflex workflow. It is far less complicated than other solutions. The result should look similar to Figure 2.30. The ball is a cloth object, so it was pulled by gravity through the smaller-diameter hole of the torus. This is the surprising, but understandable, result of a malleable cloth object.

Tweaking the cloth object parameters stiffens it up enough to bounce off the torus's surface. Observing the object and knowing the impending animation makes it a prime candidate for collision optimization.

Collisions can be costly in computation time. Syflex has the ability to select a certain set of polygons as colliding faces, while leaving the rest of the object free from the collision detection computation. This is a great way to optimize a simulation, armed with the knowledge of what polygons will be affected in the collision. Setting the collision surfaces requires an object to be a collider. Select the polygon faces of the pTorus1, as in Figure 2.31, and then select the collider node as well. At this point, we must tell Syflex that the selected polygon faces within this object are the only faces to be considered in a collision computation. Go to the Syflex menu and select Syflex > Collisions > Set Collider Faces. The torus now has roughly half its faces removed from calculation, speeding the simulation and saving valuable time and computer resources.

NOT YOUR GRANDFATHER'S SOFT BODY DYNAMICS

Syflex can be used for objects other than clothing and capes. Any polygon object can be made into a cloth object. The soft body dynamics of a Syflex cloth object can be used for Thanksgiving Day balloons, a trampoline, a ponytail, an inner tube, a seat cushion, or even a jellyfish. Any object that requires a pliable surface that interacts to collisions might benefit from Syflex. Imagine a jiggling, squishy water balloon as it rolls down short bumpy steps. Syflex works better than Maya at creating the pliable. Next time you are looking to create a soft body mesh, consider Syflex as a better alternative.

ON THE DVD

At any time, you can recall these faces by selecting the collider node and selecting Syflex > Collisions > Get Colllider Faces. The scene up to this point can be found on the companion DVD in the Chapter 2 folder. It is called bounce_2.mb.

ON THE DVD

As a test, see if you can make the ball bounce off the torus without having it squeeze through the hole in the torus. This is a great example of using a polygon mesh as a cloth object and making it deform dynamically. The answer does not lie in making the sphere larger. For clues you may want to study the sqeeze.mb scene file located on the companion DVD. This scene file offers a solution to your challenge. Squeeze.mb looks very much like the bounce_2.mb scene, and although the squeeze.mb sphere is larger, it is not the reason it does not pass through the torus.

Run the simulation. In squeeze.mb, the larger sphere bounces, wiggles, and jiggles like a water balloon. Study this file for answers to finishing your challenge. The purpose of the larger sphere is to make the next effect much more impressive. Make your sphere a little larger in your bounce_2.mb challenge if you like. This alone is not enough to make it bounce without eventually drooling through the tori hole. Gravity will overcome the sphere. Only tweaking a certain parameter will keep it bouncing, jiggling in place, and standing firm atop the torus. What parameter was changed from the bounce_2 scene to make this happen?

The goal of the squeeze.mb file was to keep it from falling through by changing a single parameter from the bounce_2.mb scene file. With this accomplished, we can force the ball through the hole by changing another parameter. Let's do that now.

1. First, change the blue shader on the torus to roughly 75% transparent and zoom in slightly closer. It should look similar to Figure 2.32. Run the simulation. The torus works successfully to stop the sphere from passing through, and the motion of the ball has a very realistic jelly-like feel to it. The hole in the torus now blocks the ball from passing. Again, it must be noted that squeeze.mb does not work because we changed the size of the sphere.
   The goal now is to make this sphere, which is significantly larger than the hole, squeeze through the smaller passage. Dynamic software is best when it's able to deal with problems in real-world terms. Let's actually pull the ball through the hole using gravity as our tool. Since gravity has already been applied to sySquishy_BallTrs, we need to adjust the gravity high enough to pull the sphere right through the hole.
2. Select the syGravity1Trs node. We want to keyframe the InGravity Y value to −.01 at frame one. This value should already be set, so just keyframe it. The Y value is the only value that needs animating. Now highlight the sySquishy_BallTrs node.
3. We want to temporarily switch Active to Off. This saves time because Syflex does not have to calculate the simulation as we jump around the Timeslider. Next, set the Timeslider to view 240 frames.
4. We need to set a new a keyframe at frame 210. The syGravity1Trs node should be set to −.1. Increasing the gravitational force from −.01 to −.1 over the course of 240 frames will eventually overtake the sphere and suck it through the torus opening. This final scene file sqeeze_final.mb is located on the companion DVD.

ON THE DVD

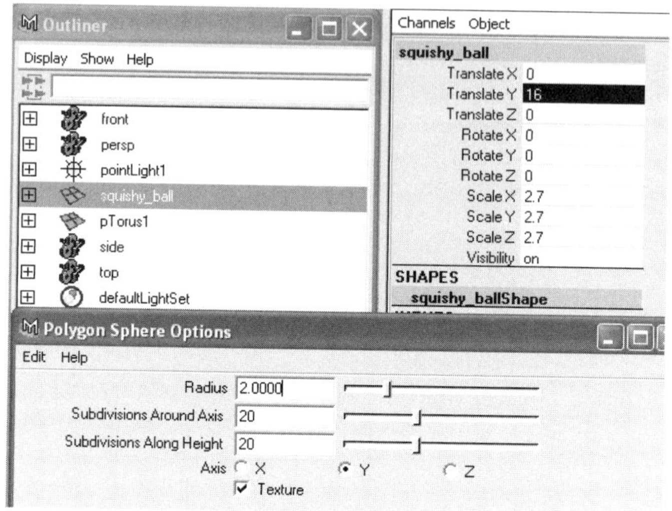

FIGURE 2.29 Values for creating, scaling, and positioning polygonal sphere.

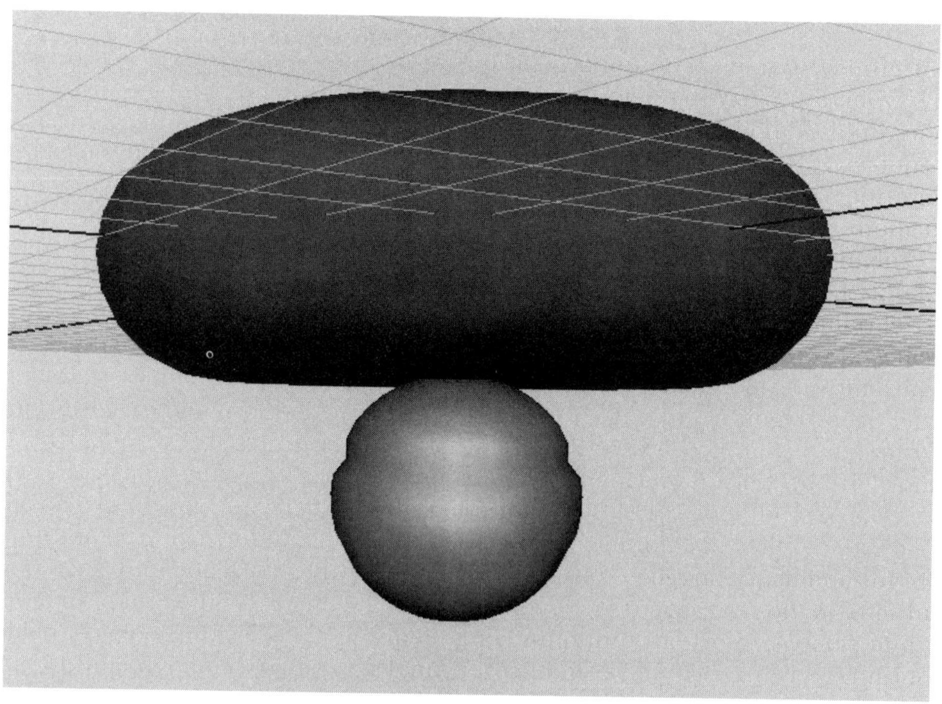

FIGURE 2.30 The cloth object squeezes through a smaller diameter hole in the torus.

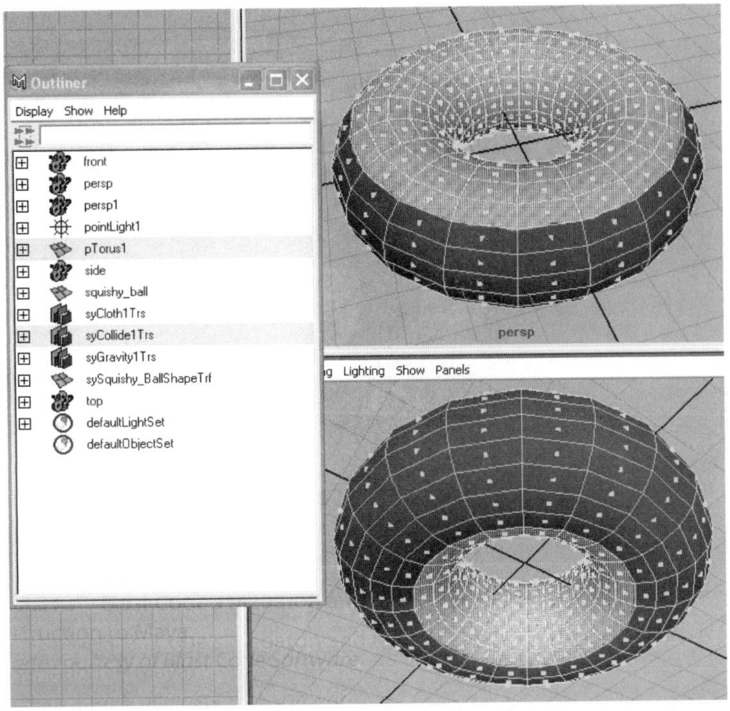

FIGURE 2.31 The top and center faces selected as the only collidable faces in this object.

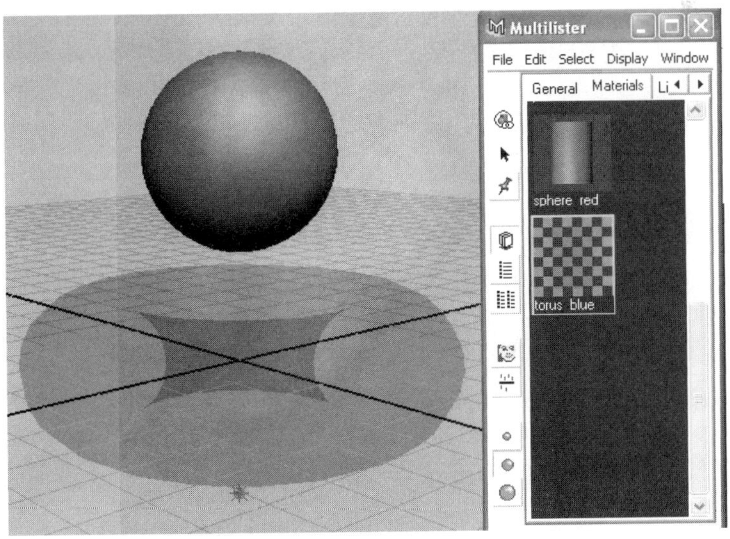

FIGURE 2.32 A transparent torus allows us to see the sphere being drawn through the torus opening.

A Simple Garment

This chapter would not be complete without an example of an article of clothing. Creating virtual cloth and clothing is usually a complex matter, but Syflex makes creating clothing a simple task. By hiding the user from complex algorithms and math, Syflex allows an artist to spend more time being creative.

ON THE DVD

Let's take a short look at creating a spinning skirt. Load the scene pleated_skirt.mb, which is located on the companion DVD. The simple pleated skirt model in Figure 2.33 has a blinn shader for catching the light as we begin to spin the skirt.

Let's start by selecting the pleated_skirt node. We need more polygons in this object to get a smooth cloth skirt. Under the Modeling menu, select Edit Polygons > Subdivide with two subdivision levels. Figure 2.34 shows the new subdivided geometry and the proper settings for the subdivide.

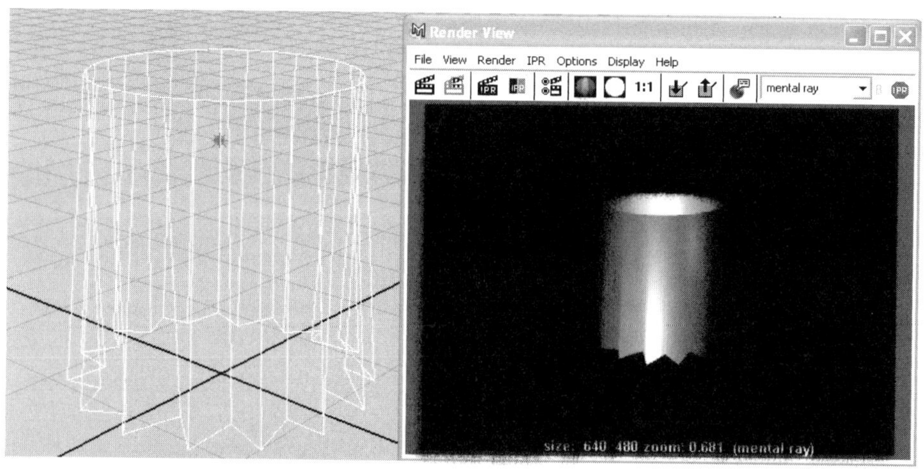

FIGURE 2.33 Polygon skirt object and render with blinn shader for highlights.

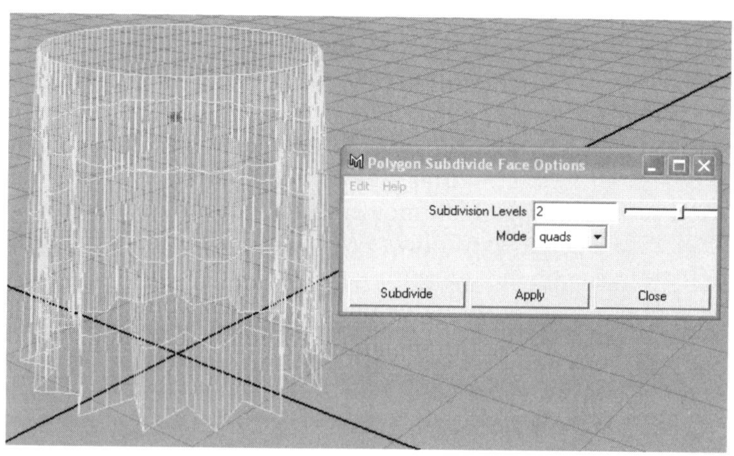

FIGURE 2.34 Polygon skirt subdivided with two subdivision levels using quads.

The skirt is now better subdivided for cloth animation. With the pleated_skirt node selected, we must go through the workflow to change it to a cloth object that can be subjected to forces. This workflow is consistent with everything we have discussed in prior tutorials.

1. Select Syflex > Cloth > Create Cloth and change the name of the resulting syCloth1ShapeTrf to sySkirt_ShapeTrf and syCloth1Trs to sySkirt_Trs.
2. Next, select the sySkirt_Trs.node and select Syflex > Forces > Create Gravity. Running the simulation now makes it obvious that we must keep part of the skirt from moving under gravity, while the rest is free to dangle.
3. Select the syCloth1ShapeTrf node and choose the top row of vertices, as shown in Figure 2.35.

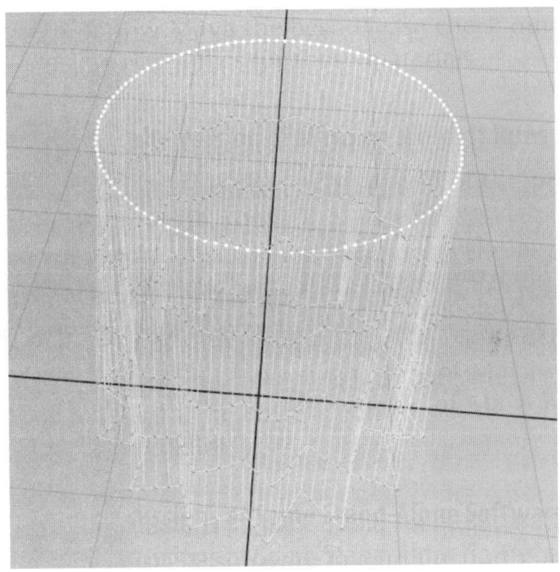

FIGURE 2.35 Top row of vertices selected for conversion to a Nail Constraint.

4. Select Syflex > Constraints > Nail. This acts as the waist. The syNail1Trs node can be animated. It is the basis for our spinning and swirling skirt motion. Save your work.

ON THE DVD

5. Load the scene dancing_skirt.mb, which is located on the companion DVD. This scene has the syNail1Trs node animated over 300 frames. The animated hip translation and rotation gives the skirt a nice dynamic dancing quality.
6. Run the simulation. The animated hip gyration gives the cloth quite a ride, but as shown in Figure 2.36, the cloth does a nice job of keeping up with the motion.

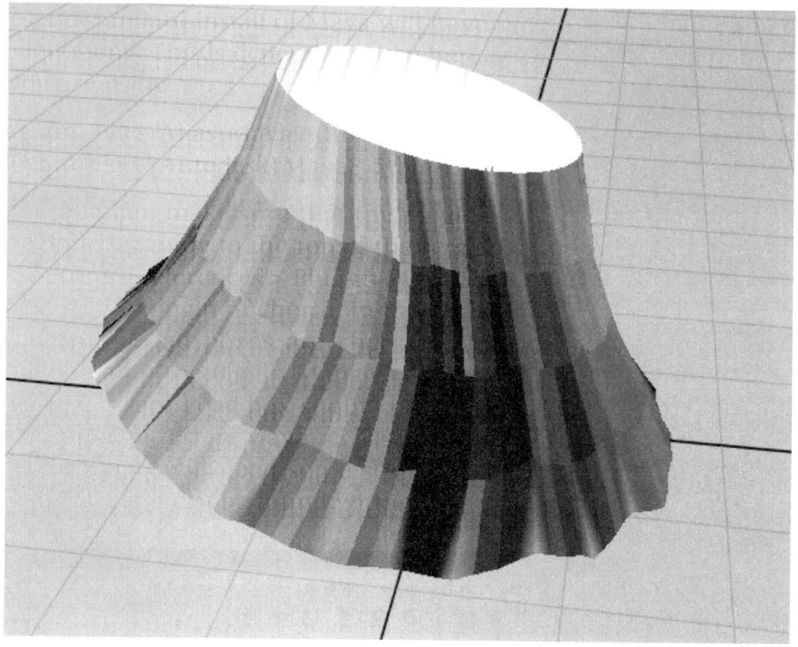

FIGURE 2.36 Frame 220 of the test simulation.

A bit of maintenance is needed for the cloth to act more realistically. Figure 2.37 shows the cloth spinning in on itself, causing severe intersecting geometry, and the polygons are visible in the final render. The skirt could be further subdivided or polygons could be smoothed, but the geometry can also be replaced with something more render-friendly and flexible.

Rewind the Timeslider to the beginning frame. We are going to use a relatively low-polygon animated skirt as a proxy that will drive a more realistic subdivision surface model.

1. With the syCloth1ShapeTrf mesh node highlighted, create a subdiv surface duplicate, making sure to keep the original selected, as shown in Figure 2.38.
2. With the polygon skirt selected, go to the top of the Maya menus and select Modify > Convert > NURBS to Subdiv to create the subdivision surface duplicate of the skirt.

This subdiv duplicate is driven by the original low-polygon cloth animation with a wrap deformer. Maya has several types of deformers to choose from. Deformers give you the ability to smoothly contort or deform geometry in a variety of ways. Deformers serve many purposes and are infinitely useful in creating animation that might otherwise be impossible by other means.

1. This can be done by selecting the new polyToSubd1 node and then the syCloth1ShapeTrf node. The order is important.

2. Amidst the Maya menus in the Animation menu set, select Create Deformers > Wrap. The subdiv surface model is now deformed by the cloth.
3. We must now hide the syCloth1ShapeTrf node by making it invisible. Select syCloth1ShapeTrf in the outliner and turn off visibility as shown in Figure 2.39. What remains is the subdiv copy of the skirt ready to render (see Figure 2.40).

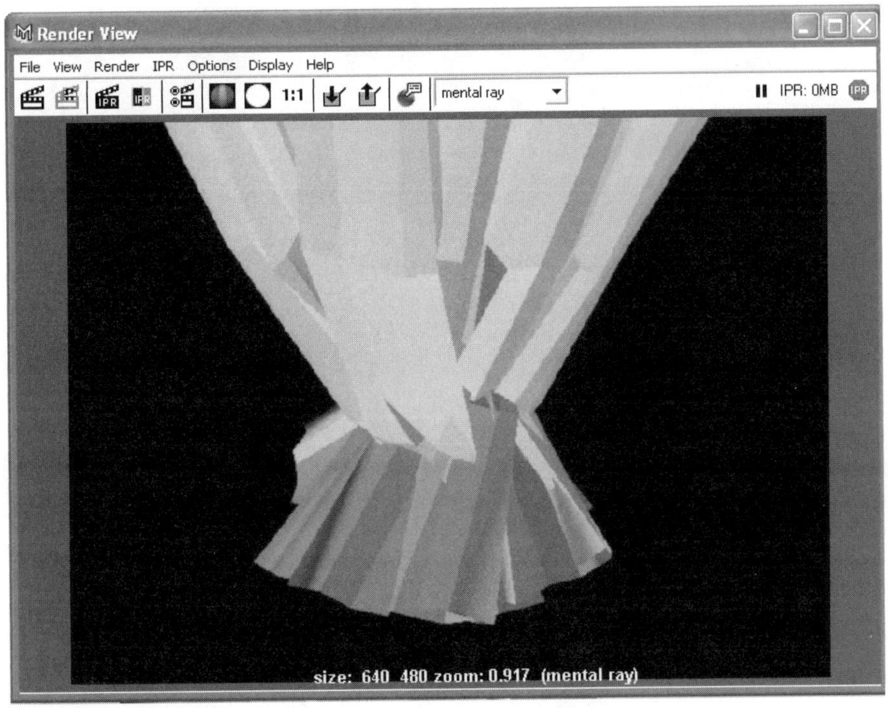

FIGURE 2.37 Polygons visible in a mental ray render.

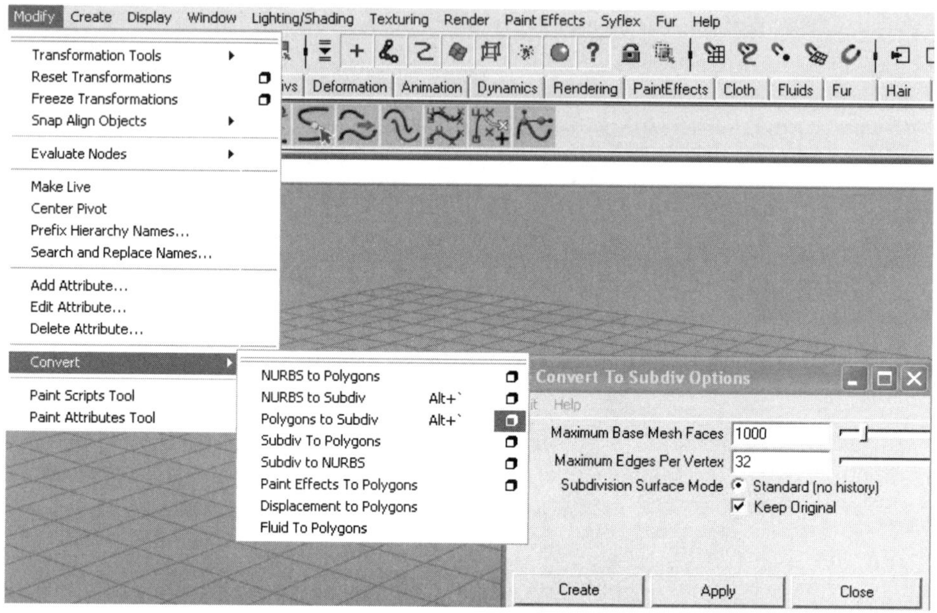

FIGURE 2.38 Creating a subdiv duplicate of the polygon mesh skirt.

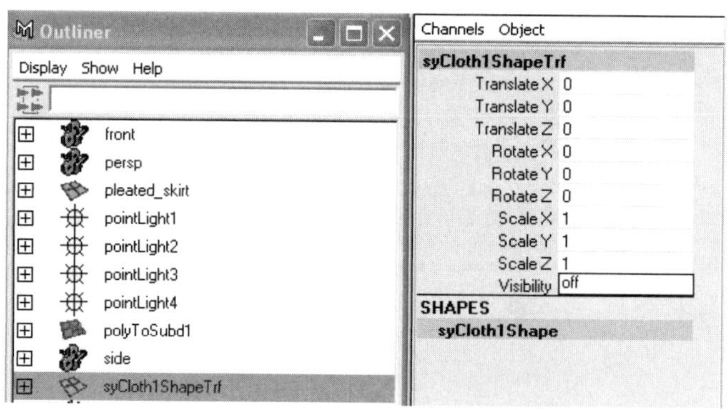

FIGURE 2.39 Polygon mesh skirt hidden from view

FIGURE 2.40 The subdiv render creates a much smoother look.

ON THE DVD

Only one more tweak must be made for our skirt to be a dancing success. The intersecting geometry shown in Figure 2.37 must still be fixed. This can be done by selecting the syCloth1Trs node and setting the Self Envelope attribute to a value of 1, as shown in Figure 2.41. When rendered out now, the intersecting geometry is gone. Figure 2.42 shows the effects of Self Envelope having a value of 1. The final scene file is located on the companion DVD in the Chapter 2 folder.

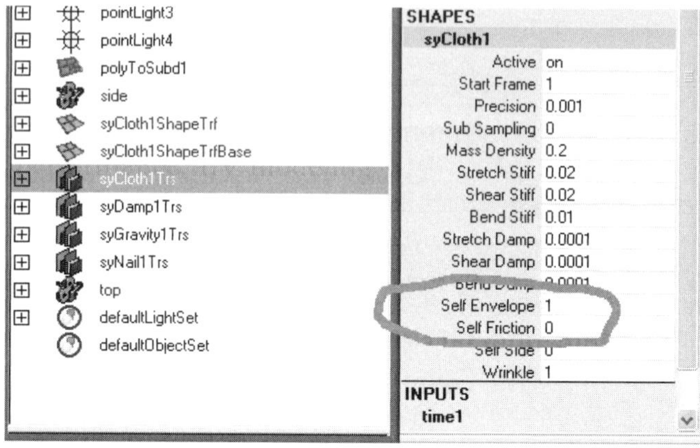

FIGURE 2.41 The Self Envelope value on syCloth1Trs set to 1.

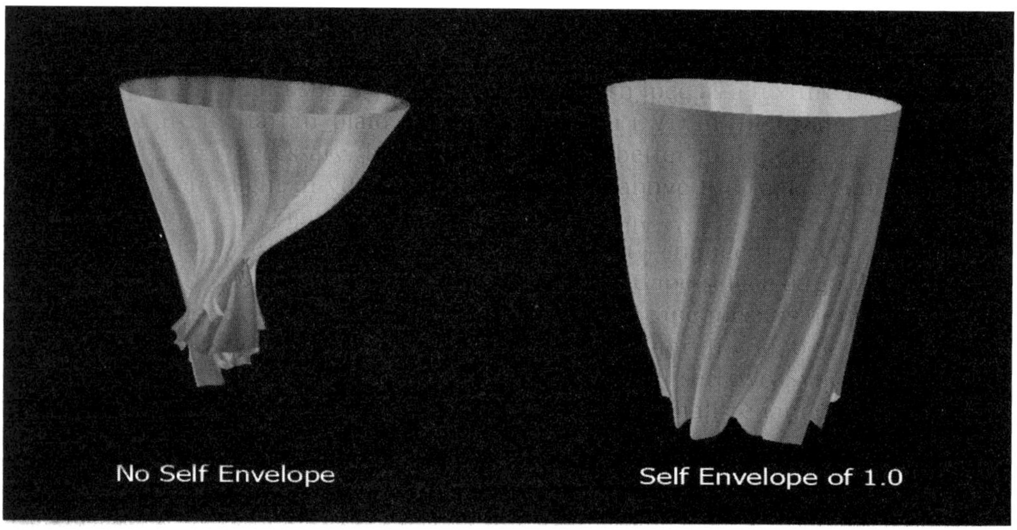

FIGURE 2.42 Identical frames rendered without Self Envelope (left) and with a value of 1 (right).

In this chapter, we learned the power of Syflex for doing cloth simulation and how versatile it is at creating other materials, such as rubber. More information on Syflex can be found in the appendix under Chapter 2. This includes links and other resources including bonus scene files not worked on in this chapter. Let's move on to something vastly different.

CHAPTER

3

HAIR AND FUR

In This Chapter

- Introduction
- A Furry Bird
- Sixties Shag Rug
- Blowing in the Wind

The bird's feathers are generated in Shave and a Haircut and are rendered in mental ray.

INTRODUCTION

The computer graphics community has set their sights on many goals. One of them has been realistic flowing hair. The magnitude of generating and rendering thousands of hair strands was a problem that seemed insurmountable. Today, computer animation and visual FX films are filled with golden locks, tufted fur, and regal manes. Innovative solutions have popped up over the past five years that have almost put the issue of hair generation to rest. Autodesk's Maya Unlimited solution is Maya Fur. A far superior Maya plugin solution is called Shave and a Haircut. This single plugin with a funny name plays tongue-in-cheek homage to the musical couplet, of unknown origin, first used in the early twentieth century. It is being used by dozens of studios and FX houses. Shave and a Haircut is full of features that overshadow the Maya Fur solution by leaps and bounds.

HAIR, HAIR, EVERYWHERE

The short list of films using Shave and a Haircut is impressive. While many studios use Maya as their primary package, they bypass Maya Fur and use Joe Alter's Shave and a Haircut plugin to elicit hair effects that suit their needs. Films such as *300, Barnyard, Charlie's Angels II, Charlotte's Web, Dr. Who, Dreamkeeper, The Exorcism of Emily Rose, Exorcist: The Beginning, Half-Life 2, Hellboy, Into the West, King Kong, The Magic Roundabout, Moongirl, Pirates of the Caribbean: At World's End, Sin City, Space Chimps, Superman Returns, Ultraviolet, Underworld Evolution, When Animals Attack!,* and *X-Men 2* have visible uses of Shave and a Haircut in action.

Among its most powerful features are ease of use, exceptional rendering, and seemingly infinite flexibility. The feature set of Shave and a Haircut is impressive and integrates with Maya seamlessly in the following areas:

- **Sculpting:** Shave and a Haircut is an aptly-named plugin. The moniker is not a clever euphemism. It truly allows the user to feel that barbershop paradigm. Hair can be grown, shaped, cut, and shaved. Its tight integration with Maya allows novel ways of texturing, shaping, and cutting hair. These tools are already familiar to you as a Maya user. Being a virtual barber is great fun.
- **Rendering:** The quality of the fur and hair rendering in Shave and a Haircut is incredibly photo-realistic. Shave and a Haircut uses its own renderer. Shave and a Haircut uses what's called *Deep Accumulation* for all shadows. Shadows are rendered first and displayed in the scene. The hair is then composited into the scene as a post process. Light penetrates within the hair mass to calculate more sophisticated and accurate shadows and self-shadowing than most other renderers do. There is little necessity for working around a situation. Maya functions, such as light properties and fog, work fine.

- **Instancing:** Shave and a Haircut has brought a great deal to the table with its package. While hair is its primary focus, it is capable of a few other neat tricks. Shave and a Haircut does not prevent your favorite renderer from being used. Hair generated in Shave and a Haircut is proprietary, but can also be converted to a mesh version object, so that any renderer could be used. Hair can also be substituted by other geometry. Instancing mesh objects can open up a world of new possibilities—a field of sunflowers, a pumpkin patch, sheep, or even pimples are all possible.
- **Surface Dynamics:** Shave and a Haircut hair strands are wired and ready for dynamics. Hair guides are created as a dynamic chain and carry their own dynamic properties contained in the normal Maya Attribute Editor. Since hair is best served on a living thing, hair is not dynamically controlled by the overall movement or transform, but rather by skin dynamics. This means that as the skin surface distorts or deforms, so does the hair it is attached to. As skin moves over bone or muscle, the dynamically-driven hair correctly imitates the action.

Let's delve into Shave and a Haircut with a quick and easy example.

A FURRY BIRD

ON THE DVD

It is very easy to get hair to grow on something quickly. Load the scene file bird_1.mb into Maya. It is located on the companion DVD in the Chapter 3 folder. A quick render should reveal our polygon model with lighting, as shown in Figure 3.1. This particular model is made of polygons, but Shave and a Haircut grows hair on just about any object type. When the plugin is loaded, Shave and a Haircut places two menus within the menus in the Maya menu bar, and they remain constant throughout all Maya menu sets. These two menu selections are shown in Figure 3.2.

RENDER TO TASTE

Don't fret if your picture does not exactly match that of the book. We regularly switch between renderers. Since Shave and a Haircut utilizes its own renderer, it doesn't matter which renderer you are using (see Chapter 4 for other renderers). The hair should always turn out just fine. Hair can be converted to mesh objects and rendered in other renderers. However, unless otherwise noted, we are rendering fur and hair in the Shave and a Haircut renderer.

FIGURE 3.1 The polygon bird model ready for hair.

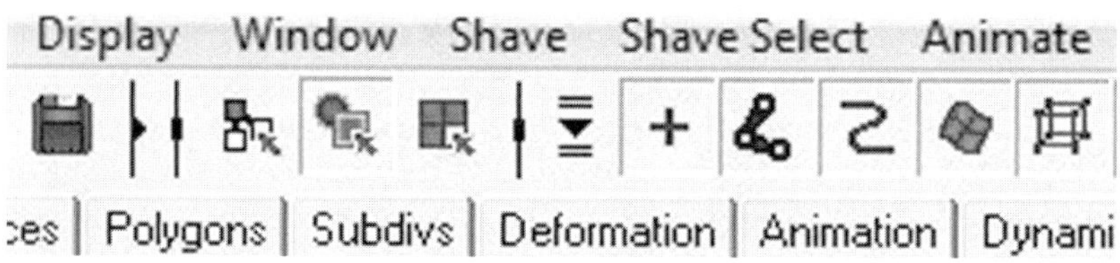

FIGURE 3.2 Shave and a Haircut's two menus are nestled among the Maya menus.

There are many ways to direct Shave and a Haircut to place hair. This time we will select specific polygons on the model that will grow hair. It may help to make the box room invisible in the Channel Editor. This may make it slightly easier to select the specific polygons. It may also be easier to select all the polygons of the head and then deselect the face polygons that should be hairless. Figure 3.3 shows two alternate views of the bird's body, with polygons deselected.

FIGURE 3.3 Two views of selected polygons shaded dark. These polygons produce hair.

With the hair polygons selected, it's a simple matter of creating a hair node for them. Go to the Shave and a Haircut menu on the Maya menu bar. Select Shave > Create New Hair, as shown in Figure 3.4. This brings up a library of preset hair types to choose from (see Figure 3.5).

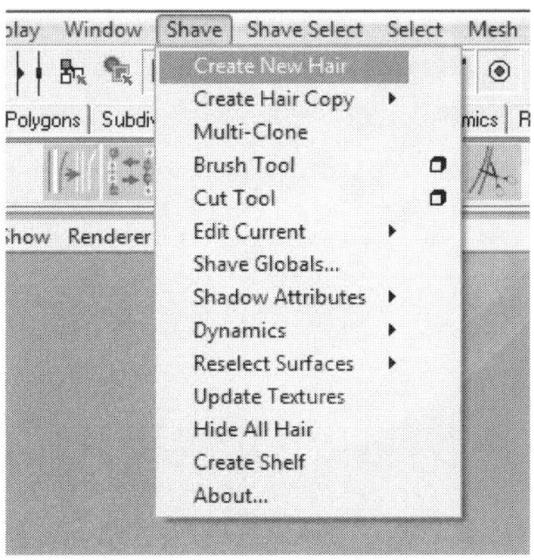

FIGURE 3.4 Shave and a Haircut's menu selection for creating a new hair node.

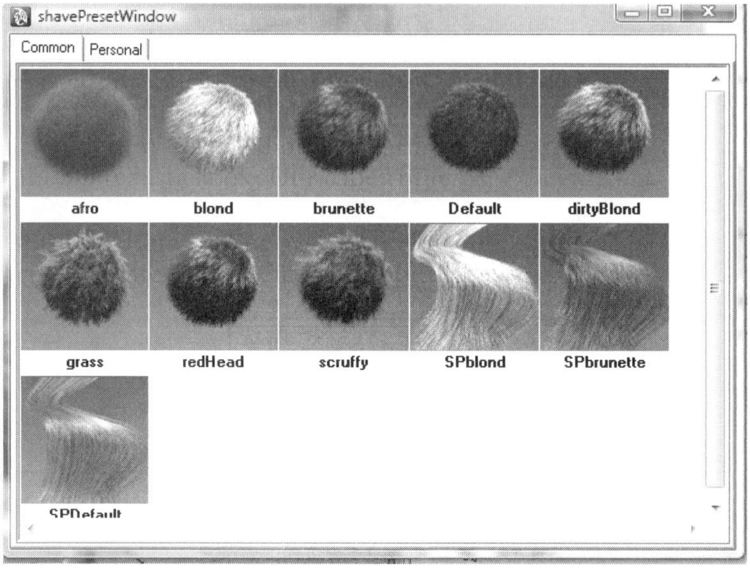

FIGURE 3.5 The pop-up window with preset hair types.

Select redhead from the presets. The bird model now looks something like Figure 3.6.

FIGURE 3.6 Hair now appears from the model and is clearly represented in the Outliner window.

The node shaveHair1 is visible and selectable from the Hypergraph or the Maya menu bar. The Shave and a Haircut's Shave Select menu, shown in Figure 3.2, lists all available hair nodes. It is focused for quickly selecting the proper node to work with. Hair is not the only item generated with a hair node. Spline curves called *guides* appear evenly spaced on the hair surface.

Select the hair node shaveHair1. In the Attribute window, under the Hair Display tab, the guides may be toggled on and off. Let's toggle the guides for shaveHair1, as shown in Figure 3.7. Hair guides are a nifty solution for handling large numbers of hairs. These guides provide a little order in the chaos of a bad hair day. Our bird looks as though he fell victim to a cartoon electrocution. Let's style his hair more appropriately. Save your work.

Good Hair Day

Guides and hairs are separate and different components of the hair node. Guides are primarily used for dynamic interactions and styling hair. The results of a dynamic interaction are translated to the hairs. Other modifications to the hair are calculated afterward. The guides do give you a reasonable representation of the hair's direction, but hairs may be set askew by other modifiers, such as displacement kink and frizz. If your hair isn't following the guides, check in the Attribute Editor to see what attributes might be making the difference.

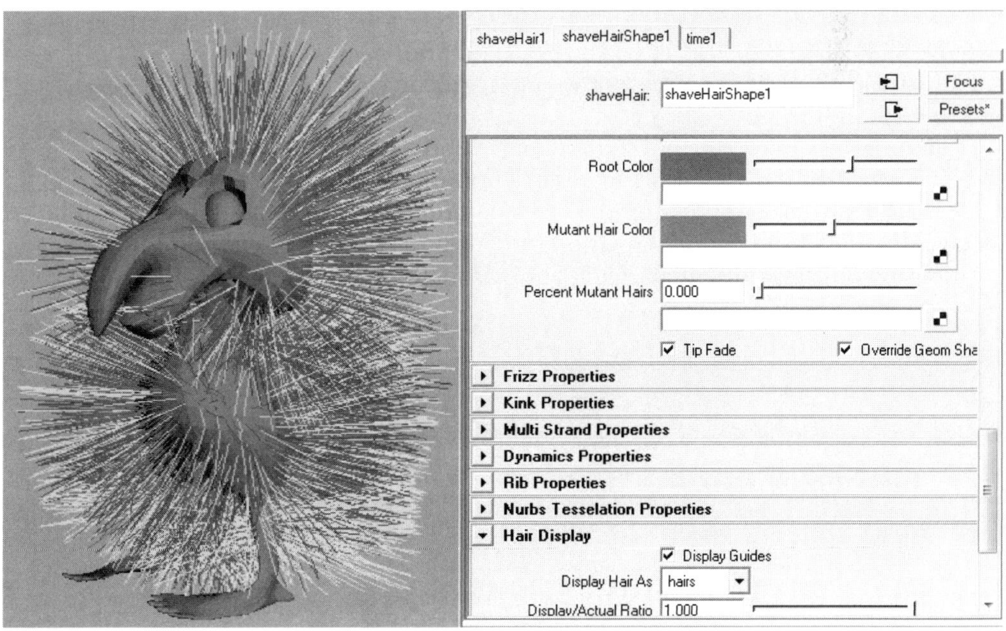

FIGURE 3.7 The all-important guides are now turned on.

ON THE DVD

Load bird_2.mb from the companion DVD in the Chapter 3 folder. This is our scene up to this point. Shave and a Haircut has tools aptly named Brush and Cut.

Skin So Smooth

The bird model is faceted partly because it was built in another program. It is always better to work with lower-resolution models. Smoothing the polygons of the models smoothes our bird's skin out. Shave and a Haircut adapts to new geometry by adding hair guides as needed.

This is where the virtual barbering takes place. Go to the Shave menu shown in Figure 3.8 and select Shave > Brush Tool. Select the option box as well. This brings up a small set of Brush functions in the Attribute Editor, as shown in Figure 3.9. The six Brush functions operate on the hair guides in some very helpful ways. Select the Translate Brush. This is all we will deal with at this point.

FIGURE 3.8 Selecting the Brush tool with option box circled.

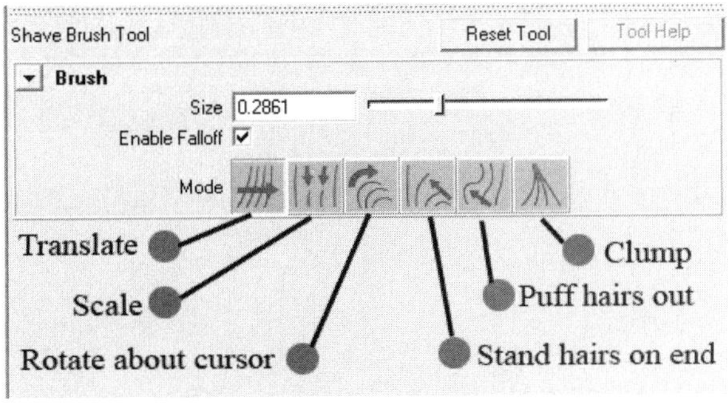

FIGURE 3.9 Brush option box with various Brush functions labeled.

ON THE DVD

Experimentation with all the brushes is the key to styling the perfect coif. Brushing virtual hair in Shave and a Haircut is a very interactive procedure. It would be difficult to convey how to do this in still images. Figure 3.10 is a frame of a movie file that shows how to tame the bird's mangled mane. The red circle in Figure 3.10 is the Brush. It is very similar to a typical Maya Brush. You can change the Brush size interactively by holding down the B key and dragging the mouse right and left. Play brushup_bird1.mov from the companion DVD in the Chapter 3 folder.

As shown in the movie, it doesn't take long to wrangle the hairs. Figure 3.11 shows a before-and-after of the quick styling. With a little practice, it becomes quite easy to design a great look for whatever beast you are working on. The difference is how you utilize the other Brush tools available.

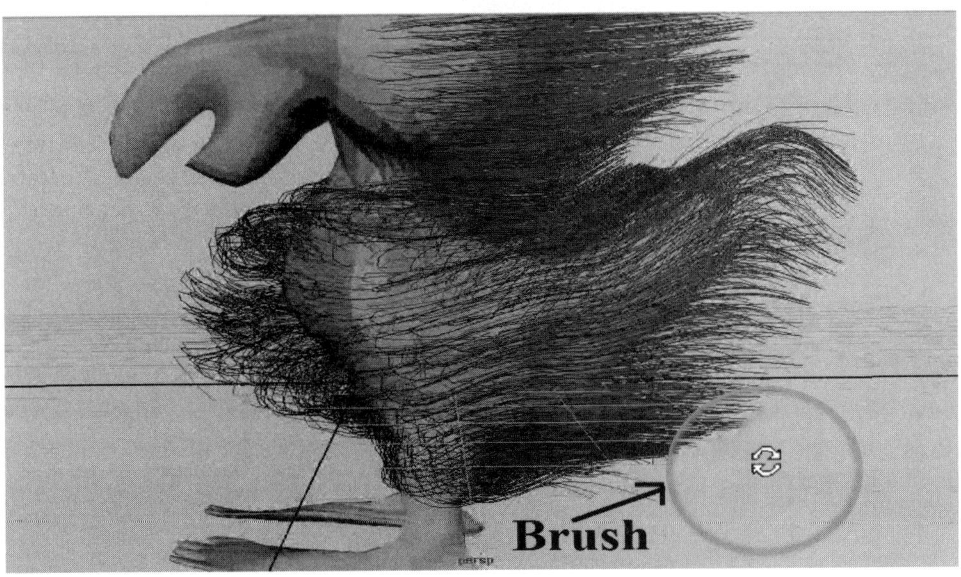

FIGURE 3.10 A familiar Maya-type Brush helps groom an unruly hairstyle.

FIGURE 3.11 A rushed styling job makes the bird almost presentable.

> ### STYLE IS EVERYTHING
>
> When styling hair with the Brush tools, it is a good idea to turn off the display for hairs. The guides are what are actually being brushed. The display becomes quite fast, and it is visibly uncluttered by hundreds of hairs.

ON THE DVD

Save your work. The result of the quick grooming from the movie is available on the companion DVD in the Chapter 3 folder as bird_3.mb. There is also a small scene file called brush_practice.mb in the Chapter 3 folder. This is a simple tuft of hair on which you can practice brushing virtual hair. The effects of the brushes are easily seen here.

Shave and a Haircut has a sizable feature set. Let's look at some of those other features.

SIXTIES SHAG RUG

Shave and a Haircut has some fun and useful features that help users get the most from their imagination. Shave and a Haircut's parameters are such that you can create something that might not otherwise have been very easy. Shag carpet, which is the scourge of good taste, was once very popular, and it's due for a comeback. Joe Alter has spent considerable time studying which components make up a hair and how it can be reproduced in the renderer. It seems that the parameters for creating perfect hair can also be used for creating other fibers.

ON THE DVD

Load peace_1.mb from the companion DVD in the Chapter 3 folder. This small square patch has a standard grass preset on it. We will use that as the starting point for creating our shag rug. Select the shaveHair1 node in either the Hypergraph or the Shave Select menu in the Maya menus at the top of the screen. The grass is too long to be a shag rug, so it should be shortened. Figure 3.12 shows the changes to be made in the shaveHair1 node under the General Properties tab in the Attribute window. Use all the parameters, but take note of a few in particular.

- The Hair Count has been raised to 60,000. This may be overkill, but the hairs are now short, which may expose the plane from which they emanate.
- The Scale is where we have actually shortened the hair fibers. Since the hair is now very short, the Hair Segments may be lowered as well.
- Rand Scale set to zero ensures consistency of the height of each fiber. There is no deviation in length to this shag rug's fibers.
- The root and tip thickness have to be adjusted to a more accurate shape and diameter. The Root Thickness is now much higher. This mimics a thicker fiber, creates more texture surface, and covers the ground plane. The tip thickness is now closer to a shag carpet fiber in thickness.

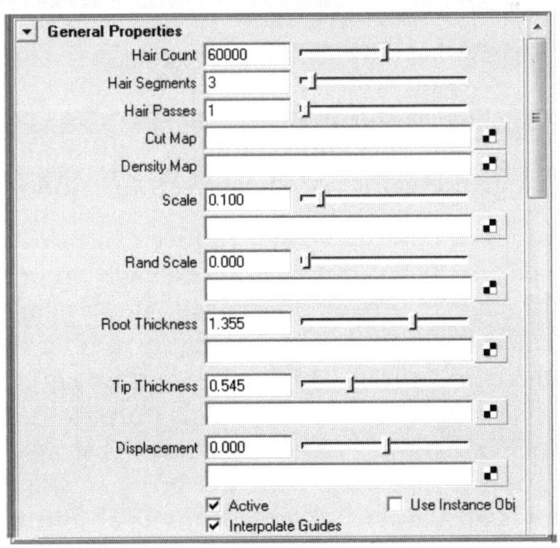

FIGURE 3.12 Proper parameters for the start of the shag rug.

Render this out at a good, low approaching angle. Figure 3.13 shows what the shag carpet should look like so far. At this point, it is certainly more like carpet than grass. The carpet is similar to sculpted pile carpet rather than a shag rug. Save your work.

FIGURE 3.13 Test render of the shag rug.

ON THE DVD

The exercise up to this point is reproduced as peace_2.mb and is located on the companion DVD in the Chapter 3 folder. A little adjusting is in order to get closer to our goal. Change the values of the shaveHair1 node to that of Figures 3.14 and 3.15.

- The number of hairs has been reduced from 60,000. There were just too many densely packed hairs in proximity to each other.
- The hair scale has been increased. It was far too short for shag rug fibers. Lengthening them and reducing their number moves us closer to our goal.
- Root Thickness and Tip Thickness are now equal values. This creates a fiber that is more like a tube than a cone. This mimics shag fiber more closely.
- Under the Kink and Frizz tabs, we have basically straightened out the fibers. The sculpted pile carpet look with the grooves was a result of these values. Figure 3.15 shows all values lowered to their absolute definable lows. Some of these values are not zero.

ON THE DVD

Render the scene. Figure 3.16 shows a much closer approximation to shag carpeting. This seems suitable. Render it from various angles to get different perspectives on it. Experimenting with the values is the key to tweaking the carpet to suit your eye. Save your work. The scene file that rendered Figure 3.16 is located on the companion DVD in the Chapter 3 folder. It is called peace_3.mb.

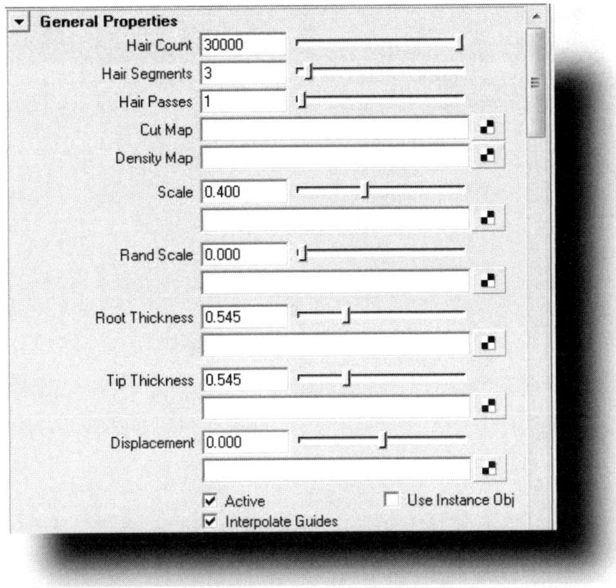

FIGURE 3.14 New values under the General Properties tab.

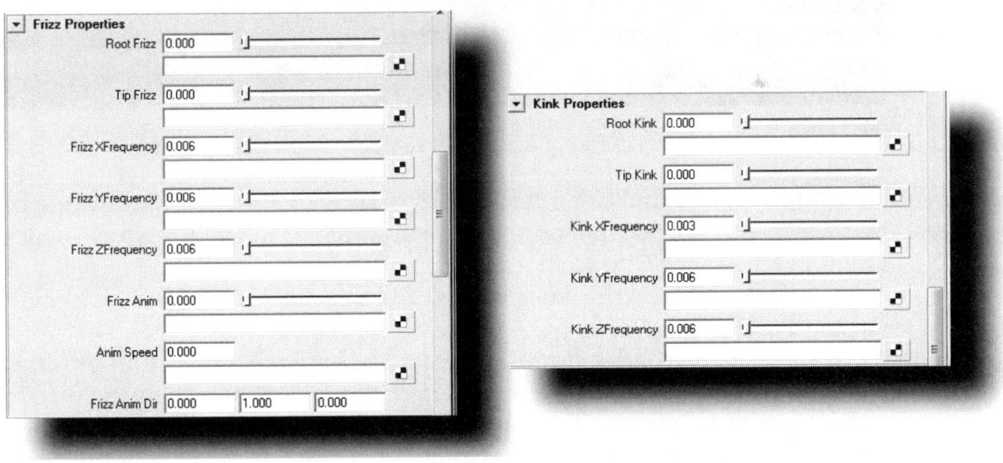

FIGURE 3.15 Lowering Frizz and Kink values straightens out the carpet fibers.

FIGURE 3.16 New values create a much more realistic look for the shag rug.

ON THE DVD

Shag is so 60s and 70s, but the color of our rug is a little drab. Some color would really spruce it up. Located on the companion DVD in the Chapter 3 folder is a scene called peace_4.mb. This scene is similar to all our prior work but has a few tweaks. In short, we reduced the fiber count, added a little kink and frizz, and made the fibers a little longer.

ON THE DVD

It's very easy to color fur in Shave and a Haircut. This is another tool that allows the user greater flexibility for achieving amazing results. We want to apply a color map to the tips of the hair. With the shaveHair1 node selected, go to the Materials tab in the Shave Attribute Editor. Under Tip Color, we want to apply a color map instead of a specific color (see Figure 3.17). Load a color map using peace_color.jpg located on the companion DVD in the Chapter 3 folder. This is the color map for the hair tips.

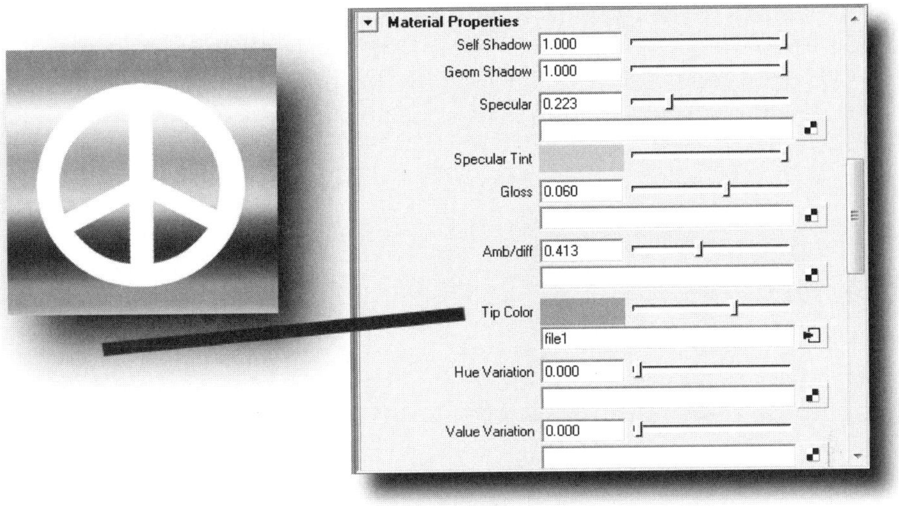

FIGURE 3.17 Peace sign file used as color map for hair's tip color.

Rendering the scene file out should yield a psychedelic shag rug that looks similar to Figure 3.18.

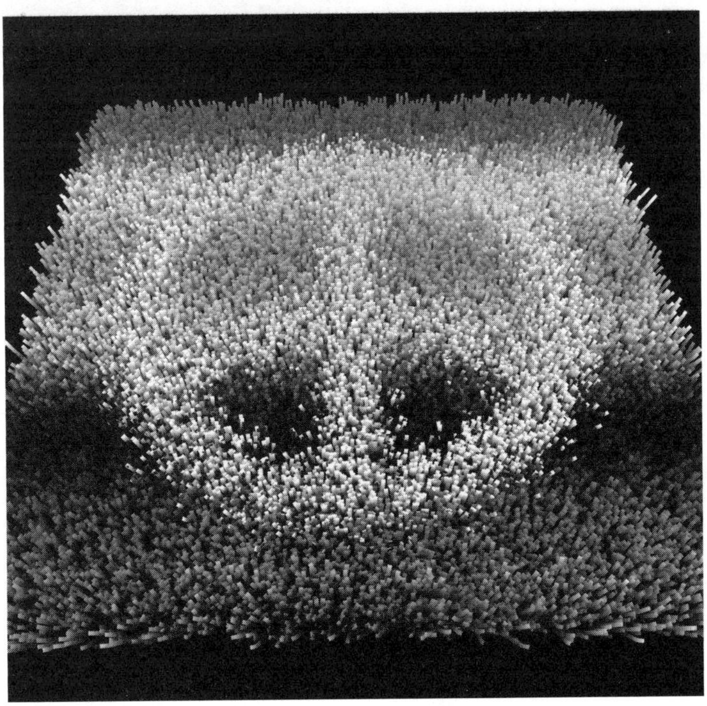

FIGURE 3.18 The shag rug with a new rainbow-colored dye job and a symbol of peace.

Color is not the only attribute that can be mapped. It is very easy to actually cut the hair based on a grayscale matte. Under the General Properties tab is the Cut Map input (see Figure 3.19). Clicking the file input tab allows you to select a map that trims the hair based on the grayscale height of the image.

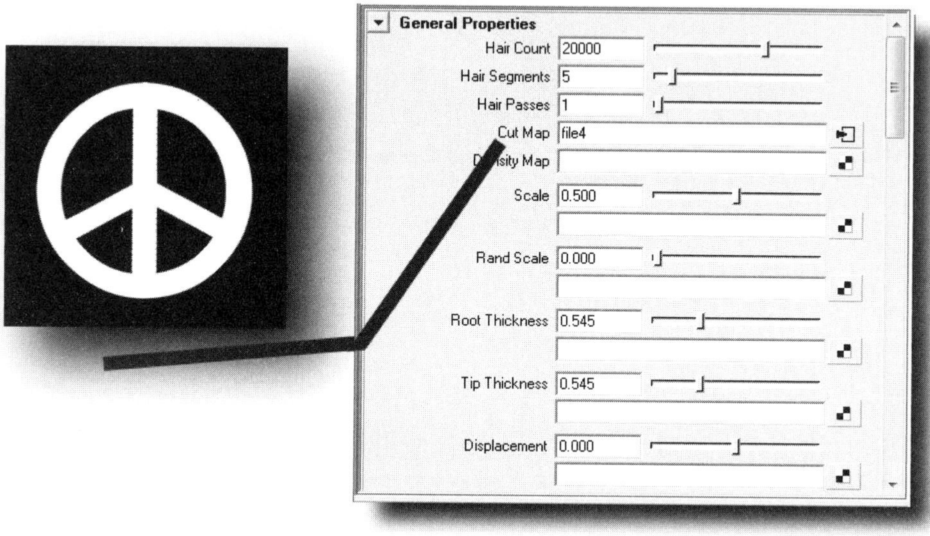

FIGURE 3.19 Cut Map input and a grayscale image as a height map to cut hair.

Shave and a Haircut interpolates height based on the grayscale values of the image. This is a very familiar concept and a staple in CG. Figure 3.20 and Figure 3.21 show the same shag rug trimmed with the Cut Maps that created them. As you can see, this can be a powerful tool.

ON THE DVD

Other parameters can be mapped as well. It's possible to map hair density, hair length, root thickness, tip thickness, and many others parameters. Figure 3.22 shows hair scale and the map that created it. Notice the length of the hair mimics the grayscale image in the upper right-hand corner of the image. This is a typical height map used in many 3D packages. Areas of pure white will generate the longest hairs while areas on the map of pure black will be the shortest hair. Any degree of gray is an interpolated value between the pure black and the pure white values of the map. There is a world of tremendous possibility here. We have included the color maps and grayscale images used in this section on the companion DVD in the Chapter 3 folder. There are also bonus materials not shown here.

FIGURE 3.20 The shag rug with a new rainbow-colored dye job and a peace symbol cut from it.

FIGURE 3.21 The opposite cut map from Figure 3.20 yields the opposite haircut.

FIGURE 3.22 The height of these shag fibers is determined by a grayscale height map.

Other features of Shave and a Haircut need to be touched on. Save your work and let's look at some hair dynamics.

BLOWING IN THE WIND

The use of computer-generated hair basically demands some sort of dynamic interaction with other objects, the elements, and themselves. If hair doesn't move, it looks like some sort of helmet or rigid "hair hat." Shave and a Haircut has a dynamics engine built in and integrates with Maya's dynamics. Let's take a quick tour of Shave and a Haircut's hair dynamics. Load the file brush_practice.mb from the companion

ON THE DVD

DVD in the Chapter 3 folder. We have previously used this to practice brushing techniques. We can use it now to see dynamics at work. The scene as it stands is nothing more than a sphere with a Shave and a Haircut hair node attached to the top polygons. Shave and a Haircut has a Live Mode that is, for all intents and purposes, real time. Select the shaveHair1 node. Once it's selected, you can turn on Live Mode. This can be found in the Shave menu at the top of the Maya screen. Select Shave > Dynamics > Live Mode, as shown in Figure 3.23. With Live Mode on, the hairs should fall down and pass right through the sphere they emanate from.

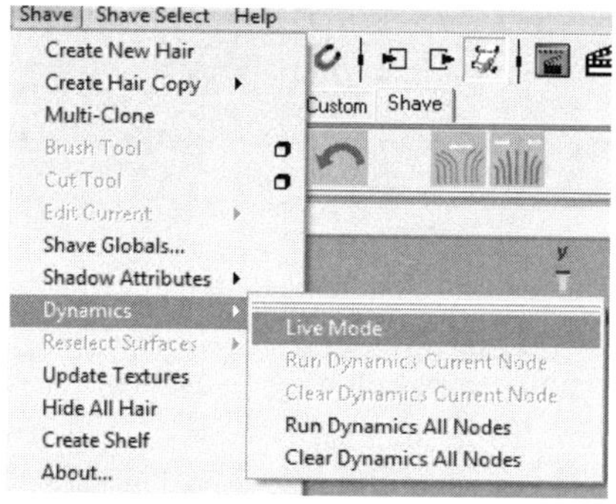

FIGURE 3.23 Live Mode allows some interesting real-time feedback.

With the shaveHair1 node selected, go to the Dynamics tab in the Attribute Editor. All the values should be set to zero as shown in Figure 3.24.

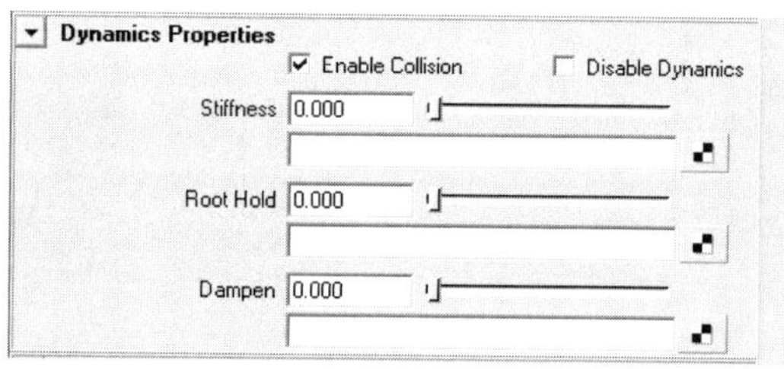

FIGURE 3.24 The Dynamics attributes of the shaveHair1 node.

ON THE DVD

Start by lightly tweaking the Dampen slider, and the hairs begin to rise. You can add a little stiffness to it as well. Sliding these values back and forth gets you real-time dynamic feedback of those values. Figure 3.25 and Figure 3.26 display the range of dynamic reaction to the Stiffness and Dampen parameters. Now, with the polygon sphere node selected, you can drag it around the screen, and the hair follows dynamically and in near real time. You can rotate and scale the sphere as well. If you get lost, the file can be found on the companion DVD in the Chapter 3 folder. It is called dynamics_1.mb. If you reload the scene file, make sure you select the hair node and turn Live Mode back on.

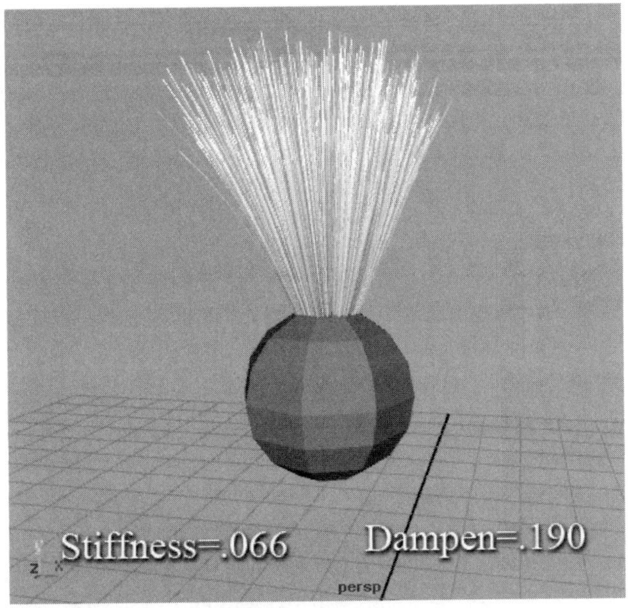

FIGURE 3.25 Stiffen value set to .066 and the Dampen value set to .190 show more rigid dynamic reaction.

FIGURE 3.26 Stiffen value set to 0.0 and the Dampen value set to .101 relaxes hair dynamics.

ON THE DVD

The problem with this is that the hair passes through the sphere. No collision is calculated. This would not be very effective as a hairstyle. Hair should not pass through the head. We can easily remedy this. Load the scene file dynamics_2.mb located on the companion DVD in the Chapter 3 folder. This is basically the same file as dynamics_1.mb, with the addition of a low-polygon copy of the sphere already in the scene. The new sphere is of equal size and position. This serves as a collision proxy for the hair. Highlight the original sphere called pSphere1 and make it invisible. With the shaveHair1 node selected, choose the polygon faces in the proxy sphere to be included in the dynamic simulation. These selected polygons, as shown in Figure 3.27, collide with the hairs and do not allow them to pass through the sphere.

FIGURE 3.27 Highlighted polygons are included in the dynamic simulation with the hair.

With the polygons and the shaveHair1 node selected, go to the Shave Menu and select Shave > Edit Current > Update Collision Mesh. This can be seen in Figure 3.28.

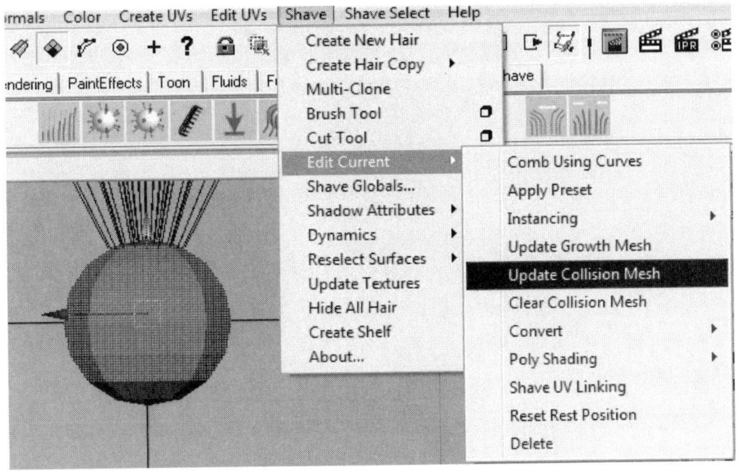

FIGURE 3.28 Selected polygons are linked dynamically to the shaveHair1 node.

ON THE DVD

There is one small problem. We have the appearance of a sphere with a tuft of hair coming from it. It's actually two spheres: one to grow the hair and one for the collision. We need to group pSphere1 and pSphere2 together. As before, go to the Maya menus. Select Shave > Dynamics > Live Mode. Select the new grouping of pSphere1 and pSphere2. You can now drag it around the screen and get real-time feedback of the hair moving. This time, however, the hair collides quite nicely with the sphere. Figures 3.29 shows how the hair collides with the sphere, while Figure 3.30 shows how the hair lays on the sphere surface observing collision detection. Save your work. For your convenience, we have included this file, called dynamics_3.mb, on the companion DVD in the Chapter 3 folder.

FIGURE 3.29 This mental ray render shows 10,000 hairs passing through the sphere's surface.

FIGURE 3.30 The hairs now obey the collision detection and rest on the sphere's surface.

We've covered some basic features of Joe Alter's Shave and a Haircut. As you work with the program, it will become apparent how much ingenuity and creative thought has gone into making this Maya plugin a big success. Its functionality is deserving of a book all to itself, but, alas, there is more plugin technology to delve into ahead. With that said, let's forge on.

CHAPTER

4 COLOR, TEXTURE, LIGHTING, AND RENDERING

In This Chapter

- Introduction
- The Right Look
- Common Rendering Terms
- Pixar's RenderMan for Maya
- RenderMan Compliance
- Light Simulators

A scene from *Ratatouille* rendered in RenderMan.
© 2007 Disney/Pixar

INTRODUCTION

The three basic stages of the CG animation process are modeling, animation, and rendering. That's a bit of oversimplification because these stages can be broken down into substeps. In the rendering stage, we must consider the lighting, texturing, and final output of the scene. In the end, the culmination of all this work is sent to a renderer. The renderer interprets all the intricacies of the models, the calculated movements of any animation, and the nuances of texture and lighting. The renderer then outputs this amalgam of virtual 3D world data into our 2D perception of that world at 24 or 30 frames per second. In gaming this holds true as well but certain considerations are made for a real-time rendering engine. This is often at 60 frames per second. It sounds complicated, but it's all worth it.

Not all renderers are created equal. They don't necessarily interpret the scene data in the same way. Maya originally had a passable renderer that received a litany of complaints. Maya is an ever-evolving project, and eventually the goal of a new renderer was reached. The highly regarded and award-winning mental ray® was eventually incorporated as part of the base Maya package. Maya now has four native renderers to choose from.

- **Maya software:** The software renderer is an all-around renderer that is quite capable of producing excellent-quality imagery. It has shortcomings such as speed, and it lacks features for producing more photo-real images such as global illumination.
- **Maya hardware:** The hardware renderer uses the capabilities of your computer's graphics card to render directly. The imagery is broadcast quality and is speedier than the software renderer. It has limitations similar to the software renderer but is a viable choice depending upon the requirements of your work.
- **Maya vector:** The vector renderer is a focused renderer that can be used to generate vector-based imagery. This renderer is great for outputting to web-ready file formats such as SWF. The vector capabilities of this renderer are often used to gain a certain stylized look such as the flatness of 2D cartoons or limited palette renderings. This renderer is great for these special needs.
- **mental ray:** mental ray has a devoted following and is a welcome addition to Maya. It addresses some of the complaints about the Maya software renderer. The mental ray renderer is capable of producing more realistic images that often require entities such as caustics, special lighting, and more realistic shadowing as shown in Figure 4.1 and Figure 4.2.

FIGURE 4.1 Two metal rings bounce and spin after being dropped as caustic reflections dance from their surfaces.

FIGURE 4.2 Shadows are cast from two marbles created from different materials.

This render in mental ray shows light passing through one of the marbles and falling on the ground plane, an effect not likely achievable in the Maya software renderer.

The Right Look

While the Maya renderer may have shortcomings, that does not disqualify it for a job. We are not taking a stand on which renderer is best. It is more a question of what are the capabilities of each and does that fit into the aesthetic of the imagery you hope to achieve. There are pros and cons to the choice of renderer that is used for any given job. One must ask several question. Does my project require photo-realistic imagery or a more artistic representation of the world? Does this renderer create the effect and stylistic tone I am looking for? Am I using a renderer that is overkill for the job at hand? Often the Maya hardware renderer does a fantastic job of producing the quality of look required. Using the Maya software renderer over the Maya hardware renderer may be time-consuming. Fine photo-real images are possible in the Maya software renderer, but you may require the alternate quality and feature set of mental ray to gain the desired look and feel for your images. There is a world of possibilities, and a balance of technology, capability, quality, and time should ultimately help you choose your renderer.

Renderers can make all the difference in the world to your image. In many ways, the renderer is the last and most important piece of the virtual world or scene you have built. The deft placement of lighting and the careful and deliberate texturing of models is vital. The same scene will take on a drastically different ambiance based on these factors. The renderer you use will be important as well. In fact, the renderer will help determine how you exploit lighting and texturing in a scene. Figure 4.3, Figure 4.4, and Figure 4.5 show the same scene rendered by Maya's native mental ray renderer, software renderer, and vector renderer, respectively.

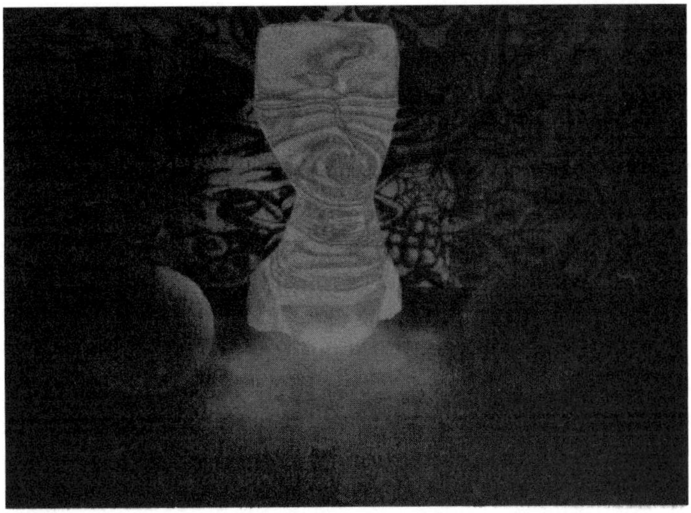

FIGURE 4.3 Two point lights and one spotlight illuminate this scene using the mental ray renderer.

The point lights are nearly nonexistent in intensity and are placed in front of the spheres at a 0.1 intensity. The spotlight, with an intensity of 0.9, is behind the Tiki figure's head. Mental ray's global illumination, caustics, and final gathering were used to render this scene. The low light is much less of a concern when using global illumination, as the light bounces from object to object sharing its energy. The spotlight passing from behind the figure produces caustic reflections at its base.

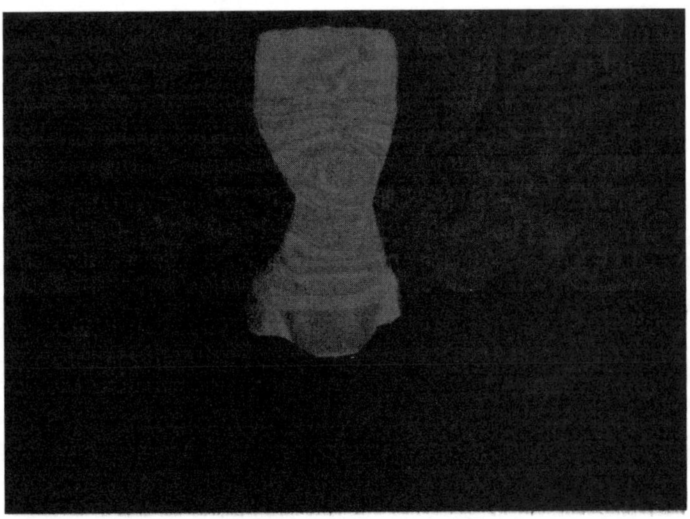

FIGURE 4.4 The same scene using the same lighting conditions as the mental ray render shows a substantial difference when raytraced in the Maya software renderer.

While the spotlight barely illuminates the Tiki figure, the two point lights are, for all intents and purposes, useless. The spotlight does generate enough light to see that the software renderer has calculated the raytraced refractions of the Tiki figure.

FIGURE 4.5 With the variable settings of Maya's vector renderer, the limited palette produces imagery more consistent with Flash vector graphics.

The vector renderer parameters can be adjusted for a range of looks, including outlined objects, a broader color palette, and more image detail. The two point lights' intensities were increased from 0.1 to 1.0 for this vector render, or else the entire image would have rendered black.

There are third-party considerations for rendering the final output of your masterpiece. The choice of a renderer is usually made based on a variety of reasons, including time, quality, subject matter, simplicity, cost, and the desire to create the impossible. The choice of a renderer may also be determined by the type of project you are working on. Ultra-photo-real renderers may make for amazing animation or visual effects, but time constraints may make that impractical. On the other hand, these renderers are becoming a mainstay for product visualization, architectural visualization, and design. Again, it is the balance between the practical and probable versus aesthetic and artistic. We will take a succinct look at some of the possibilities and a few alternative ways of achieving that final result.

Common Rendering Terms

As you delve into the intricacies and features of any renderer, you will most likely come in contact with some common terms. Let's take a brief look at some of the most common advanced technical terms that produce the most dramatic effects. This is by no means a complete glossary of terms, but gives a background for some of the text to follow.

- **Photo-realistic:** For our purposes the terms *photo-real, photo-realistic,* and *photo-realism* are used when describing an image that appears to be an authentic representation of the real world. The creation of a photo-real image takes into account lighting and shading to produce an image of painstaking detail fooling the eye into believing it is seeing a photograph.
- **Ray tracing:** This rendering technique calculates the path of individual light rays as they bounce through a scene and return to the camera (eye). Ray tracing is used to create a more photo-realistic image by calculating refraction, reflection, and reasonably accurate shadows.
- **Refraction:** Refraction is a term borrowed from physics that describes the change in direction of light as it passes through or is absorbed by a material. This is best seen in the distortion of an image seen through glass, crystal, or even water. Many materials have an index of refraction value that determines with precise accuracy how much light is altered when passing through a medium.
- **Reflection:** In contrast to refraction, reflection is the path that light takes as it partially or wholly bounces from a surface. A surface that reflects light will mirror its surroundings in whole or in part based on the wavelengths of light absorbed and bounced from a surface.
- **Caustics:** *Caustics* is a term used to describe the refractive and reflective anomalies that are caused by light passing through or bouncing off a curved surface, causing light to become focused. This is most famously seen as the dancing light at the bottom of a swimming pool on a sunny day. This can also be seen in the focused reflected light from a shiny metallic wedding band on a tabletop.
- **Global illumination (GI):** For the sake of avoiding a long technical explanation, we will lump global illumination, radiosity, and final gathering under one umbrella. These terms are related to the calculation of bounced light between surfaces. Often referred to as secondary lighting, global illumination calculates the shared energy of light between objects in a scene. These techniques are used for creating a much more realistic lighting model. The surface colors of a red sphere, white sphere, and yellow ground plane will bounce and bleed into each other's surfaces, adding to the overall lighting of the scene. Although subtle, the effect can lend itself to a more accurate and photo-real image.
- **Radiosity:** *See* global illumination.
- **Final gather:** *See* global illumination.
- **HDRI:** High dynamic range imaging (HDRI) is closely related to global illumination. The HDRI format represents a far broader range of the color spectrum, culminating in images that consider radiance and luminance in addition to RGB

values. HDRI images are not represented properly on a monitor and are not correctly distinguished. The extra information embedded in HDRI can be used by a software renderer to represent global scene lighting more properly.

- **Deep shadows:** This method for calculating shadows takes into account varying depths of self-shadowing of a pixel and variable transparencies and volumes such as fog and smoke. This technique produces more accurate and realistic self-shadowing results while rendering significantly faster, and also it takes into account motion blur.
- **Subsurface scattering (SSS):** SSS is a technique for calculating the transfer of light through translucent surfaces. Light penetrating the surface of materials such as marble, wax, or even skin, tends to bounce within the material before exiting. These calculations produce very real approximations of this phenomenon and take on stunning visual meaning. A human ear is a good example of how SSS represents the thin membrane of the ear as backlight passes through it.
- **Z-buffer:** A z-buffer or z-depth introduces another value to the single surface pixel. Along with the RGB values that constitute a pixel's color, z-depth contains a value of the pixel's distance from the eye or camera.
- **Alpha channels:** Similar to z-depth, the alpha channel calculates the opacity or transparency of a pixel. This value can range from 100 percent transparent to 100 percent opaque. Alpha channels are grayscale values and are embedded in various image formats, such as tiff, iff, and targa. Images containing these channels are very valuable for compositing images together for the final scene.
- **Bump mapping:** This technique calculates bumpy textured surfaces and uses deviations in the surface normals to create 3D bumps, scratches, markings, and anomalies. This is a 2D effect that is lost by observing the profile or silhouette of an object.
- **Displacement mapping:** Unlike bump mapping, displacement mapping actually alters the surface geometry of an object and is discernible from the profile or silhouette of the displaced geometry.
- **Render passes:** A good renderer can render an image into separate components. These render passes are invaluable in the final composite of a frame. A typical set of render passes may include, but is not limited to, a beauty pass, alpha pass, refraction pass, reflection pass, shadow pass, specular pass, diffusion pass, z-depth, and color pass. The renderer creates a separate file for each pass per frame, and the composite brings them together to form the final image. This is a necessity in high-caliber effects work. One advantage to this is render time. A single frame may take 40 minutes or longer to render. When a shot must be tweaked to perfection, the single components necessary for the proper change may take a fraction of the time. Once rendered, these new passes replace the old ones in the composite for near instant feedback. Individual passes may also be directly altered in the composite, saving a re-render of the passes in question. This type of micromanaging of the single image generates a great deal of data. A program such as RenderMan Pro Server is an ideal tool for maximizing the efficiency of these projects.

- **Compositing:** Compositing joins the various components of a single frame to produce the final image. This may include the various render passes mentioned above but also the incorporation of this CG data into a live action plate. A variety of programs do this type of work. A list can be found at www.bigheadekitty.com/compositors.
- **RIB:** The RIB (RenderMan Interface Bytestream) file format is Pixar's proprietary file format that contains geometry, shaders, lighting, camera data, and much more. RIB files written in accordance with the RenderMan Interface Specification can be sent to a RenderMan-compliant renderer to produce the image described in the RIB file.

PIXAR'S RENDERMAN FOR MAYA

If there is a single rendering technology that most animators and visual effects artists would choose to be stranded on a desert island with, that would be Pixar's RenderMan. This Academy Award–winning software is the rendering system that is the overwhelming preference at most major Hollywood FX houses. The imagery generated by RenderMan is of a superior and consistent quality and continues to be the most reliable renderer. That's a tremendous advantage and a necessity when a film is using RenderMan as its core. Pixar is a unique mix of film production studio and software developer. RenderMan is time tested and continuously being developed in production at Pixar.

Three main products from Pixar may constitute a Maya rendering pipeline.

- RenderMan Studio is a complete set of tools for creating the amazing imagery seen in so many Hollywood films.
- RenderMan for Maya is a plugin for Maya that seamlessly integrates the powerful functions of RenderMan into the Maya interface.
- RenderMan Pro Server can turn a desktop computer or server into a finely-tuned RenderMan server.

PRACTICE MAKES PERFECT

The value of a renderer's reputation for being a stalwart contributor to a film can't be understated. It has to be a dependable link in the creative workflow. RenderMan was originally built upon a long lineage of in-house productions at Pixar. Pixar began developing in-house shorts as a way of displaying its own hardware and software technology. Many of these shorts have garnered Oscar nominations and other awards. Pixar also created some groundbreaking and award-winning commercials that included spots for Listerine and Lifesavers candy. In 1995, Pixar released its first full-length film. *Toy Story* became the first fully computer-generated film in history. It went on to garner a host of awards, including a Special Achievement Award from the Academy of Motion Picture Arts and Sciences. *Toy Story* became the catalyst for a new age of animated features. It is interesting to see the development of RenderMan over the years from Pixar's earliest short to their latest film. RenderMan is truly a time-tested and production-savvy renderer, in no small part due to its programmers overcoming the technical challenges presented by their own film work. For an interesting look at the progression of the Pixar short, check out *Pixar Short Films Collection*, Vol. 1. You'll be glad you did. This DVD collection can be found at better online and brick-and-mortar DVD outlets.

A lingering misunderstanding surrounds the semantics of the term *RenderMan* and its slack usage. This is, in part, due to other software packages taking advantage of a standard published and owned by Pixar. RenderMan, or RenderMan Interface Specification, is a set of requirements that describes a 3D scene and its components. Developed by Pixar, the RenderMan Interface Specification was designed to standardize a 3D scene description and to stave off obsolescence by advances in future rendering technology. The term *RenderMan* used in PhotoRealistic RenderMan (PRMan) is Pixar's actual renderer, which is based on its own RenderMan Interface Specification. A renderer that is RenderMan-compliant adheres to the stringent RenderMan Interface Specification, although it can use any number of different rendering algorithms. We will mention one of these a bit later in this chapter. The current version of the RenderMan Interface Specification is available on their website at renderman.pixar.com/products/rispec/index.htm. It requires a serious knowledge of computer graphics programming and is not for the novice. It is, however, an amazing read.

The Maya implementation of RenderMan, called, simply, RenderMan for Maya, plugs into Maya seamlessly and adheres to the RenderMan Interface Specification. Scenes set up in Maya can be rendered directly to PRMan, which is embedded as a seamless part of Maya. As with the native Maya renderers, the selection of RenderMan can be made in the Render Globals as shown in Figure 4.6. Figure 4.7 shows a RenderMan scene in the Maya interface.

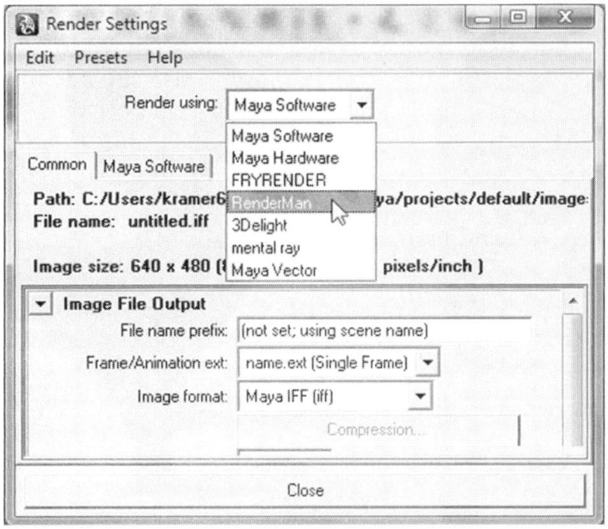

FIGURE 4.6 Selection of the RenderMan renderer is done in Render Globals, as is the case with the native Maya Renders.

FIGURE 4.7 A favorite find at SIGGRAPH, this Pixar tchotchke of the famous Utah Teapot of CG lore is rendered in Maya for RenderMan.
© 2007 Pixar

There is a standard and pro implementation of RenderMan for Maya. The Pro version is part of RenderMan Studio and RenderMan Pro Server. The substantial difference between the two is the ability to use the advanced features for writing custom tools, effects, and shaders. The interaction with the RenderMan renderer is flawless. Maya materials are converted for use in RenderMan. Almost all of what is familiar to the Maya user can be sent to RenderMan. This includes the native Maya systems such as Maya Fur, Maya Hair, Maya Paint Effects, and software particles (see Figure 4.8 and Figure 4.9).

FIGURE 4.8 Maya Hair and Maya Fur can be rendered in RenderMan

FIGURE 4.9 Maya Particles can be rendered with RenderMan.

What makes RenderMan such a lauded renderer is its ability to created rich 3D scene files. This is done through its RenderMan Shader Language, which is very similar to the C programming language. Volumes have been written on the subject of RenderMan, so there is no need to try to present a complete picture of it here. For the purposes of this chapter, it is enough to know that Pixar has created a very good implementation of RenderMan for Maya, and it certainly merits your further investigation. A few other software products link Maya to RenderMan. Let's take a brief look at these tools.

AN INTERVIEW WITH CHRIS FORD
PIXAR ANIMATION STUDIOS' RENDERMAN BUSINESS DIRECTOR

The CG field is a rather small community. People come and go. I was happy to see that Chris Ford had found a home at Pixar as their RenderMan business director. I met Chris many years ago and have always marveled at some technology he was displaying or insight he shared. I was interested in his thoughts on RenderMan and Pixar's achievements, and posed some questions to him.

How did Pixar get its start?

Pixar was created as an independent company in 1986 out of the computer graphics division of Lucasfilm Ltd. From the beginning, Pixar has blended both

continued

art and pioneering technology to create some of the most successful animated films of all time, including *Toy Story*, *Finding Nemo*, *The Incredibles*, *Cars*, and most recently *Ratatouille*, together grossing more than $4 billion at the worldwide box office to date. Since 1986, Pixar has also developed many key technological innovations in CG film production, including the RenderMan renderer that remains the primary rendering application used in cinematic feature animation and visual effects.

Pixar has received several Academy Award considerations on multiple fronts. What were they for?

Pixar has won 20 Academy Awards to date for both its movies and its technology. For RenderMan specifically, in 1993, the Academy of Motion Picture Arts and Sciences honored the developers of RenderMan with a Scientific and Engineering Achievement Award for their contribution to the motion picture industry. An Academy Award of Merit (Oscar) was also awarded "for significant advancements to the field of motion picture rendering as exemplified in Pixar's RenderMan" as part of the 73rd Scientific and Technical Academy Awards ceremony presentation on March 3, 2001. This was the first Oscar awarded to a software package for its outstanding contributions to the field.

Does RenderMan benefit from your production challenges? Can you cite any examples?

RenderMan's ongoing development directly benefits from 20 years of accumulated production expertise at Pixar. RenderMan is unique in that it is the product of a major film studio and is stress tested not only by the demands of Pixar's own films, but also by the majority of visual effects studios. This intensity of testing and user feedback, focused on one common core technology, has no parallel and is fundamental to RenderMan's stability and reputation. The cinematic introduction of hair/fur, the fast processing of super-large datasets, and photorealistic motion-blur and depth of field are but a small sample of many production challenges overcome.

What really distinguishes RenderMan from other renderers?

Pixar's RenderMan is fundamentally responsible for the revolution in computer-generated cinematic imagery over the past 20 years and has consistently broken new ground. Beyond key functional areas such as motion blur, depth of field, displacements, deep shadows, and many other specific features, RenderMan is above all distinguished by its reliability proven in hundreds of motion pictures. Developing a renderer is one thing. Developing a production solid renderer that can predictably deliver on time and budget to a consistent level of quality is a completely different order of achievement. RenderMan is solely focused on the demands of cutting-edge feature film quality and will continue that tradition into the future.

RenderMan is used to generate things that are not usually associated with shaders, such as terrain. Can you cite a few examples?

A key component of Pixar's RenderMan is the RenderMan specification—the RI Spec, which provides information to describe geometry and shaders in 3D and is where RenderMan really stands out as a flexible solution. Very frequently in production, custom tools are developed to create procedural effects using this specification. These types of effects might range from anything from terrain to fur to bustling cities to downy feathers, effects that are far too complicated to model by hand. These effects also generate huge amounts of data, putting enormous demands on the rendering architecture, and rendering highly-scaled datasets is where RenderMan particularly excels.

What was the most unusual, creative, challenging, or inventive use of RenderMan?

Every production has its quota of new surprises and challenges, often down to each individual shot. The answer then to which shot is most creative or challenging is usually all of them! This is why RenderMan has been developed to be flexible enough to allow movie-makers and technical directors to be clever for themselves. RenderMan has been developed, with great pains, to advance the key concept that the renderer shouldn't impose arbitrary limitations on the creative and technical processes of making a film.

Where do you see CG lacking right now? What hurdles need to be addressed?

In the world of Pixar's RenderMan, we see a consistent demand for more education. There are many studios ramping up to take on large feature film projects who find themselves looking for well-qualified technical directors. Unfortunately, there are not enough to go around. To address this, we've been working with schools and universities to add production-focused RenderMan training to their curriculum. To help with this goal, we've recently released our RenderMan Certified Courseware, which reveals the details of how leading studios actually use RenderMan and which is a highly valuable tool for schools, studios, and individuals.

What's down the road for Pixar and your software?

As you know, Pixar is currently working on a number of animated feature films, all of which will be rendered using RenderMan. The images that Pixar puts on the big screen are ultimately limited by the capabilities of the rendering technology, and that's why Pixar is committed to pushing the state of the art in this area—simply, it is what we live and breathe. A recent example of innovation is the use of stereoscopic rendering to create a number of forthcoming 3D films in which RenderMan is optimized to produce the imagery at a high degree of computing efficiency.

RenderMan Compliance

RenderMan for Maya, while being able to take advantage of PRMan, cannot read or write RIB files. It internally converts work done in the Maya interface to be used by the renderer. Output to PRMan through Maya allows the imagery produced to take advantage of the quality and speed of the renderer. More expert qualities, such as writing RIB files, are part of the RenderMan for Maya Pro. This is certainly an impetus for upgrading. There are, however, other Maya-specific products capable of using RenderMan. One of these products is Animal Logic's MayaMan. This Maya plugin translates a Maya scene into Pixar's RIB format and converts your materials into RenderMan shaders. Animal Logic is another one of those production house–software developers that makes the fruits of their labor available to the rest of us. MayaMan has been used on the bulk of their production work in film and television over the past decade. Their film work includes *Happy Feet, 300, 28 Weeks Later, Fool's Gold, The Matrix, Moulin Rouge!,* and *World Trade Center*. Animal Logic also uses MayaMan in their commercial work, as seen in their work for Smirnoff and Toyota, as well as music videos. Stills from this work are shown in Figure 4.10, Figure 4.11, and Figure 4.12.

FIGURE 4.10 Smirnoff Ice "Icicle" commercial. *Image courtesy of Animal Logic*

In Figure 4.10, in an ice-covered cave, hundreds of Smirnoff Ice bottles are frozen to the ceiling as stalactites. Suddenly, one breaks off, crashing into the ground, creating an instant party. Animal Logic created an entire CG environment for the ad, with only a few small live action elements incorporated in the first few shots. The team created the cave, the CG icicles and bottles, as well as the shattering effect when one bottle falls and breaks through the ice.

FIGURE 4.11 Ice vehicle from a Toyota Prado commercial.
Image courtesy of Animal Logic

The graceful, gliding, four-wheel drive vehicle made of ice shown in Figure 4.11 was needed for Toyota Prado's latest television commercial, "Ice Sculptures," directed by Bruce Hunt through @radical.media. Animal Logic created the 3D computer-generated ice car and carefully choreographed its movement as it glides across various road surfaces, verging on being out of control.

FIGURE 4.12 A scene from Telemetry Orchestra's music video "Under the Cherry Tree."
Image courtesy of Animal Logic

MayaMan is not specifically a renderer, but like RenderMan for Maya, it allows Maya users to take advantage of RenderMan-compliant rendering solutions such as PRMan, 3Delight, Air, and others. It translates Maya materials, geometry, lighting, cameras, and more. Unlike RenderMan for Maya, which renders within Maya using the embedded PRMan, MayaMan can write Maya scene files out to the RIB format for use in other renderers. Additionally, MayaMan can read and attach external custom RenderMan shaders to objects within a Maya scene. RenderMan for Maya cannot do this unless you are using RenderMan for Maya Pro, which is bundled with RenderMan Pro Server or RenderMan Studio.

Quite a few RenderMan-compliant renderers are out there. One of those renderers is 3Delight from dna research. 3Delight integrates smoothly into the Maya interface, as shown in Figure 4.13 and Figure 4.14. It renders within Maya with its own renderer, or scenes can be exported as RIB files and rendered in another RenderMan-compliant renderer. As with MayaMan, both Maya materials and RenderMan shaders can be assigned to objects within the Maya scene.

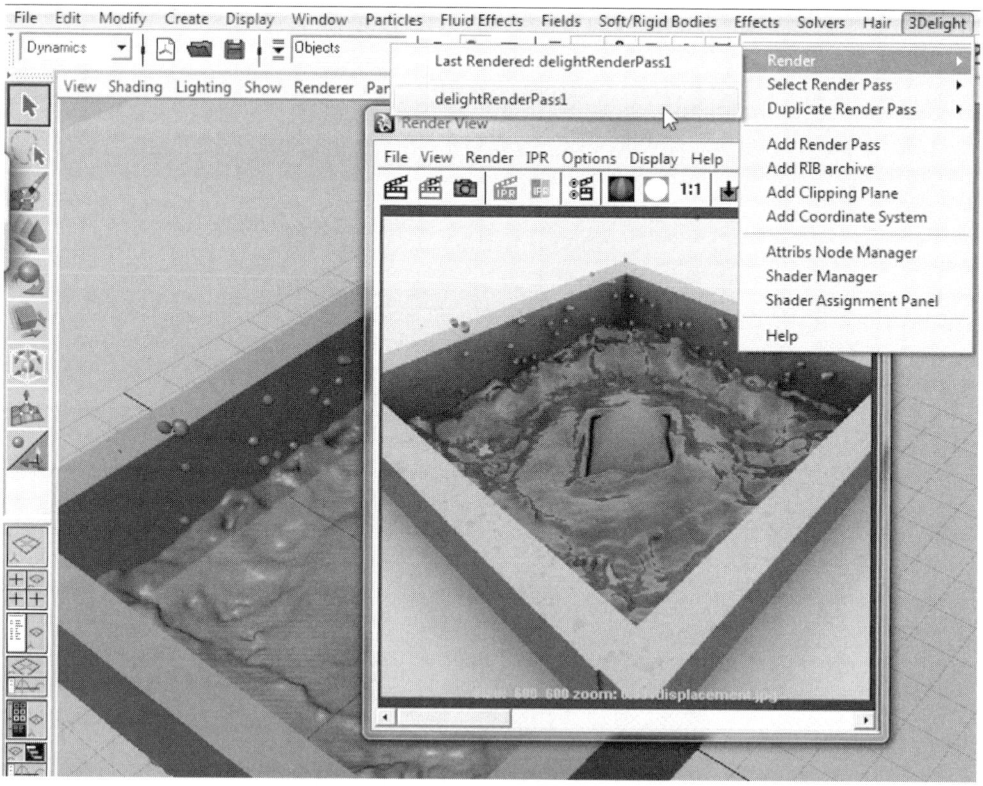

FIGURE 4.13 Rendering of specific render passes within the Maya Interface with 3Delight.

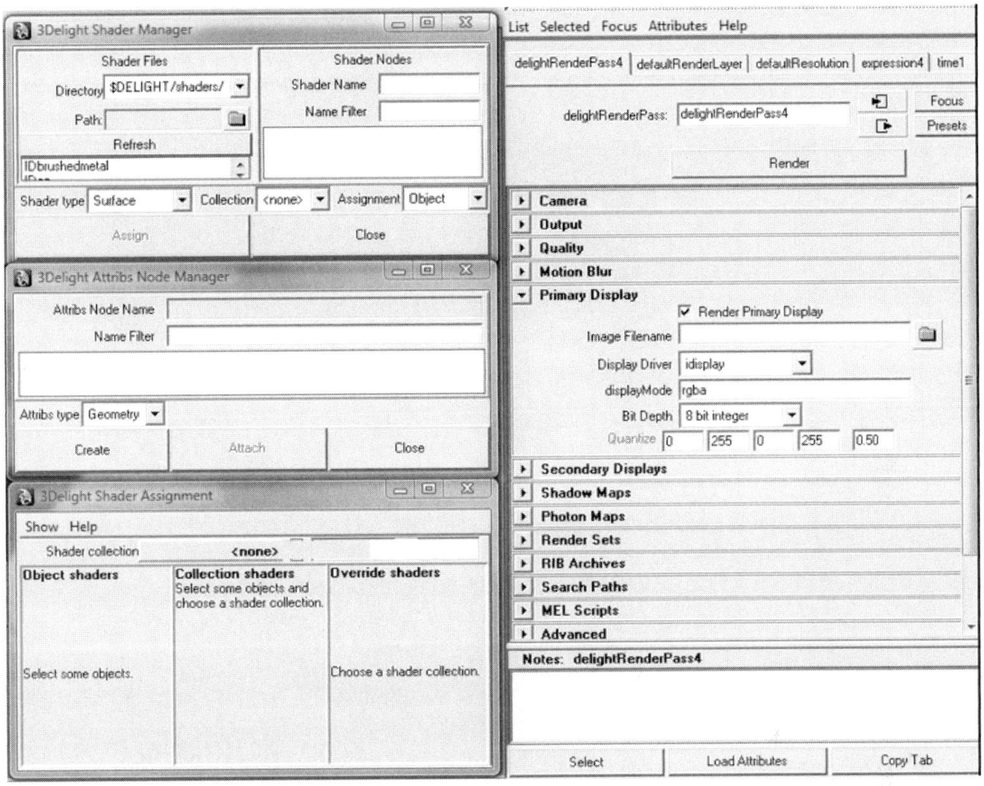

FIGURE 4.14 The 3Delight Shader Manager, 3Delight Shader Assignment, and 3Delight Attribs Node Manager are part of the 3Delight interface within Maya.

3Delight can achieve some very realistic imagery and has tools such as very high-quality displacement mapping, depth of field, motion blur, ray tracing and shadow maps, subsurface scattering on a per object basis, global illumination supporting HDRI, and final gathering. Figure 4.15, Figure 4.16, and Figure 4.17 are rendered directly within Maya using 3Delight.

FIGURE 4.15 Global illumination was used taking advantage of HDRI image-based lighting. The water surface is generated as a result of displacement mapping, while the particle splashes were extra geometry created in RealFlow.

FIGURE 4.16 This scene image from *Monolith* was modeled in Blast Code and rendered in 3Delight within the Maya interface.

FIGURE 4.17 Another Scene from Mark Smith's animation project *Monolith* rendered in 3Delight in the Maya interface. The scene is rendered using HDRI-based lighting.

AMAZING ANIMATION

SIGGRAPH is a place to see the latest in computer graphics technology. In 1995, dna research, created by Pierre Lachapelle in association with TFX Animation, in Montreal Canada, wowed SIGGRAPH 1995 with a trailer to a film called *The Boxer*. The animation was far more advanced than anything else around. The piece was rendered in RenderMan and was exceptional on many levels. The software team at dna research has been developing 3Delight for many years, and it is now used in their production work. 3Delight has been involved in some other groundbreaking projects. These include Storm Studio's *Free Jimmy* (www.freejimmy.com; not for children or the faint of heart but truly amazing) and the IMAX film *Adventures in Animation 3D* (www.adventuresinanimation.com). These are highly recommended for any CG enthusiast.

Additionally, 3Delight has been utilized in *The Chronicles of Narnia*, *X-Men: The Last Stand*, *The Fantastic Four*, *Final Destination 3*, *The Woods*, *Bailey's Billions*, *Superman Returns*, and *Charlotte's Web*.

That's a brief look at some RenderMan-compliant Maya programs. Another type of renderer deals with the physical properties of light in a different way. Let's take a quick look at physically-based light simulation for Maya.

Light Simulators

In a separate class of renderer, physically-based light simulation is different in that it takes the paradigm of photography. Terms such as *lumens, wattage, lens, spectral dispersion, focal length, candela control, efficacy, fresnel reflection,* and *temperature* are the norm. These renderers are more properly called physically-based, unbiased spectral renderers. The images produced from these types of renderers look very real. Renderers such as Next Limit Technologies' Maxwell Render and Feversoft's fryrender are becoming favorite renderers in the architectural and product design worlds. The calculations of these renderers are based on the real behavior of light. The term *unbiased* refers to the accuracy of the renderings, which is devoid of the trickery other rendering packages use to create realism. The calculations can come at a cost in rendering time, so the design and architectural firms that use them are more concerned about the accuracy of a still image than full-blown animation. Although it is not impossible to produce animation with these renderers, it can border on painstakingly long. The imagery produced is quite remarkable, however.

Maxwell Render is one of a series of physically accurate simulation programs available from Next Limit Technologies. Their Academy Award–winning software RealFlow is discussed in Chapter 5, "Water, Waves, and Other Matter." Maxwell Render is named in honor of James Clerk Maxwell, a Scottish theoretical physicist, and his work with the physics of light. Maxwell Render is a plugin that introduces physically-based lighting to Maya. Scenes set up within Maya can have Maxwell-specific materials applied to them and sent to Maxwell Render. Figure 4.18 shows a Maya scene in the Maxwell Render interface.

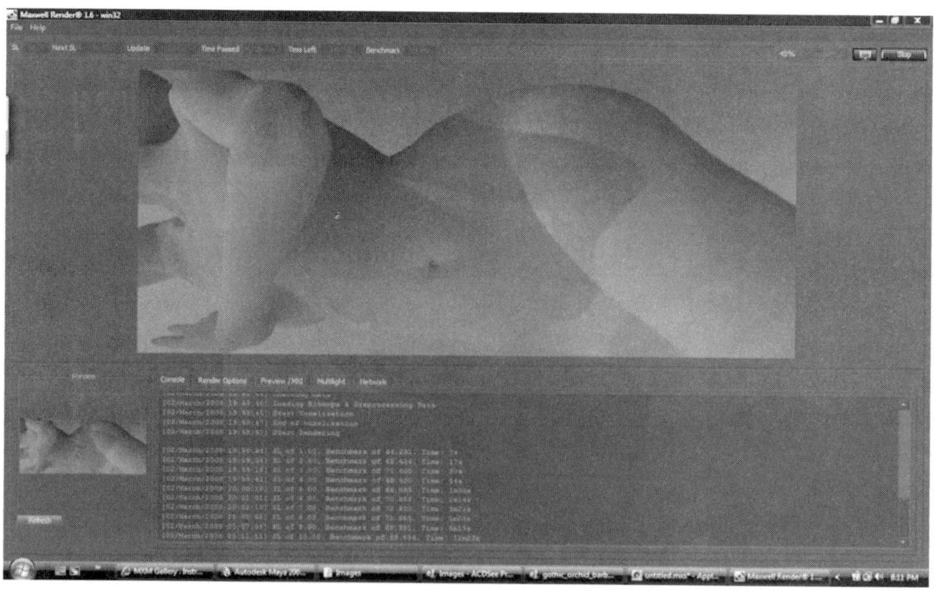

FIGURE 4.18 A scene modeled and lit in Maya is sent to Maxwell Render for rendering and further tweaking.

Proprietary shaders can be created in Maxwell Render and assigned to the geometry in a Maya scene. Figure 4.19 shows a Maxwell Render interface for loading and adjusting materials. Figure 4.20 shows the completed piece after rendering and touch-ups. Next Limits has a Maxwell Render site. There you can download a few thousand amazing and imaginative Maxwell Render materials. It will become apparent looking through the catalog of materials that the collection has a bias toward the design and architecture fields. Check it out at mxmgallery.maxwellrender.com/index.php.

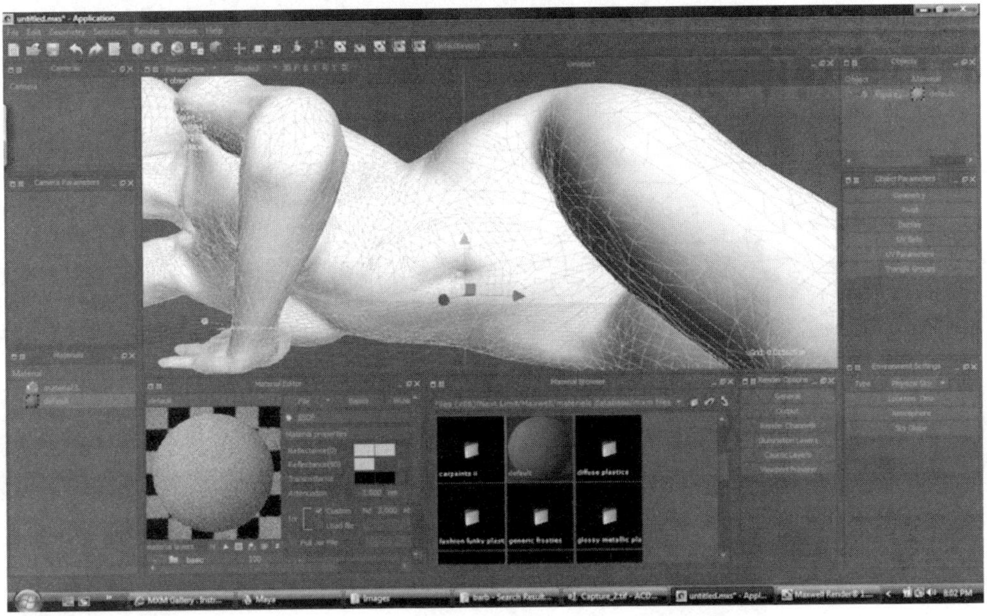

FIGURE 4.19 Materials can be created, tweaked, or loaded from a vast materials repository for use in Maya scenes.

FIGURE 4.20 The final image, Blue Barb, rendered in Maxwell Render was adjusted slightly in Photoshop to add barbed wire and change it to a black-and-white image.

Maxwell Render deals with materials such as glasses and metals with physical accuracy. Shadows, objects as light emitters, and depth of field are present in Figure 4.21. Maxwell Render renders the entire image at once, constantly refreshing the image for further accuracy. Images can be set for predetermined rendering times.

FIGURE 4.21 This hastily assembled scene was stopped before its predetermined rendering time. Although unfinished, the light emitters, various materials, shadows, and depth of field begin to emerge.

A lot is involved in a program like this, but depending on your needs, it may be worthwhile to investigate its potential. Its feature set goes beyond the scope of a chapter such as this. One last intriguing feature worth mentioning, however, is Multilight. This feature is a boon to rendering technology and may be especially useful in the architectural field. Multilight allows the user to alter the intensities of the various lights in a scene. This can be done during the render or after its completion. Depending on how many lights are in a scene, possibly thousands of lighting scenarios can be tested and saved. Tweaks to the lighting are done in virtual real time. This is not unlike working with IPR in Maya. Figure 4.22 shows the Multilight control panel with sliders for film ISO, shutter control, and the adjustment of five individual lights. Figure 4.23, Figure 4.24, Figure 4.25, Figure 4.26, and Figure 4.27 show five separate changes to the lighting in a scene. These five adjustments were rendered and saved in about a minute.

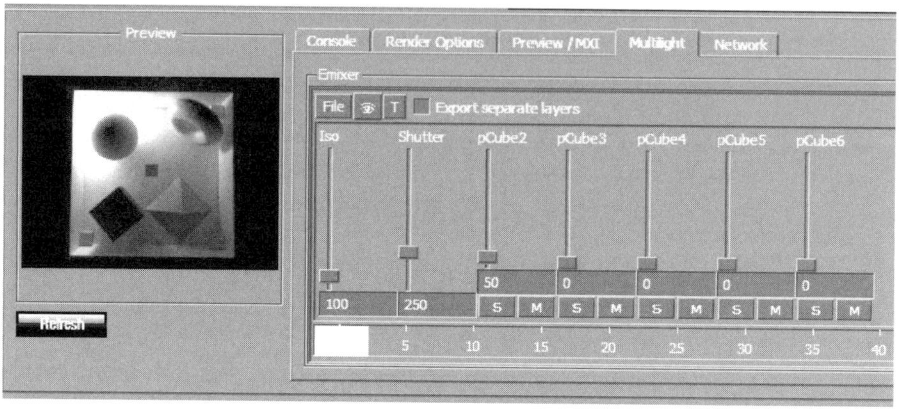

FIGURE 4.22 The Multilight control panel allows the individual adjustment of all lights in a scene. The five small cube light emitters' intensities can be adjusted individually, along with the film ISO and shutter aperture. This is an invaluable feature for the architectural industry.

FIGURE 4.23 Simple lighting scenario composed of five small cube light emitters.

FIGURE 4.24 A real-time lighting adjustment made to the original rendering in Figure 4.23. Sliders assigned to each light in the scene can be individually adjusted and reviewed in real time.

FIGURE 4.25 A real-time lighting adjustment made to the original rendering in Figure 4.23. The scene's ISO number, which is just like that of real photographic film. The ISO (International Standards Organization) gauges film speed. A slider can adjust the ISO or exposure of the entire scene.

FIGURE 4.26 Yet another real-time lighting adjustment made to the original rendering in Figure 4.23. This Multilight technique is incredibly helpful for architectural renderings where a single render can then be used to produce countless lighting scenarios for a client in real time.

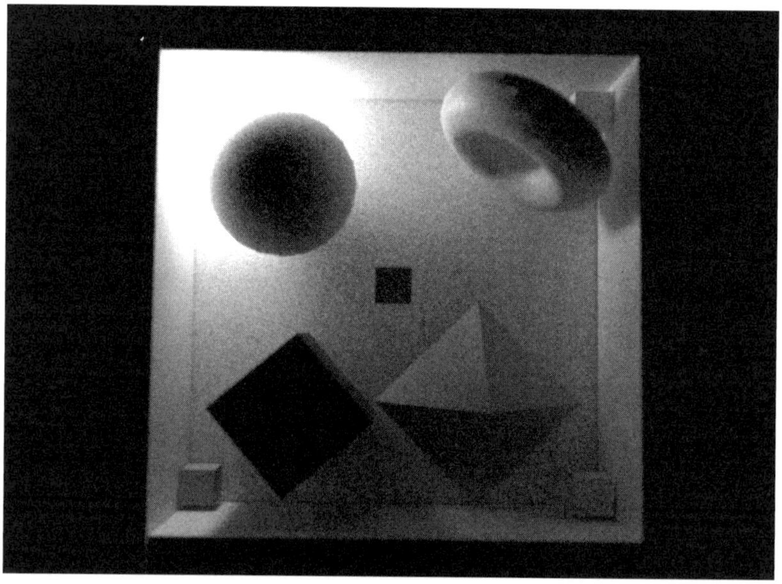

FIGURE 4.27 Depending on the number of lights in a scene there are countless possibilities for altering the original lighting via Multilight. A real-time lighting adjustment made to the original rendering in Figure 4.23 can include daytime and nighttime lighting.

Maxwell Render is not the only physically-based unbiased spectral renderer. Fryrender from Feversoft also hopes to stake a claim in the Maya market. Fryrender is very similar to Maxwell Render. They share the same archetype of a photographer or spectral light physicist. fryrender is a plugin for Maya that allows you to set up a scene in Maya, add fryrender-specific materials, and send it off to fryrender for rendering. Figure 4.28 shows a test scene in the Maya interface. Figure 4.29 shows the test scene in the fryrender interface, and Figure 4.30 shows the fruits of the experiment.

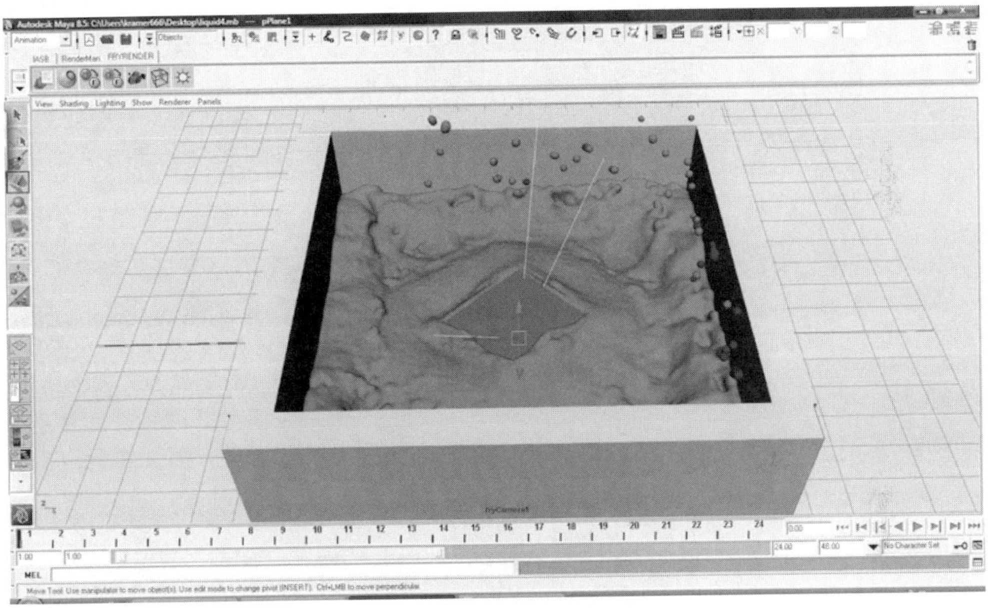

FIGURE 4.28 An experimental scene repurposed from the original 3Delight scene is used to check how fryrender and 3Delight compare. Fryrender was used to mimic the rendering results in 3Delight.

FIGURE 4.29 The experimental scene in the fryrender application. The challenge was to approximate the look of 3Delight, which is an inherently different type of renderer from fryrender.

FIGURE 4.30 In this instance, the final render in fryrender compares favorably to the one rendered in 3Delight.

Fryrender uses its own camera for Maya scenes. A library of scenes can be drawn from and assigned to the various objects in the Maya scene. Fryrender converts Maya materials to fryrender materials. Figure 4.31shows the stand-alone Fryrender Material Editor for developing new materials or altering old ones. Figure 4.32 shows a standard swatch rendering for determining the look of the material you are constructing. Fryrender has a similar material repository to Maxwell Render. It is for registered users of fryrender and can be found at http://materials.fryrender.com/#home.

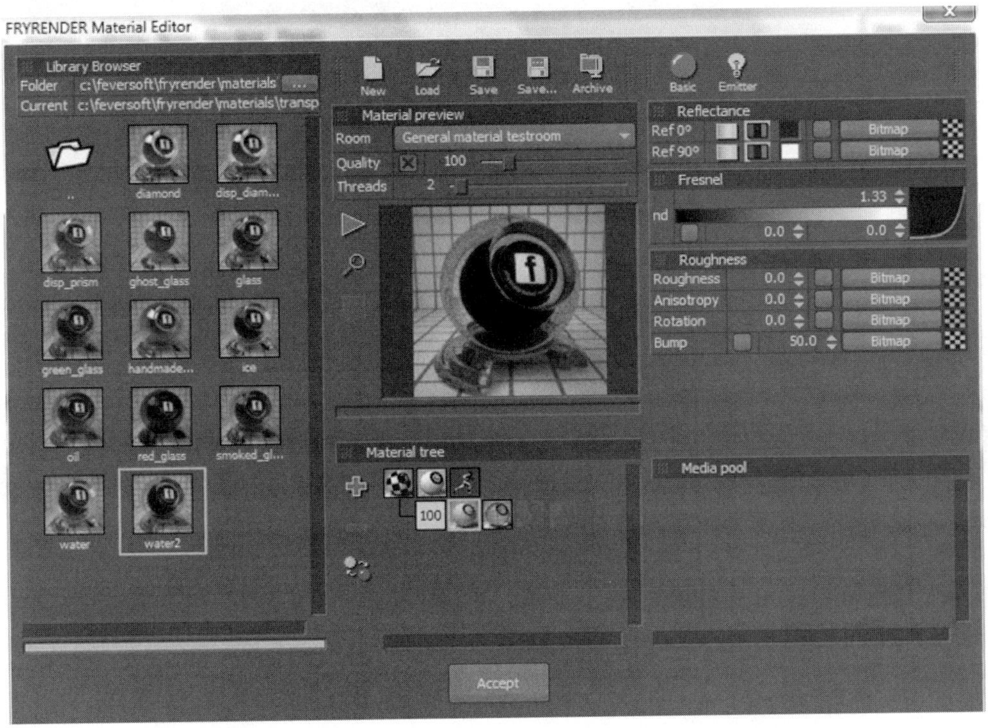

FIGURE 4.31 The Fryrender Material Editor is used to design materials for use in Maya.

FIGURE 4.32 The Fryrender Material Pop-Up renders a standard object for determining the look of the newly designed material. This render is then stored as a swatch representing that shader in the material library. An online repository for user-created materials is available to registered fryrender users at http://materials.fryrender.com/#home.

It should be noted that both fryrender and Maxwell Render are integrated plugins to Maya, but each company has created plugins for use with other packages such as Autodesk 3ds Max, Lightwave 3D, Rhinoceros 3D, CINEMA 4D, Softimage XSI, and others. Fryrender has many of the same features that Maxwell Render has. It calculates caustics, HDRI image-based lighting, full global illumination, mesh objects as light sources, and motion blur. Figure 4.33 shows a fryrender image showcasing subsurface scattering. The list of features goes on and on. Fryrender has a feature similar to Maxwell Render's Multilight functions called *Layer Blending*. One unique feature is the ability to adjust the physical sky and environment properties in a graphical or numerical way. The Fryrender Physical Atmosphere Editor can change the environment lighting by adjusting real-world figures such as longitude, latitude, heading, day, month, and year.

FIGURE 4.33 Fryrender can render subsurface scattering with very realistic results.

FIGURE 4.34 The Fryrender Physical Atmosphere Editor is a graphical way of adjusting the physical sky environment. Values such as longitude, latitude, heading, day, month, and year can be input.

Physically-based unbiased renderers are extremely photo-real. The learning curve is less intimidating than it sounds. It is a new way of thinking about laying a scene out. When correctly adjusted, the imagery that they produce is virtually indistinguishable from a real photo. If you are using Maya for design or architecture, consider looking at fryrender or Maxwell Render as your alternative Maya solution.

RenderMan is the industry standard and has a great deal to offer. The network rendering and organization of render passes, the speed versus quality ratio, the consistency and reliability of the image, the hardcore programming feature set, and its industry-wide support are worth a look, depending on your work as an artist or production facility requirements. There are also the software packages with varying degrees of RenderMan compliancy and Maya support to consider. To have these options as a Maya user is invaluable. Following is a list of the companies written about in this chapter. There are also a few Maya renderers and plugins listed that were not mentioned in this text. They are all worthy of consideration when you are looking for an alternative rendering solution for your Maya work. There are also links to Maya-specific information when applicable. Color versions of many of the images in this and other chapters can be found on the book's Web site at www.bigheadedkitty.com/index.php under the Maya Plugin Power Images menu selection.

It is certainly worth investigating alternative renderers for your work in Maya. Whether you create photo-real architecture stills or full-blown film resolution animation, there are quite a few choices for the Maya user. Below is a short list of links to a variety of rendering options currently available. The list is divided into renderers that comply with the RenderMan Interface Specification and those that do not.

Non-RenderMan Compliant Renderers

- mental images
  - mental ray
  - www.mentalimages.com/2_1_0_mentalray/index.html
- Next Limit Technologies
  - Maxwell Render
  - www.maxwellrender.com/plugins/maya/index.php
  - www.maxwellrender.com/news/maya_video.html
  - mxmgallery.maxwellrender.com/index.php
- Feversoft
  - Fryrender 1.9
  - www.fryrender.com/#home/index
- cebas computer GmbH
  - finalRender Stage-2 for Maya
  - www.cebas.com/news/read.php?UD=10-7888-33-788&NID=244
  - www.finalrender.com/products/products.php?UD=10-7888-35-788&PID=52
- Illuminate Labs
  - Turtle 4.1 for Maya
  - www.illuminatelabs.com

- NVIDIA Corporation
  - Gelato/Gelato Pro 2.2 Mango Plugin
  - www.nvidia.com/object/gz_features_benefits.html
  - www.nvidia.com/object/legal_info.html
- Luxology, LLC
  - Modo 3.01
  - www.luxology.com/whatismodo/
- e-on software
  - Vue 6
  - www.e-onsoftware.com/products/
  - www.e-onsoftware.com/support/f.a.q/?page=vue6xstreamFAQ

RenderMan Compliant Renderers

- Pixar
  - RenderMan for Maya
  - renderman.pixar.com/products/tools/rfm_webinfopage.html
  - renderman.pixar.com/products/whatsrenderman/index.htm
- dna research
  - 3Delight for Maya
  - www.3delight.com/en/index.php/products/3delight_for_maya
  - www.3delight.com/en/index.php/products/3delight_for_maya/tutorials
- Animal Logic
  - MayaMan
  - www.animallogic.com/#Products,MayaMan,OVERVIEW
- SiTex Graphics
  - Air
  - www.sitexgraphics.com/html/air.html

This is not a complete list of rendering possibilities. There are several new renderers that are in various stages of development. We will update this list as we learn of new releases and options. These links may be accessed directly at www.bigheadedkitty.com/render.

We have talked quite a bit about rendering, but it is time to move on. Chapter 5 will deal with the exciting world of fluid dynamics.

CHAPTER

5

WATER, WAVES, AND OTHER MATTER

In This Chapter

- Introduction
- The Elephant and the Umbrella
- High-Voltage Wet Maps
- The Wakes of Loch Ness

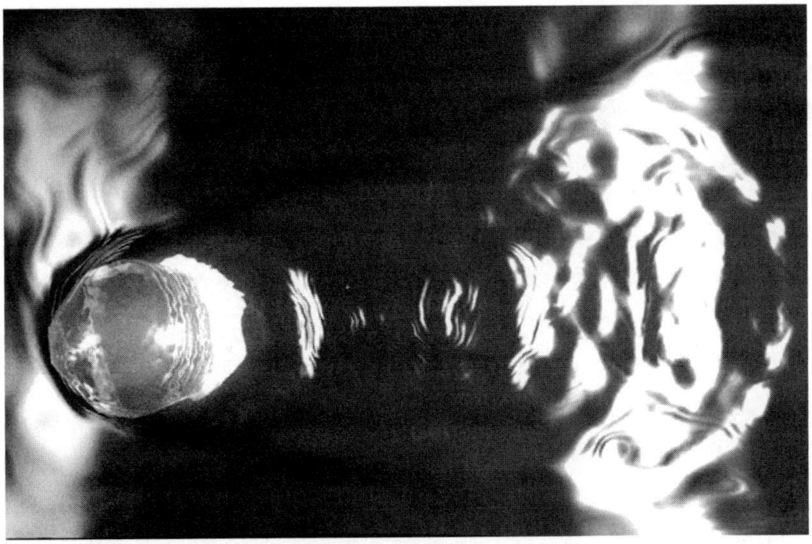

A faceted crystal soccer ball rolls through a silvery liquid leaving a wake as it rolls. The dynamic roll and collision was created in Maya and imported into RealFlow for interaction with the shallow pool.

INTRODUCTION

Computer-generated (CG) liquids have advanced over the course of many years. Maya has tools for creating liquid and gas, but they had seemed rather impractical at this point. Next Limit has been paddling away at realistic CG fluid simulation for years, and the results speak for themselves. RealFlow (RF) is the integration of once separate programs, RealWave (RW) and RF.

This package offers a veritable water park of animation tools. *Liquid* is a broad term that includes all types of fluids and gases, with wide-ranging properties. Motor oil, cake batter, mud, slime, and perhaps even mist are all fluids. RF's incorporation of RW allows the user to create very realistic fluid surface animation. A stormy sea or a still Scottish loch are easy to create. Dynamics are the key to the lifelike and nuanced motion of an RF simulation. RF has a superior set of tools for attaining a proper and very accurate result. The basis for such animations is primarily generated by particle systems. Particle dynamics can calculate object collision, mesh interaction, self-collision, and the standard fields and forces. RF also introduces other less well-known forces, such as surface tension, Coriolis fields, and temperature. The dynamics in RF are a complete system, which also accounts for hard and soft body simulations. All this interaction can lead to amazing results.

It is always a pleasure when you can sit down with the creators of a favorite program and pick their brains. RF is such a well-developed application that I wondered what the genesis of RF was and what was next for Next Limit. I posed a few questions to Nicole van der Burg, PR coordinator of Next Limit for the answers.

AN INTERVIEW WITH NICOLE VAN DER BURG PR COORDINATOR OF NEXT LIMIT

How did Next Limit get its start?

Next Limit Technologies was founded in 1998 by two young engineers: Victor Gonzalez and Ignacio Vargas. They were enthusiastic about creating new and innovative tools combining science and visualization for the CG market. Hard work led to the release of their first product, RealFlow. Today, Victor and Ignacio lead a team of the best young professionals in the industry. RealFlow4 was released in 2006. A new product, Maxwell Render, was developed in 2005 and released in 2006. The first unbiased rendering engine on the market, Maxwell Render was received as a revolution in the rendering world and continues to provide innovative solutions to its dedicated user base.

What was the genesis of your software?

The mission of Next Limit Technologies is to provide cutting edge simulation technologies for a broad range of applications in computer graphics, science, and engineering. Next Limit boasts a young, multidisciplinary team with expertise in physics, mathematics, computer graphics, engineering, and visualization. They all share a common vision for the creation of new products that connect science, simulation, and visualization, using novel paradigms and innovative methodologies.

What types of companies would benefit from your software?
Maxwell Render is mainly focused on architecture, product visualization, engineering, and design markets. Any studio or individual trying to create photorealistic images in an easy, physically correct manner would benefit greatly from the use of Maxwell Render. RealFlow is focused on fluid and dynamics simulation and visual effects for feature films and commercials. Any studio in need of high-end, off-the-shelf, professional fluid and dynamics simulations would benefit greatly from the use of RealFlow.

Where can the use of your software be seen?
RealFlow has been used in numerous films: *Primeval, Poseidon, The Guardian, Meet the Robinsons, 300, The Da Vinci Code, Charlie and the Chocolate Factory, Ice Age: The Meltdown, Slither, Constantine, X-Men: The Last Stand, Robots, Lord of the Rings: The Return of the King, Water Giant,* and more. RealFlow is the fluid simulator of choice for many studios and has been used in commercials for Heineken, Sony, Pontiac, Martini, Dockers, and Amp'd Mobile. RealFlow4 was used to simulate the fluids in the music video for U2 and Greenday's "The Saints Are Coming." RealFlow clients include Disney Feature Animation, National Geographic, Spacelabs Healthcare, Pixar, and Luma Pictures. Maxwell Render has not yet been used in films. However, it is constantly being used by up-scale architectural visualization firms including CityScape in London. Maxwell Render clients include Adidas, BMW, Ford, Hewlett-Packard, Motorola, Nokia, SEGA, Nike, Porsche, Walt Disney, IKEA, and H&M.

What's down the road for your company and software?
While we have only just released an update for RealFlow4, our development team has already started work on a new toolkit for shading RealFlow particles in large quantities through RenderMan renderers. These tools solve meshing issues and the related problem of creating very heavy and hard-to-handle files. The new toolkit offers two different approaches to render a scene in RF4 without having to make a mesh. The first approach, called FlowTracer, is a ray-marching technique that samples part of the fluid to construct information about the whole, at render time. The second approach covers FlowParticler and FlowMesher, which both generate various types of geometry (polygonal meshes, sprites, points) at render time.

Maxwell Render is a young product with a bright future ahead. Our development team is currently working on Maxwell Displacement, which will be different from any displacement presently known, and on a radically improved physical sky model.

RF is a stand-alone program but supports Maya by supplying plugins that load the proprietary data format it generates. This sequential data can come in the form of meshes and particles. Workflow between Maya and RF most often goes something like this.

- **Create scene in Maya:** The scene contains polygon objects that set the environment with which the RF simulation will interact. This does not have to be a static scene. It can contain animation. For instance, a rotating water wheel fills well water and then dispenses it in a fixed pail.
- **Export Maya scene:** The Maya scene file is saved as an RF proprietary file.
- **Load Maya scene into RF:** The proprietary scene file exported from Maya serves as the basis for interaction with RF dynamics. All polygon objects and any animation are now available in the RF environment and subject to RF dynamics.
- **Create RF dynamics:** Utilize RF to create dynamic interaction with the imported scene.
- **Run simulation and export relevant data:** Particle and mesh data are calculated and exported on a frame-by-frame basis.
- **Re-import scene file into Maya:** The previously created and exported scene file is imported back into Maya. Maya to RF import plugins are used to load particle and mesh data previously exported from RF.

Let's take a look at what Maya and RF can accomplish together.

The Elephant and the Umbrella

Creating quick and reasonably impressive animation can be accomplished simply. Let's start in RF itself and create an animation of an elephant spraying water into the air and the water landing on an umbrella. Assuming that you have loaded the Next Limit RF plugins correctly, there should be a Next Limit menu at the top of the screen amidst the rest of the Maya menus, as shown in Figure 5.1. If not, you should select the three plugins in the Plugin Manager, highlighted in Figure 5.2. The function of these plugins is straightforward.

- **RealflowMesher.mll:** This loads meshes generated by RF back into Maya.
- **RealflowParticler.mll:** This loads RF particles into Maya native particles.
- **sdTranslator.mll:** The RF sd file format allows Maya to export and import scene information

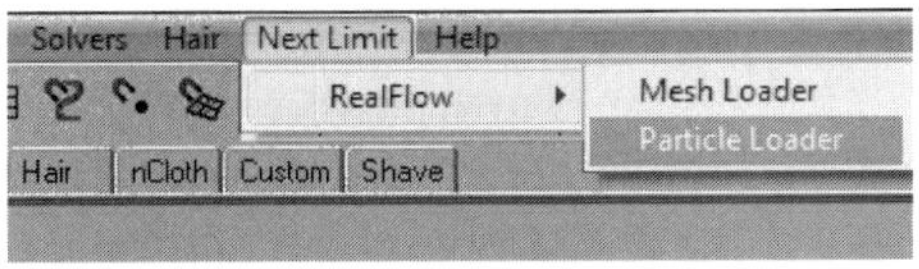

FIGURE 5.1 The opened Next Limit menu as it appears in Maya's menu bar.

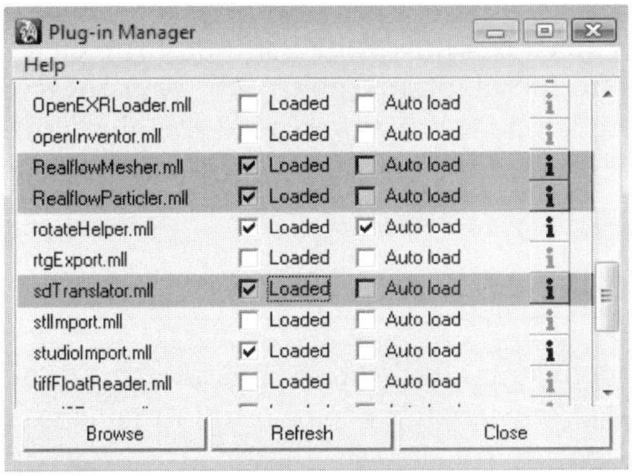

FIGURE 5.2 The Maya Plugin Manager with the three required RF plugins highlighted.

ON THE DVD

The first thing we need to do is create a scene in Maya for import into stand-alone RF. On the companion DVD in the Chapter 5 folder is a scene file called elephant.mb. Load that scene, which shows an elephant facing an umbrella. It should look something like Figure 5.3. This is the important first step of integration between Maya and RF.

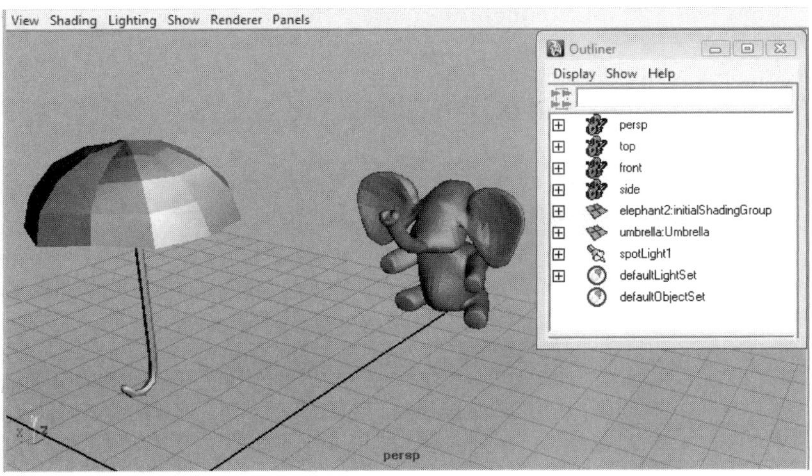

FIGURE 5.3 The elephant.mb scene file as loaded and unmodified.

The RF sd file format stores object, camera, and animation information. RF works best with triangulated polygons, so any objects that are involved in a dynamic reaction should be comprised of triangles. Objects that are not interacting dynamically are not bound by this stipulation. The umbrella is the only object in the scene that will have any particle interaction. The elephant model is merely the aesthetic proxy water source. We need the elephant to gauge where we shall place the emitter in the scene. The problem is the number of polygons in the elephant model that are unnecessarily slowing down the scene simulation time.

ON THE DVD

We only need to know the position of the elephant's trunk. Close the scene and load the scene file elephant_point.mb from the companion DVD in the Chapter 5 folder. The red cube that has replaced the elephant marks the position and angle of the tip of the elephant's trunk. We will use this scene in RF.

KEEP COUNT OF THOSE POLYS

RF is very efficient, even when the calculations being asked of it are intense. It's always good practice to keep in mind the polygon count in a scene. Even when polygons play no role in a simulation, the program considers them. The elephant model is the source of the water, but he is initially unnecessary for the simulation. The end goal is to combine the fluid dynamics from RF with the scene originally built in Maya. These two items get merged back into Maya for rendering and anything else that is necessary to accomplish the goal of the scene.

In the File menu, select Export Selection and choose the sd file type. Save the file as umbrella.sd. We now have our Maya file ready for import into RF. We can leave Maya for a while and launch RealFlow 4.x (RF4). On start-up of RF4, the program will ask you to open or create a new project. Create a project called umbrella. RF now creates a project file with a set of subfolders. These subfolders hold the various types of data that can be generated from RF. Figure 5.4 shows the Project Management window and the directory structure it creates.

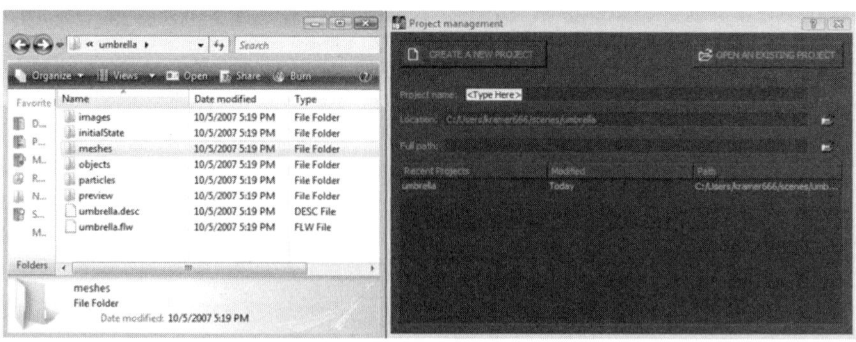

FIGURE 5.4 The Project Management window and the project directory it creates.

ON THE DVD

First, we want to make sure we are in the proper orientation mode for Maya. At the top of the RF screen select File > Preferences. This brings up the Preferences window. Under the General tab in the Preferences window is a setting for world axis setup. It is important to create data in the proper Maya Y-up orientation. We can now import the sd file that we exported from Maya. At the top of the RF screen, we once again access the File menu, this time to import our previously exported file. Go to File > Import > Import Object and navigate to umbrella.sd. If you got stuck or didn't export your file correctly, you can find it on the companion DVD in the Chapter 5 folder. You should now be able to see your 3D scene represented in the RF windows.

Getting around the 3D world in RF is the same as in Maya, so you should be comfortable from the start. Manipulating objects (translation, rotation, scaling) takes a little getting used to. The W, E, and R keys toggle between translation, rotation, and scaling, respectively. The icons at the top of the screen, as shown in Figure 5.5, perform the same functions.

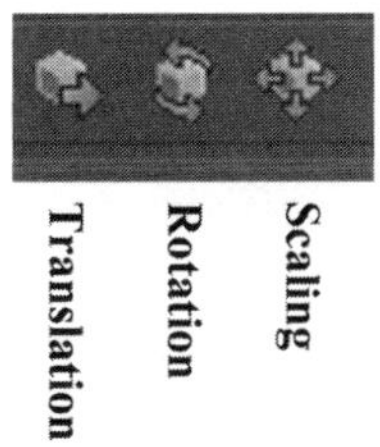

FIGURE 5.5 Translation, rotation, and scaling icons at the top of the RF screen.

An Ample Toolbox

The bulk of any work done in RF deals with particle emissions in various forms and the forces that manipulate them. RF has a substantial toolbox for getting almost any job done properly. Emitters such as Circle, Square, Sphere, Linear, Triangle, Spline, Cylinder, Bitmap, Object, Fill Object, RW_Splash, RW_Particles, Fibers, Binary Loader, and NBinary Loader all have unique abilities and are immensely powerful. Daemons such as Attractor, Magic, Heater, Wind, Vortex, Gravity, Drag, Coriolis, and Texture Gizmo are a few of the forces that can be introduced into the RF world.

Our goal is to generate water and have it hit the top of the umbrella. The cube that is our proxy for the tip of the elephant's trunk is the launching point for the water. We must add an emitter into the scene to generate those particles. At the top of the RF screen is a set of icons shown in Figure 5.6.

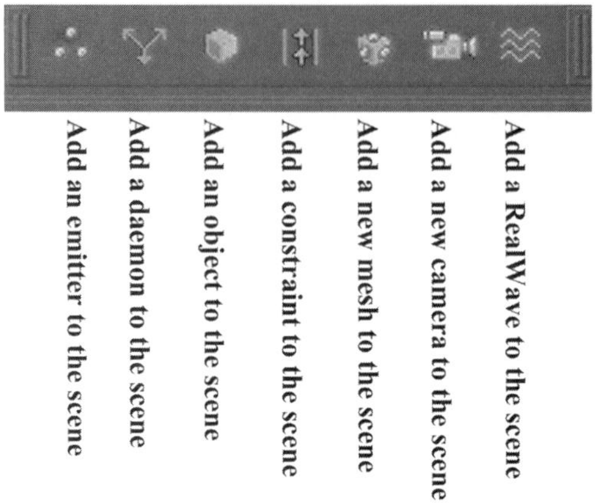

FIGURE 5.6 Icon bank at the top of the screen holds the key to the bulk of RF's functionality.

You'll want to work in the perspective window. In the upper-left corner of the four viewport windows (perspective,top, front, and side views) are two tiny icons which allow you to change the viewport configurations from single view to quad view. Changing the quad view to a single view will make it easier to work in the larger workspace. It may also be helpful to change from wireframe mode. Pressing the 7, 8, 9, and 0 keys toggles the scene into various states of display. This functionality can also be found in the View menu at the top of the screen, where it is possible to toggle individual elements of a scene to various display states. We are going to add a circle emitter to the scene. Click the Add Emitter icon and select the circle. A circle emitter is just that: a circle from which the particles will emanate. The particles will flow from the circle emitter in a round column like water pours from the circular pipe of a spigot. Your scene should look something like Figure 5.7.

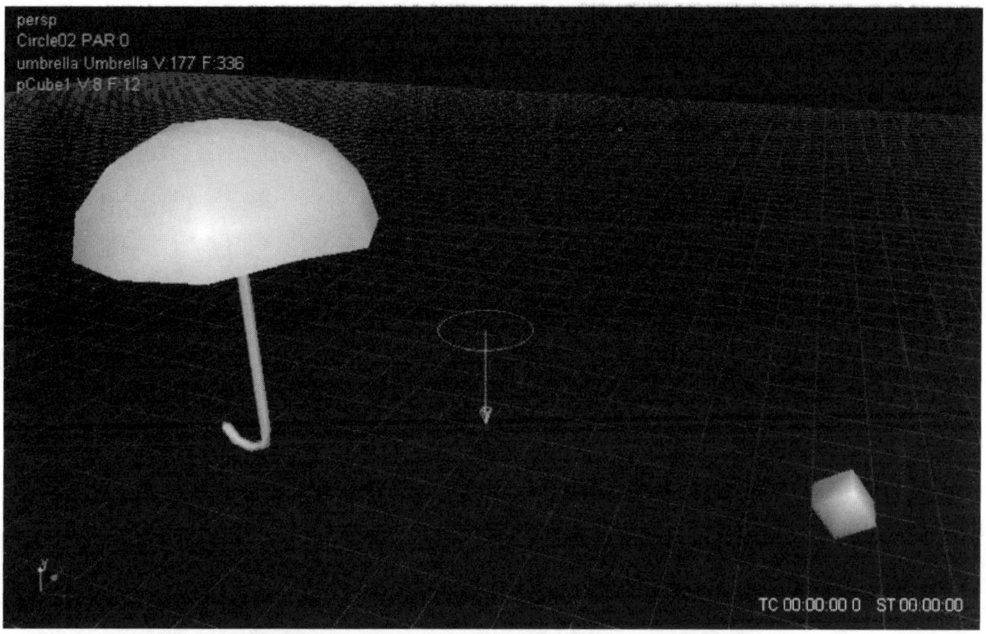

FIGURE 5.7 The umbrella scene with umbrella, trunk proxy cube, and circle emitter.

At the bottom of the screen, there is a timeline and two buttons: Simulate and Reset. Click on the Simulate button, and the result particles will start coming from the circle emitter. When you have seen enough or the simulation has run its course, click on Reset to turn things back to zero. We want to place the circle emitter at the point of the proxy object. The circle emitter has a directional flow arrow that is visible even when deselected. This shows the direction of the emitted particles. Move the emitter into position near the proxy and take into consideration that we want the particles to shoot skyward. When you are finished, run the simulation again. If all goes well, you should have something that resembles Figure 5.8.

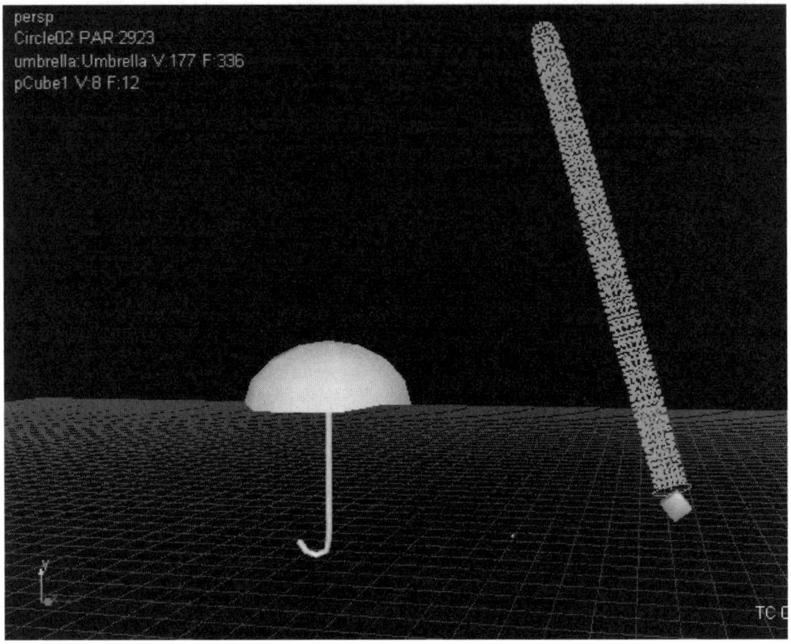

FIGURE 5.8 The umbrella scene begins to take shape, but is not without problems.

The first thing you'll notice is that the particles seem to go on endlessly. We can fix this by affecting the scene with gravity. This will clue us in to whether our elephant has good aim or not. At the top of the screen amidst the bank of icons is the Add New Daemon icon, as shown in Figure 5.6. Clicking on the Add New Daemon icon brings up a full list of choices. Select Gravity. Once this is done, you can run the simulation again. If you're lucky, you will see particles bouncing off the top of the umbrella. It is more likely that you will have a scene that looks like Figure 5.9.

FIGURE 5.9 The particles dribble from the emitter.

The particles seem to barely travel inches before they plummet to earth. The particles are dribbling instead of being shot forcefully from the elephant's trunk. This can be helped by changing the speed of the particles. On the right side of the RF screen is a bank of windows. Figure 5.10 shows what the umbrella scene looks like up to this point.

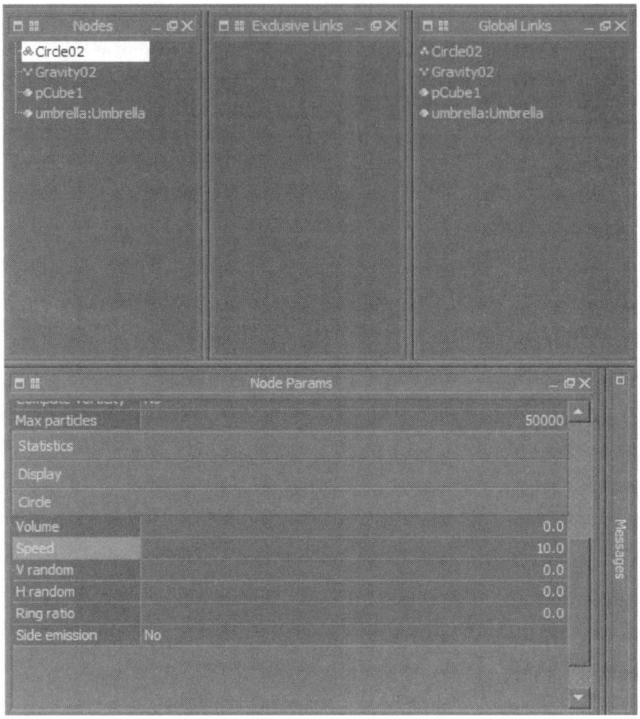

FIGURE 5.10 RF's Node, Exclusive Links, Global Links, and Node Params windows

The Nodes window is a handy list of the elements in the scene. It can be used much like Maya's Outliner window to select elements. The currently selected Circle02 shown in Figure 5.10 is the emitter in this scene. Your name may vary slightly, depending on if you have added and then deleted emitters. Also shown in Figure 5.10 is the Node Params window. It shows a multitude of parameter options for the currently selected node, in this case the circle emitter in the scene. As shown, the speed variable of the circle emitter has been changed from its default to a value of 10. Running the simulation again should garner more respectable results, as shown in Figure 5.11.

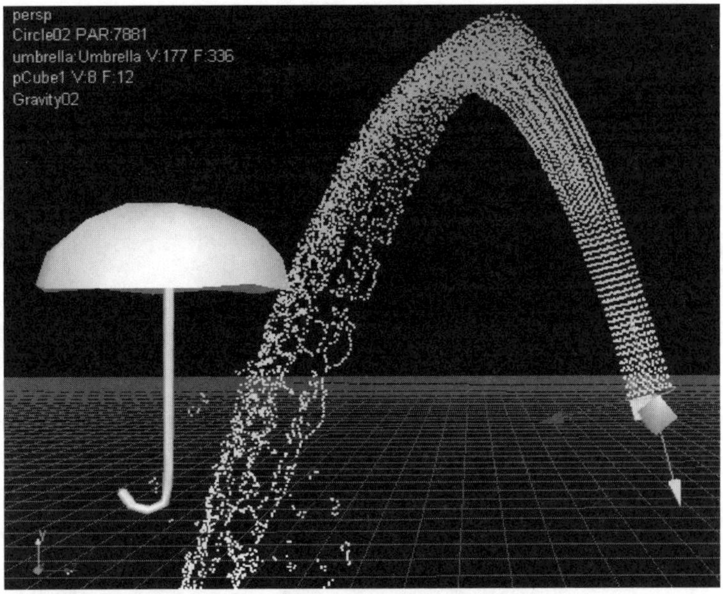

FIGURE 5.11 Adjusting the particle speed shoots the particles much higher and farther.

A careful series of speed adjustments and tweaking the position, rotation, and scaling of the emitter results in a thoroughly wet umbrella and a fine dynamic reaction. The scaling of the emitter to a more oval shape, a closer approximation to the proxy object, and a particle speed adjustment yields an acceptable result, as shown in Figure 5.12.

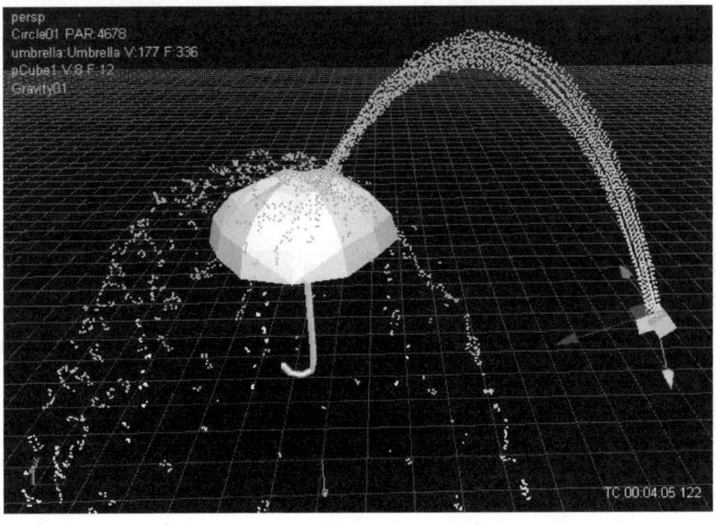

FIGURE 5.12 Minor adjustments lead to the successful interaction of water and umbrella.

At the top of the screen amidst the bank of icons is the Add New Mesh icon, as shown in Figure 5.6. Clicking on the Add New Mesh icon places a new node in the scene, called a *mesh*. This Mesh node can be used to generate an actual polygon mesh from the particle data. Once the mesh is added to the scene, right-click on the mesh02 listing in the Nodes window, which brings up a pull-down menu. Select Insert Fluids, which will list all the available particle emitters in the scene. We want to associate the mesh with the particle emitter. Highlight the Circle Emitter node and hit OK. This will now generate a mesh based on the particles generated from this emitter. This can be seen in Figure 5.13.

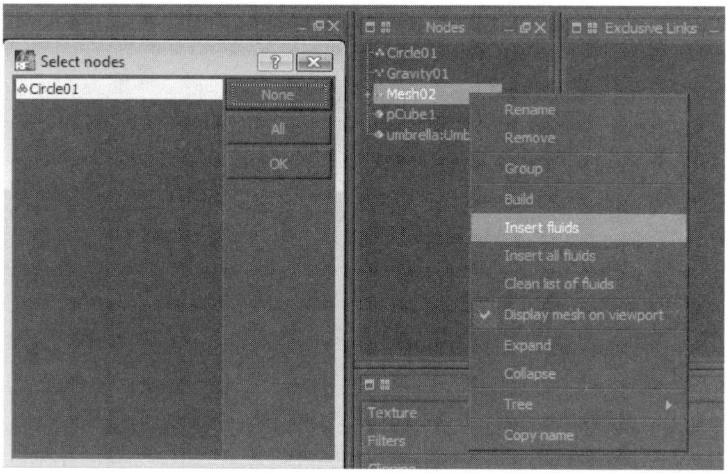

FIGURE 5.13 The Mesh node can be used to generate polygonal meshes from particles.

Selecting the Circle node associates it with the Mesh node. Resetting and rerunning the simulation bares the visible signs of a mesh cage around the particles emitted. The new mesh is shown in Figure 5.14.

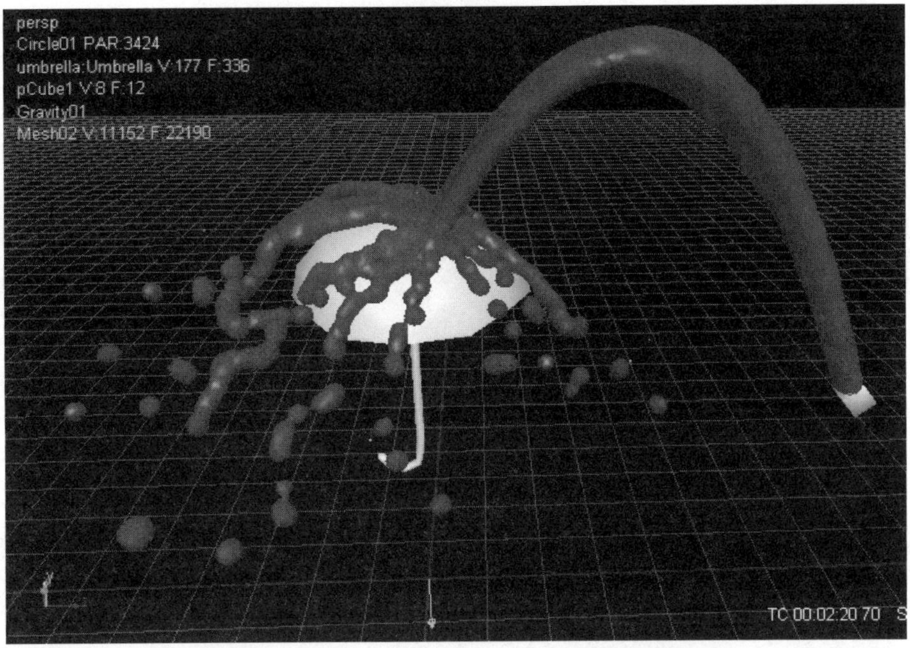

FIGURE 5.14 Polygonal water spray rendered in blue is generated based upon the particles.

After we have established a satisfactory simulation, the various forms of data need to be saved for import back into Maya. During a simulation, a wide variety of data are generated. The Maya scene and what we hope to accomplish with RF determines what kind of data we save out. Pressing F12 brings up the Export Central window. This can also be found in the Export menu at the top of the screen. The Export Central window lists the elements in the scene that can be used to generate data. In Export Central, emitters from the scene are listed. The sole emitter, Circle01, is listed.

Clicking the tiny + sign before it opens up a list of formats that particle data may be saved as. Select the .bin format checkbox if it is not already selected. This is the format we will use to import back into Maya. When imported into Maya, these data will be standard Maya particles. These particles can then be rendered as any of the different types of hardware and software options available to particles in Maya. Below that in the Export Central window are the meshes. Clicking the tiny + sign before them opens up a list of formats that mesh data may be saved as. For our purposes, the .bin format will serve nicely. Figure 5.15 shows the proper selection checked off in the Export Central window.

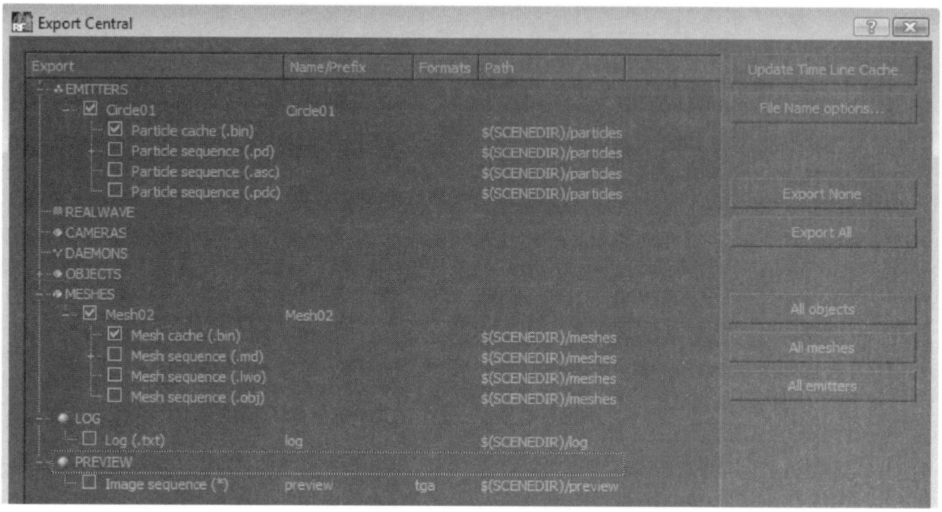

FIGURE 5.15 The Export Central window with mesh and particle data types selected for output.

EXPORTING DATA, SAVING TIME

The Export Central window is your key for selecting the data types that you are looking to generate. Each time you run a simulation the data is generated but not saved. You will test and test again until you have finely tweaked your scene but there will be no data saved unless those data types are checked in the Export Central window. Some simulations can take a long time to calculate therefore it's a good idea to set up your exports when nearing the end of your final simulation. Depending on what your scene entails the simulation may take considerable time to render. As fast as RF is at doing all these amazing calculations it would be painful to have to re-run the simulation because you forgot to set up your needed data types in the Export Central window. Saving the data per frame doesn't really steal a great deal of RF's resources. If you have data set up for export in the Export Central window it will be overwritten each time you reset and rerun the scene. This tip could wind up saving an afternoon's worth of render time.

There is one more touch to make in this scene. Sometimes particles are no longer needed once they are generated. There is no floor in this scene, so particles will continue to fall. There are also particles that may fall wildly out of bounds. A Volume daemon within a scene can set up boundaries for particle generation. As before, select the Add New Daemon icon from the bank of icons shown in Figure 5.6. Clicking on the Add New Daemon icon brings up a full list of choices. Select Volume. A bounding box will appear in the scene. This can be scaled to surround the emitter, particles, and umbrella. Any particles that fall outside of the volume are eliminated.

This is a great tool that can be used effectively to eliminate errant particles and reduce calculation time. Figure 5.16 shows the effective elimination of particles. What is most noticeable are the particles that seem to disappear near the ground plane.

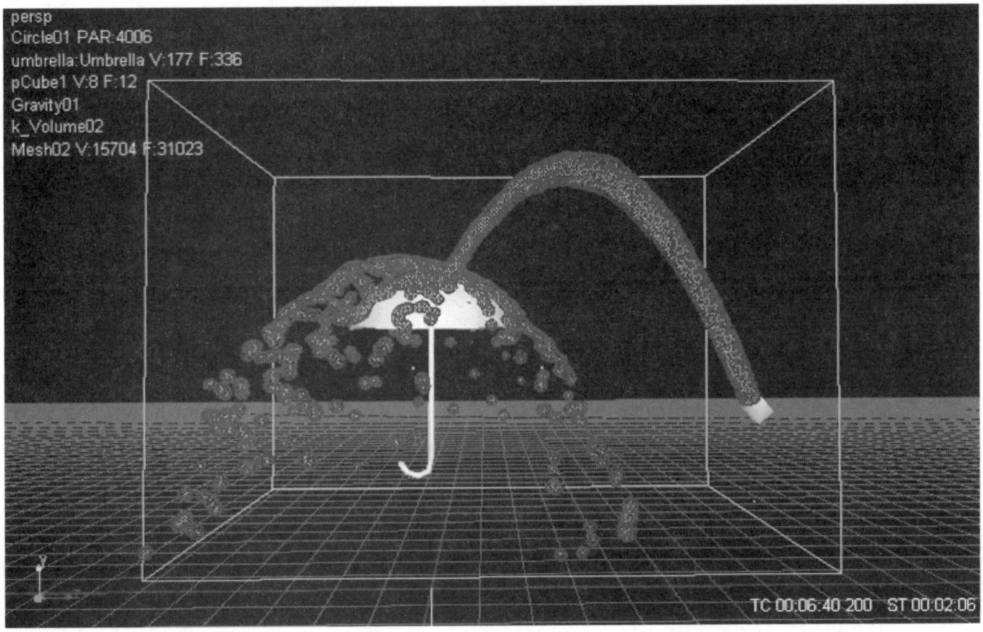

FIGURE 5.16 Particles falling outside the Volume daemon are eliminated from the scene.

With the Volume daemon in place and the desired output data selected in the Export Central window double checked, the simulation can now be run for its full 200-frame length. Clicking on the Simulate button saves 200 frames of the selected data types for import into Maya. Once the simulation has run it's course, it can be scrolled through, and the dynamics can be viewed in real time from the cache.

That completes the dynamic simulation in RF. Start Maya again, and we will utilize the efforts from our RF simulation. We must now load the Maya scene for which the RF data were created.

ON THE DVD

On the companion DVD in the Chapter 5 folder is the original scene file called elephant.mb. Load that scene. Don't load the elephant_point.mb scene file. That scene file has served its purpose. Here again we see an elephant facing an umbrella. As seen earlier in Figure 5.1, select Next Limit > RealFlow > Particle Loader and direct the plugin to your project's particle folder. This may be something like (user)/scenes/umbrella/particles. You can also load the particles from the companion DVD-ROM in the Chapter 5 folder, scenes/umbrella/particles. The files are named and numbered as umbrella######.bin. Once the particles are loaded, run the simulation. Make sure the Timeslider is set to the number of particle frames loaded. If all is successful, your scene should look something like Figure 5.17.

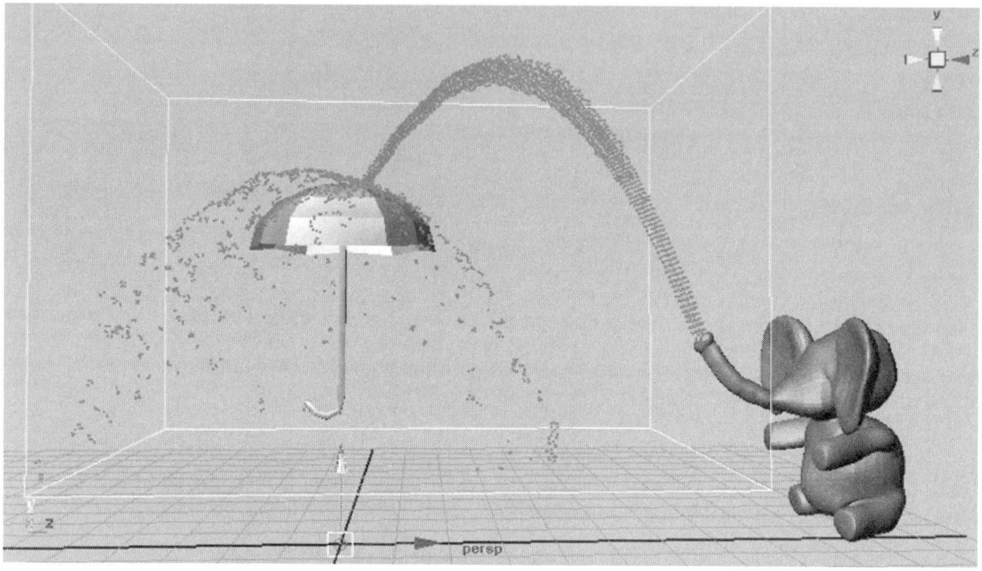

FIGURE 5.17 Particles generated in RF are imported successfully into Maya.

ON THE DVD

The particles are loaded as what could be considered a 3D composite of elements from multiple sources. These particles are Maya particles, so they can be rendered as Maya hardware or software particles. These options may be viable for the scene and look we are hoping to achieve. There is also the option of utilizing the meshes that were generated in RF. In the Outliner window, select and delete both the RealFlowEmitter and the RealFlowParticle nodes. As shown earlier in Figure 5.1, select the RealFlow menu at the top of the Maya screen. This time, select Mesh Loader and direct the plugin to your project's meshes folder. This may be something like (user)/scenes/umbrella/meshes. You can also load the particles from the companion DVD-ROM in the Chapter 5 folder. They can be found in the scenes/umbrella/meshes directory. The files are named and numbered as meshbrella#####.bin. As you run the animation this time, a series of meshes now represent the water that is being shot from the elephant's trunk. In Figure 5.18, the meshes formed from the particles in the RF simulation offer a polygonal solution as well.

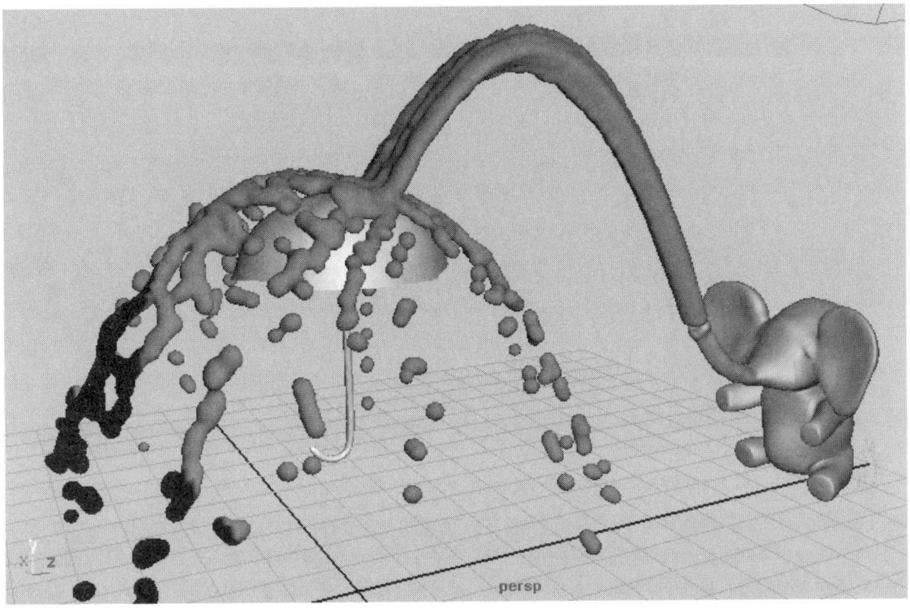

FIGURE 5.18 Particles generated as a mesh sequence offer a new set of possibilities.

It is easy to begin to see the potential in a program like this. It is accurate and exceedingly fast, considering the calculations taking place. Let's take a look at a nice feature of RF that adds yet another dimension to its toolset.

High-Voltage Wet Maps

Next Limit has added the concept of "wet maps" to RF. There is a lot of potential to eke out another layer of realism in a fluid dynamics animation. Let's look at how to generate a wet map and how it can be utilized. Again, we start within Maya to set up a scene with which to interact. Create a polygon plane with the dimensions shown in Figure 5.19. Make sure you select the Create UV's option box.

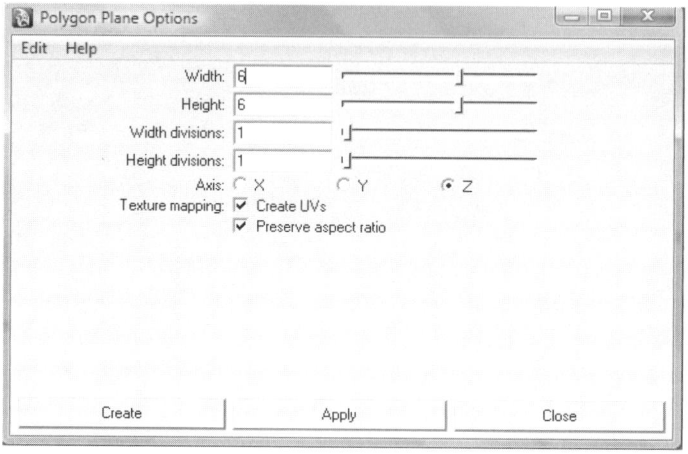

FIGURE 5.19 A polygon plane created with UVs.

We also want to make sure this plane is created with triangles. This can be done by selecting Mesh > Triangulate under the Polygons menu. This ensures good particle interaction in RF. Next, let's apply a texture to the plane.

Wet Maps and UVs

Wet maps are only generated on surfaces with UVs. If wet maps are not generating properly or not generating at all, a lack of UVs is usually the culprit. Any objects used to generate wet maps must have UV sets and textures applied to them prior to saving the sd file out to RF.

ON THE DVD

We are actually making a metal sign that should not be getting wet. Create a phong shader with a file as the color map. The file sign1.jpg is on the companion DVD in the Chapter 5 folder. Additionally, let's tilt the plane −20 X degrees to hold onto that water a little longer. When all is complete, the scene should look like Figure 5.20.

FIGURE 5.20 The very dry warning sign is almost ready for export to RF.

ON THE DVD

At this point, the scene is nearly complete. Let's throw a little extra interaction into the mix. On the companion DVD in the Chapter 5 folder is a Maya scene file called doors.mb. Load it. Since your warning sign should be on the origin, the doors should fit nicely. The Timeslider should be set to 500 frames. Play the animation back. The additional animation will be imported into RF as part of the dynamic simulation. In the File menu, select File > Export All and select the Option box. In General Options, make sure that the sd file format is selected. Click on Export All and save the file as warning_sign.sd. Notice as the file is exported that it runs through the animation. It is saving the animation information in the sd file for use in RF.

ON THE DVD

That's it. We can now import this scene into RF for further enhancements. If you got lost, both files, warning_sign.mb and warning_sign.sd, are on the companion DVD in the Chapter 5 folder. Additionally, there are the texture files for creating your own screen from scratch.

Close Maya. It won't be needed for a while. Launch RF. If you have been following along, create the new project directory warning_sign in the scenes directory, along with the umbrella project. When you create a project, RF creates the project's own separate set of subdirectories and an RF scene file designated by .flw. The warning_sign.sd file can now be imported into the project. In the File menu at the top of the RF screen, go to File > Import > Import Object and navigate to the warning_sign.sd file you just exported from Maya. Once imported, your RF scene should look something like Figure 5.21.

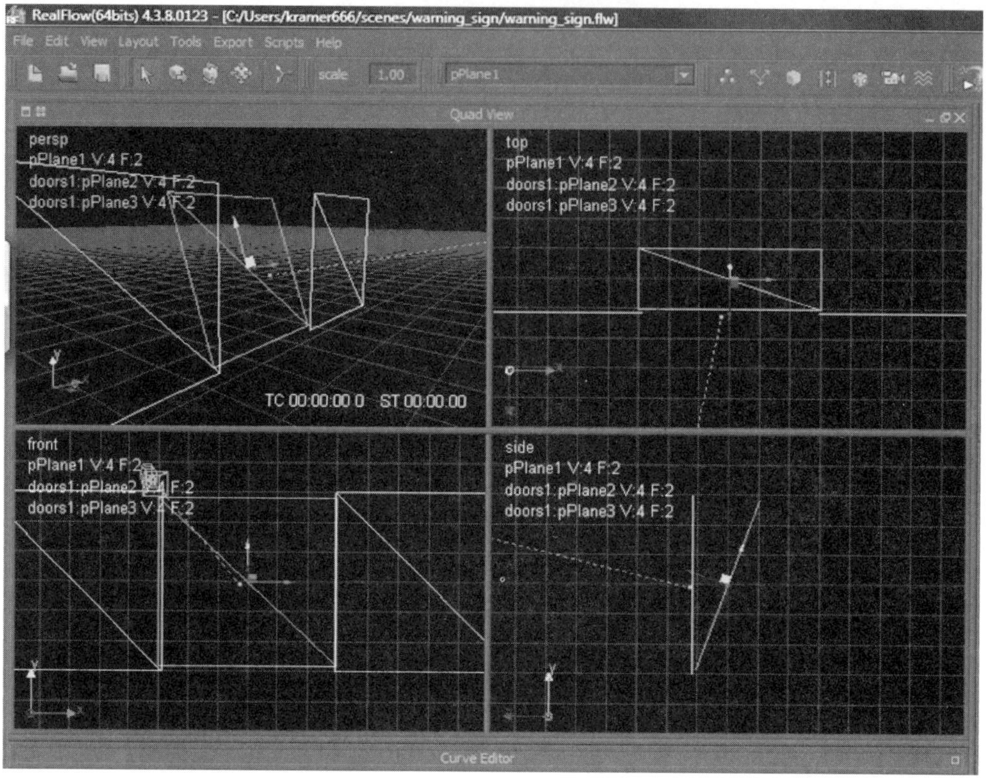

FIGURE 5.21 The Maya-exported sd file as it appears in RF.

We can expand the view by clicking on the red highlighted button shown in Figure 5.22. Selecting the Single View option expands the view so that it is easier to work with.

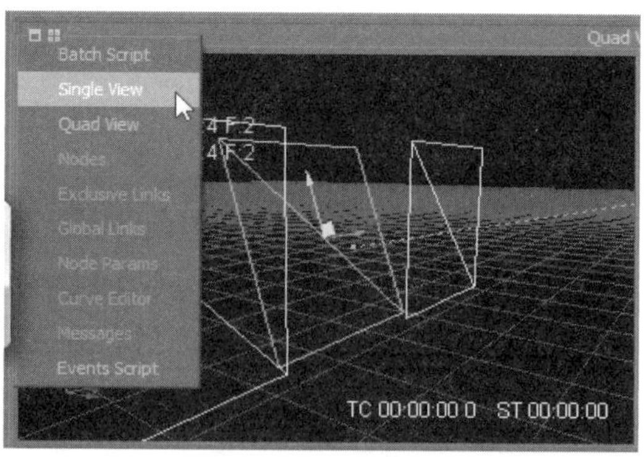

FIGURE 5.22 Expansion to a single view makes it easier to see.

We can further enhance how we view the scene by turning on flat shading and textures. This is important for the following reasons:

- We want to see if the UV texture coordinates transferred correctly from Maya.
- We want a visual cue that wet maps are being generated.

Pressing the 9 key on the keyboard turns on flat shading. Pressing Ctrl+Alt+F turns on textures. This can also be done on a single element or scene from the View menu at the top of the RF screen. The scene should look similar to Figure 5.23, as it did in Maya. The Timeslider and controls are very similar to Maya's. It is easy to scroll through or play back the imported animation as well.

FIGURE 5.23 The Maya scene now resides correctly in RF.

To generate a wet map, we must generate particles getting a surface wet. We will focus on getting the "KEEP DRY" sign wet. This time we will use a linear emitter for our particles. At the top of the RF screen is a set of icons shown in Figure 5.6. Select Add a New Emitter and choose Linear as the type. Position the Linear emitter so that it will launch its particles toward the sign. Test your emission by running the simulation. Your scene so far should resemble Figure 5.24. Gravity should exist in this scene as well. It will help to leave wet map streaks as the water particles slip down the sign. Gravity can be added by clicking on the Add New Daemon icon, as shown in Figure 5.6. This selection is also shown in Figure 5.25 along with its listing in the Nodes window.

Particle Flows and Arrows

Remember that you can tell which is the particle emission direction of an emitter by the smaller green arrow.

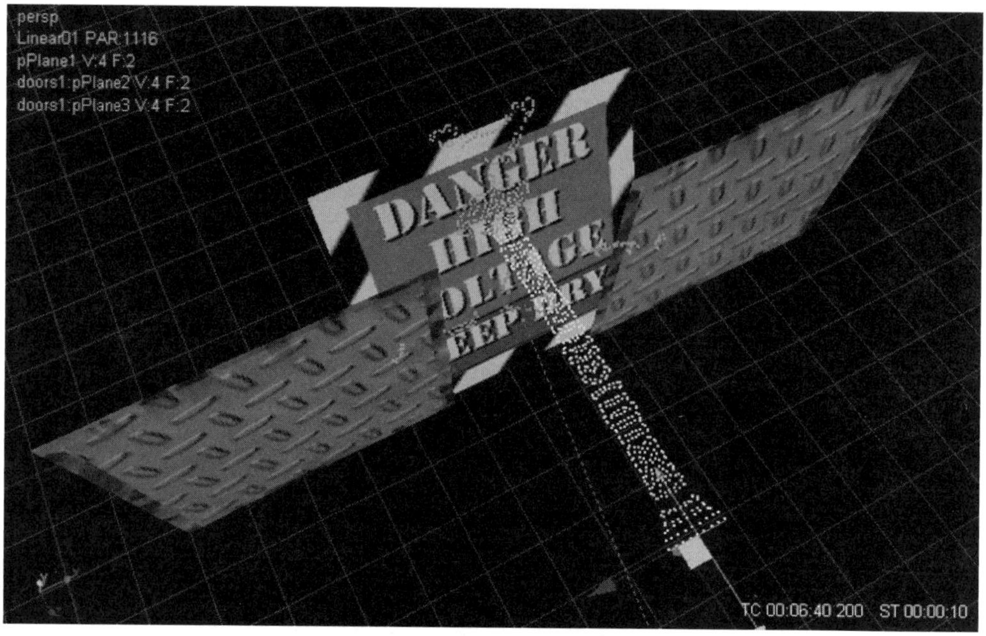

FIGURE 5.24 The linear emission of particle impacts for the high-voltage sign.

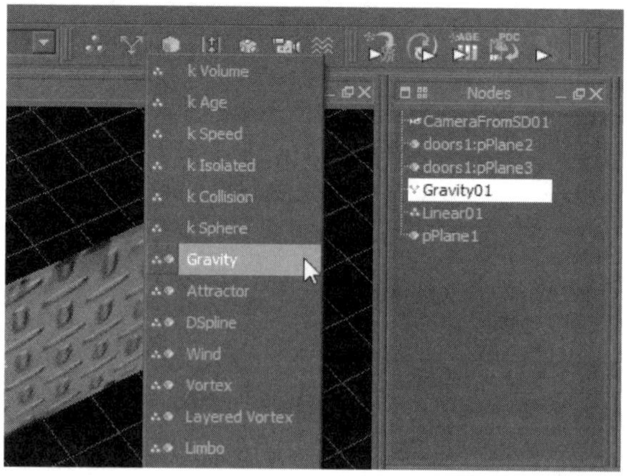

FIGURE 5.25 Adding a Gravity daemon to the scene.

As happened in the umbrella demo, the gravity has caused the particles to miss the mark. A careful adjustment of the position of the emitter and the speed of the particles will have the particles reaching the sign in short order. To make the scene even more interesting, the emitter's position can be animated. By sliding through the Timeslider and setting keyframes, the emitter can be repositioned and rotated over time. Moving the Timeslider to a frame and right-clicking the emitter brings up a menu for adding keyframes for position, rotation, and scaling. This is shown in Figure 5.26.

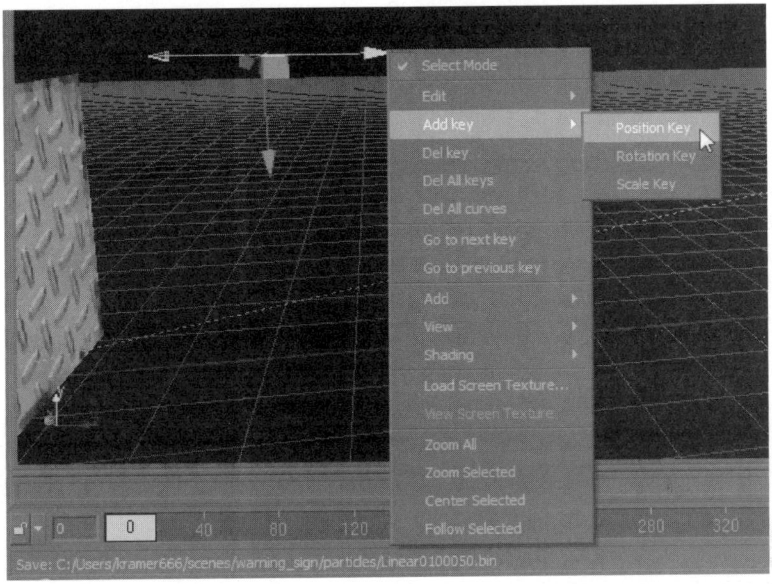

FIGURE 5.26 Adding keyframes to reposition and rotate the emitter at frame 0.

ON THE DVD

Adjust the emitter animation every 100 frames to spray particles over a wider area. Scroll through the Timeslider to see if you have successfully animated the emitter. Save your work by selecting the File menu at the top of the RF screen. Go to File > Save Project. You can also save a working version of your scene by selecting File > Save As. Load the warning_sign2.flw project from the companion DVD in the Chapter 5 folder. This is a 300-frame version of the work to this point. This can be done by going to File > Open Project and directing the browser to the scenes/warning_sign/ folder on the DVD-ROM.

The Ins and Outs of Wet Maps

Wet maps are grayscale images that are produced based on the impact of particles on a UV surface. Looking much like a matte, these sequential files can be used as a specular map, diffuse map, or any other kind of map to alter the rendered surface shader. A wet map has a few parameters that can be used to alter its appearance and effect.

Any object that has a texture applied in RF has configurable parameters under the Texture tab in the Node Params window. Most of these parameters deal with wet maps. By toggling WetDry Texture on, five values become unghosted.

- @resolution sets the output resolution of the wet maps. These images are square and sequential. One particle is going to leave a one-pixel spot, so adjusting the final map resolution bears consideration.
- @filter loops # is the number of iterations the filter will be applied. This can be computationally time-consuming. Higher values make the map fade to black more quickly.
- @filter strength is a Gaussian blur that helps smooth the pixel marks.
- @pixel strength is the brightness of the pixel spot left on collision with the surface.
- @ageing determines the length of time the wet map effect lasts. If a wet map flickers, this is an indication that the ageing is set too low.

At this point, we want to make sure that we are going to create wet maps for the warning sign. Select Plane1 from the Nodes window or select it directly. Under the Node Params window is a Texture tab. Clicking on that opens up a list of adjustable parameters. Next to the WetDry texture parameter is the word "No." Clicking on the word will toggle it to "Yes" and indicates to RF that we want to save wet maps for this texture. Notice that the warning sign has gone black. This is an indication that RF is now displaying wet maps. Run the simulation and stop it around frame 45. If you maneuver closer to the black warning sign, you will see the streaky wet marks left by the impact of the particles. This can also be seen on the backside of the warning sign. Figure 5.27 and Figure 5.28 show the wet map generated at frame 45.

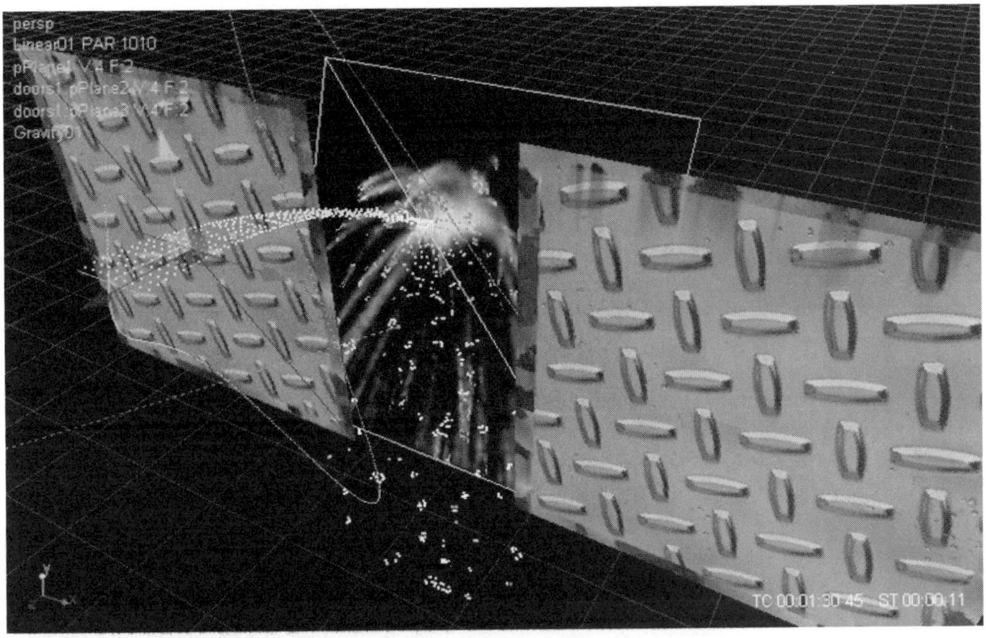

FIGURE 5.27 The streaks of the newly generated wet map are clearly visible on the warning sign.

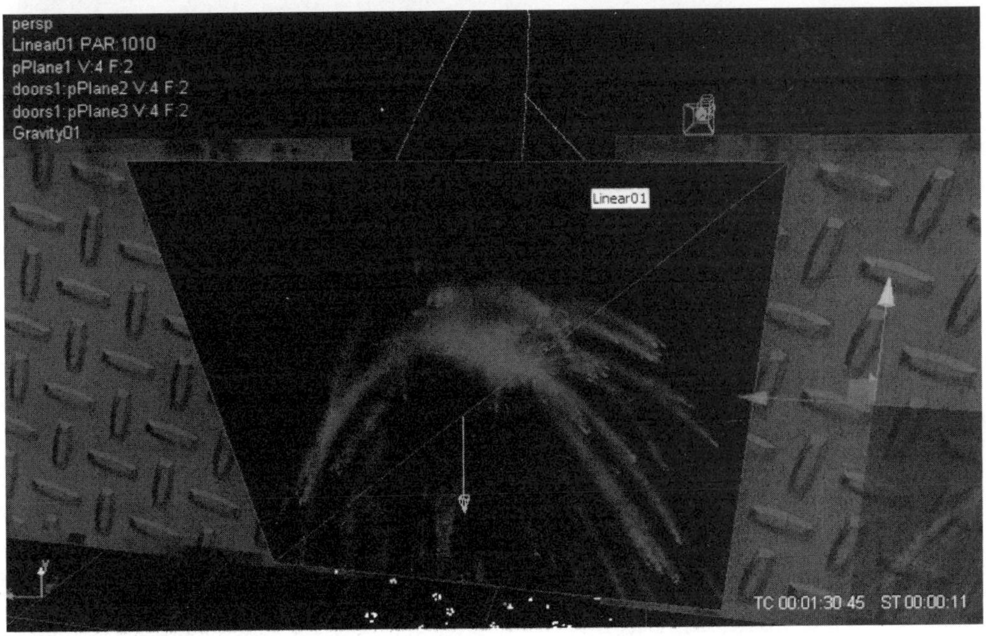

FIGURE 5.28 A better angle of the wet map can be seen on the reverse side of the sign.

RF generates all kinds of data. It's up to the artist how a scene is constructed and what data are needed to accomplish this task. The ability to selectively choose what data are saved is very helpful. Let's add a mesh generator to this equation (better safe than sorry if you have the available time to render it). As before, at the top of the screen amidst the bank of icons is the Add New Mesh icon, as shown in Figure 5.6.

1. Clicking on the Add New Mesh icon places a new node in the scene, called a *mesh*.
2. After the mesh is added to the scene, right-click on the mesh01 listing in the Nodes window. This brings up a pull-down menu.
3. Select Insert Fluids, which will list all the available particle emitters in the scene. We want to associate the mesh with the particle emitter.
4. Highlight the Linear01 node and press OK. This will now generate a mesh based on the particles generated from this emitter. This process can be seen in Figure 5.29. Resetting and rerunning the simulation should now produce a mesh representative of the particles generated.

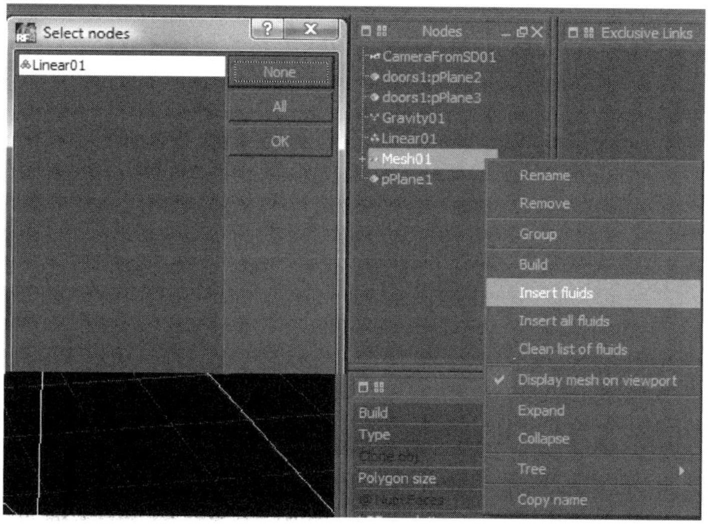

FIGURE 5.29 Linking the particle emitter to the Mesh01 node generates mesh data.

ON THE DVD

Save your work to this point. Load the warning_sign3.flw project from the companion DVD in the Chapter 5 folder. This is the same 300-frame version of the work to this point. This scene file has an added volume daemon. The bounding box of the daemon forces the destruction of any particles (and therefore meshes) that fall outside the volume. We did this with the umbrella scene as well. It is a terrific tool for quickly eliminating particles and meshes that no longer serve a function and only add to the computation time.

There is nothing more to do now than export the data that you need to generate. Pressing F12 brings up the Export Central window. This time mesh data and wet maps are all that are needed for this scene. Figure 5.30 shows the Export Central window with these two data types selected for output.

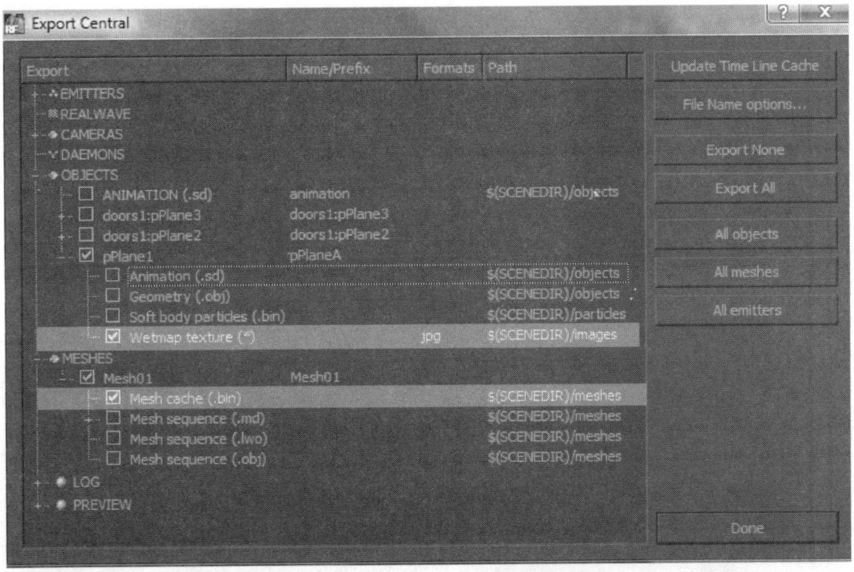

FIGURE 5.30 The Export Central window with two data types highlighted for

It Pays to Rename

Errors can occur when you try to import certain data types generated in RF into Maya. The error occurs due to the expectations of Maya's naming conventions. RF designates each node with a name with digits (for example, pPlane01, pPlane02...) to distinguish like nodes. This can confuse Maya when you are trying to import sequential data. This can be remedied by designating like nodes as pPlaneA, pPlaneB, and so on. This tends to matter less with data imported from a Maya/RF plugin, but data such as wet maps, which are used with shaders, do get confused. Changes can be made in the Export Central window under the File Name options tab.

The simulation can now be run for its full 300-frame length. Clicking on the Simulate button saves 300 frames of the selected data for import into Maya. After the simulation has run its course, it can be scrolled through, and the dynamics can be viewed in real time from the cache.

ON THE DVD

That completes the dynamic simulation in RF. Start Maya again, and we will begin to assemble the parts of the final Maya scene. On the companion DVD in the Chapter 5 folder is the scene file called warning_sign2.mb. It is nearly identical to the original scene file, with the exception of a shader. Load that scene. As shown earlier in Figure 5.1, select Next Limit > RealFlow > Mesh Loader and direct the plugin to your project's particle folder. This may be something like (user)/scenes/warning_sign/meshes. You can also load the particles from the companion DVD in the Chapter 5 folder, scenes/warning_sign/meshes. The files are named and numbered as mesh#######.bin. Once the meshes are loaded, run the simulation. Make sure the Timeslider is set to the number of mesh frames loaded, which is 300. It may be better to actually scratch through with the Timeslider. If all is successful, your scene should look something like Figure 5.31.

FIGURE 5.31 The meshes generated in RF are successfully imported into Maya.

ON THE DVD

The scene is shaping up just fine. We want to add the wet maps to the warning sign now. The use of the wet maps is wide open for interpretation. They can be added to the shader's diffusion, specularity, reflection, or just about anything that can be mapped. Let's alter the bump map of the warning sign shader to affect the surface with bumps. This will distort the surface, and the phong shading will catch highlights. Pull up the Multilister and select the phong shader that is currently used for the sign's color map. This technique is no more difficult than adding an image as a bump map. Select File for the bump map image and direct the browser to (user)/scenes/warning_sign/images. You can also load the wet map images from the companion DVD in the Chapter 5 folder, scenes/warning_sign/images. The files are named and numbered as pPlaneA####.jpg. Make sure to toggle the Use Image Sequence box on. It may be best to temporarily make the meshes invisible. Render out frame 240. The result should be similar to Figure 5.32.

FIGURE 5.32 The addition of the wet map as a bump map seems to melt and peel the sign.

ON THE DVD

The effect should look rather interesting. The phong shader being bump mapped looks very similar to water beading on the surface of the sign. The effect is not perfect but lends itself more to melting or having the paint bubble away from heat. As you can see, there are innumerable ways to alter the shader with the wet maps, depending on the type of look you hope to achieve. The results can be amazing. The added ability to generate wet maps in RF can be extremely useful, yet it is surprisingly easy to produce these maps. Figure 5.33 shows the finished scene. The scene file warning_sign3.mb on the companion DVD in the Chapter 5 folder has additional tweaks to the sign shader, and the mesh has been shaded as a hot oil type liquid.

FIGURE 5.33 The final scene showing the hot oil marking the warning sign.

Now let's take a look at generating wakes in a Scottish loch.

The Wakes of Loch Ness

Next Limit used to have a wave-generating program called RW. This has since been incorporated into RF. RW permits the user to create some particularly fascinating waves. Let's work a simple tutorial on generating wakes in a lake. Figure 5.34 shows various states of the Loch Ness monster. The highest-resolution model of Nessie, to the far right, may be used as the final model, once the waves have been generated in RF. The middle model is a lower-resolution proxy of the higher-resolution model. The far-left model is the proxy for use in RF and was built to avoid complications associated with Nessie's pointy back spikes.

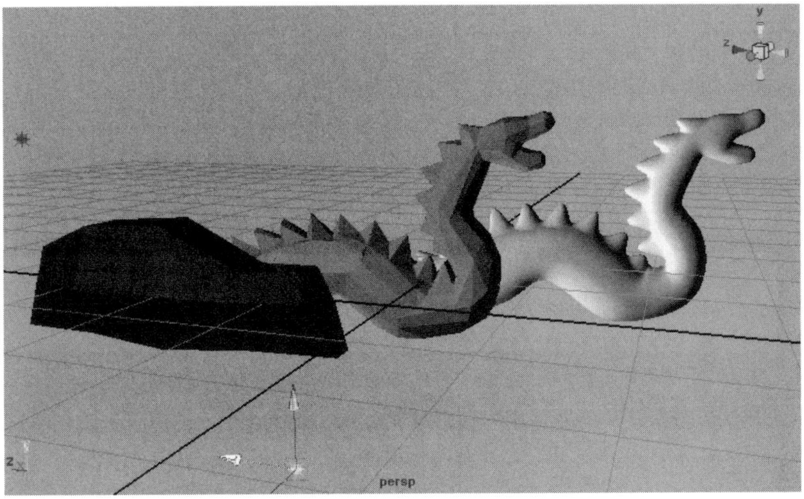

FIGURE 5.34 Multiple Nessie models serve different purposes for this scene.

ON THE DVD

Start RF and create a project called *nessie*. Import the model super_low_ness.obj, which is on the companion DVD in the Chapter 5 folder. This will serve as our temporary monster. At the top of the RF screen is the set of icons shown in Figure 5.6. Click on the Add a RealWave to the Scene icon. An RW plane is placed in the scene. Under the Nodes window, the RW plane is listed as Realwave01. Right-click on the node and rename it Loch_Ness. In the Node Params window under the Node tab, change the Z scale of the RW plane to 20. The image should look like Figure 5.35.

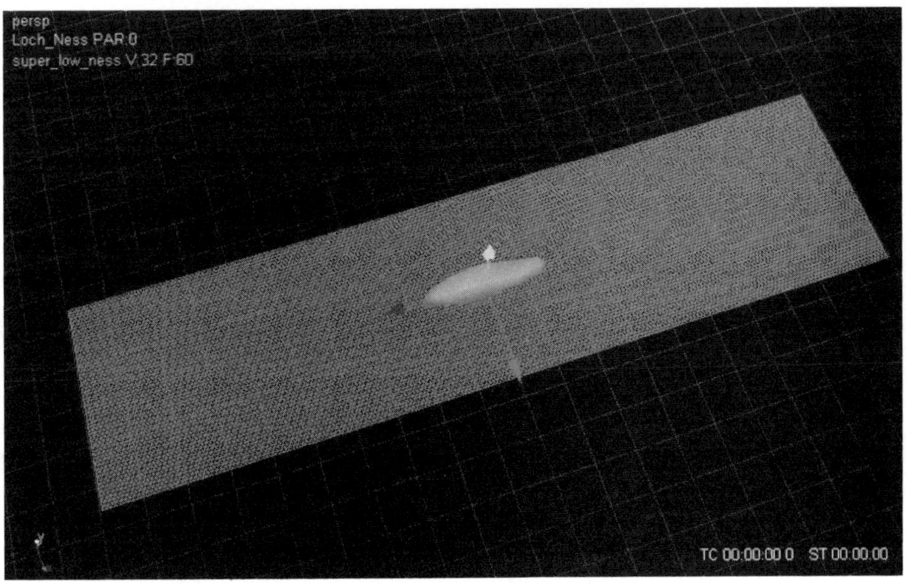

FIGURE 5.35 The RW plane is scaled in the Z direction.

With the Timeslider set to 0, translate Nessie to the far left of the RW plane. Right-click on the model and keyframe its position, as shown in Figure 5.36. At frame 200 move Nessie to the far right side of the RW plane.

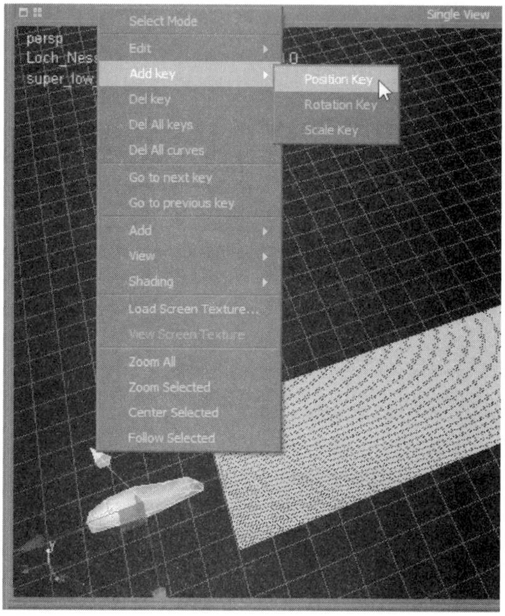

FIGURE 5.36 Nessie keyframed at frame 0 on the far left of RW plane.

Right-click on the model again and keyframe this position, as shown in Figure 5.37.

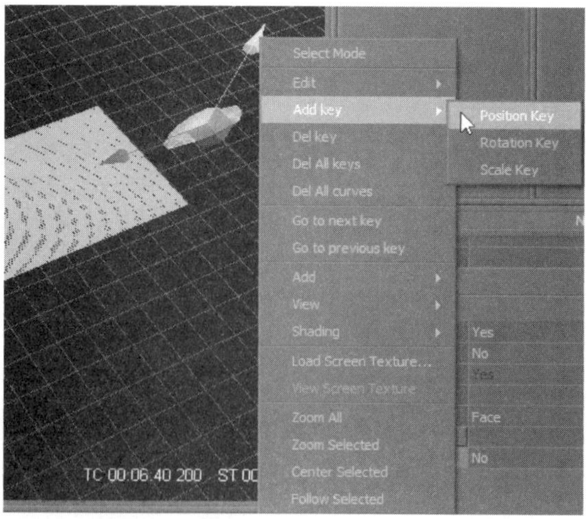

FIGURE 5.37 Nessie keyframed at frame 200 on the far right of RW plane.

Running the simulation now should yield a result, although it may be slight. This can be tweaked to give us the look we need. We can add a small amount of fractal disturbance to the water. Right-click on the Loch_Ness listing in the Nodes panel. Select Loch_Ness > Add Wave > Fractal as shown in Figure 5.38. The fractal wave will displace the wave with a complex fractal pattern. This fractal has several parameters for adjusting its weight, height, speed, slope, and octaves. Another type of wave is the spectrum wave that generates sinusoidal waves with varying frequencies, scale, and number of samples. Think of this as ripples in a sine pattern. Another type of wave is a control points wave. This wave allows the users to select vertices in the wave mesh that move up and down. Waves emanate in an ever expanding set of circles from the control point vertices like a stone thrown in a still pond. These waves propagate.

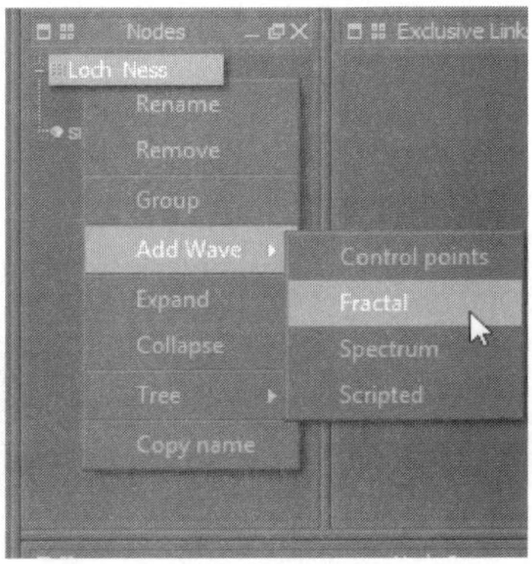

FIGURE 5.38 Adding a fractal disturbance makes the wave movement more realistic.

Select the newly created Fractal01 node from the Nodes panel and adjust its parameters as shown in Figure 5.39 of the Node Params window.

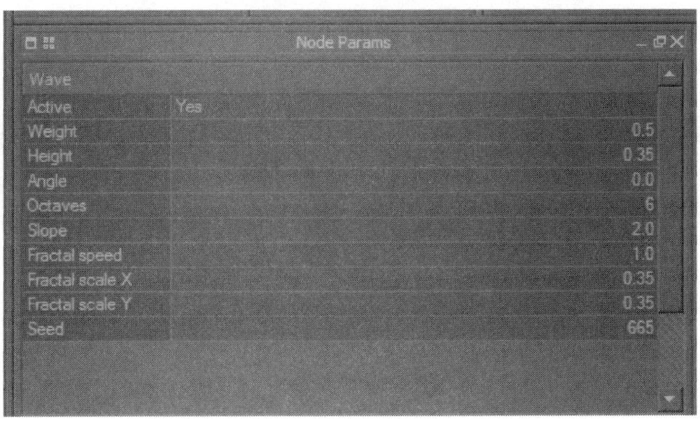

FIGURE 5.39 Adjustment of the Fractal01 node parameters.

Select the Nessie model and open the RealWave tab in the Node Params window. Tweak the parameters as shown in Figure 5.40 and run the simulation again. This should give a more sophisticated-looking wake as shown in Figure 5.41.

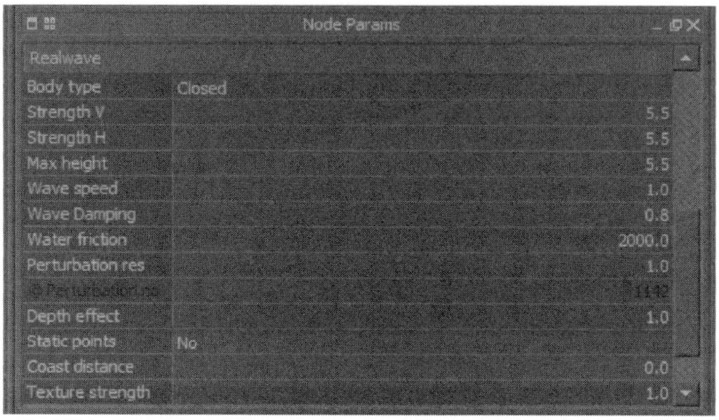

FIGURE 5.40 Further adjustments to the RW node for yielding a better-looking wake.

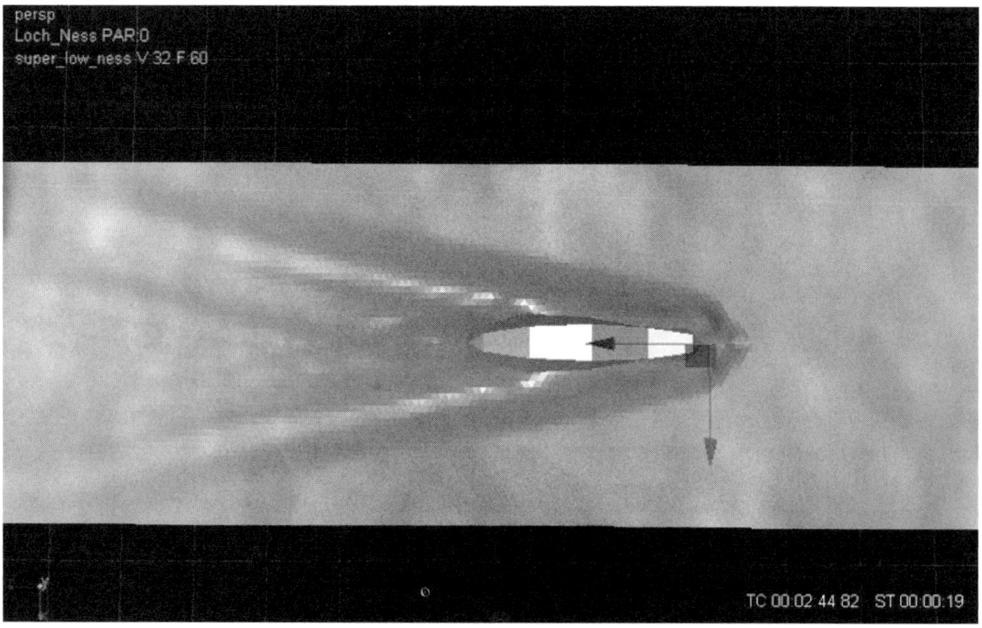

FIGURE 5.41 The results of the RW node adjustments.

At this point, we should be reasonably happy with the results of the simulation. The data we need for use in Maya are minimal, and we really only need the surface deformation of the RW. Pressing F12 brings up the Export Central window, where we will focus on the REALWAVE listing. Clicking the tiny + sign before it opens up a list of formats that RW data may be saved as. Select the .bin format and change the Name/Prefix in the File Name options box to the right in the Export Central window to Loch_Ness. This is the format we will use to import back into Maya. Figure 5.42 shows the Export Central window with the proper data selected for this exercise.

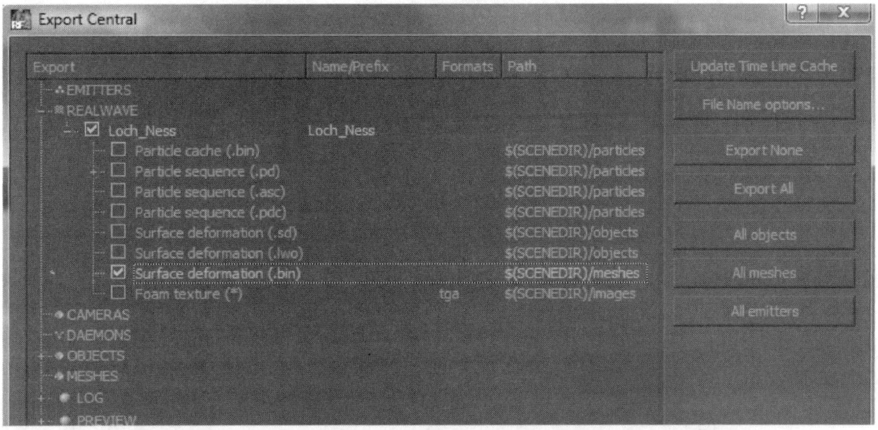

FIGURE 5.42 The RW surface deformation selected for export in the Export Central window.

ON THE DVD

Save your work and load Maya. We need to import our new data into Maya. As seen earlier in Figure 5.1, select Next Limit > RealFlow > Mesh Loader and direct the plugin to your project's meshes folder. This may be something like (user)/scenes/nessie/meshes. You can also load the particles from the companion DVD in the Chapter 5 folder, scenes/nessie/meshes. The files are named and numbered as Loch_Ness#####.bin. As reference, you can also load the nessie proxy into the scene. This can be done by importing the .sd file super_low_ness.sd, which is in your (user)/scenes/nessie/objects directory. Remember that this time you are using File > Import from the Maya menu. After the meshes are loaded, run the simulation. Make sure that the Timeslider is set to the number of meshes generated, which is 200. If all is successful, your scene should look something like Figure 5.43.

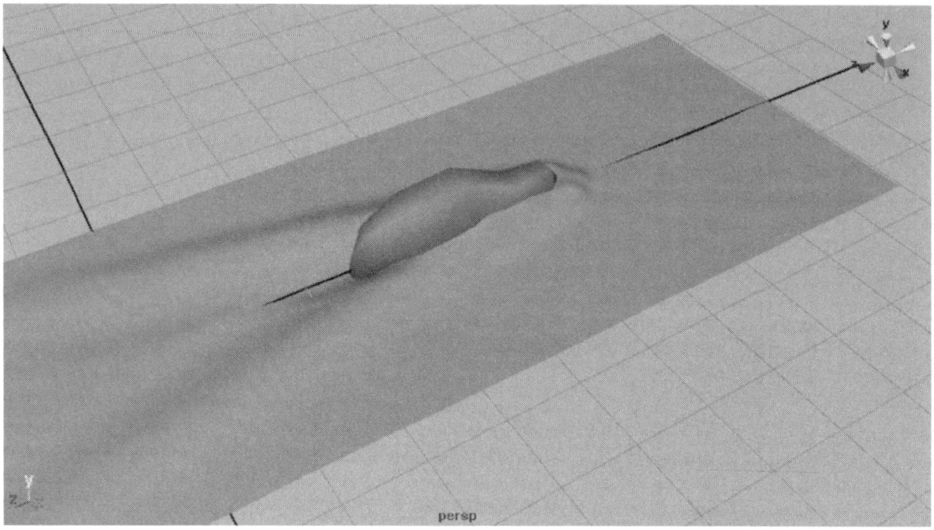

FIGURE 5.43 The successful import of RF-generated data into Maya.

The headless proxy Nessie is replaced by a low-poly Nessie model for the final render, which can be seen in Figure 5.44.

FIGURE 5.44 A slightly higher-resolution Nessie model replaces its proxy for the final scene.

ON THE DVD

This is a great example to show off the power and potential of RF. Two bonus RF and Maya scenes are on the companion DVD in the Chapter 5 folder. Both scenes, soccer_roll and Aquafuel, which are shown in Figures 5.45 and 5.46, are there to study.

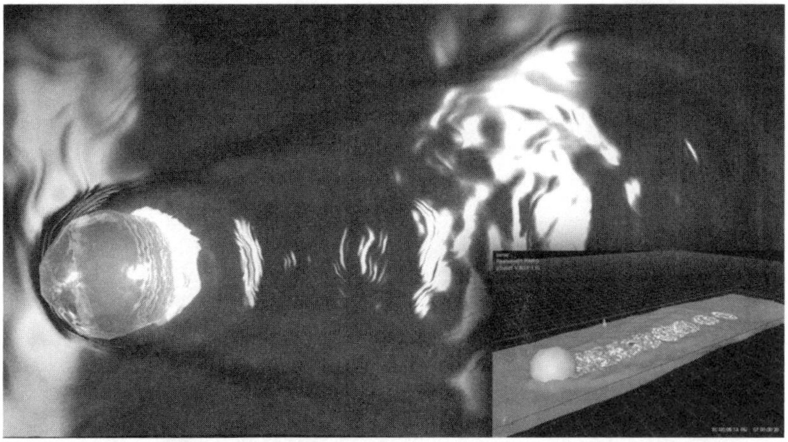

FIGURE 5.45 Bonus scene: a ball rolling through puddle generates foam textures and wakes.

FIGURE 5.46 Bonus scene: bitmap texture can be used as emitters for interesting results.

An entire book could be written on RF, but it's time to move on. The next chapter addresses a plugin for the 3D character.

CHAPTER

6

CHARACTERS

In This Chapter

- Introduction
- Rigging Allen the Alien
- Testing Movement of the Rig

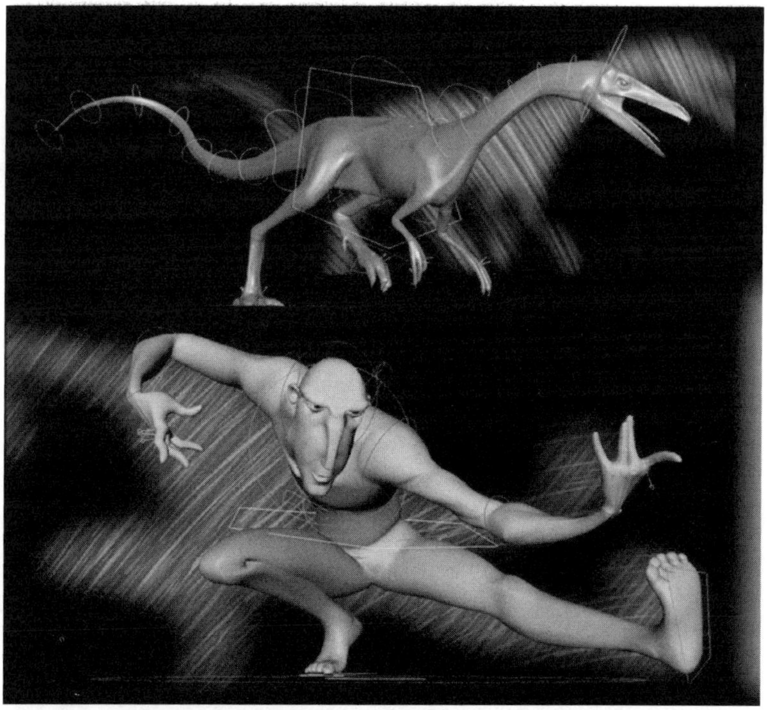

Nimble and expertly rigged bipeds and quadrupeds are easy to create in Anzovin Studio's Setup Machine 2.
Character images courtesy of Anzovin Studio

INTRODUCTION

Maya plays a big role in character animation. One of the toughest challenges is rigging the character for good clean animation. This requires access to the parts of your character that will bring it to life. The Setup Machine 2 (TSM2) is a Maya plugin from Anzovin Studio that makes the rigging process much easier. Most character rigs for films and TV are highly sophisticated manipulation tools. When a character takes a starring role, it needs to remain easy to use, masking the technical hurdles inherent in this type of work. It is not uncommon to have animators who are less technology minded and more aware of the nuances of animation. Character animation is an art unto itself.

TSM2 allows the user to create an efficient character rig with relative ease. It creates a character with basic rig staples such as skin weighting and eliminates the need to consider technical challenges such as pole vectors and joint orientation. A novice can have a character up and running in short order, while a more seasoned rigger has a terrific starting point for enhancements. TSM2 provides the tools necessary to create nonhuman forms such as quadrupeds, creatures with tails, and even an octopus (see Figure 6.1).

FIGURE 6.1 Human and creature rigs are possible in The Setup Machine 2.
Images courtesy of Anzovin Studio

Executing TSM2's installer program is simple. After installation, make sure that the plugin is loaded and recognized by Maya. This can be done by going to the top of the screen in the Maya menus and selecting Window > Setting/Preferences > Plug-in Manager. Make sure that both the Loaded and Auto load boxes are selected next to TSM2.mll. After installation, Maya will have two new menus labeled The Setup Machine and TSM Controls.

Let's use this chapter and TSM2 to create a basic character rig and pose our character.

Rigging Allen the Alien

ON THE DVD

We will create a simple rig for a small humanoid alien. First, import the OBJ mesh allen.OBJ from the companion DVD in the Chapter 6 folder. Your scene should look something like Figure 6.2.

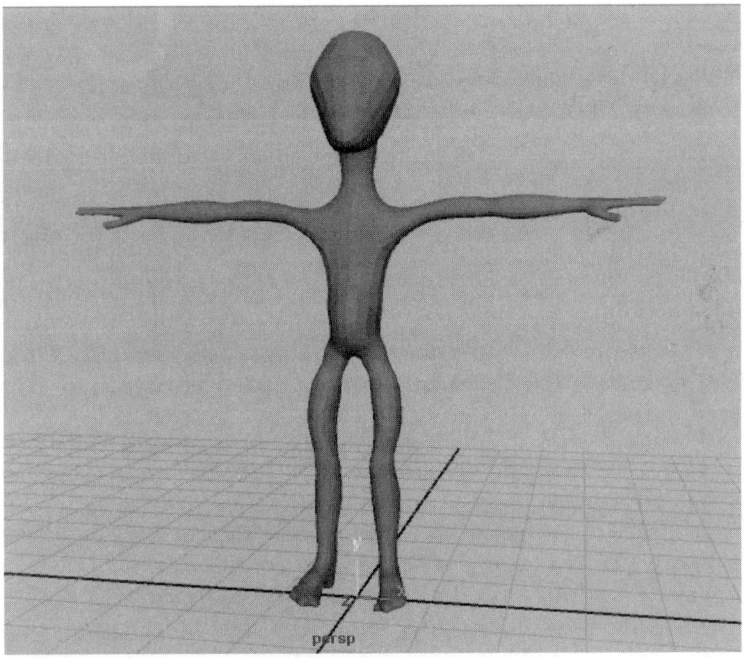

FIGURE 6.2 The alien model imported into Maya and ready for rigging.

A simple workflow for rigging a character in TSM2 is as follows:

1. Load your character mesh into the scene.
2. Describe your rig, thereby creating the widgets necessary for your character's form.
3. Load the widgets into the scene.

4. Adjust the scaling and positioning of the widgets to conform to the scale and position of the mesh character.
5. Apply the rig to the mesh, creating your jointed and weighted character.
6. Save your rigged character.
7. Make any corrections to the weighting of your rig. This is an inevitable part of the process.
8. Resave your character.

SAVE VERSUS SAVE AS: KNOW THE DIFFERENCE

Save your work often. Rigs cannot be undone, so a prudent use of the Save As command is in order. Keep a copy of your mesh and rigs for safety's sake. It is discouraging and costly to lose time-consuming work due to overwriting a file. Save As is a universal function in almost every program. Using Save overwrites the file that is loaded. Save As makes it easy to rename the scene file, thus creating valuable backups and versions of the same scene.

TSM2 uses a system of widgets that represent the various parts of a rig. Each widget contains all the joint information for that section of the rig. Think of the widgets as representations of the various body parts that compose your character. TSM2 uses the widgets to make it easy for the user to define a rig by hiding the tedium, technicalities, and functionality that can make rigging a character confusing. When the TSM2 rig is loaded, it is composed of simple color-coded geometry that represents arms, legs, head, neck, torso, and even a tail. Once the mesh has been loaded into the scene, you can begin the rigging process by describing the widgets that will ultimately comprise the rig of your character. Follow these steps.

1. Go to The Setup Machine menu at the top of the screen with the Maya menus and choose The Setup Machine > Pre-Rig > Build Biped and select the option box.
2. This allows you to define or describe the widgets necessary for your character. The option box tells TSM2 the number of fingers for your biped plus the option of a thumb and tail. In this instance, we are creating four fingers and a thumb for the rig. This can be seen in Figure 6.3. Figure 6.4 shows the color-coded biped widgets created in the scene. Notice that it is much larger than the mesh.

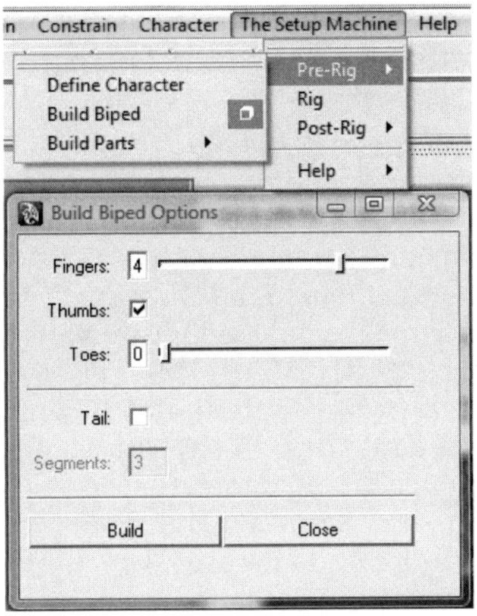

FIGURE 6.3 The bipedal widgets are defined and created for the scene.

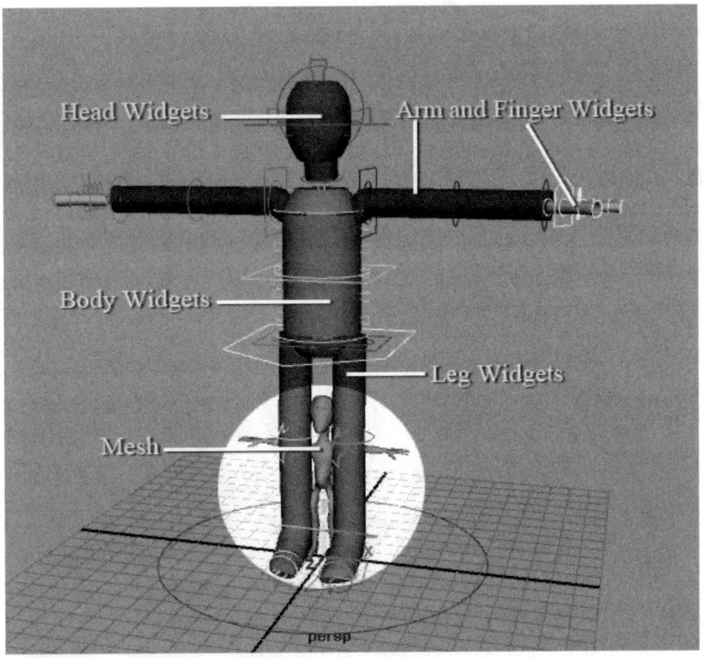

FIGURE 6.4 The biped widgets currently tower over the mesh object.

Three Fingers Versus Four Fingers

While it may be argued that it is less prevalent these days, there has been a long history and curious phenomenon of animated characters possessing only three fingers and a thumb. The most widely held reason for this is simple. It is easier to draw characters with one less digit. This seems to have stemmed from the early days of animation. Hand-drawing animation cels is a time-consuming task. The chance to take time off the animation process, by drawing one less finger, is welcome. Mickey Mouse, Mighty Mouse, Bugs Bunny, and Snoopy all had three fingers. Lest you think this is confined to animals, Elmer Fudd, the Simpsons, and Family Guy all have three digits plus a thumb. Fred Flintstsone and Barney Rubble are similarly afflicted.

Another reason often cited is that imaginary characters are not necessarily bound by the same constraints as real ones. Most people don't notice this feature, or lack thereof, anyway. This must explain why most people don't notice that Fred, Barney, Wilma, Betty, and the rest of the Stone Age gang only have three toes.

The widgets must now be scaled to fit over the mesh character. As an analogy, think of the widgets as a suit. The stiff and rigid mesh will be enveloped by the widget suit. Two controls are used for this. At the feet of the widgets is a large circle. This is the Character Control. At mid-torso level is the Upper Body Control, as shown in Figure 6.5. Selecting either the Character Control or the Upper Body Control will present the same translation, rotation, and scaling manipulators that any Maya object will have. Translate the Character Control to match the bottom of the alien model's feet. Once this is done, uniformly scaling down the rig with the Character Control will get you closer to matching the rig to the model. At this point, translate the Upper Body Control of the rig to better match the mesh alien's hip.

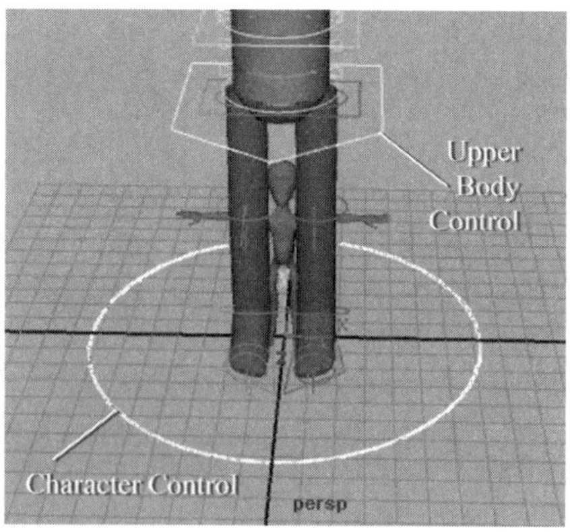

FIGURE 6.5 The Character and Upper Body Controls are used to scale and translate the widgets.

After scaling the widgets down to size, your character should look similar to Figure 6.6.

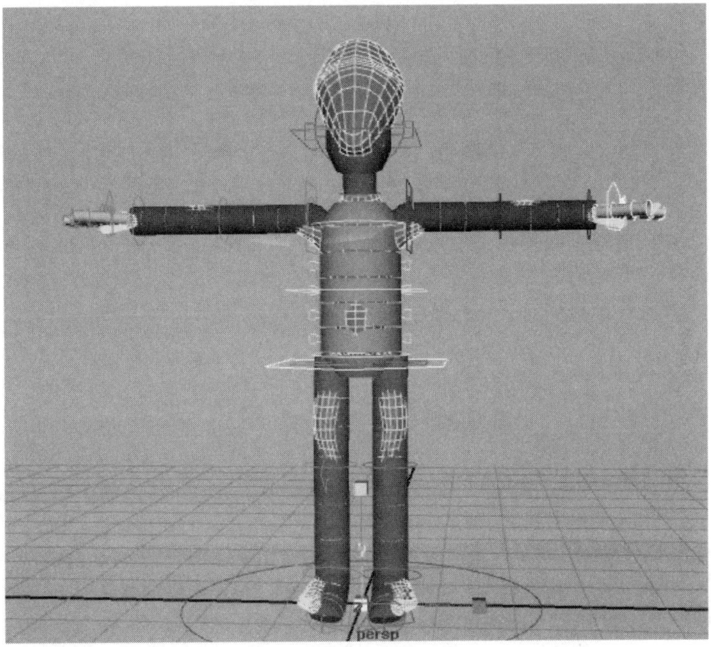

FIGURE 6.6 After scaling, the mesh and widgets should share approximately the same space.

UNIFORM VERSUS NONUNIFORM SCALING

When using the Character Control and the Upper Body Control for scaling and translating the widgets, don't scale it nonuniformly. In other words, don't scale XYZ separately (see Figure 6.7).

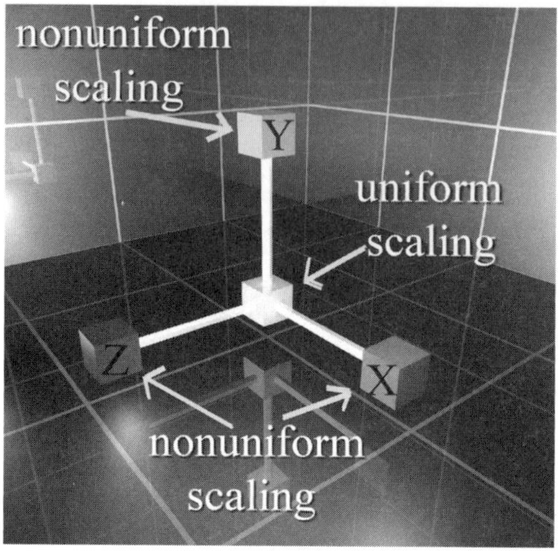

FIGURE 6.7 Uniform versus nonuniform scaling.

The next step is to adjust the individual widgets to conform better with the mesh. Widgets have two controls: the System Moving Control and the Fit Controls. The System Moving Control is used to manipulate the entire widget as a whole and is represented as a square. The Fit Controls, represented as circles, are used to finely hone the widget's shape. This is shown in Figure 6.8.

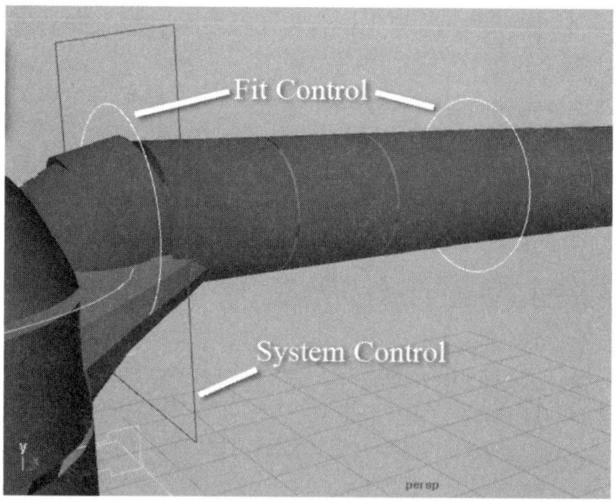

FIGURE 6.8 The System Moving and Fit Controls of the arm.

The controls for setting up the rig can be categorized into three main groups. Among these are widgets, System Controls, and Fit Controls. Widgets are represented by the nurbs-based and color-coded cylindrical shapes that are an approximation of the mesh. These widgets need to be fitted around the various mesh sections. Think of them as tight-fitting armor suit sections. These widgets are the basis from which the final working rig is established. The color codes represent the different sections of the body.

- Red widgets are used to control the head and neck.
- Blue widgets are used to control the arms.
- The yellow widgets are representative of the hands and fingers.
- The green widgets control the spine/torso of the mesh.
- Purple widgets control the legs.

The System Controls and Fit Controls are an integral part of each widget's section. They are used to conform the widgets to the mesh. The System Controls are intended to position the widget's sections in place more appropriately. These controls are square and are used for translating the entire color-coded widget section. These controls may also be uniformly scaled.

The Fit Controls are used to properly position the individual subsets of a widget into place. In the case of the leg widgets, the Fit Controls help to better position the thigh/hip, knee, ankle/heel, ball of the foot, and toes. They usually denote where TSM2 will place joints in the final rig. Fit Controls adjust the cylindrical nurbs pieces that constitute the entire color-coded widget section. These controls are usually circular, with one notable exception on the foot, and may be nonuniformly scaled to fit the mesh. The Fit Control of the foot is the only noncircular Fit Control and can be seen in Figure 6.9. The individual cylindrical nurbs sections of a widget may also be separately manipulated to position them better around the mesh.

Scaling Is Critical

As with the Character Control and the Upper Body Control, there are issues with nonuniform scaling. The widget's System Moving Controls should only be uniformly scaled. Nonuniform scaling of this control may lead to unexpected rigging results. The Fit Controls do not have this distinction and may be nonuniformly scaled.

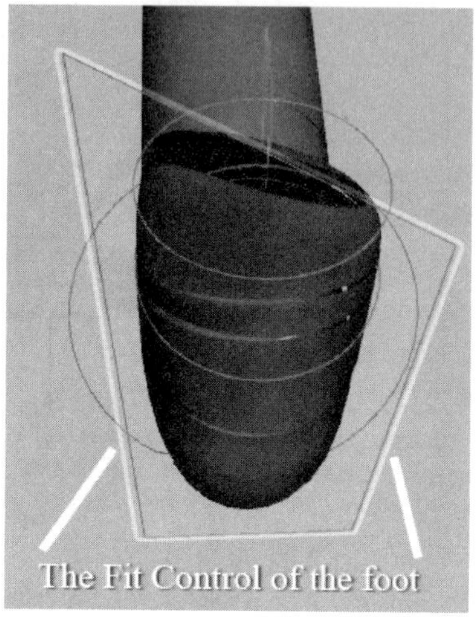

FIGURE 6.9 The foot Fit Control is the only noncircular Fit Control in TSM2.

Next, we want to tweak the widgets to conform better to the mesh. It is always best to start by positioning the hip first. This is where the body meets the legs and where your character will bend. Select the Upper Body Control and move it to where your character's hips will be (see Figure 6.10).

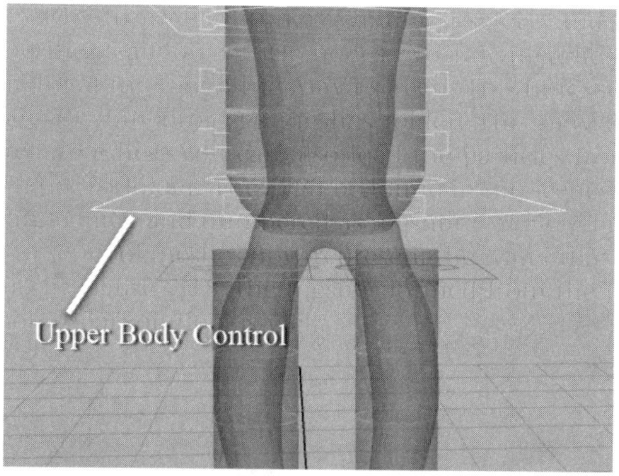

FIGURE 6.10 Positioning the Upper Body Control to set the position of the hips.

Next, position the legs by selecting the square System Moving Control of the legs. If you scale it, remember the rules for nonuniform scaling. The legs should be placed in a similar fashion to Figure 6.11.

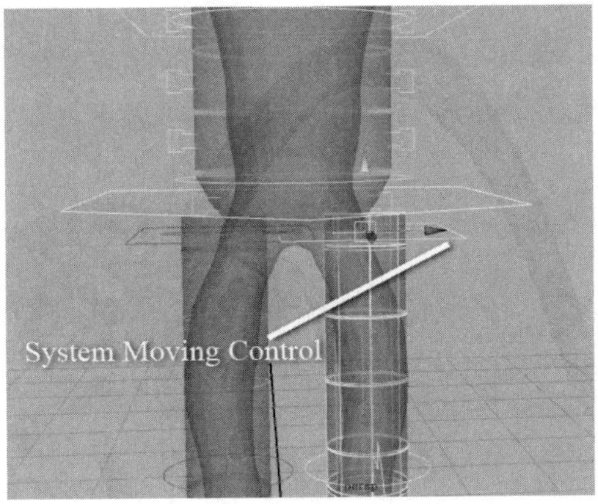

FIGURE 6.11 Set the leg's position near the hips by selecting its System Moving Control.

THE RIGHT HAND KNOWS WHAT THE LEFT HAND IS DOING

The head and body widgets are singular, but there are two arm, leg, and hand widgets. Any translation or scaling done on the widgets of the left side of the character's body will be mirrored on the right. As viewed in this scene, the body's left side is on the viewer's right.

We must now position the upper body to encompass the shoulders. The placement of the hips may have shifted the spine. The shoulders may need adjustment. This can be done by selecting the upper body's Fit Control and moving it into position. Figures 6.12 and 6.13 show this movement.

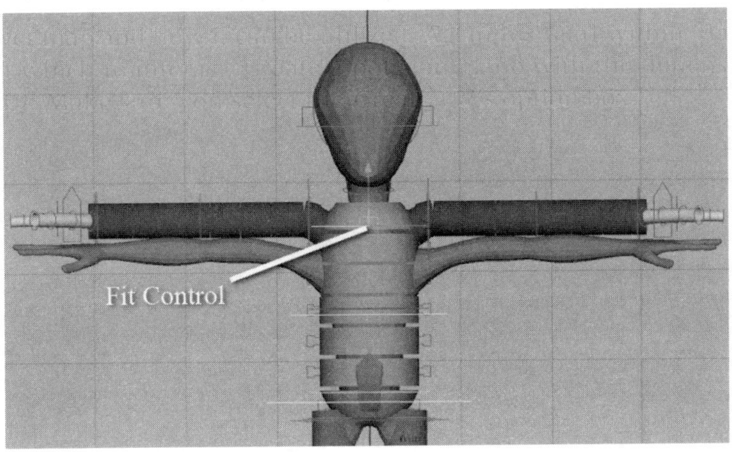

FIGURE 6.12 The Fit Control of the upper chest.

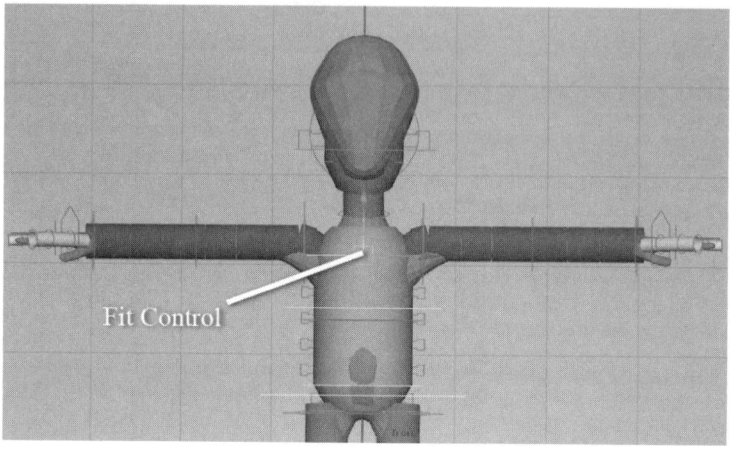

FIGURE 6.13 Repositioning the upper chest and aligning the shoulders and arms.

DIFFERENT VIEWS

Depending on what you are trying to manipulate, it is helpful to switch between wireframe, flat shading, and X-ray shading in the viewports. One shading view may be easier than another to manipulate the various components of the widgets. It is also more helpful to stay primarily within the orthogonal views.

Next, we can set the head and neck widgets into position. Allen has a longer-than-average neck. Adjust the individual neck widgets to cover the neck. The individual pieces can be translated and scaled nonuniformly to fit around the Allen mesh. Now scale the head widgets to cover Allen's head. In the front view, make sure the Fit Control encompasses his face. The most important area is the chin. The Fit Control should clear the bottom of Allen's chin, or else there will be weighting distortions when the head is turned certain ways. Use Figure 6.14 and Figure 6.15 as guides.

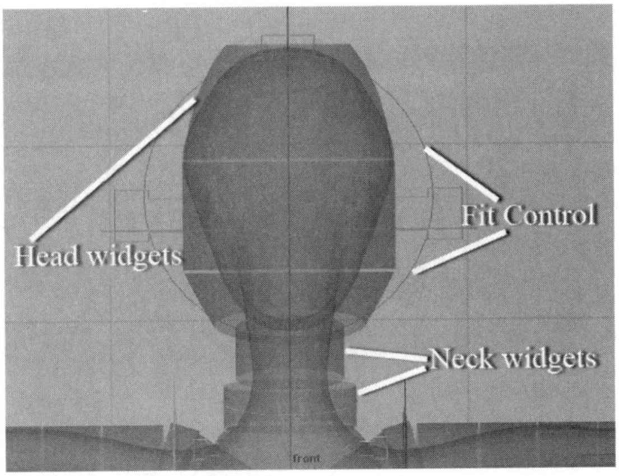

FIGURE 6.14 The front X-ray view of Allen's neck shows how the widgets can fit properly.

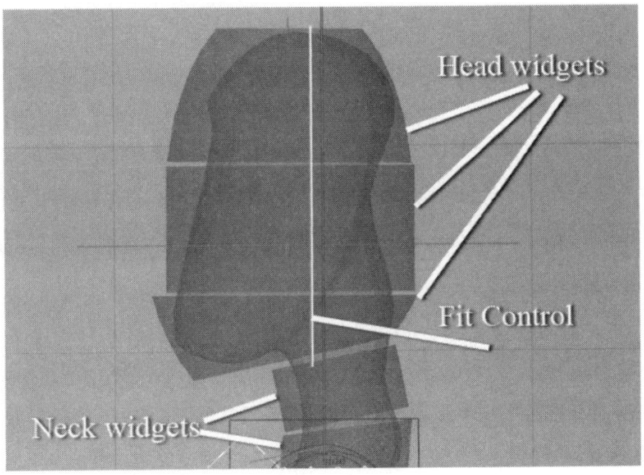

FIGURE 6.15 Side view of widget placement around the mesh head and neck of the alien model.

Close Enough

While it may be good practice, the mesh geometry does not have to be completely enveloped in the widgets. Often, the geometry will poke through the widgets. You'll have to toy with it to find out what works best. Saving the scene in stages allows you to go back and retry placement. To be safe, save at least each set of adjustments. This will give you plenty to fall back on if you need to reconsider the placement of any of the widgets. The Save As command is a good friend.

Let's concentrate on the legs and feet. Position the foot widgets in place around the foot. Depending on how you originally scaled down the entire widget rig, they may fit by merely translating the Fit Control of the foot. If you intend to do walk cycles, don't rotate the Fit Control of the foot. You can scale and translate the individual foot widgets to encapsulate the geometry of the foot inside the purple foot widgets. You can even adjust the CVs to get a tighter fit. Figure 6.16 and Figure 6.17 show the adjusted widgets in the X-ray shading mode. CVs are the individual control vertices that define a NURBS' surface.

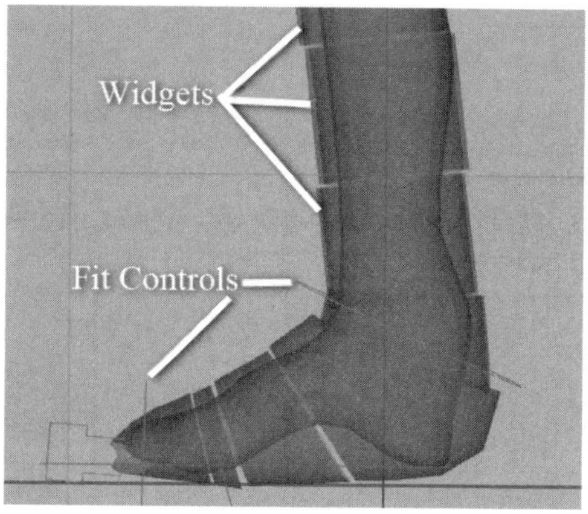

FIGURE 6.16 X-ray shading of the feet. The Fit Controls will become joints of the foot.

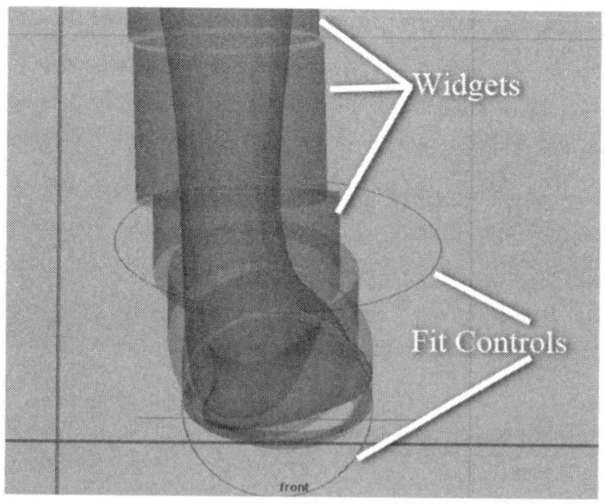

FIGURE 6.17 X-ray shading of the front orthogonal view of widgets encapsulating the mesh foot.

Figure 6.18 is a perspective view of the feet without X-ray shading. Allen has an oddly shaped foot, so it may be a bit more difficult to get the proper widget shapes in place. Notice the placement of the circular Fit Controls of the foot. These will be the toe, ball of the foot, and ankle joints, respectively.

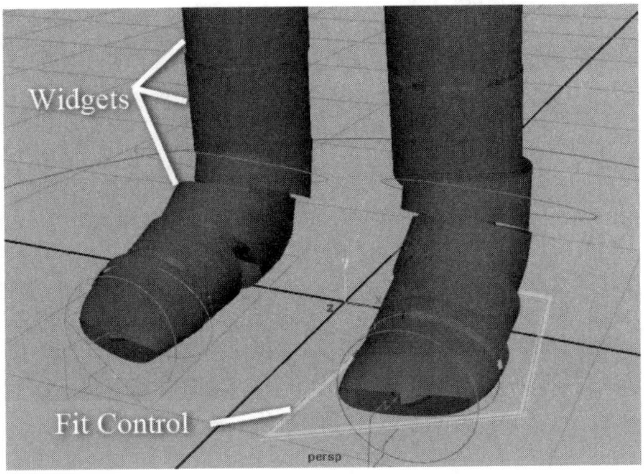

FIGURE 6.18 Smooth shaded view of widgets properly enveloping the mesh feet.

Mirror, Mirror

When working on individual widgets, scaling, rotation, and translation do not mirror. Most of the time, this can be overcome by selecting the opposing widget on the other side and performing the action on both items. In the case of Allen the Alien, this will work in the YZ directions but not in X. The X plane is the direction of the mirror, so nonuniform scaling, translation, and rotation in X need to be mirrored actions. Precise placement and adjustments on the right can be mimicked and mirrored in the Channel box.

Now let's finish up the legs. A quick repositioning of the widgets should be fairly simple. The mesh model is a little bowlegged, so there will be a bit more repositioning of the X-plane widgets. This requires a little extra work, as individual widgets won't have their manipulations mirrored in X. Remember the placement of the Fit Control of the knee. This will become the knee joint of the character (see Figure 6.19).

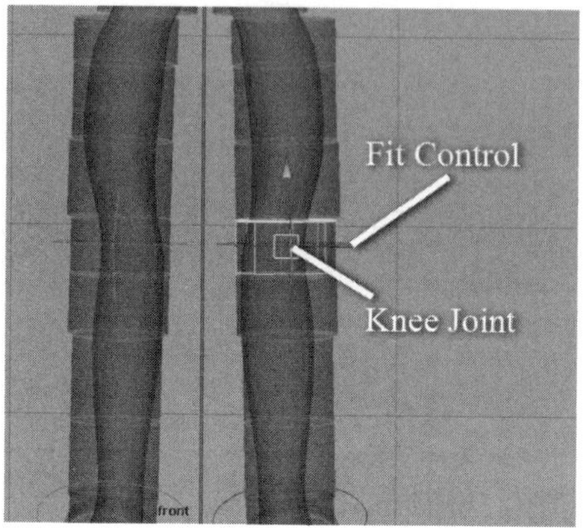

FIGURE 6.19 Front X-ray-shaded view of the final widget's placement.

Also, remember to save this scene prior to setting the rig. The odd nature of the bowed legs leading into the hips may need reevaluation. See Figures 6.20 and 6.21 for perspective and side views of the finished legs. The arrows coming from the knee point the direction of the joint.

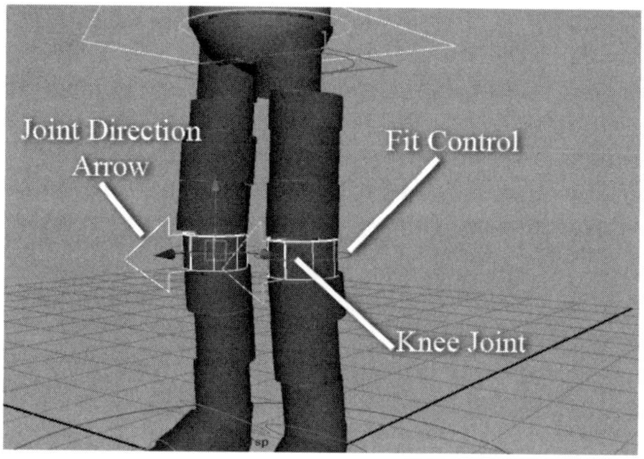

FIGURE 6.20 Shaded perspective view of widgets of the legs and knee joint direction arrows.

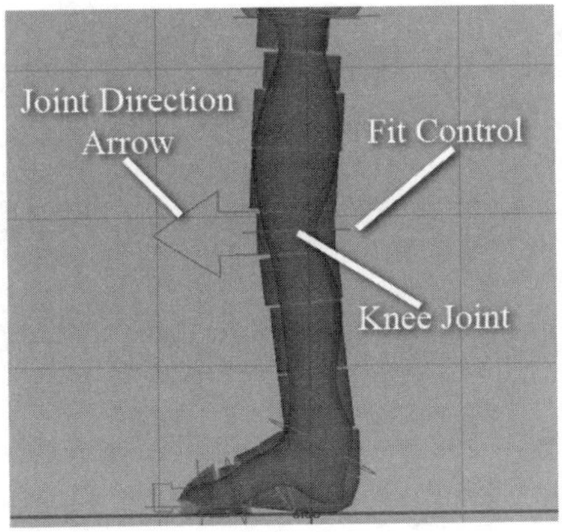

FIGURE 6.21 Side view of widgets and knee joint direction arrows.

The meeting of the legs and hips is one last thing to consider. Widgets can interpenetrate each other. Figure 6.22 shows the hip and the overlap that occurs with the upper body. This is a fairly good starting point for a hip. Note the Upper Body Control's proximity to the top Fit Control and System Control of the legs.

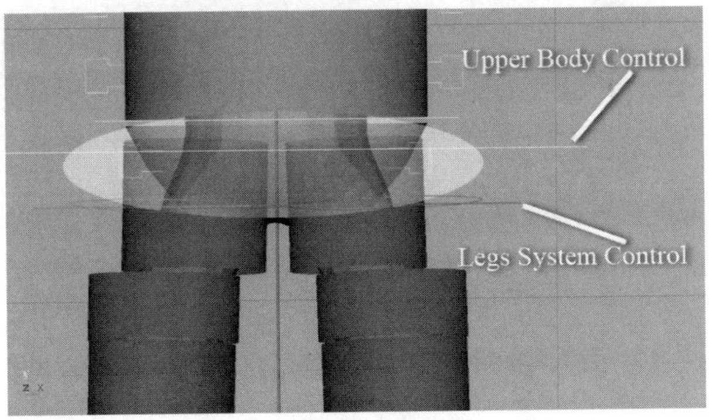

FIGURE 6.22 The leg's Fit and System Controls and the intersection of the leg and body widgets.

The arms are next. Place the arm widgets around the arms of the mesh. Note that the elbows have a point direction as well as the knees. Try to keep the joint direction in its initial position. Drag the System Control of the arm into position so that it interpenetrates with the upper body. This will create the shoulder. This is done because the shoulder is a complicated joint that connects the arm to the torso. Movement at this joint will move a small portion of the torso, creating a more realistic movement. Move the Fit Controls of the shoulder, elbow, and wrist into position at the appropriate spots on the mesh. Figure 6.23 and Figure 6.24 show the proper way to set the widgets and joints of the arm. Save your work.

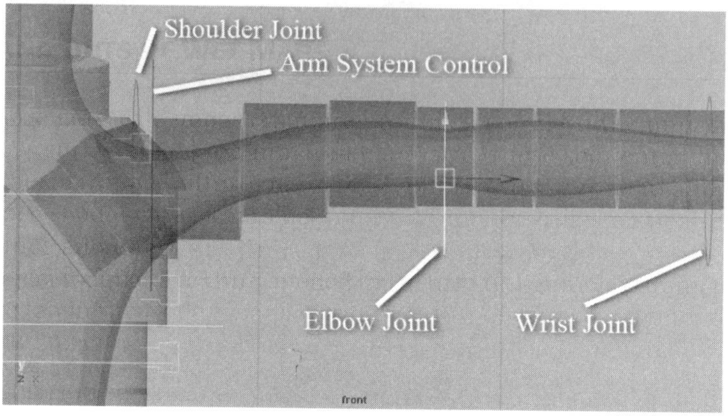

FIGURE 6.23 Front view of widgets with shoulder, elbow, and wrist joints placed accordingly.

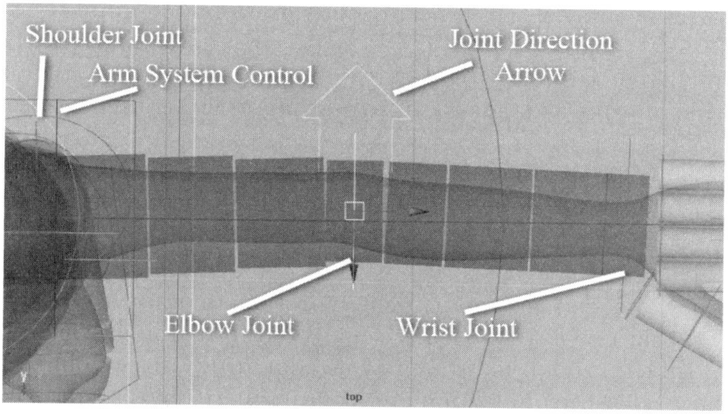

FIGURE 6.24 Top view of arm widgets with joints and elbow directional arrow.

Finally, we move on to the hands. The fingers and thumb each have their own separate System Control, as you might expect. They have a slightly different shape than the normal square System Control. They are the same shape as the Upper Body Control (see Figure 6.25). Uniformly scale each finger widget down and fit them over the mesh fingers.

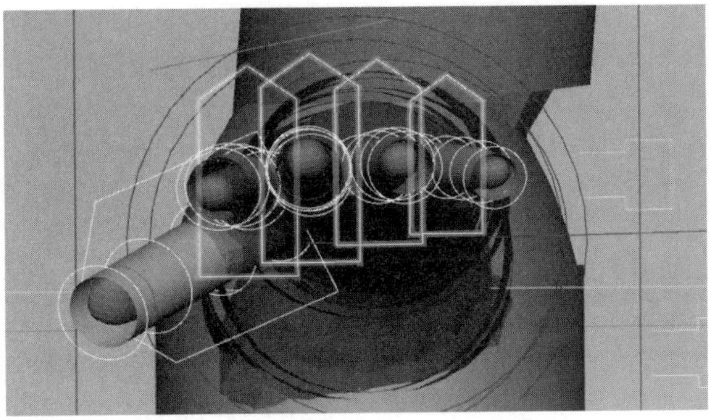

FIGURE 6.25 The four "house-shaped" System Controls of the fingers are outlined.

Place the finger widgets well into the hand and move the individual Fit Controls of the fingers into position for the knuckles, as shown in Figure 6.26.

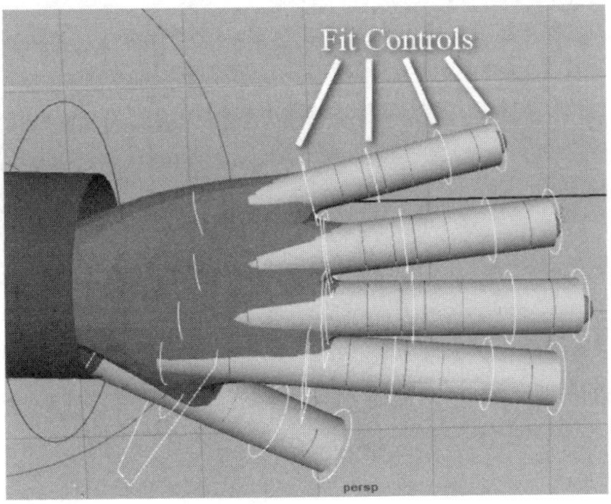

FIGURE 6.26 Top view of arm widgets with joints and elbow directional arrow.

The same operation applies to the thumb as well. Set the thumb into the hand. The only exception is to rotate the System Control of the thumb. Our thumbs are opposable and bend differently than the rest of the digits of the hand. This is so we can grasp things. Rotating the System Control gives the thumb a better rotation for grasping (see Figure 6.27).

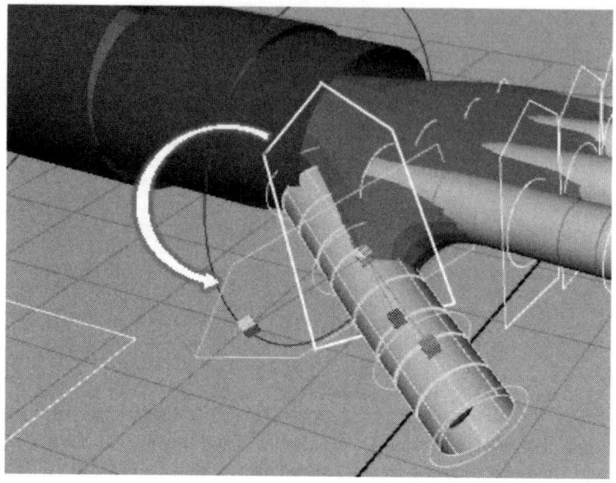

FIGURE 6.27 Thumb widgets and rotation of the thumb System Control for better grasping.

Now we are ready to let TSM2 rig the character from the placement of the widgets. We must tell TSM2 what mesh it will rig. Select the mesh from the Outliner window. Go to The Setup Machine menu in the Maya menus and select The Setup Machine > Pre-Rig > Define Character, as shown in Figure 6.28.

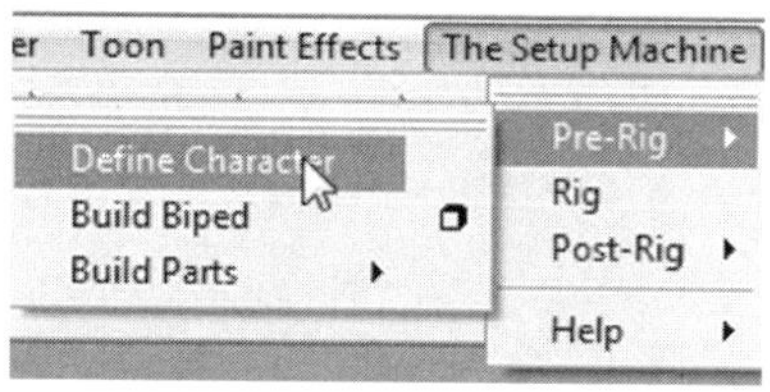

FIGURE 6.28 Defining the mesh object for TSM2.

This is immediately followed by selecting the Rig command. This can be done by going to The Setup Machine menu and selecting The Setup Machine > Rig. TSM2 will alert you to the fact that the rigging it creates is not undoable. Choosing Rig in the warning box sets the rigging process in motion. This can be seen in Figure 6.29.

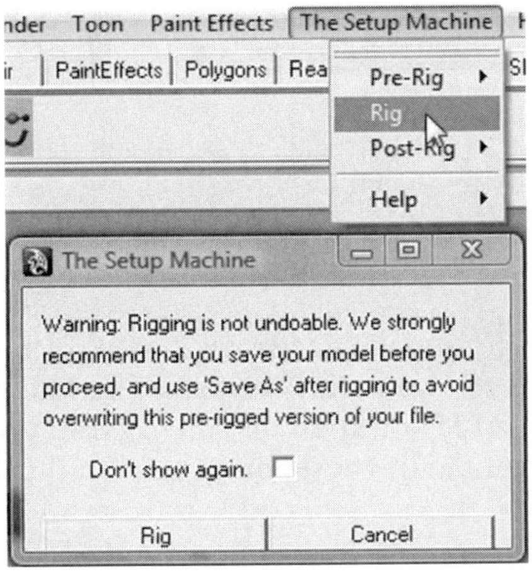

FIGURE 6.29 The Rig command warns you of its irreversibility and then rigs your character.

TSM2 takes a few seconds to calculate the rig and then returns with a fully rigged character, as shown in Figure 6.30.

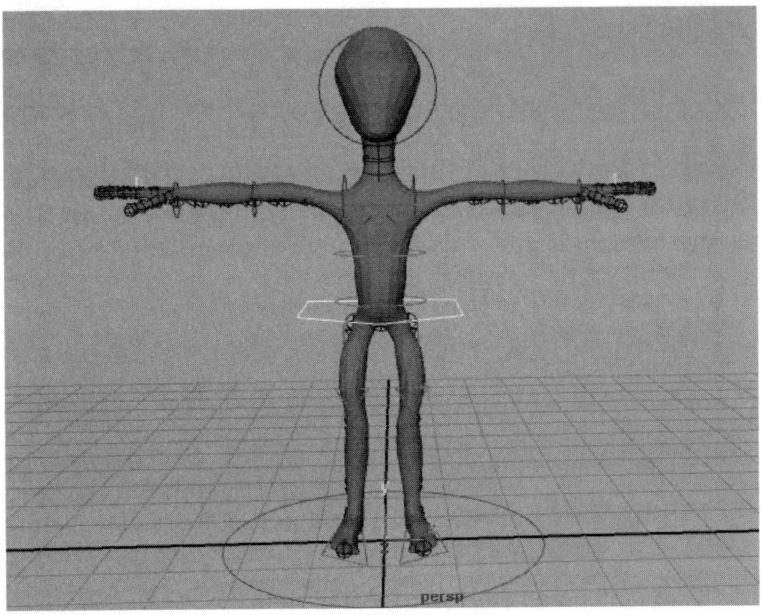

FIGURE 6.30 TSM2 returns a fully rigged and weighted character.

Test, Test, and Retest

If TSM2 doesn't take a few seconds of calculation time and returns immediately without a rig, then in all likelihood, something is wrong with the widgets. This seems to be mostly caused by accidental nonuniform scaling. This is the perfect time to go back to one of your many saved versions. At any time during the widget placement, you can calculate the rig. The widgets don't have to be fully set up for you to get a sense of the rig to any point. It is good practice to try to create a rig at every save point. Once a section of widgets has been placed into position, save the file and then test the rig. If there is an error, this is a great time to discover a problem. These interim rigs don't need to be saved, as they may be rather useless, but they will confirm that you are going in the right direction. If you are successful, it is easy to reload the saved widgets scene, change another section of widgets, save, and retest. This method can save valuable time.

ON THE DVD

Congratulations. The rig is complete. You can find the completed rig, allen2.mb, on the companion DVD-ROM in the Chapter 6 folder.

Testing Movement of the Rig

The rig, once completed, has forward kinematics as well as inverse kinematics. It is also conveniently weighted. This rig can now be used in any version of Maya and can be enhanced with additional character modeling techniques. Many users use TSM2's rigs as a jumping-off point for adding the personal touches to their animated characters. One of the really interesting things about TSM2 is its ability to auto-weight the rig. It is a simple matter of painting weights to change how your character reacts to certain movements.

Without a single enhancement, the rig is amazing. It affords the animator a lot of flexibility for proper movement and position. It is easy to tell that TSM2 was written by an animator.

If you are unfamiliar with character animation, let's take a brief look at what rigging the character has given us. Let's pose Allen the Alien.

Making Allen sit down is a simple matter of selecting his Upper Body Control, as shown in Figure 6.31, and translating by dragging it down and to the right. He should bend with ease at the hips and knees.

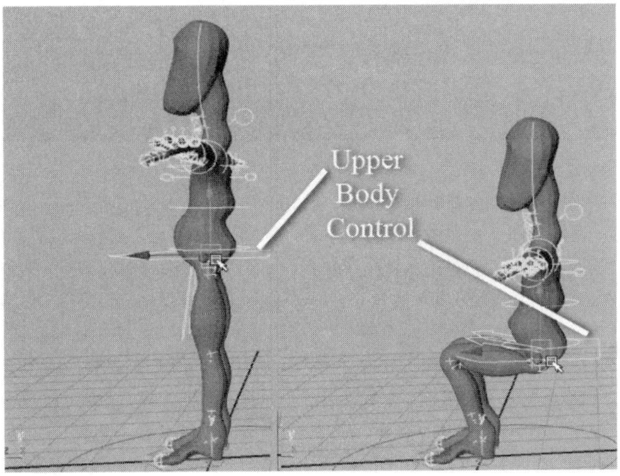

FIGURE 6.31 Selecting the Upper Body Control can easily make Allen take a seat.

Allen's arms can be moved at the shoulder, elbow, and wrist by selecting the corresponding handles, pressing the E key on the keyboard, and rotating the joints (see Figures 6.32 and 6.33).

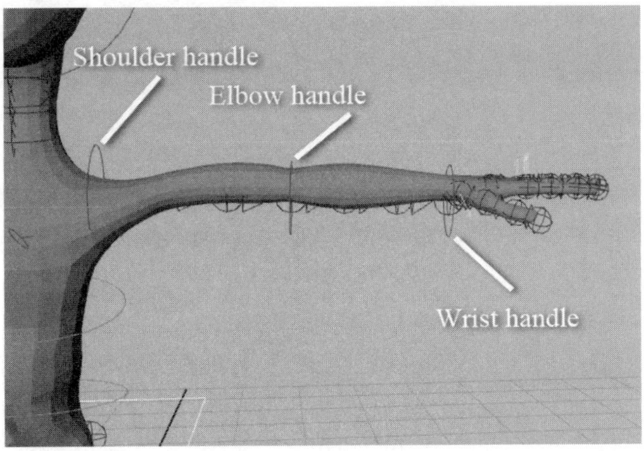

FIGURE 6.32 The shoulder, elbow, and wrist handles can be used to pose Allen's arm.

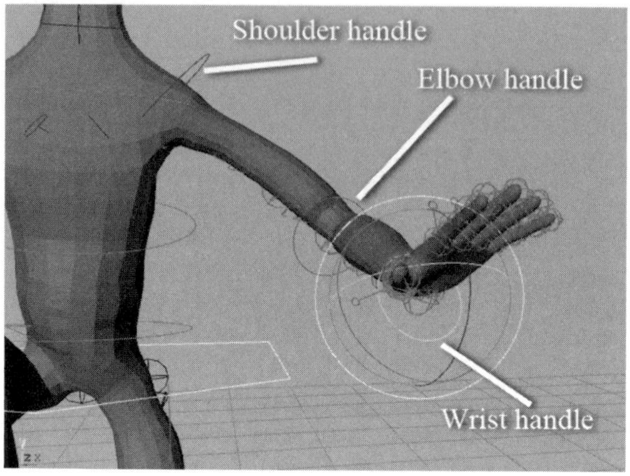

FIGURE 6.33 The arm posed by rotation of the joint handles of the shoulder, elbow, and wrist.

Selecting the nonstandard foot System Control and dragging it backward makes the model appear to lunge, as shown in Figures 6.34 and 6.35.

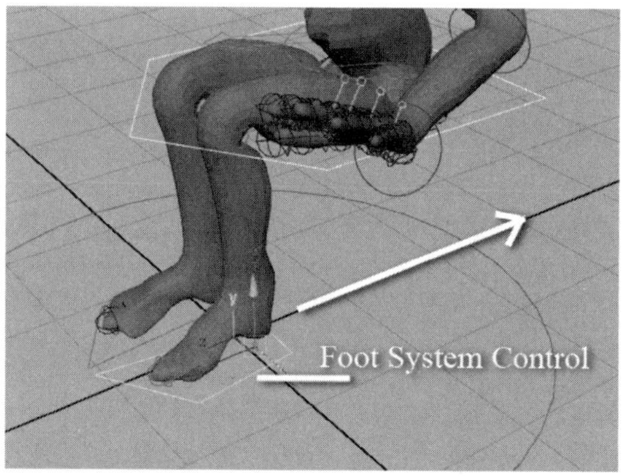

FIGURE 6.34 Selection of the foot System Control allows for full movement of the leg.

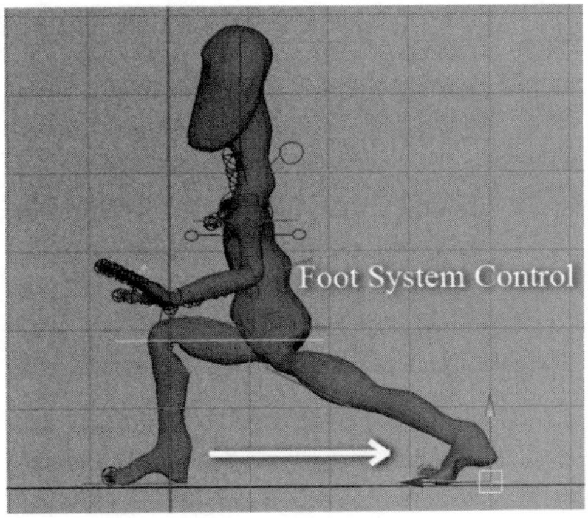

FIGURE 6.35 The side view shows how the translation of the foot can make Allen appear to lunge.

There are two useful handles on the torso of the mesh model. Select them at the same time and drag them forward. This gives a more realistic lung movement (see Figures 6.36 and 6.37).

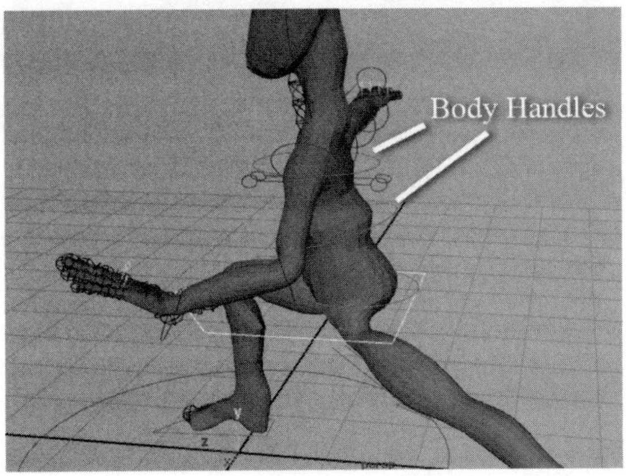

FIGURE 6.36 Selection of the two torso handles of the rig.

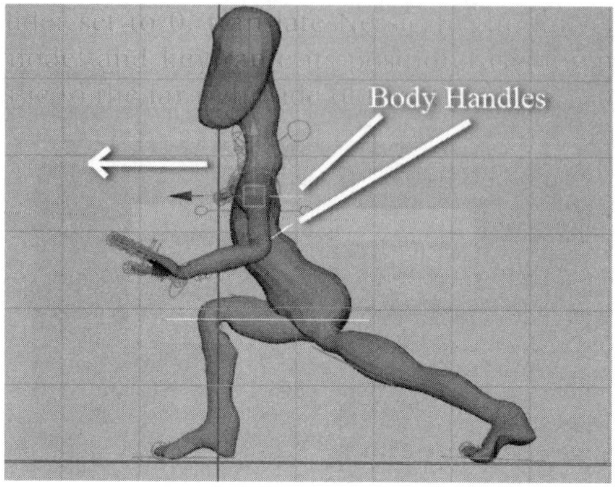

FIGURE 6.37 Moving both handles forward gives the lunge a better look.

A final touch to our pose involves the head. Select the head handle of the head and press E on the keyboard, as shown in Figure 6.38.

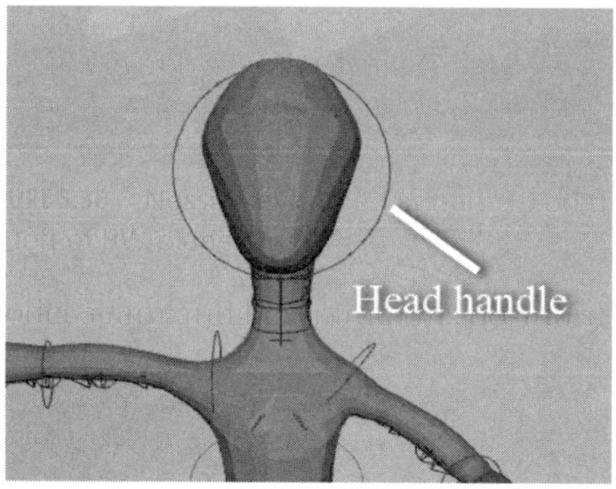

FIGURE 6.38 Selection of the head handle of the rig.

Rotating Allen's head forward makes him appear to be struggling to push something heavy (see Figure 6.39).

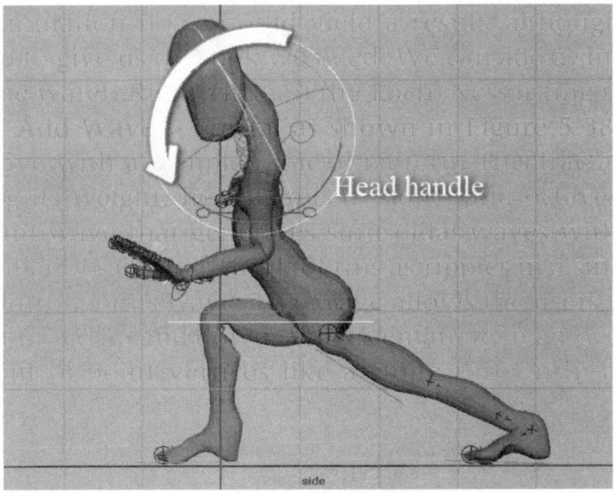

FIGURE 6.39 The rotation of the alien's head makes him seem to struggle against a heavy weight.

Congratulations! You have posed the rig. While not a course in character animation, this chapter does give the beginner a head start in the right direction. Character animation is a terrific process to experience, and having a good rig goes a long way to achieving success. Figure 6.40 is a frame from Allen the Alien's first animated sequence. This image can be seen in color in the color gallery.

FIGURE 6.40 Allen the Alien's first animated sequence.

Interview with Raf Anzovin
President and Creative Director of Anzovin Studio

I am thoroughly impressed with the ease of use of TSM2 and wanted to know more about Anzovin Studio. Raf Anzovin is the president and creative director of Anzovin Studio, and he was kind enough to answer a few questions.

How did you get your start in CG—or a little company history?
I've been animating, in one form or another, since I was 14. Since I was home-schooled, I had a lot of time on my hands to pursue my own interests, and I was able, with the help of my father, Steve Anzovin, to take them in a professional direction fairly quickly.

Anzovin Studio was declared in existence in 1999, and since then, in addition to our plugin business, we've done a lot of commercials, made-for-TV movies, and game cinematics.

What was the genesis of your software?
I used to do a lot of rigging, and I enjoyed trying to come up with better controls for the animator (who was usually also me) to use. I went down a lot of blind alleys that way, but I ended up with something that I really liked. But once the engineering had been done, actually applying it to multiple characters was a chore.

This was back in 2000, when auto-rigging wasn't as common an idea as it is now, and I was using Hash's Animation:Master at the time. A:M has a text-based file format, so I, along with John Wilson, who was one of my students at the time, figured we could write an applet that would take basic bone positions in the character and construct a rig around them. The applet had to parse the text file, make its changes, and then spit out a new one.

We wrote it in, believe it or not, Macromedia Director. Horrifically primitive as that sounds, it was actually quite well received by users. We eventually ditched the whole text-file-parsing part and wrote the next version as a real plugin. Then, to expand our market, we tried porting it to other software. The Lightwave version fizzled, but the Maya version of TSM met with some success.

It didn't really take off till we released TSM2 for Maya, though. At that point, I'd had a look at some really advanced rigging, primarily the "broken rig" created by the Disney studio for Chicken Little and showcased at SIGGRAPH 2005. Clearly, character rigging was undergoing a massive paradigm shift, changing from something with limited controls designed to rotate rigid body parts to something that was as flexible and elegant as the animator's imagination. I tried to incorporate as much of that elegance as I could into the design of TSM2, and the result is that we've met with quite a bit of success as one of the top commercial auto-rigging solutions.

What types of companies would benefit from your software?
Large animation studios have their own rigging departments, staffed with rigging experts. Smaller animation studios, freelancers, and students, though, generally don't have that luxury. Any animator who has ever had to struggle through creating his own rig simply to get to the point where he could animate can benefit from The Setup Machine.

Who uses your software?
The majority of our user base is freelance animators and students, but quite a few small studios, and even a couple of larger ones, have ordered our product.

Where can the use of your software be seen?
http://www.ceres.com

What was the most unusual, creative, or inventive use of your code?
Hmmm . . . that's a tough one. TSM2 is designed to do pretty much just one thing—rig character bodies—and hasn't got a wide range of possible applications outside of that, so we haven't really seen too much really strange stuff done with the rigs.

Where do you see CG lacking right now?
There's such a tremendous focus on detail and "realism" that the larger importance of composition, clarity, and good filmmaking are often lost. Go to any CG gallery and you'll see images stuffed to the edges with detail, but go to any painting gallery and you'll see images with very little detail that are far more beautiful and compelling. This is generally true in CG films versus traditional animation as well (with some notable exceptions, of course).

What's down the road for your company and software?
Lots of stuff! By the time your readers see this, we'll already have released The Face Machine, the facial-rigging companion to TSM2. From there, we have several other products on the drawing board, including a ground-up rewrite of Maya joints and IK we're tentatively calling Anzovin Rig Tools.

ON THE DVD

This chapter was a brief primer for TSM2 for Maya. You can see that it is very easy to rig and pose a character using TSM2. It's an inexpensive tool for jumpstarting your next character project. We have only scratched the surface of this amazing plugin. Also included on the companion DVD-ROM in the Chapter 6 folder is a wolf rig created in TSM2 by Anzovin Studio. You can refer to the DVD-ROM links for other information on Anzovin Studio. There is more to investigate in the next chapter. Let's move on to a new way to record motion capture in Chapter 7.

CHAPTER

7

A HOST OF HELPERS

In This Chapter

- Introduction
- Four Wheeling
- Camera Tricks

INTRODUCTION

In this chapter we look at a series of plugins that help the user previsualize certain animation scenarios. As the name implies, Craft Director Tools puts previsualization power in the hands of a film or media director. The ability to interactively describe actions to your team in the "previz" stage of an effect shot or animation sequence can save vast amounts of time and money. Certain areas of computer animation can be tedious and necessary, so the use of these plugins can greatly increase productivity. Craft Director Tools from Craft Animations consists of plugins for controlling prerigged craft, both procedurally and in a unique motion capture, gaming-style paradigm. The use of procedural animation to drive animation scenarios, in conjunction with the ability to interactively plot the course of a vehicle or camera, is unique. Craft Director Tools adds a whole new layer of realism and spontaneity to animation. While removing the drudgery of rigging, an animator can spend more time being creative. Cars, trucks, tanks, missiles, helicopters, jets, and camera motion can be automated and vastly improved over other methods. A group of the Craft Director Tools plugins deals with four-wheeled vehicles. If a scene calls for a dune buggy to barrel through an obstacle-laden canyon road, the simple workflow would entail the following information:

- Importing a terrain and canyon model and obstacles
- Importing a prerigged Craft Director Tools four-wheeler model, as shown in Figure 7.1
- Creating an association with the terrain and the prerigged model
- Animating the four-wheeler through the terrain via the use of an external device such as a joystick, recording the movement as motion-captured data
- Replace the prerigged proxy vehicle, terrain, and obstacle with higher resolutions of the final scene

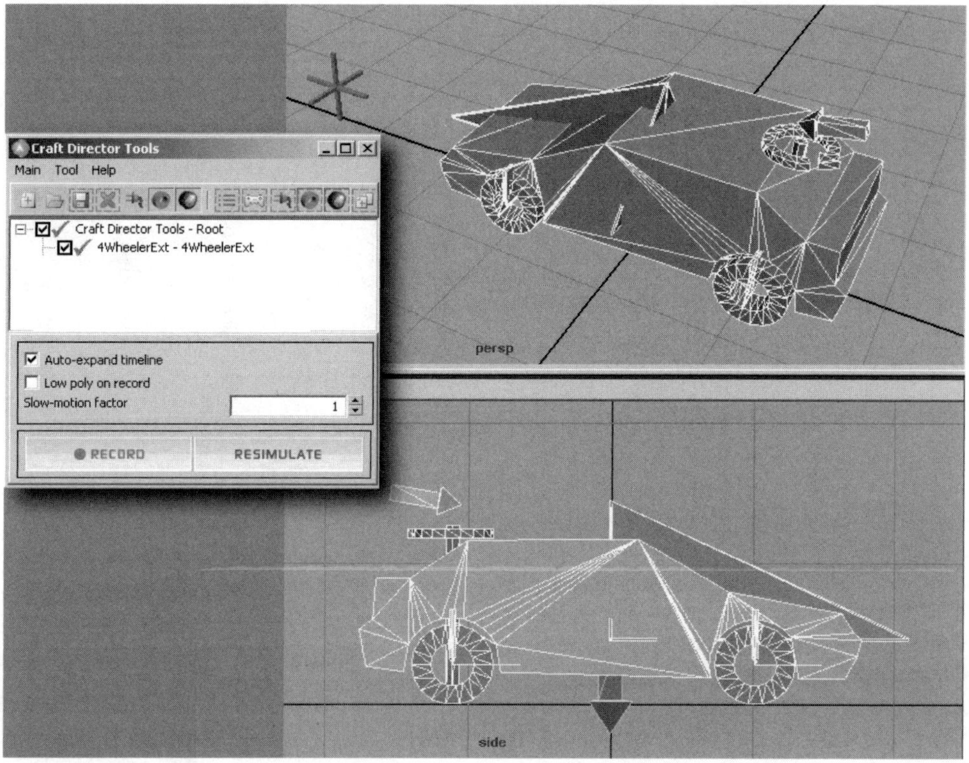

FIGURE 7.1 Craft Director Tools' prerigged four-wheel vehicle proxy model.

The vehicle's motion over the terrain is bound by various physics properties, not merely the contour surface of the terrain, but bouncing, accelerating, decelerating, and generally acting as weighty real-life vehicles do. The conditions are highly configurable. As you will see, Craft Director Tools rigs can mimic a broad range of vehicle types and conditions. This interactive simulation is tantamount to the instant replay in video games, which reenacts the last few seconds of your gameplay, prior to your demise. The ability to give the director of your film hands-on interactive control, to drive the virtual car in his scene, is truly placing the power of direction where it needs to be. It becomes a great director's tool to express what is needed in a given scene, whether as a previsualization plan for live action or CG integration. Other vehicles such as two-wheeled vehicles, towing trailers, and a provision for extra wheels round out the wheeled Craft Director Tools plugins Craft Director Tools category. Figure 7.2 and Figure 7.3 show the two-wheel vehicles and trailer rigs, respectively.

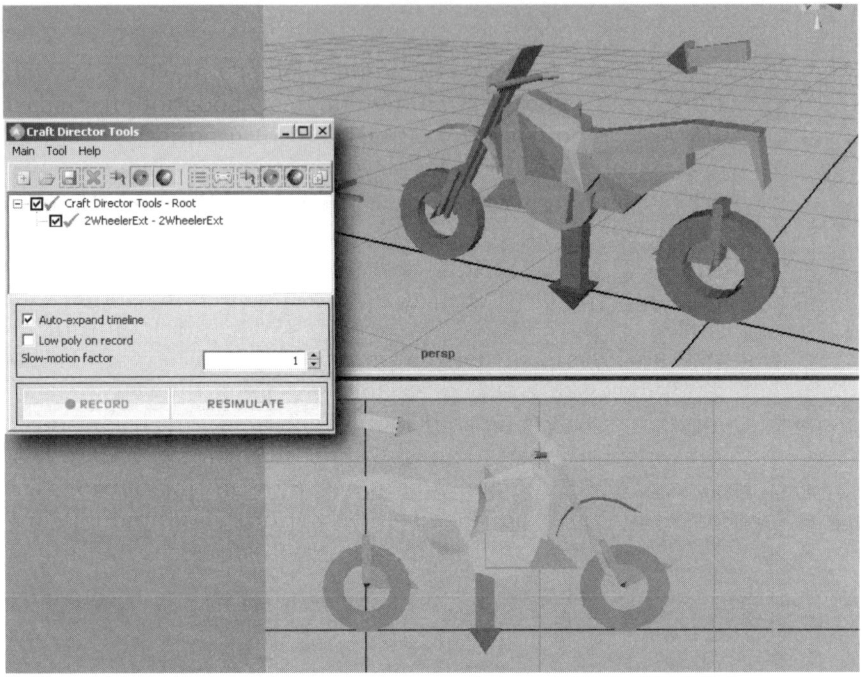

FIGURE 7.2 Craft Director Tools' prerigged two-wheel vehicle proxy model.

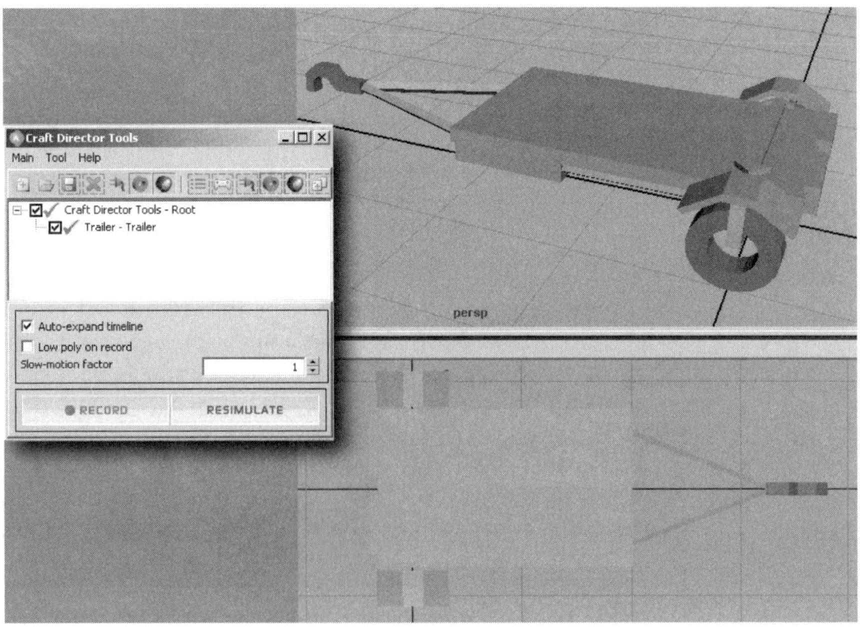

FIGURE 7.3 Craft Director Tools' specialized tow trailer rig.

COLOR GALLERY

Two metal rings bounce and spin after being dropped, as caustic reflections dance from their surfaces. This was rendered in mental ray.
Image © 2007 Mark Jennings Smith

This image is a frame from the final animation of "Allen the Alien" from Chapter 6. Allen was built in Maya and rigged using Anzovin Studio's The Setup Machine 2.
Image © 2007 Mark Jennings Smith

A scene from the animated feature *Ratatouille* rendered in RenderMan. *© 2007 Disney/Pixar*

Next Limit's Maxwell Render creates fantastic photo-realistic renderings by the correct simulation of light. This image is called "Selfillumination." *Image courtesy of André Kutscherauer (www.ak3d.de)*

This bust of a chimp was created with ZBrush by Ty Shelton. *Image courtesy of www.tyshelton.com*

Smirnoff Ice "Icicle" commercial. In an ice-covered cave, hundreds of Smirnoff Ice bottles are frozen to the ceiling as stalactites. Suddenly, one breaks off, crashing into the ground, creating an instant party. Animal Logic created an entire CG environment for the ad, with only a few small live action elements incorporated in the first few shots. The team created the cave, the CG icicles and bottles, as well as the shattering effect when one bottle falls and breaks through the ice. *Image courtesy of Animal Logic*

This scene originally created using RealFlow in Maya and rendered in mental ray for Maya was successfully transferred to 3ds Max v9 using PolyTrans. The file was rendered in Max's mental ray renderer after some minor tweaking. It is virtually identical to its counterpart rendering in Maya's mental ray. *Image © 2007 Mark Jennings Smith*

The different examples of stitching on this leather ball add an extra level of detail using Seamour.
Image courtesy of Matthias F. Richter (ticket01.com)

The baseball crashing through the pane of glass was created using Blast Code's Megaton.
Image Courtesy of Blast Code Software (www.blastcode.com)

A scene from Mark Smith's animation project *Monolith* rendered in 3Delight in the Maya interface. The scene is rendered using HDRI-based lighting.
Image © 2007 Mark Jennings Smith

This image was modeled using ticket01's Wire and rendered using fryrender. Notice this extruded cheese food render uses subsurface scattering with very realistic results.
Image © 2007 Mark Jennings Smith

The rainbow-colored shag rug from Chapter 3 uses Shave and a Haircut to create the rug's fibers.
Image © 2007 Mark Jennings Smith

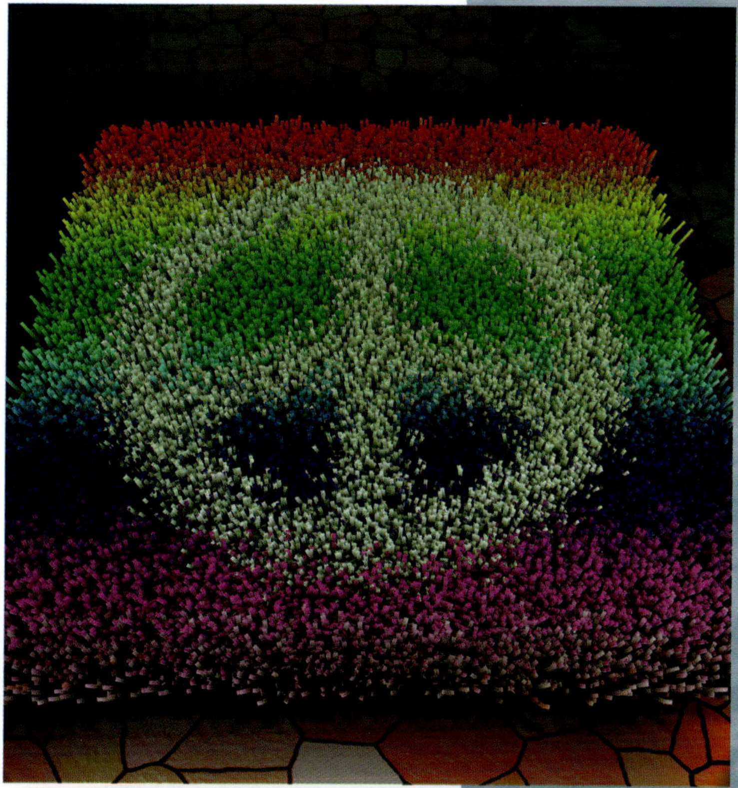

A Syflex-generated sun dress moves dynamically and keeps Sylene covered.
Image courtesy of Syflex LLC

This render in mental ray shows light passing through one of the marbles and falling on the ground plane, an effect not likely achievable in the Maya software renderer. Notice that the surface colors of the marbles add to the lighting energy in the scene.
Image © 2007 Mark Jennings Smith

Ice vehicle from a Toyota Prado commercial. The graceful, gliding, four-wheel-drive vehicle made of ice was needed for Toyota Prado's latest television commercial, "Ice Sculptures," directed by Bruce Hunt through @radical.media. Animal Logic created the 3D computer-generated ice car and carefully choreographed its movement as it glides across various road surfaces, verging on being out of control.
Image courtesy of Animal Logic

The still image "Blue Barb" was modeled and lit in Maya and sent to Maxwell Render for re-rendering, lighting, and further tweaking. The final image was adjusted slightly in Photoshop to add barbed wire and convert it to a black-and-white image.
Image © 2007 Mark Jennings Smith

This image shows a frame from one of the exercises from Chapter 5. RealFlow was used to create the hot oil splashing against the warning sign.
Image © 2007 Mark Jennings Smith

This image is a scene from Mark Smith's animation project *Monolith*. The Monolith was modeled in Maya and disassembled using Blast Code's Megaton. It was rendered in 3Delight within the Maya interface.
Image © 2007 Mark Jennings Smith

The final render of the Maya-originated dice scene in Vue 6 xStream's renderer. The global illumination and caustic reflections of the dice and water make for a realistic image.
Image © 2007 Mark Jennings Smith

This abstract form modeled in Maya and exported via PolyTrans as a .obj, is shaded, lit, and rendered in Vue 6 with global illumination.
Image © 2007 Mark Jennings Smith

This image entitled "Steel Knot" is a terrific example of a model created with Wire.
Image courtesy of Matthias F. Richter (ticket01.com)

Global illumination was used to take advantage of HDRI image-based lighting. The water surface is generated as a result of displacement mapping, while the particle splashes were extra geometry created in RealFlow. This image was rendered using 3Delight within Maya.
Image © 2007 Mark Jennings Smith

Craft Animation also has tools for aircraft. It is possible to control airplanes, helicopters, jet aircraft, and even missiles. Figures 7.4 and 7.5 show the default rigs of airplanes and helicopters, respectively. To get the most out of these plugins, it's best to have a good input device to control these rigs. These rigs have a wide range of interactively controllable parameters, so very accurate simulations can be created.

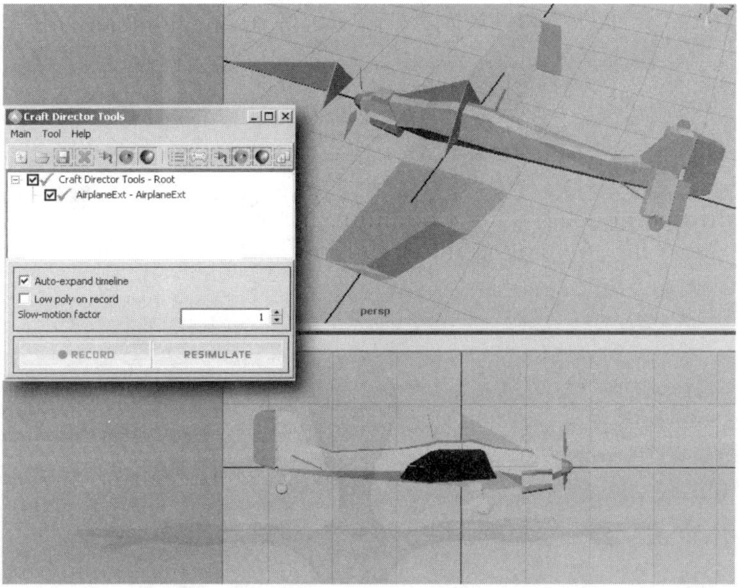

FIGURE 7.4 Craft Director Tools' airplane rig.

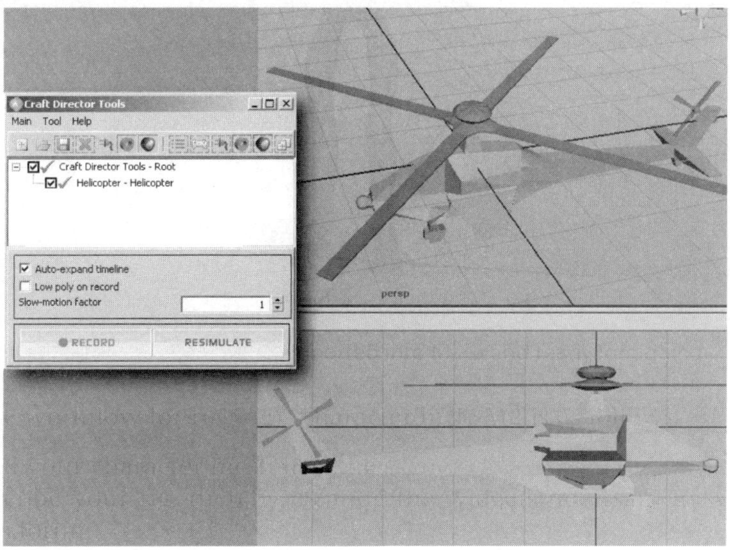

FIGURE 7.5 Craft Director Tools' default helicopter rig.

Any flight sim fanatic has a decent input device for controlling virtual flights. Those same input controllers allow the most thorough use of the controls of these rigs. Rudder, aileron, and elevator controls ensure accuracy. There are also autonomous controls that can be used to keep the flight in check. Figure 7.6 shows a short list of interactive controls that are possible for an airplane rig.

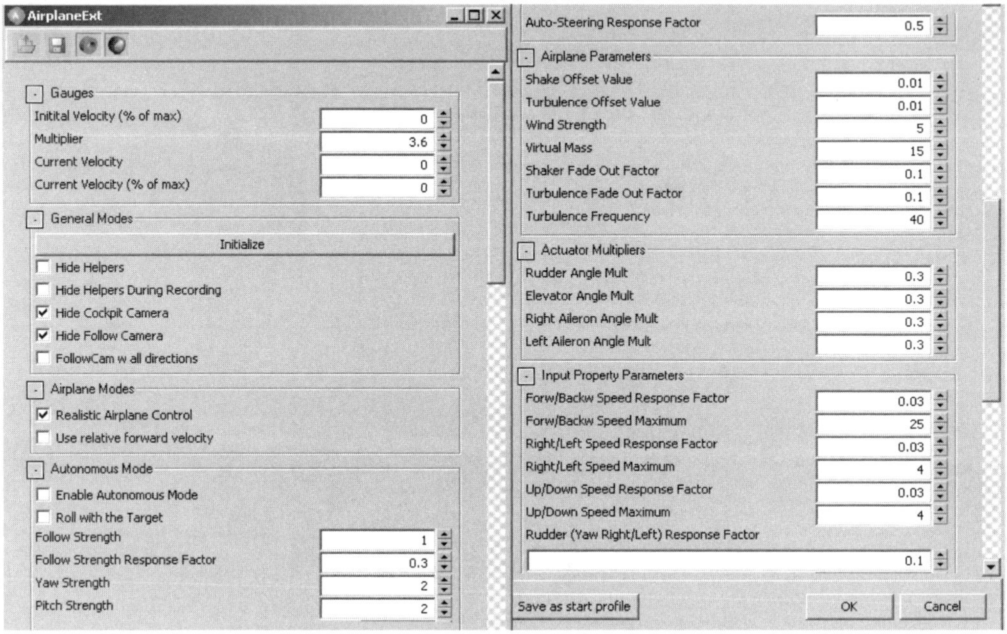

FIGURE 7.6 Some of the interactive controllable parameters of the airplane rig.

TAKING CONTROL

The input control devices for use with Craft Director Tools are wide open. Keyboard, mouse, gamepads, and joysticks can be used. In fact, any DirectX device can be used. The device you use is partially dependent on the sophistication of the animation you are hoping to achieve. A gamepad such as the Thrustmaster Dual Analog 3, as seen in Figure 7.7, may be all that is required. A full-blown flight sim control system can be used to mimic actual controls of a plane. There are devices that look just like the yoke, rudder pedals, and throttle controls of an airplane. For automobiles and the like, there are devices that mimic the controls of an auto, such as steering wheels, brakes, and acceleration pedals. These types of devices are readily available and most often used by hard-core gamers who are interested in an authentic experience. Any combination of devices can be used, and it is very easy to assign the rig controls to your choice of device. You can get a better idea of what these devices look like and are used for by investigating the links below.

http://www.saitek.com/uk/prod/pcgc.htm
http://www.thrustmaster.com/product-selection.aspx
http://www.chproducts.com/retail/index.html

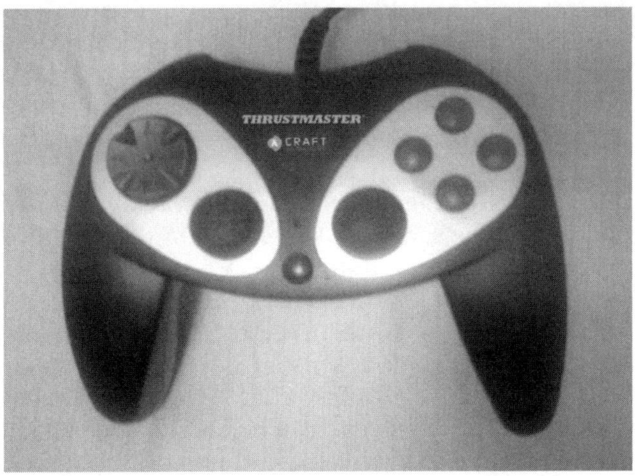

FIGURE 7.7 The Thrustmaster Dual Analog 3 Gamepad was one of the input devices used for this chapter.

With these tools, the demise of King Kong from the buzzing biplanes, a death-defying air race, or perhaps even the famous Beggar's Canyon race in *Star Wars Episode 1: The Phantom Menace* could have utilized the aircraft rigs in Craft Director Tools.

A unique Craft Director Tools plugin deals specifically with missiles, rockets, and projectiles. Craft Missile helps simulate the specific physics of these types of objects. This tool gives the user tighter control over the movement of these projectiles.

Another set of Craft Director Tools plugins involves cameras. These camera plugins can add a new sense of reality to an animation in subtle yet distinctive ways. There is no denying the engaging feel of a handheld camera shot or the claustrophobic feel of the head-mounted helmet-cam. Good use of dramatic camera shots can breathe untold life into a scene. There are eight camera helpers in the Craft Director Tools plugin set, and all can be used to achieve interesting cinematic results.

- Craft AutoFocusCam allows the user to create real-time focusing effects intelligently and automatically. The camera's focus can be switched slowly or snapped quickly between two points. This can be done between mobile or static points and can have dramatic results. This plugin creates real-time control of focus and zoom with the use of an input device such as a joystick.
- Craft AutoZoomCam is a passive or automatic camera that zooms the camera in direct relation to the distance of the camera and the designated target object. The camera automatically adjusts to keep the target in exact proportion within the frame at all times. The AutoZoomCam can be bound to other cameras for interesting effects. Think Alfred Hitchcock here.
- Craft SphereCam follows the target object, always keeping it at the center of its spherical motion track. In other words, the camera moves along the surface of a sphere with the target object at its center. This could be used as an impossibly mobile form of a human head-mounted camera or used as a unique sweeping camera shot of an aircraft, viewing the action from any angle. Camera movement, zoom, and spherical distance can all be adjusted in real time via an input device such as a gamepad or joystick.
- Craft HumanizerCam creates a handheld camera look. Oddly enough, this is one of Craft's passive cameras. There is no interactive input on this camera. The HumanizerCam adds the nuances of a handheld shot to a camera, which is otherwise difficult to animate by hand. It is amazing how this small detail can add great power to a shot and increase the realism and urgency in a scene.
- Craft ObserverCam is a real-time control camera that combines several technologies to produce a well-rounded multipurpose observation camera. It can be moved in all directions and can be bound to moving objects. It does not recreate realistic movement, but camera shake can be added to it. A nice feature is its ability to switch between multiple cameras in a shot. The all-purpose nature of the ObserverCam could lend itself to creative repurposing of the camera, configuring otherwise difficult setups and defining real-world camera rigs.
- Craft DigitizerCam is a dedicated camera specifically designed for use with a MicroScribe digitizer arm from Immersion (http://www.immersion.com/digitizer/). This camera is controlled by precise and accurate interactive movements of the digitizer arm within the viewport. It can be linked to other objects and can be combined with other Craft cameras.

- Craft ZeroGCam simulates the weightless movement of zero gravity. At first glance, it seems like it would have very narrow usage, but it provides some very fluid and interesting shots. The camera wafts in zero gravity but has controls for slowing, stopping, and reversing its motions and direction. Think of this as reverse thrusters. Imagine playing *Asteroids*, with the ship as the camera, and you may begin to see, or perhaps *feel*, how it can be used. This is a highly interactive camera, with a 3D mouse being the most appropriate control device. Once mastered, the Craft ZeroGCam can be a really nifty tool for that unique flowing shot.
- Craft SoftMotionCam takes the hard edge off some camera movement. Under certain conditions that cameras may face, such as chaotic stability and shaky, abnormal movements, the SoftMotionCam can smooth out the rough spots. This can be thought of as a sort of digital steady cam, creating more fluid, smooth, and natural camera motion. This passive camera can be added after the fact or used during real-time recording. It is invaluable in stabilizing an otherwise bumpy camera shot.

CAN'T WE ALL JUST GET ALONG?

The power of the Craft Director Tools begins to shine when the plugins are combined within a scene. The use of the AutoFocusCam, for instance, in conjunction with two high-speed Craft Director Tools-controlled jeeps, jockeying for position in a race across the sandy dunes, can have remarkable impact on the scene. The selection of parameters for the various tools allows the physics to be adjusted to suit the animation. A lumbering weighty vehicle, an agile dirt bike, or the smooth, slow bouncing of a moon rover are all possible. These facets, combined with the interesting use of Craft Director Tools-controlled cameras, can bring a scene to new heights of impact and realism. Layered effects combined with real-time interactivity can yield awesome and unexpected results.

Some other useful plugins are available in the Craft Director Tools toolbox. The Craft DirectInputLink is a direct link to an input device, such as a gamepad or joystick, and the objects within your scene. The movement of a character's eyes or the movement of a pinball through a maze can be directly controlled by the user and recorded in real time. This has infinite possibilities and is very easy to set up.

One other plugin worth mentioning is the Craft Gyro. This tool is designed to maintain certain aspects of an object's position and rotation. It can be used to set up a stable platform for a camera or to keep an object from straying too far from a specific translational or rotational plane.

These tools all have a great deal of value, but their use can be hard to appreciate without some proper examples. Let's take a look at some practical uses of the Craft Director Tools arsenal.

FOUR WHEELING

ON THE DVD

Let's start by using the Craft Director Tools to control a four-wheel vehicle on a bumpy terrain. Load the vroom_1.mb scene on the companion DVD-ROM in the Chapter 7 folder. Your scene should look something like Figure 7.8.

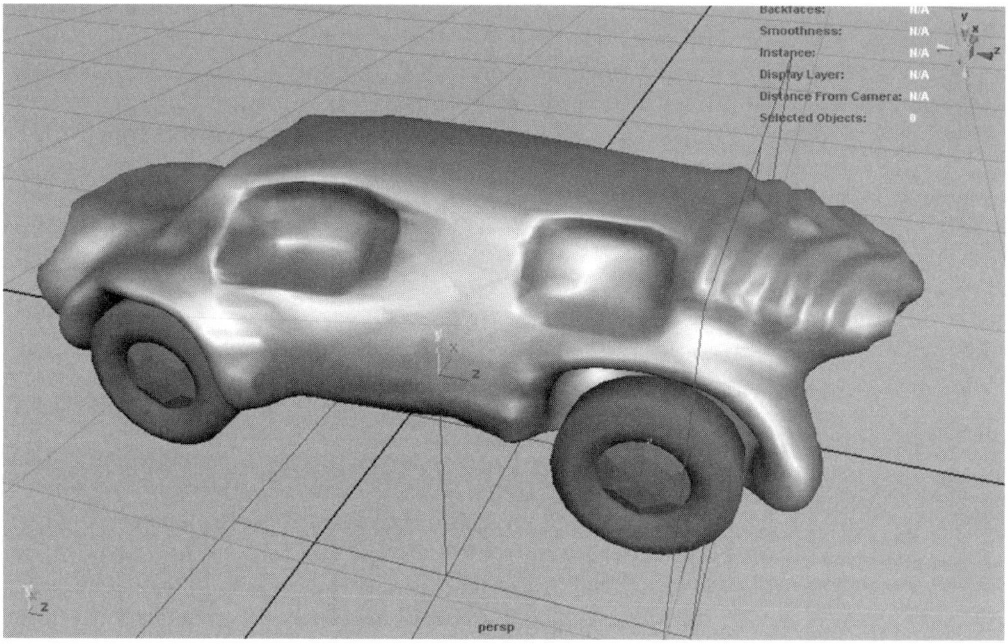

FIGURE 7.8 A simple clown-like car and a bumpy terrain serve as a starting point.

All of the Craft Director Tools come as separate plugins or bundles, depending on the Craft Director Tools category of action you are hoping to achieve from the package. The downloadable demo has all of the current plugins plus some useful freebies. Each plugin or bundle has an individual key allowing its use. Installing Craft Director Tools is as easy as executing the installer program. After installation, make sure the plugin is loaded and recognized by Maya. This can be done by going to the top of the screen in the Maya menus and selecting Window > Setting/Preferences > Plug-in Manager. Make sure that both the Loaded and Auto load boxes are selected next to the Craft Maya Adapter.mll. Figure 7.9 shows the selection of the plugin manager and the listing of the Craft Director Tools plugin.

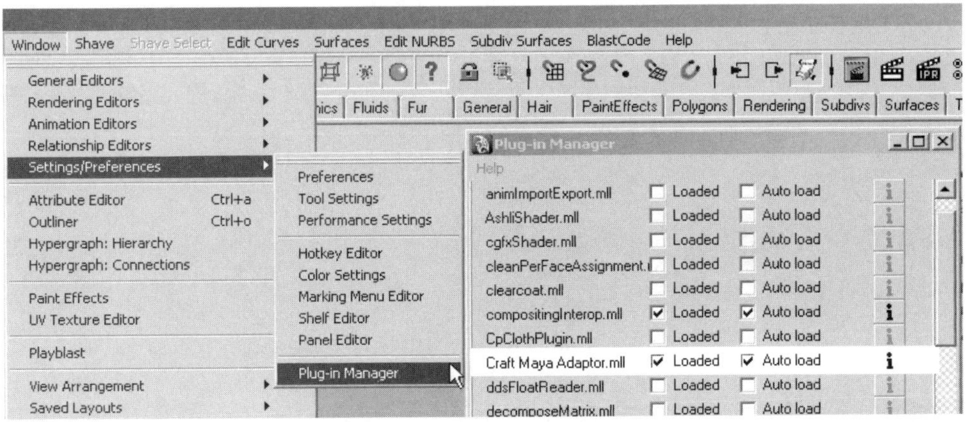

FIGURE 7.9 Checking the Plug-in Manager to verify that Craft Director Tools is loaded for use.

Craft Director Tools can now be accessed within its own Maya Tool Shelf tab. Each plugin asks for a license key the first time it is loaded. Click on the orange Craft Director Tools icon in the tool shelf. This brings up a Craft Director Tools window from which most of the interaction between user and plugin occurs. Select Main > New from the Craft Director Tools Window. This will bring up a Create window that lists all the tools available to you. You want to select 4WheelerExt from the list of tools. Figure 7.10 shows the selection of the 4-Wheeler tool from the Create window. The Craft Director Tools 4-Wheeler chassis now appears in the scene at the origin and should

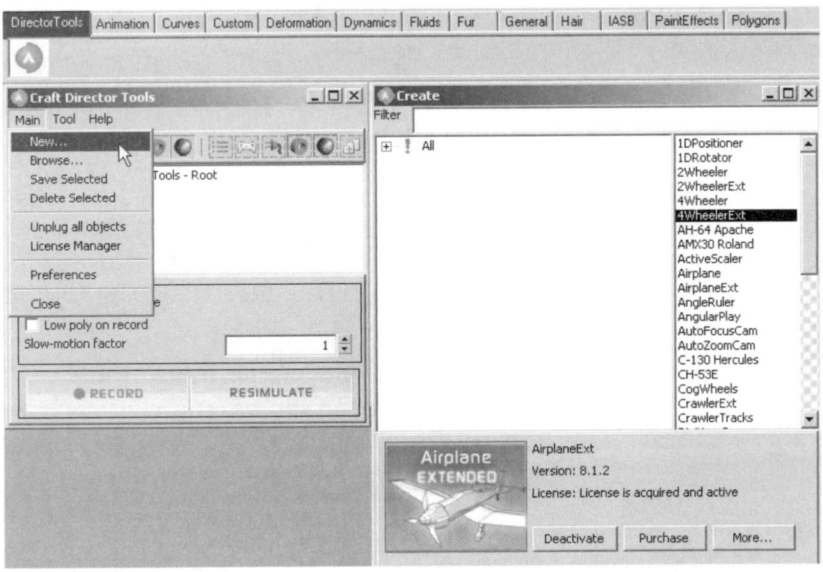

FIGURE 7.10 The selection of the 4-Wheeler Extended plugin from the Create window.

look very much like Figure 7.11. This physics-based rig is the driving force behind the control of our clown car. We must associate the Craft Director Tools rig with our clown car by first scaling the rig and then parenting them together. Take the following steps to rig the clown car for motion.

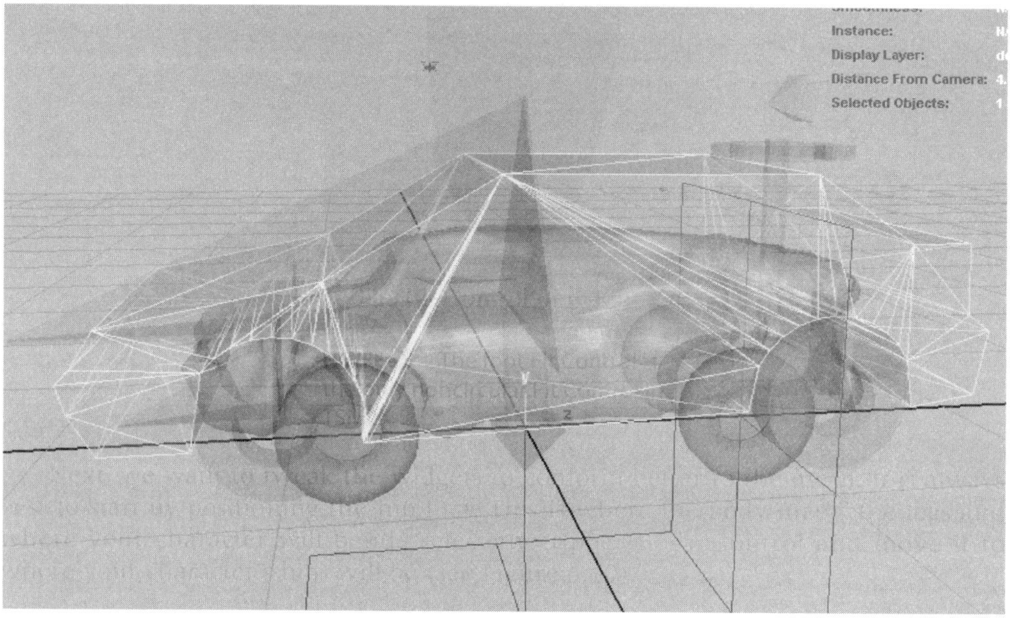

FIGURE 7.11 With X-ray shading mode turned on in the viewports, the newly loaded Craft Director Tools chassis can be seen within the clown car.

1. Move the Craft 4-Wheeler Extended's chassis so that it is placed in the same position and has the same size as the clown car.
2. Scale the Craft 4-Wheeler Extended's chassis so that it fits the scale of the clown car. Reposition the Craft Director Tools rig's wheels to that of their counterparts on the clown car. Use the Align tool to center the Craft Director Tools wheels, labeled CCarExtended_01_WheelMesh_00 to 03. The Align tool is in the Maya menus under Modify > Align Tool. Make certain that the wheels are centered in all axes.

At this point, both chassis should match each other, with both car bodies scaled to fit and the wheels sharing the same centered space. The rigs should look like Figure 7.12.

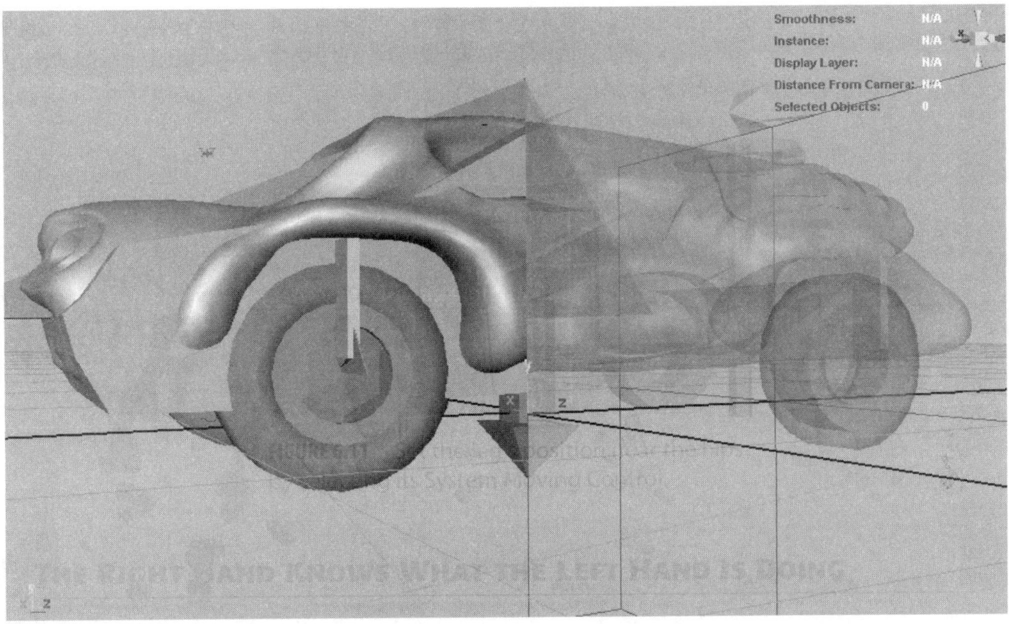

FIGURE 7.12 X-ray shading mode in the viewports allows you to gain a clearer picture of the perfectly aligned car chassis within the clown car.

3. We can now scale the wheels of the Craft Director Tools rig to the clown car wheels. Select the wheels labeled CCarExtended_01_WheelMesh_00 to 03 and scale them to their corresponding clown tires.
4. We want to associate the various car parts so that the rig can control the clown car properly. Parent the clown car chassis to the Craft Director Tools rig chassis.
5. Parent each clown car wheel to its related Craft Director Tools rig tire (CCarExtended_01_WheelMesh_00 to 03).

One Size Fits All

The 4-Wheeler rig is very adaptable to the size and proportions of the four-wheeled model you will be controlling. Bear in mind that the rig uses sophisticated physics to simulate the weight and inertia of real-world vehicles. For this obvious reason, the wheels of your model should be separate entities from the vehicle body. The rig will then be able to transfer the proper motion to your model for incredibly realistic animation.

ON THE DVD

At this point, the only thing left to do is link our rig to a terrain or pathway. The scene has a terrain mesh that has been made invisible. If you are confident in your rigging, make the terrain visible and follow along. If you have gotten lost, save your work and load the vroom_2.mb scene on the companion DVD in the Chapter 7 folder. This scene contains the work up to this point. Find the terrain mesh and make it visible.

At the bottom of the Craft Director Tools rig is a 3D mesh arrow. This is the GravityDirectionMesh. Select this object and parent it to your newly revealed terrain mesh. The terrain mesh now becomes the parent of the GravityDirectionMesh. This will keep the car hugging the road and following its contours. Figure 7.13 shows the GravityDirectionMesh selected in the view and highlighted in wireframe.

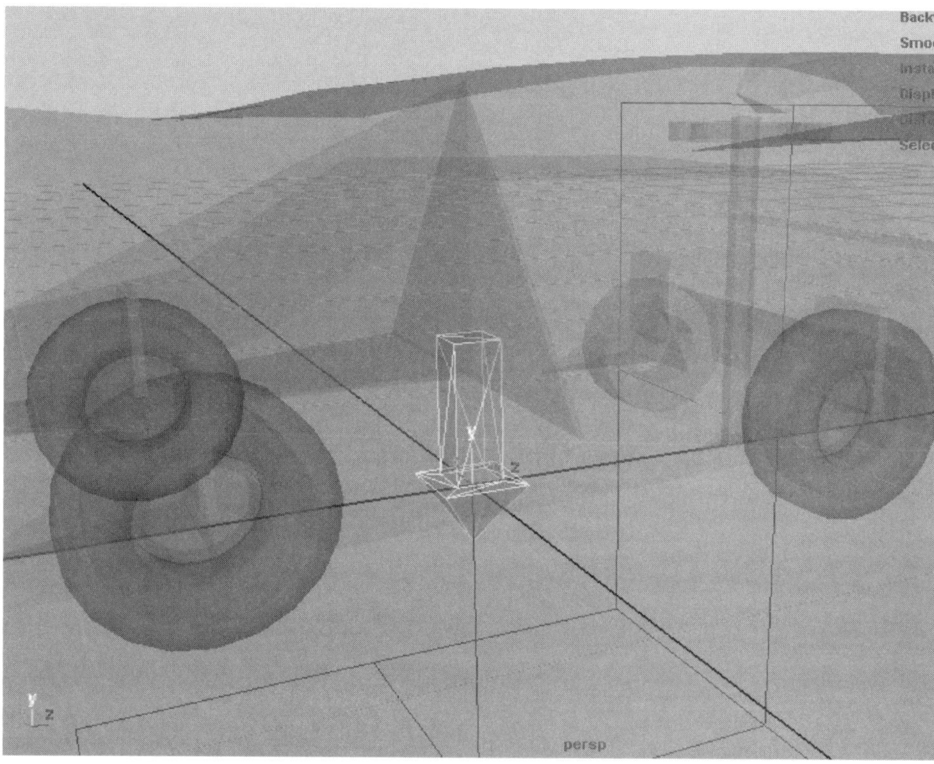

FIGURE 7.13 X-ray shading mode within the viewports allows us to see the rig and its wireframe representation of the GravityDirectionMesh node inside the clown car model.

IN CASE YOU DIDN'T PAY ATTENTION IN PHYSICS CLASS

It's hard to see the full impact Craft Director Tools can have until you start to actually use them. There are two standout areas that are the obvious and unique features of Craft Director Tools. The main focus is to provide physics-based timing and reactions for your models while injecting the paradigm of real-time interaction with your models.

The 4-Wheeler Extended plugin provides the vehicle rig with physics, which makes a driving automobile very real. The presets allow your model to take on the sluggishness of a weighty humvee or the light and bouncy parameters of a moon buggy. The key lies in the suspension, which has all the parameters available to create the kind of vehicle you need to simulate. The car's reactive suspension control provides acceleration, deceleration, skidding, sliding, and braking. The weight of your vehicle flows over the suspension with accurate motion. The lift and landing, as your sand buggy takes to the air, is physically convincing.

The interactive real-time component allows a wide assortment of control devices. The flight sim fanatic uses the finest control for his experience, by adapting an analog device for control of yoke, throttle, and rudder pedals. The virtual road racer can control his experience via an analog steering wheel, gear shift, and braking and acceleration pedals. The configuration menu allows for accurate control and adjustment of many parameters. Mice, keyboards, joysticks, and gamepads can be configured easily and simply. While this may seem complicated, it isn't.

Now we will configure the rig for an input device and provide parameters for its suspension to get it to react properly to its surroundings and vehicle type. If the Craft Director Tools window is not open, open it by clicking on the orange Craft Director Tools icon in its own tool shelf labeled Director Tools. The window should appear as shown in Figure 7.14.

FIGURE 7.14 The Craft Director Tools' main interface window.

Highlight the newly listed 4WheelerExt rig that now appears in the Craft Director Tools window. At the top of the Craft Director Tools window, select the Tool > Configure to bring up a new window that has a wide array of parameters for configuring the suspension of the clown car. This can be seen in Figure 7.15.

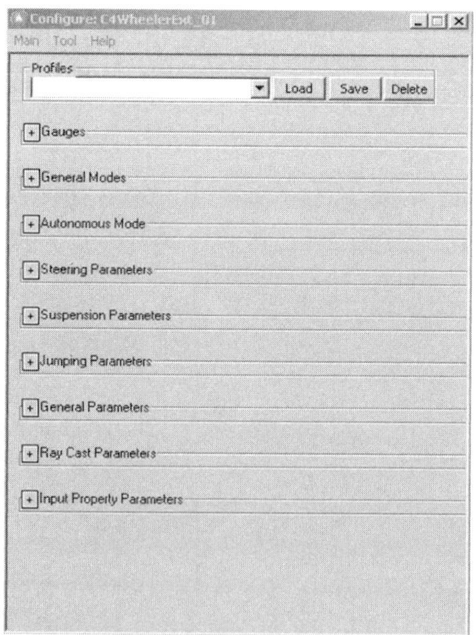

FIGURE 7.15 The Craft Director Tools' Configure window.

KEEP ON TRUCKIN'

You may wonder if there are any provisions for other types of wheeled vehicles, such as a larger truck, 18-wheeler, or truck with tow. The aforementioned Craft Trailer plugin and another plugin called the Craft ExtraWheel plugin are the building blocks for creating larger vehicles and other vehicle scenarios. The plugins work quite nicely together, so the proper combination of these plugins can be used to produce any necessary simulation rig.

Click the open folder icon at the top of the Configurations window. This will launch a new window containing preset suspension types that can be applied to your rig. The presets range from the light-gravity jumping moon buggy to a heavy, overburdened humvee. Let's select the heavy car preset for this test. Click the OK button, and the parameters of the heavy car will be applied to the clown car. The next step is to assign an external control system to the car. At the top of the Craft Director Tools window is the Tool menu. Selecting Tool > Input Settings from the menu brings up the Input Settings window. Click the open folder icon at the top left of the Input Settings window. This brings up the Profile window, which is a list of possible input types. Select example:keyboard and click OK, as shown in Figure 7.16.

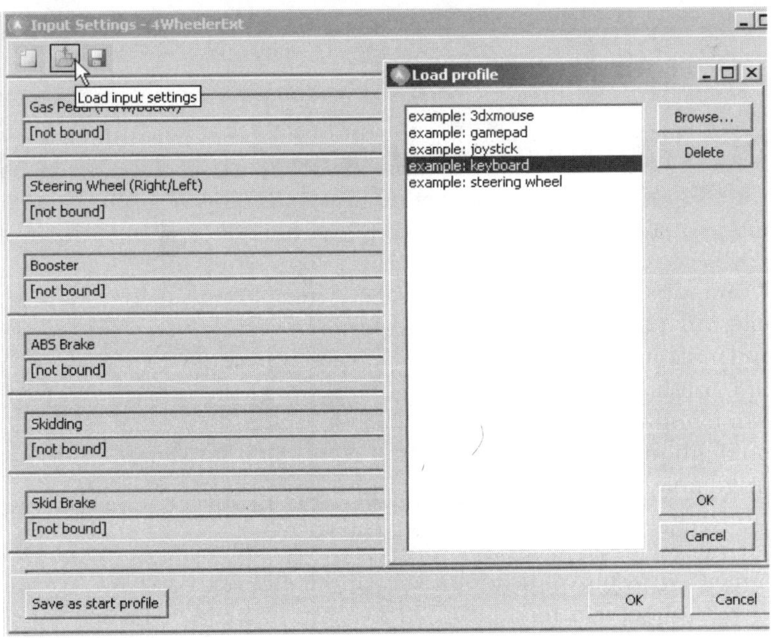

FIGURE 7.16 Select the keyboard as the input control device from the Profile window.

Anyone who has played computer games has had the opportunity to use a keyboard as the input device. Since everyone has a keyboard, let's stick with the basics. Figure 7.17 shows a closer view of the keyboard Input parameters and the keys to which they are bound. Select Load and close the window.

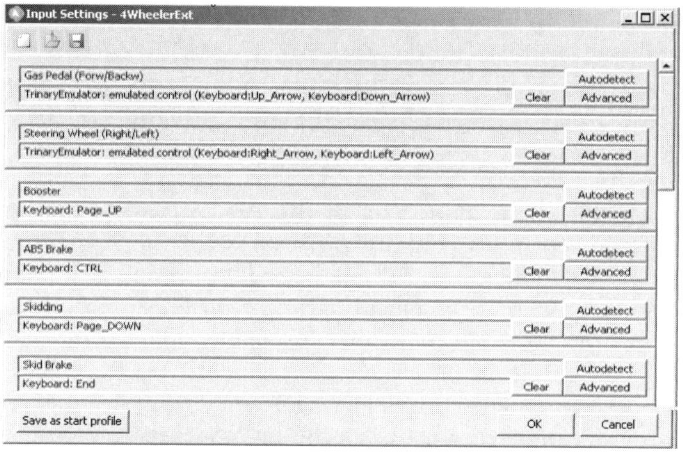

FIGURE 7.17 Several control functions of the Heavy Car are bound to keyboard keys for driving.

More Memory for Mocap

The purpose of the Craft Director Tools plugins is to derive real-time input or "desktop mocap" data of a final model by use of the physics-bound Craft Director Tools chassis rig. It is a good idea habitually to optimize your scene. The best way to do this is temporarily hide, or making invisible, the high-polygon-count objects not vital to the recording. This frees some memory and makes for a smoother recording. There is also a free plugin called *Craft Bounding Poly* that reduces high-polygon-count objects and scenes and recreates the original objects upon rendering out the recorded animation.

A quick view of the input settings and their functions makes for a better simulation.

- **Gas Pedal (Forw/Backw):** Accelerates the vehicle forward or backward using the up and down keyboard arrows
- **Steering Wheel (Right/Left):** Steers the vehicle right or left using the right and left keyboard arrows
- **Booster:** Thrusts the vehicle forward with an additional burst of velocity (good for jumps)
- **ABS Brake:** Works to bring the vehicle to a halt without dangerous sideways sliding or uncontrolled movement

- **Skidding:** Controls rear wheel skidding (think *Tokyo Drift* or *Atari Ice Race*)
- **Skid Brake:** Locks up the wheels until the vehicle comes to a rest
- **Gravel Shake Amplitude:** Simulates traveling on a gravel surface changing its amplitude in real time
- **Burnout:** Spins the rear wheels like the burnout start of a dragster
- **External Force:** Creates an external force on the Craft Car Extended/4-wheeler node that points in the same direction as the CCarExtended_01_ExternalForceMesh node; could be used for the simulation of changing gears or cargo shifting

The Craft Director Tools 4-Wheeler Ext rig comes with three cameras. It becomes helpful, if not necessary, to use them, as it may become impossible to keep up with fined-tuned and accurate driving.

- **TopCam:** This camera follows the vehicle from above, locking squarely on the car's rooftop. This is ideal for maneuvering through obstacle-laden courses that require a heads-up of what lies ahead.
- **FollowCam:** This camera tails the car from a third-person vantage point.
- **DriverCam:** This camera has the POV of the driver but can be altered if needed.

We are now ready to drive the car and record our steps. In the Craft Director Tools main window, there are a few important and useful functions. The red Record button starts and stops the recording of the simulation. The Slow-motion factor is important, as it slows the entire action recording time. This is invaluable, especially when learning. It also helps to steer more precise and accurate routes. The Auto-expand timeline box toggles changes to the timeline as needed, depending on the number of frames that are being recorded. The Low Poly on Record tool toggles higher-resolution models to a low-resolution proxy to allow for better real-time feedback while recording. You can also temporarily select and hide the clown car body and clown car tires, as this will optimize recording as well. At the top of the window, selecting Main > Preferences brings up some options. They include Start Countdown and End Countdown time, which allow the user to create a buffer for readying themselves prior to running the simulation. This gives the user a chance to get his hands on the controls, as seen in Figure 7.18.

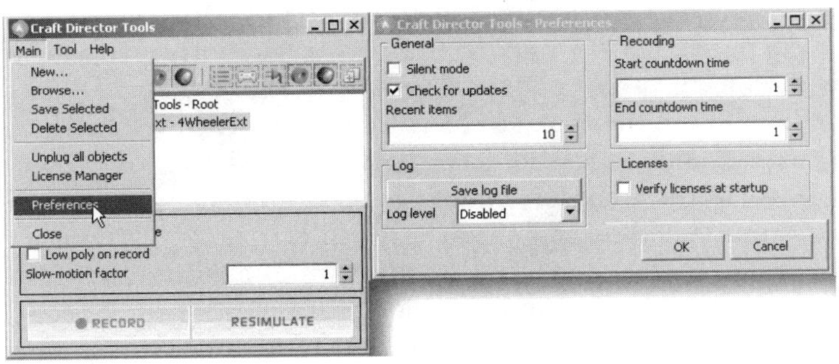

FIGURE 7.18 The Record panel of the Craft Director Tools' main window and Preferences.

Click Record and start driving (see Figure 7.19). As you drive, notice how the weighty chassis shifts its weight over the suspension. Speeding up and braking hard shift the chassis forward and then rest it in place. The suspension works as it should. Stop the recording and return the Timeslider to the beginning. You can now record over the last session. Once you get the hang of it, load different preset suspensions, reinitialize, and see how the adjusted physics performs in contrast.

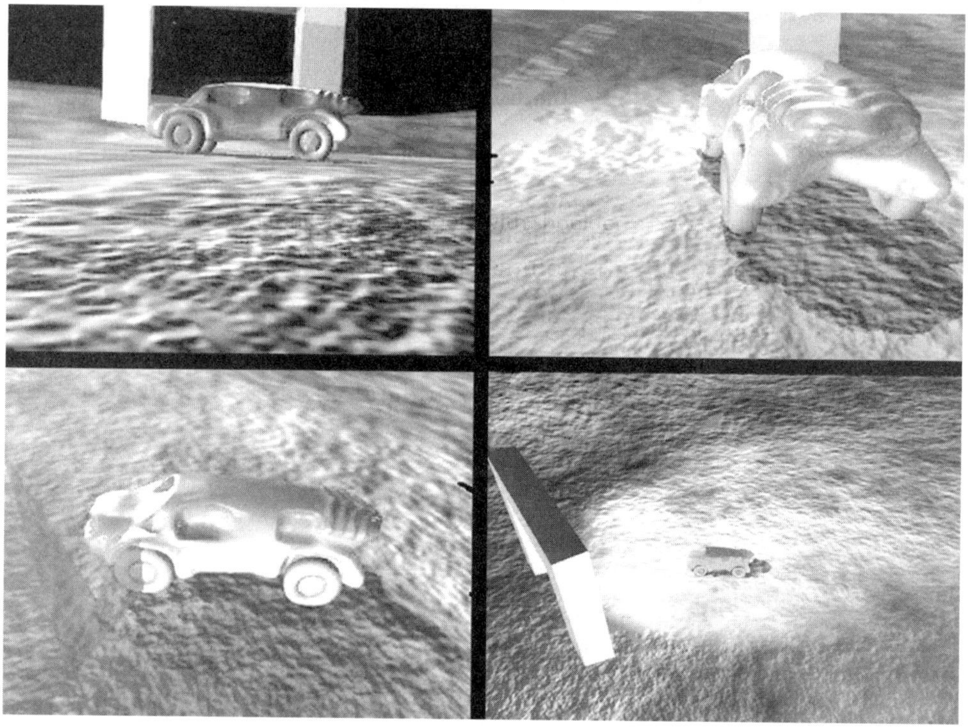

FIGURE 7.19 Four shots of the clown car in action.

ON THE DVD

Hidden from view is a group node called *Obstacles*. Unhide this group and try to maneuver the vehicle through those arches. Once you feel you have captured the perfect performance, unhide the clown geometry and render the scene. The Craft Director Tools proxy rig will not render. This is an excellent but simplistic example, and it will become apparent as you investigate these plugins why they are becoming so popular and successful. Save your work. The vroom_3.mb scene on the companion DVD in the Chapter 7 folder is the completed scene, with a short drive through the terrain avoiding the obstacles. Run through the Timeslider to see it in action. If you need accuracy beyond the direct input abilities of a human driver, Craft Director Tools has an autonomous mode that follows a target mesh while traveling along a spline path. While the rig follows the target mesh through its splined course, it can veer from the path with input device intervention. As soon as the controls are released, the car will return smoothly to its spline course.

At first glance, it seems like a great deal of work to get the job done. On the contrary, as you work with the plugins, the value becomes quite apparent. The provisions provided in the rigs, and in conjunction with other rigs, allow the users to build complex, exact, and logical simulations, which would otherwise be arduous and inaccurate. The addition of other Craft Director Tools, such as the camera plugins, can create an even more impressive scene. Let's take a quick look at some of the camera tools offered by Craft.

CAMERA TRICKS

It's amazing how the tiniest subtlety and nuance of effects trickery can have a major impact on the realism and perception of an animated scene. As in practical filming, good camera work speaks volumes about the tempo, emotion, and urgency of a sequence. In animation and visual effects, good camera work provides another layer of realism that helps suspend disbelief. The series of Craft Director Tools cameras fills a void for good camera work in Maya, while making it easy to use.

ON THE DVD

Load the scene called bee.mb from the companion DVD in the Chapter 7 folder. We can use this small flower scene to test some of the simpler cameras. Once loaded, your scene should look like Figure 7.20.

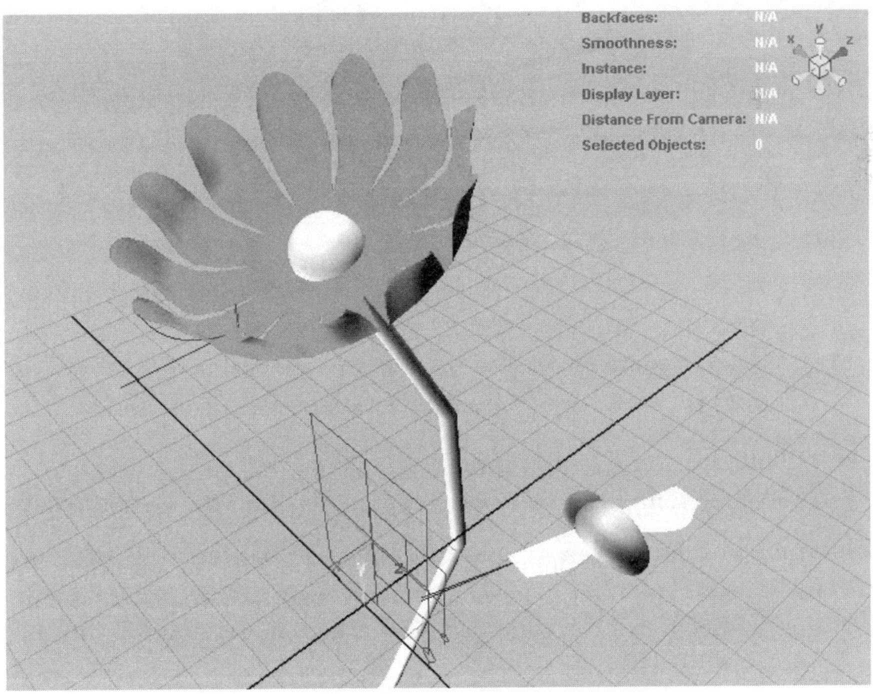

FIGURE 7.20 The flower scene as a practice arena for testing cameras.

One of the Craft cameras that has interesting applications is the SphereCam. This camera creates a spherical orbit for the camera to travel around. By setting the camera target, the user can control the spherical motion centered on a fixed point. As before, select the orange Craft Director Tool icon in the tool shelf. This brings up the Craft Director Tools main window. Select Main > New... from the Craft Director Tools Window. Again, this will bring up a Create window that lists all the tools available to you. You want to select SphereCam from the list of tools and then click the Create button, as shown in Figure 7.21.

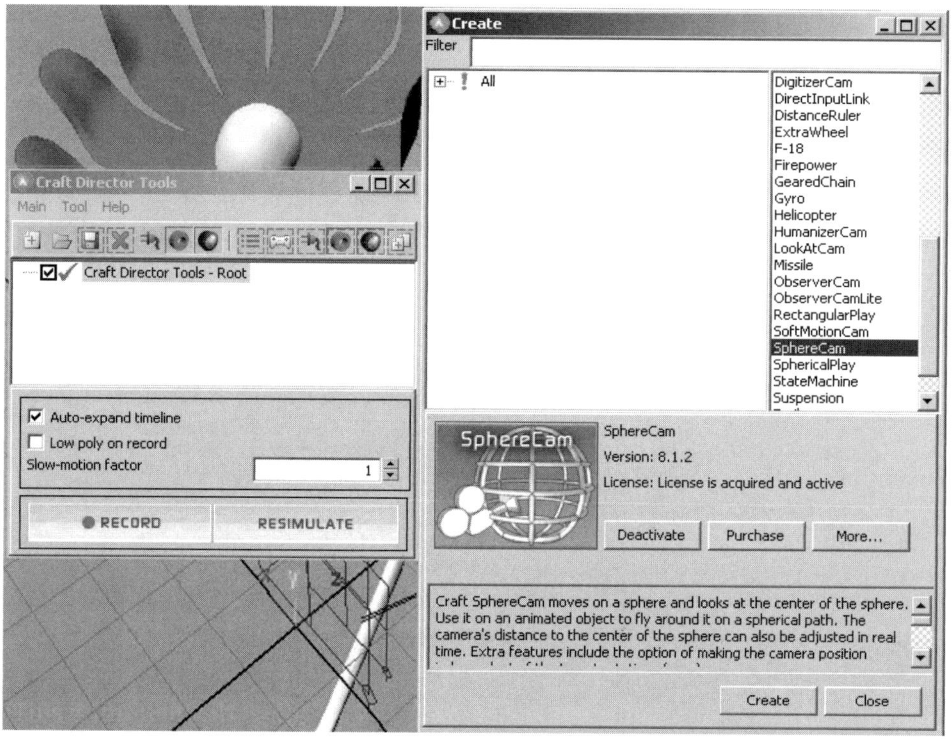

FIGURE 7.21 Choosing the SphereCam from the animated tools selection window.

If you have not used this plugin before, the program will ask you for the key. The SphereCam has two main components. Find the CSphereCam_01_TargetMesh node and center it on the middle of the flower stem. The SphereCam_01_TargetMesh is the focal point around which the SphereCam orbits. Figure 7.22 shows the SphereCam, the CSphereCam_01_TargetMesh node, and the flower model from the perspective of the camera's view. The SphereCam now needs to be configured for use with an input device.

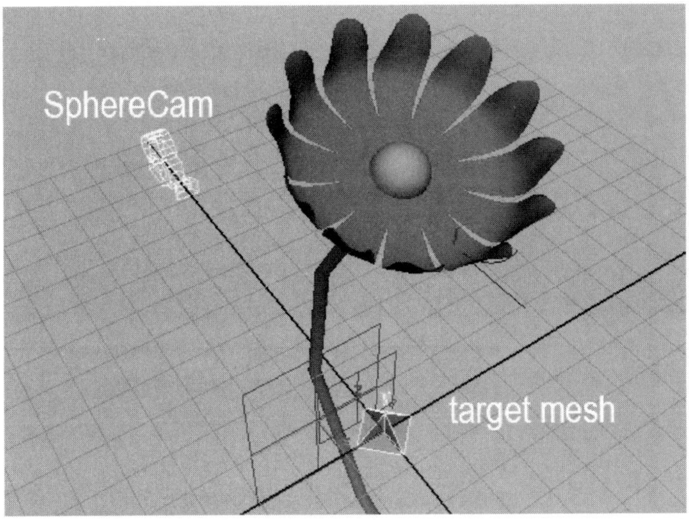

FIGURE 7.22 The diamond-shaped TargetMesh node is centered within the scene along with the camera.

Highlight the newly listed SphereCam rig that now appears in the Craft Director Tools window. At the top of the Craft Director Tools window, select the Tool > Input settings to bring up a new window that has the parameters for configuring the input devices of the SphereCam. Click the open folder icon at the top of the SphereCam Input Settings window. This will launch a new window containing device profiles. This time a gamepad device is in order. Select example:gamepad from the Profiles window and click OK. The SphereCam can now be controlled via a gampad device. Figure 7.23 shows the gamepad input selection and some of the default corresponding control actions on the gamepad.

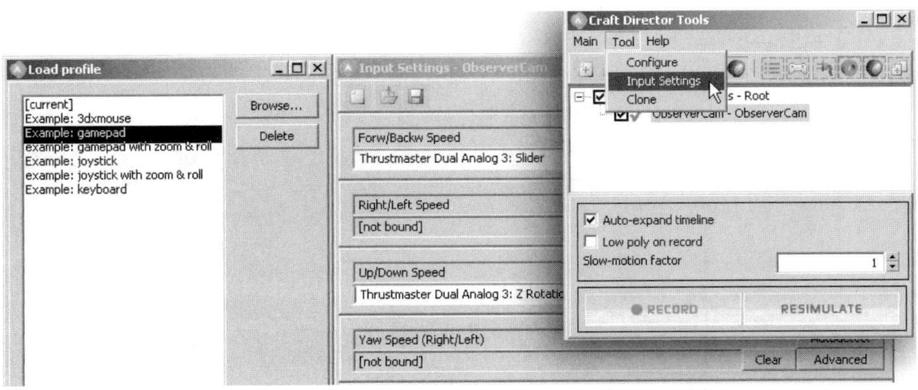

FIGURE 7.23 Changing the input settings to use a video game controller.

ON THE DVD

At this point, you can start recording camera motion. Remember to select the SphereCam in the viewports Panels menu, as shown in Figure 7.24. Clicking on the Record button, as shown in Figure 7.18, begins recording keyframes. Move the camera in full spherical motion around the target centered at the origin. Once you have recorded enough frames, click on Stop. You can play back what was recorded by resetting the Timeslider and playing it back. Re-recording is as simple as recording over the last keyframes. A version of this scene file, bee2.mb is available on the companion DVD-ROM in the Chapter 7 folder. This scene file contains an example of camera motion recorded with the SphereCam. There is no doubt that practice makes perfect here, but the output is well worth the effort.

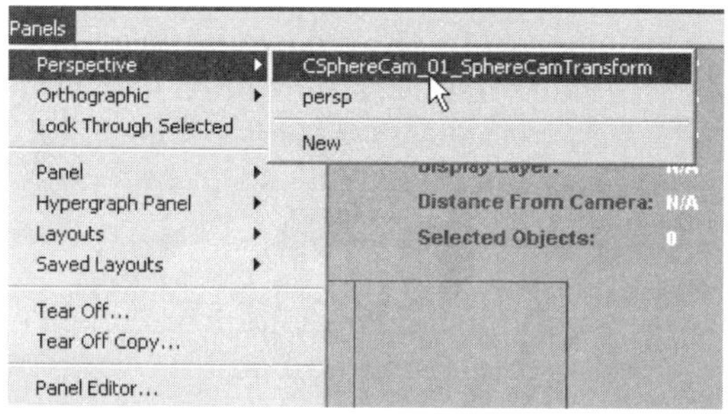

FIGURE 7.24 Selecting the proper camera for the interactive real-time filming.

ON THE DVD

This scene file also contains a small animated bee. Although rudimentary, it opens up interesting possibilities for parenting objects to cameras. The bee parented to the CSphereCam_01_SphereCamTransform and conveniently positioned in front of the SphereCam lens, as shown in Figure 7.25, creates the BeeCam. The scene file, beeCam.mb, on the companion DVD-ROM in the Chapter 7 folder shows an example of the BeeCam at work. The SphereCam seems a perfect use for the erratic movement of a bee's flight around a flower. It might be pointed out that the petal animation and wing beating may detract from the overall recording. In reality, it should be done with low-resolution, nonanimated objects that are replaced later.

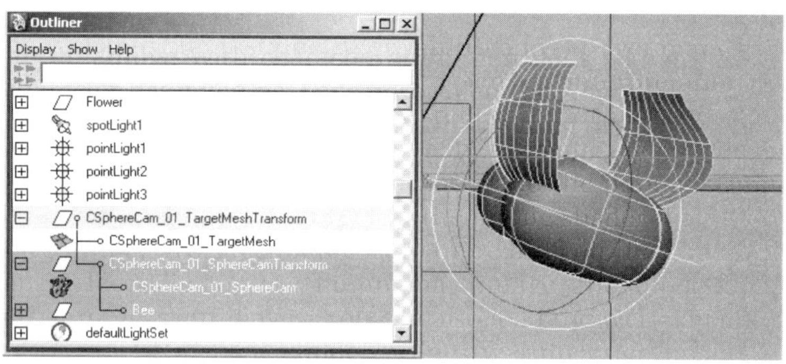

FIGURE 7.25 Parenting the bee to the CSphereCam_01_SphereCamTransform node for the BeeCam.

ON THE DVD

Let's try a scene with a different type of Craft Director Tools camera. Load the scene file focus.mb from the companion DVD in the Chapter 7 folder. The scene should look something like Figure 7.26. The series of three sketches in frames is deliberately arranged to make cinematic use of the Craft Director Tools AutoFocusCam. This camera provides external interactive real-time control over depth-of-field focus.

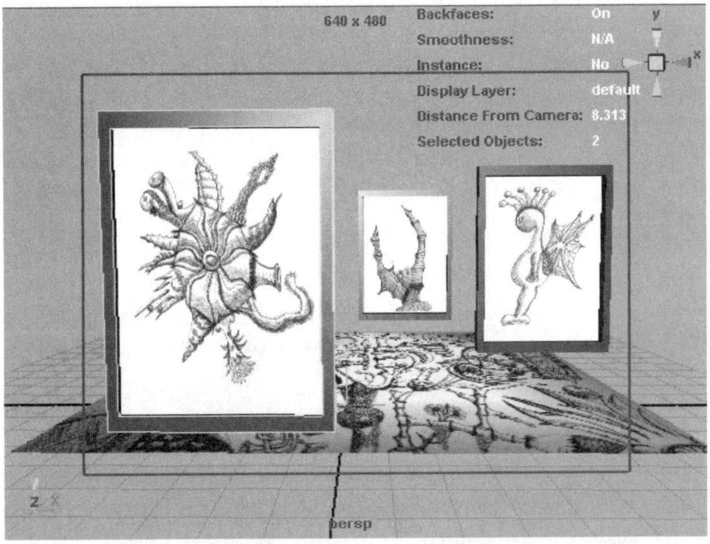

FIGURE 7.26 The gallery of three framed images provides positions to test depth of field.

Once again, let's add a camera to the scene. In the Craft Director Tools main window, select Main > New. This brings up the Create window.

Scroll down until you find the AutoFocusCam, select it and press Create. Remember, you may need to activate it first with an authorization key. The AutoFocusCam has four main components. Figure 7.27 shows the AutoFocusCam, FocalTarget_1, FocalTarget_2, and the CurrFocalPoint node.

FIGURE 7.27 The AutoFocusCam's four components are highlighted and selected in the Outliner.

The AutoFocusCam now needs to be configured for use with an input device. Highlight the newly listed AutoFocusCam rig that now appears in the Craft Director Tools window. At the top of the Craft Director Tools window, select the Tool > Input settings to bring up a new window that has the parameters for configuring the input devices of the AutoFocusCam. Click the open folder icon at the top of the SphereCam Input Settings window. This will launch a new window containing device profiles. Select the example:keyboard device and press OK. The keyboard seems to be a good choice of input device for controlling the AutoFocusCam's functions. The SphereCam can now be controlled via a keyboard. Figure 7.28 shows the Profile window and Input settings window of the AutoFocusCam. The focal position of the AutoFocusCam is controlled in real time by the left and right arrows keys of the keyboard, while zooming is controlled by the up and down keys.

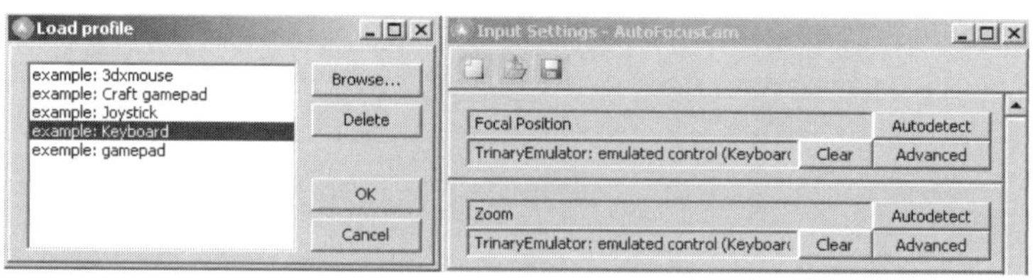

FIGURE 7.28 The keyboard is selected as the input device for controlling the AutoFocusCam.

This camera changes its focal point between the two user-determined focal targets in the scene. We must select both focal points first. FocalTarget_1 and FocalTarget_2 should be set at the furthest gallery portrait in the scene and the closest one.

Select the AutoFocusCam and position it first, followed by each focal target object, and place them as shown in Figure 7.29. The CurrFocalPoint is the interactive node here. It travels between FocalTarget_1 and FocalTarget_2 via interactive keyboard control, thus changing the camera's depth of field. There is no need to position the CurrFocalPoint, as it sets itself in position.

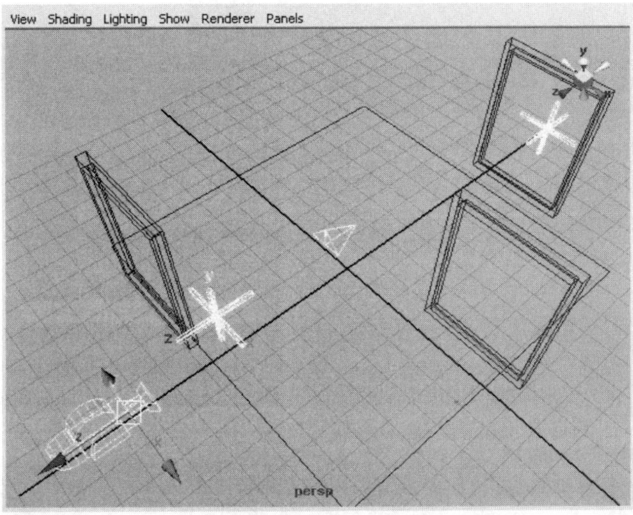

FIGURE 7.29 The far and near focal points are set and represented by the tri-axial 3D geometry, while the skewed pyramid geometry is the interactive point of focus for the camera.

Remember that you need to select your AutoFocusCam for rendering. You need to turn on depth of field, which is off by default. Select the AutoFocusCam, and toggle the Depth of Field box on, as shown in Figure 7.30.

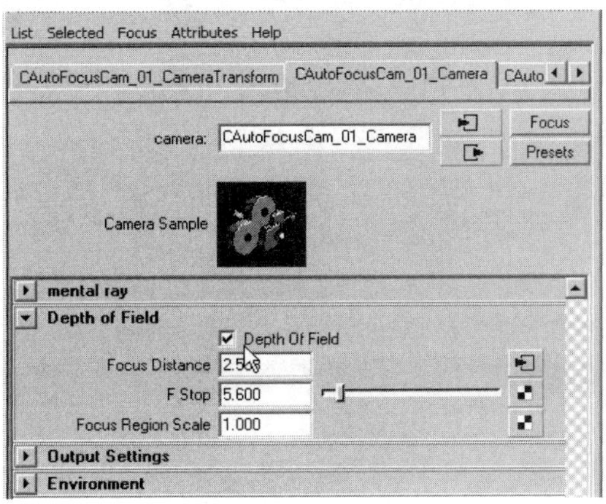

FIGURE 7.30 Toggling on the Depth of Field box ensures that the camera will render the depth of field.

Now you are ready to animate the focal point. You can begin recording by clicking on the Record button on the Craft Director Tools main window or pressing the spacebar. The best way to approach this scene is to view it from the AutoFocusCam, as well as from the orthographic side view. This gives you a visual cue as to the position of the CurrFocalPoint. Keep in mind that the AutoFocusCam has controls for zooming, as well as for changing the focal point of the camera.

You Are Being Watched

Remember that Maya can render multiple cameras at a time. By default, Maya renders the Perspective camera, as well as the AutoFocusCam. It is easy to check for renderable cameras in the Render Globals, delete the Perspective camera, and select the cameras you need rendered.

ON THE DVD

The scene focus2.mb located on the companion DVD-ROM in the Chapter 7 folder is a 900-frame animation of this exercise. Although the zoom was left untouched, the focal point was moved to gain sharp focus of the three images, independently, over time. Figure 7.31 shows four frames from this render.

FIGURE 7.31 Rendered frames show the depth of field changing over time as the CurrFocalPoint travels between the far and near focal points.

ON THE DVD

Let's discuss one more interesting camera before we end this chapter. We will use it by way of binding the camera to another. Load the helicopter.mb scene on the companion DVD-ROM in the Chapter 7 folder. The scene should look like Figure 7.32.

The Human Touch

Individual Craft Director Tools were designed to be layered upon each other. Very interesting and realistic effects can be achieved by combining certain elements. The ObserverCam, which is a general-purpose camera for viewing in all directions while moving through something, can be combined with the HumanizerCam to get a very rich handheld camera feel. The settings range from warm to earthquake and have a dramatic and immediate impact on the final filmed scene. This camera has a very realistic feel that feels, well, human. The Craft Gyro can be used in concert with a number of other tools for extra stability. Overall, these plugins work very well together.

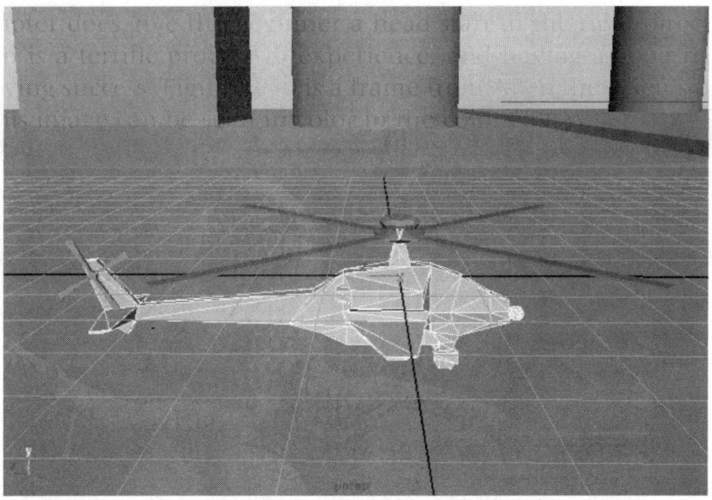

FIGURE 7.32 A training ground for your first Craft Director Tools helicopter flight.

This scene is a cityscape for testing your helicopter flight. The Craft Director Tools helicopter is already in the scene. It should be configured to suit your particular input device. Highlight the Helicopter rig listing in the Craft Director Tools window and select the Tool > Input settings to bring up a new window that has the parameters for configuring the input devices of the helicopter. Click the open folder icon at the top of the Helicopter Input Settings window. This will launch a new window containing device profiles. Select example:gamepad from the Profiles window and click OK. Now configure the Helicopter by selecting Tools > Configure from the Craft Director Tools window and select Ordinary from the profiles listing. Click OK. After you have completed this, select CHelicopter_01_CockpitCam, which is a view from the seat of the helicopter. The CHelicopter_01_FollowCam follows the helicopter flight from a safe distance. When you are ready, click the Record button in the Craft Director Tools main window and take flight. It takes a little while to adjust to the controls, but eventually it becomes second nature. It becomes clear as you utilize these tools that there is a distinct advantage to this method of animation. The time savings can be enormous. After you have flown around successfully, save your work.

ON THE DVD

The helicopter2.mb scene on the companion DVD in the Chapter 7 folder has a recorded flight of about 3,000 frames. Select the CHelicopter_01_FollowCamTransform from the Panels menu of the current viewport. This switches the view of the helicopter's flight to the FollowCam. Play back the 3,000 animation frames using the Timeslider playback controls. It does take some coordination and practice. Now select the CHelicopter_01_CockpitCamTransform from the Panels menu. Play this animation back to get a feel for what it might look like from the cockpit. The motion, while perhaps not quite like professional flying, will serve our purpose.

The use of a handheld shot is a way of inviting the audience into the shot. A handheld camera creates a feeling of urgency. Let's add a HumanizerCam to the shot. From the Craft Director Tools window, select Main > New. This will bring up a Create window that lists all the tools available to you. We want to select HumanizerCam from the list of tools. With the new HumanizerCam selected, choose Tool > Configure from the Craft Director Tools window. At the top-left corner of the HumanizerCam configuration window, select the open folder icon to get a list of profiles (see Figure 7.33).

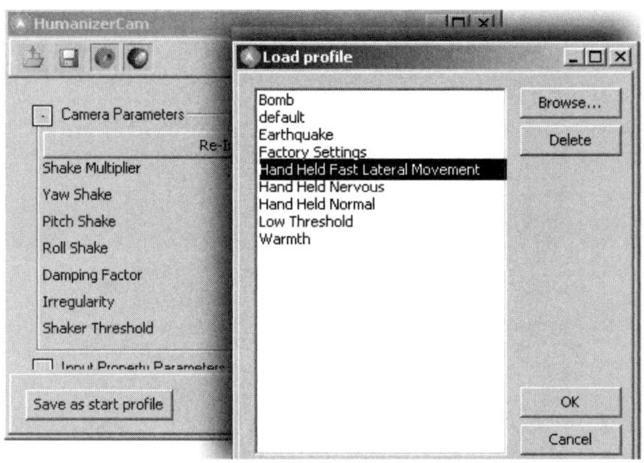

FIGURE 7.33 A list of preset profiles for the HumanizerCam.

As you can see, there is an interesting list of profiles. Select Hand Held Fast Lateral Movement and click the OK button. The HumanizerCam must be parented to the helicopter. This can be done in the Outliner by selecting CHumanizerCam_01_HumanizerCamTransform followed by the CHelicopter_01_MainBodyMeshTransform and pressing the P key. This parents the two cameras to each other. Figure 7.34 shows the Outliner window with the proper nodes selected.

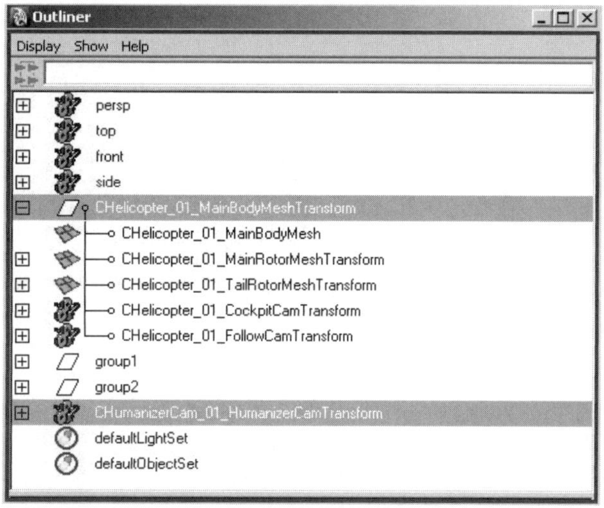

FIGURE 7.34 The Outliner window with the two camera nodes selected for parenting.

ON THE DVD

We can now record the result of the HumanizerCam. Make sure your camera view is set to HumanizerCam. Select the HumanizerCam in the Craft Director Tools main window and click the Record button. The shot now takes on the human element. The change can be minimal, but the overall effect truly enriches the shot. Included on the DVD-ROM in the Chapter 7 folder are several small movies of the same flight. They are located in the HumanCam folder. Each movie has a different HumanCam profile and thus a slightly different result. There is also a side-by-side comparison movie called HumanCam.avi.

The irony in using these special "humanizing cameras" is that the original flight was controlled by a human using a gamepad. This made the flight very rocky at times. The movie file CockPitCam.avi is the original gamepad-captured flight.

ON THE DVD

Craft has another camera called the *SoftMotionCam*. This camera acts as a steady cam. There are two components to the SoftMotionCam: the AttachedCam and the FollowCam. Let's see if we can soften some of the erratic movements of the original gamepad-captured footage. Load the scene file helicopter3.mb locted on the DVD-ROM in the Chapter 7 folder. Scrubbing through the Timeslider reveals the original gamepad capture. It's very irregular, to say the least. With this motion being the driving force, we will add another camera to the scene. From the Craft Director Tools window select Main > New. This will bring up a Create window that lists all the tools available to you. This time, load the Craft SoftMotion-Cam from the selection list, as shown in Figure 7.35. This camera is passive and works without interactive influence. The AttachedCam and the Follow-Cam components initially share the same space and view as the CockpitCam.

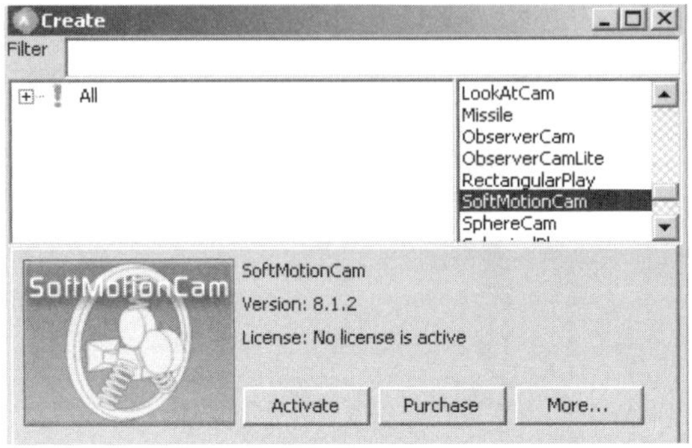

FIGURE 7.35 Selection of the SoftMotionCam from the tools list.

Select the CSoftMotionCam from the Craft Director Tools main menu and then select Configure. In the Configure window, select FollowCam from the Profiles pull-down menu. Load it. The FollowCam is already configured to follow the AttachedCam. We need to parent the AttachedCam to the helicopter. As shown in Figure 7.36, in the Outliner window, select the CSoftMotionCam_01_AttachedCam followed by the CHelicopter_01_MainBodyMeshTransform and press the P key to parent them together. This guides the AttachedCam with the previously recorded motion of the helicopter.

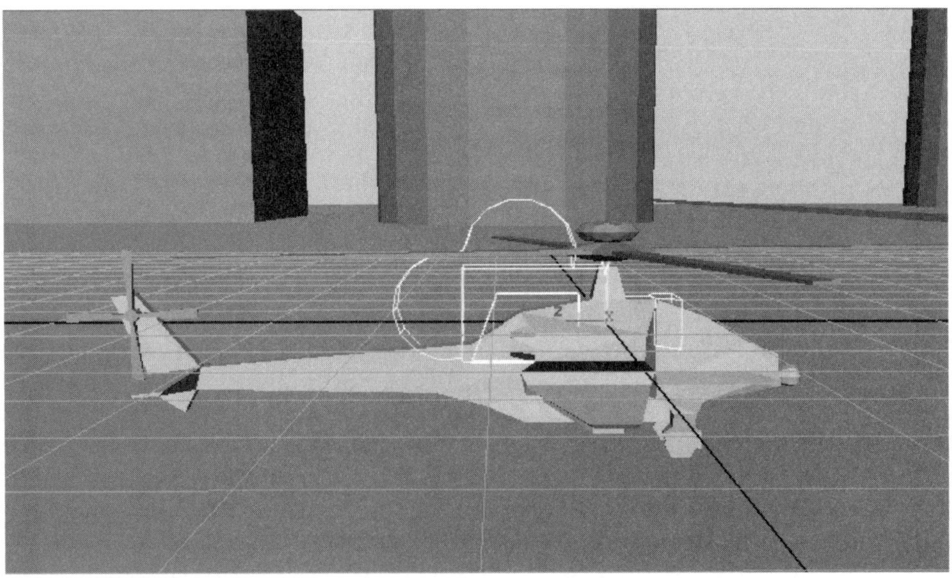

FIGURE 7.36 The CSoftMotionCam_01_AttachedCam is now attached to the helicopter mesh for a soft, windshield view from the chopper.

ON THE DVD

Change the camera view in the Panels menu to that of the FollowCam. Make the helicopter mesh invisible. Click Record in the Craft Director Tools main window. The result is a significantly smoother camera shot than the original. On the DVD in the Chapter 7 folder are two scene files (Helicopter_Soft_Follow.mb and Helicopter_Soft_Steady.mb) that use the SoftMotionCam to produce smoother results than the original helicopter shot. You will also find accompanying movies.

RIGS AND THINGS

Craft Animation has a slew of new controller rig systems on the verge of release. Craft Utilities StateMachine will be used for rigging machine systems, such as robot arms and other response-dependent machine functions. Craft Firepower can help create animation for weapons such as guns, canons, turrets, and Craft Director Tools catapults and even rainfall. They also have a small library of free plugins that have interesting applications. We'll cover one of them in Chapter 9, "Miscellaneous Tools." Several markets can get a great deal of use from the Craft Director Tools tools. Craft Animation has also released several professionally modeled and textured rigs. They include the AH-64 Apache helicopter, the AMX-30 Roland tank, the C-130 Hercules transport plane, CH53E Super Stallion helicopter, F-18 fighter jet, M1 Abrams Tank, MH60A Blackhawk helicopter, and the UH60F Seahawk helicopter. The company is also beginning custom modeling and rigging.

So much is involved in the Craft Director Tools arsenal, and it is so diverse that we could not begin to cover it all. These are powerful helpers that can ease a variety of difficult situations and deserve further investigation on your part. We have much ground to cover yet, so let's jump to the next chapter and discover the dynamics of destruction in Maya.

CHAPTER

8 DYNAMIC DESTRUCTION

In This Chapter

- Introduction
- The Easy Exploding Wall
- Creating Cracks
- Collision, Gravity, and Secondary Debris

Four stages of the destruction of a home, reminiscent of the old atomic bomb testing in Nevada in the 1950s. This sequence was done using Blast Code's Megaton.
Image courtesy of Blast Code Software

INTRODUCTION

Everyone loves a good movie explosion or some random destruction in his or her escapism. Even if the story may beg for it, it's not always very practical, safe, or cost efficient. Often, explosions are a "one-shot" situation, filmed from many angles at once. This is done to get the maximum footage of an event that only lasts a few seconds. There is no movie budget we know of that allows for building, destroying, and rebuilding a building until the director is satisfied. Explosions are not the only form of destruction in a film. Destruction can take many forms. Wouldn't it be great if destruction could be simulated in 3D animation. A baseball crashing through a window, a car crashing through a wooden fence, the ground cracking during an earthquake, a glass shattering from a fall, or a wrecking ball tearing down a wall are all forms of destruction that can be simulated safely, efficiently, and repetitively. There are a few tools in Maya to help with the task, but it is an intensely difficult procedure. Enter Blast Code from Hermosa Beach, California, which has released two products that take the burden out of destroying everything in your path. There are two versions of the Blast Code plugin: Kiloton and Megaton. For this chapter, we'll use Megaton, which has a few more high-end features.

Before we get started on our path of destruction, let's look at the basic workflow of Blast Code. Three basic mesh components make up whatever it is you are destroying.

- Slabs are the resultant mesh objects derived from a control surface. They possess a thickness and are an interactive component created from your initial intended target of destruction.
- Sweeps are another interactive component derived from the initial control surface. Sweeps are derived from curves on the initial control surface.
- Glue objects are the third interactive mesh component. This geometry is not derived from the control surface, but is attached to the control surface to complement the destruction of an object built from slabs and sweeps.

Figure 8.1 shows a typical destruction scene set up using slabs as walls, sweeps for ceiling supports, and a glue object beach ball.

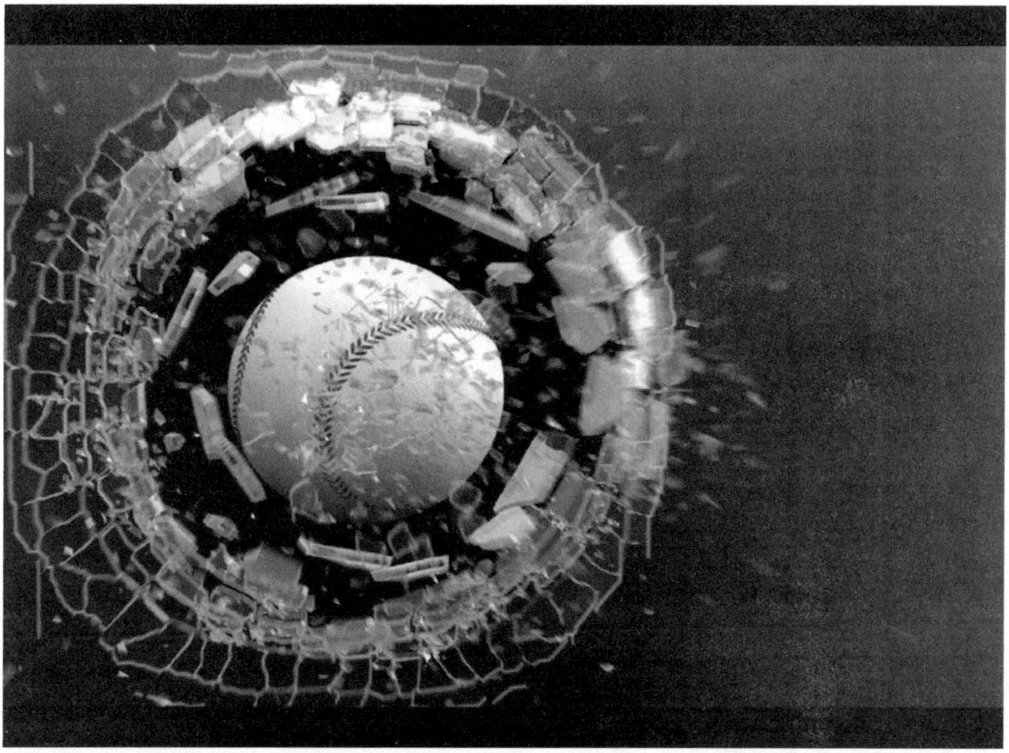

FIGURE 8.1 Scene composed of slabs, sweeps, and a glue object set for destruction.

It's not really as confusing as it sounds. Blast Code is brilliant at creating destruction, and it harbors a host of features that allow you to create ever more complex damage scenarios as you learn. Creating a blast object is a matter of creating a model of NURBS surfaces. These "control surfaces" are the starting point of a blast from which attached meshes are extruded and swept into the actual destructible 3D model. The control surfaces are not part of the final render, but are the influencing factor over the renderable meshes. The control surfaces hold the information about the blast, such as how it cracks apart, the shape and intensity of a blast wave, and secondary debris. The workflow for creating destruction is straightforward.

- The model to be destroyed is built from NURBS surfaces and designated control surfaces. These control surfaces beget the actual destroyable geometry.
- Some or all of these damage objects can be assigned cracking patterns, which designate how the objects break apart. Cracking patterns can be generated at random or precisely plotted by carefully creating a crack map in any paint program.
- Explosive forces or fields are placed in the scene to facilitate the destruction of the previously created model.
- Forces such as gravity and collision are then applied to generate a much more realistic and dramatic result.

Blast Code has been used in films such as Peter Jackson's remake of *King Kong* and Twentieth Century Fox's *X-Men 3* with great success. Let's investigate Blast Code for ourselves (see Figure 8.2).

FIGURE 8.2 A baseball dynamically crashes through a window pane.
Image Courtesy of Blast Code Software

THE EASY EXPLODING WALL

Let's jump right into the destruction of a small stone wall. You will begin to see how the workflow makes sense and how it differs from the usual way we approach this in Maya. It will also become clear how quickly we can get amazing results. Boot up your copy of Maya, and we can begin. As always, it's assumed that you have installed your copy of Blast Code software correctly. Start by creating a NURBS plane with the parameters, as shown in Figure 8.3, and then translate and rotate the NURBS plane, as shown in Figure 8.4.

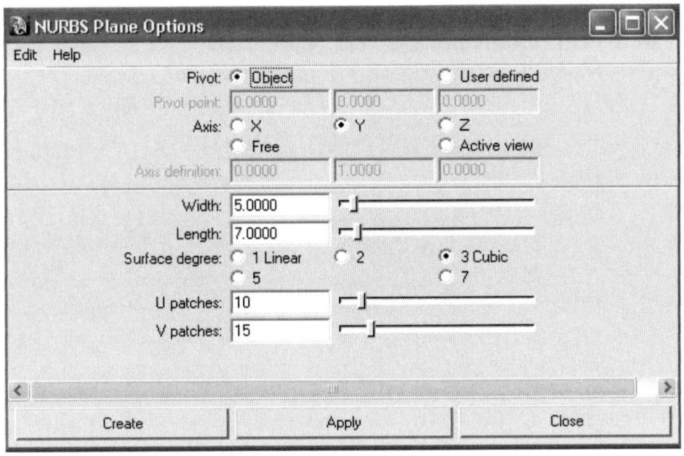

FIGURE 8.3 The parameters for nurbsPlane1.

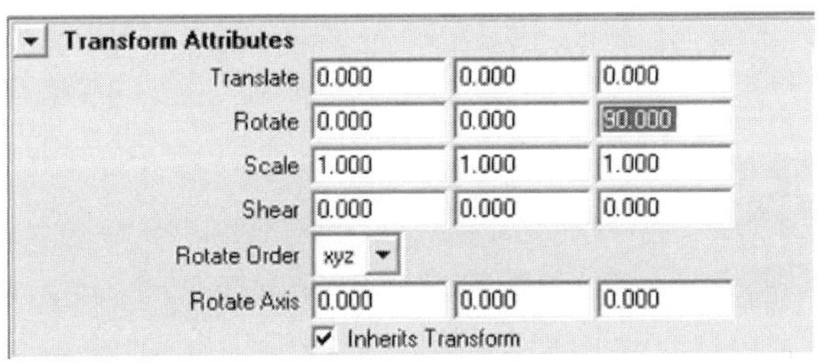

FIGURE 8.4 The rotation for nurbsPlane1.

The plugin is very well integrated into the Maya workflow, so it appears as normal as any other set of functions and menus. It appears as a separate Blast Code menu at the top of the screen, near the Help Menu, with the rest of Maya's menu selections. It should look similar to Figure 8.5.

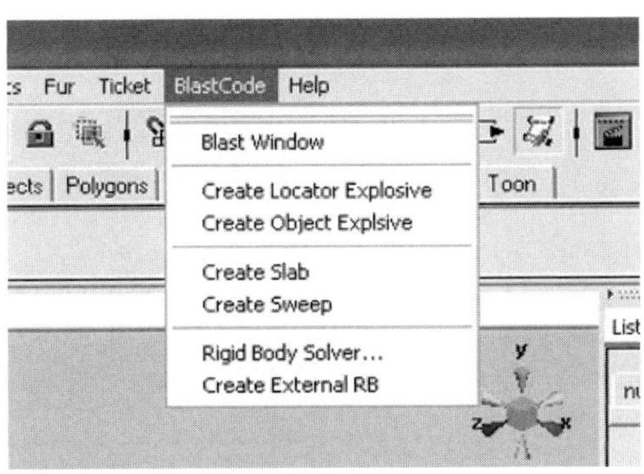

FIGURE 8.5 The Blast Code Menu and submenu selections.

This NURBS plane becomes the control surface that guides the destruction of our wall. In this example, we will be destroying a single standing wall. We must first indicate to Maya and Blast Code that this plane is a control surface. With the NURBS plane selected, go to the Blast Code menu and select the Blast window option, as shown in Figure 8.5. This opens the mail controls of Blast Code into its own dialog box (see Figure 8.6).

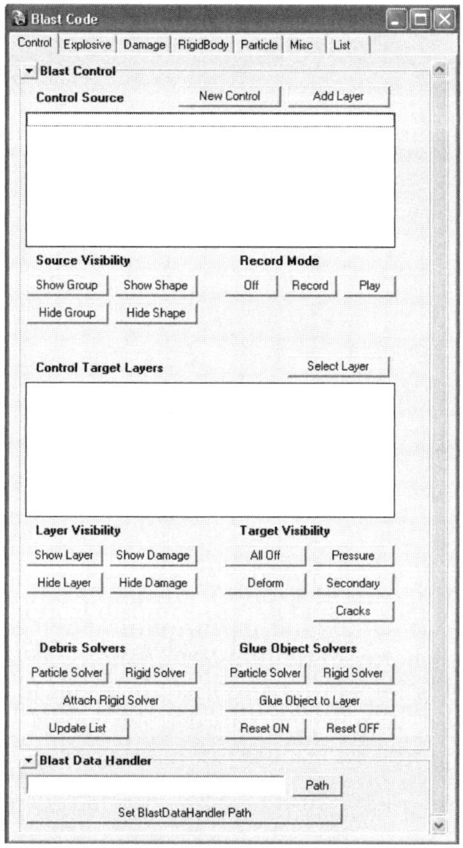

FIGURE 8.6 The main working area of Blast Code is the Blast Code dialog box.

With the NURBS plane still selected, click the New Control button in the Blast window. Blast Code lists our NURBS plane in the Control Source window. It also creates a control layer for our NURBS plane in the Control Target Layer. The NURBS plane (nurbsPlane1) and its accompanying target layer (BLayer1) are now listed in the Blast window, as shown in Figure 8.7.

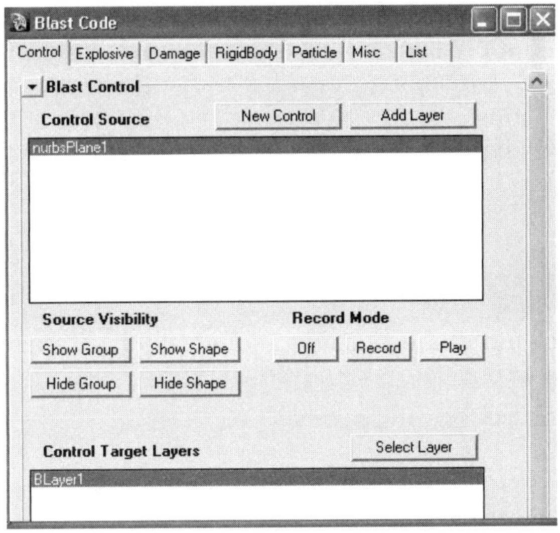

FIGURE 8.7 The newly created control surface for nurbsPlane1.

Now that the NURBS plane is designated as a control surface, an explosive force can be added. In the Blast window, there are several tabs labeled as in Figure 8.8. Select the Explosive tab and then click the Locator Explosive button. This places an explosive force in the scene labeled Explosive1, which is now listed in the Explosive window. Below the Explosive window is the Source Control Surface window, which lists nurbsPlane1 as the only control surface currently available in the scene. The red X next to nurbsPlane1 indicates that it does not have an explosive force attached to it (see Figure 8.8).

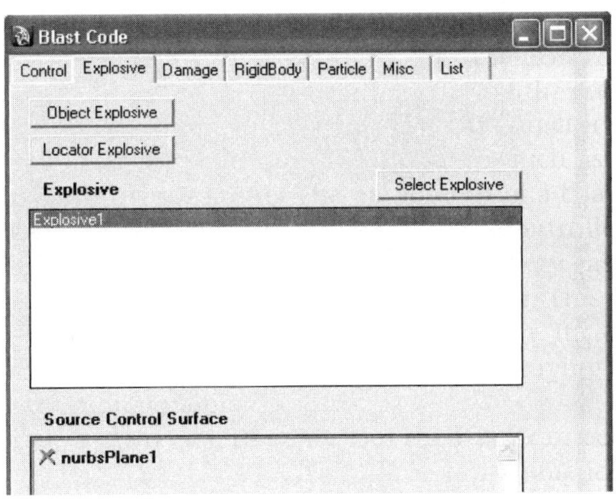

FIGURE 8.8 The Blast Code window's tabs. Explosive1 force is not yet attached to nurbsPlane1.

Explosive1 must now be attached to the nurbsPlane1. The Explosive1 force must be associated with nurbsPlane1 by selecting the explosive and clicking on nurbsPlane1. This changes the red X to a green check mark and turns the nurbsPlane1 wireframe to pink, indicating that the two items are now associated with one another (see Figure 8.9).

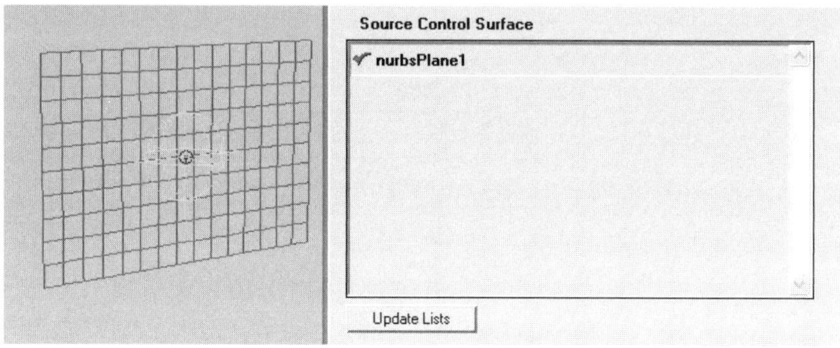

FIGURE 8.9 The nurbsPlane control surface is now associated with the explosive force.

If you created nurbsPlane1 along the origin, the explosive should have appeared there as well. It is possible to see the effects that the explosive starts to have on the control surface. Manually slide through the Timeslider frame by frame. The results of the explosive force become apparent quickly. Figures 8.10 and 8.11 show the effect of the blast wave on the nurbsPlane1 control surface.

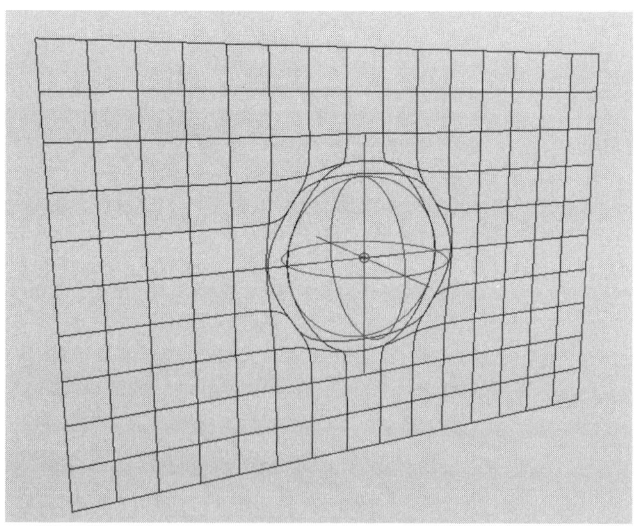

FIGURE 8.10 The effect of the blast wave on nurbsPlane1 at frame 2.

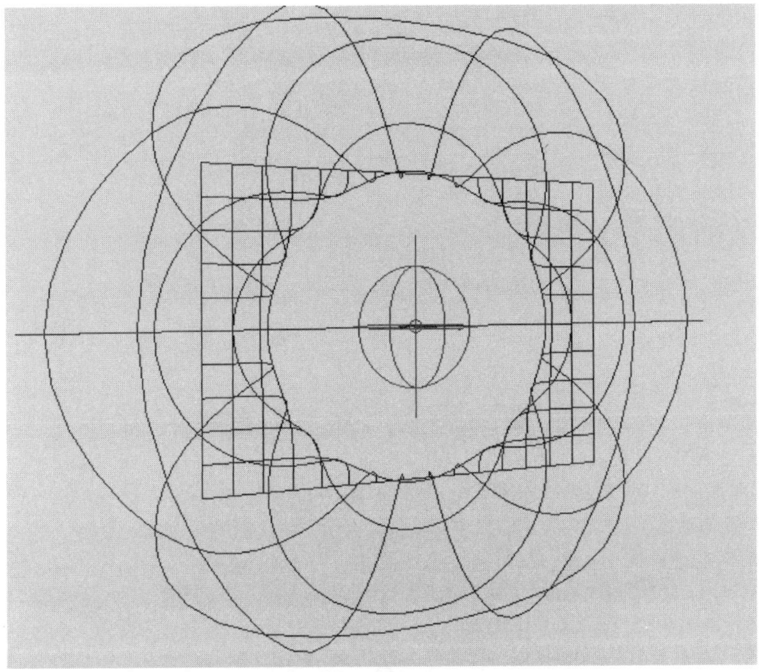

FIGURE 8.11 The effect of the blast wave on nurbsPlane1 at frame 3.

ON THE DVD

Save your scene and load the bomb_burst1.mb scene on the companion DVD in the Chapter 8 folder. It is the scene up to this point, and it will allow us to keep on the same page. Minute changes in parameters can create huge differences in results.

Now that we have the catalyst for the wall's destruction, let's begin to construct our wall. For this example, we will build our wall from slabs. As you may recall, slabs are one of the three mesh components you can utilize to build destructible forms in Blast Code. The nurbsPlane1 control source is used to create the actual solid wall we intend to destroy. (I know you're getting impatient. Hold on. We will be blowing something up shortly.) The control source can be hidden at this point. It is crucial to the explosion, but it would only be an eyesore right now. In the Blast Code window under the Control tab, select BLayer1 and click the All Off button under Target Visibility (see Figure 8.12). The nurbsPlane1 control layer BLayer1 is now hidden from view.

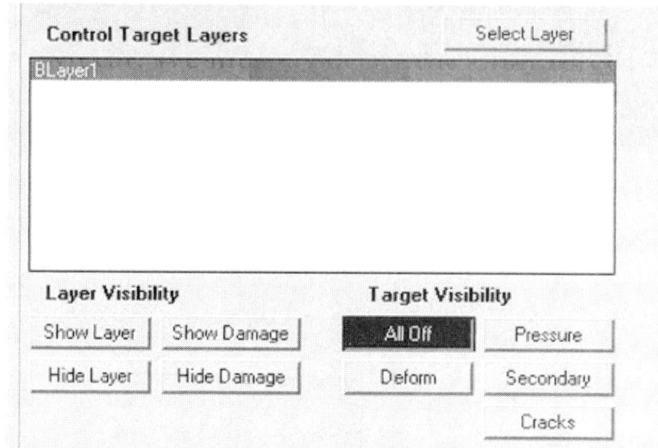

FIGURE 8.12 Turning the control layer off hides it from view.

Now we can create our 3D mesh wall. Select the BLayer1 control source. We find it easier to keep the Outliner window handy. Just remember to select the BLayer1 node within the nurbsPlane1 node. The Outliner gives a representative list of all components in the scene without you having to select the different tabs in the Blast window (see Figure 8.13).

FIGURE 8.13 The proper node is easily selectable within the Outliner.

With the hidden BLayer1 selected, click the Create Slab button in the Blast Code window under the Damage tab. This creates slab geometry from the hidden control layer (see Figure 8.14). If no meshes appear after generating the slabs from the control surface, reset the time in the Timeslider to the beginning of the simulation.

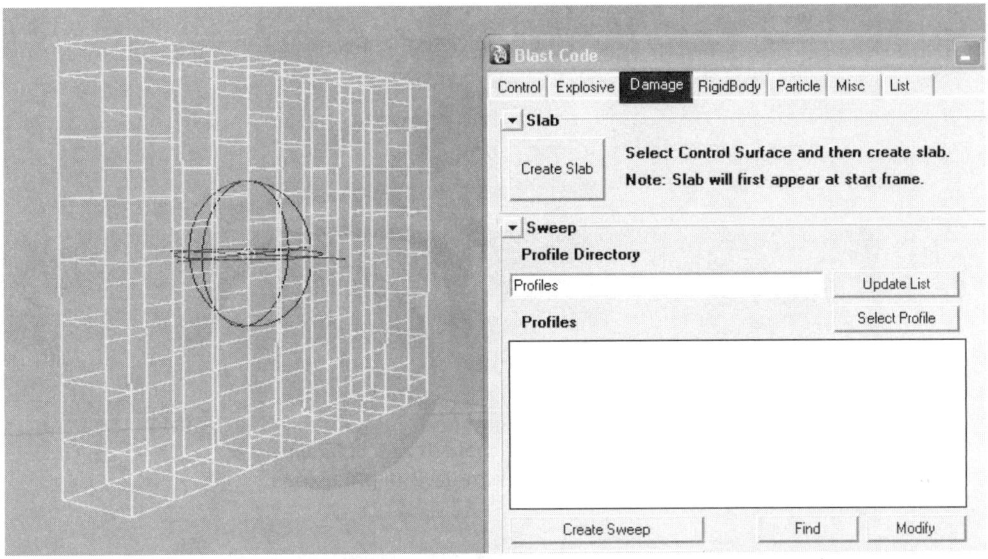

FIGURE 8.14 Slab geometry is created from the hidden control surface.

The wall is beginning to take a more damageable form. A new node called Object1 under the BLayer1 node has been created. Select that node in the Outliner window. In the Attribute Editor is a tab labeled Slab1. Adjustments can be made to the slabs here. One of particular interest is the Mesh Thickness. Adjusting this provides an interactive view of the slab's thickness. Figure 8.15 shows the result of changing Mesh Thickness.

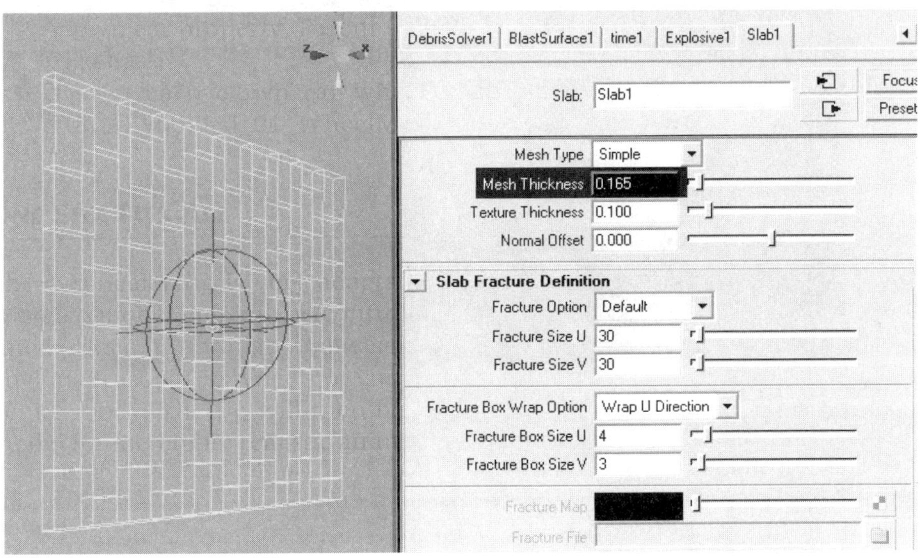

FIGURE 8.15 Mesh Thickness adjustments.

ON THE DVD

At this point, we need to shade the wall. Save your scene and load the bomb_burst2.mb scene on the companion DVD in the Chapter 8 folder. Alternatively, you can import the scene wall_shader_lighting1.mb, also on the companion DVD-ROM in the Chapter 8 folder, which contains just the lighting and a tiled pool house wall shader. If you only import the scene, drag the wall_shader onto the slabs and render it. You should have something like Figure 8.16.

FIGURE 8.16 The properly lit and shaded wall model ready for destruction.

In shaded mode, tick through the Timeslider again. You will notice three things. First, we finally have some destruction. Second, the blast seems to have emanated from the middle of the wall. Last, the chunks flying from the explosion are not shaded. These new pieces are generated as a result of the deformation of the control surface and are visible in Figure 8.17a.

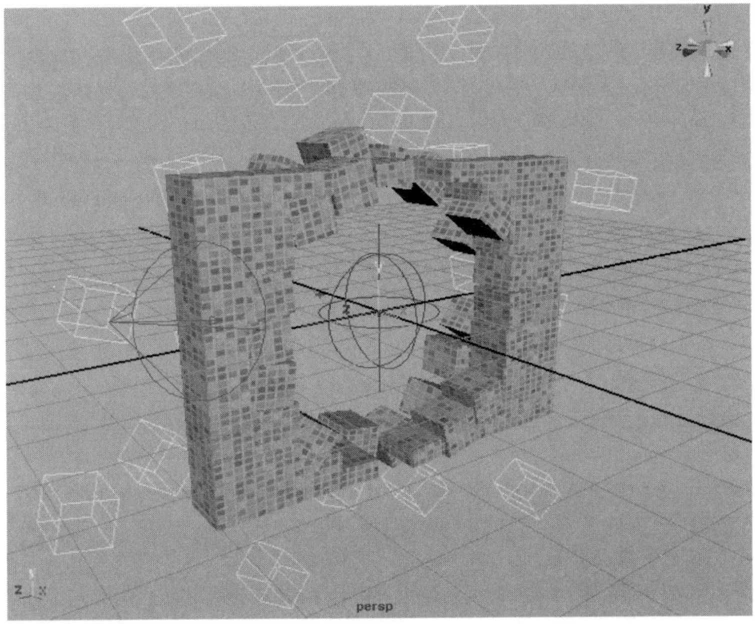

FIGURE 8.17A The model now in mid-destruction generates nonshaded pieces as a result of the deformation of the control surface.

Tick through the simulation from frame 1. Once the unshaded pieces appear, select them and drop the wall shader on them as well. With the imported lighting and shader, frame 3 should look similar to Figure 8.17b. The rendered version should look similar to Figure 8.17c.

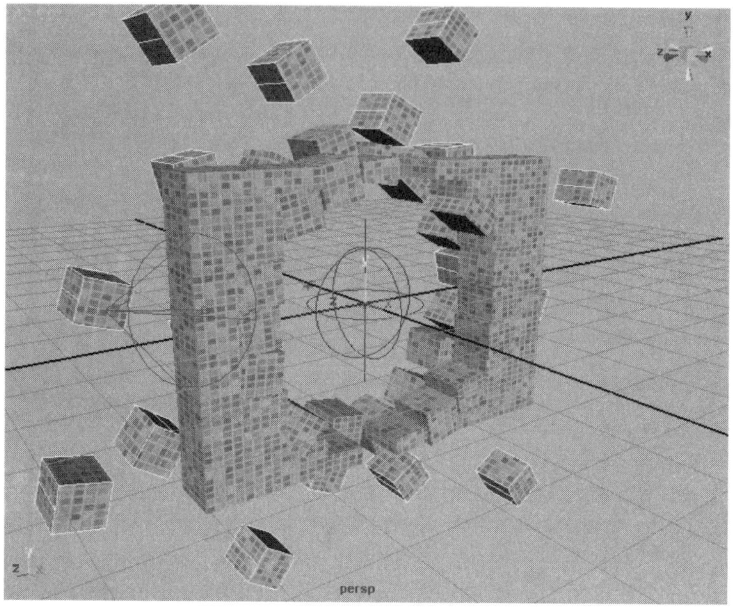

FIGURE 8.17B The back-lit and shaded wall model with all pieces now shaded explodes, albeit incorrectly.

FIGURE 8.17C A fully rendered version shows all pieces are now shaded.

The result of the blast appears as though the explosion emanated from the surface of the wall. The bricks react to the force as though the explosive device were attached to the wall. Moving the explosive element directly affects the way the wall breaks apart. Select the BombLocator1 node from the Outliner window and change its X position to −4.0, as shown in Figure 8.18. The bomb should now be positioned as in Figure 8.19a. The bomb's blast wave will become more apparent after repositioning the BombLocator1 node.

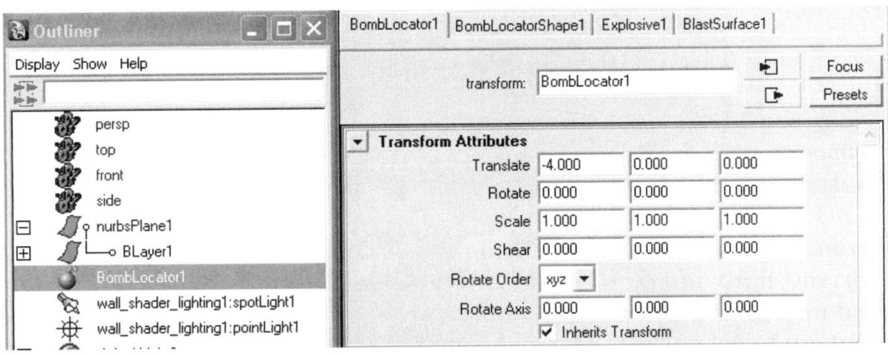

FIGURE 8.18 Adjusting the BombLocator1 node −4 in the X axis alters the blast pattern.

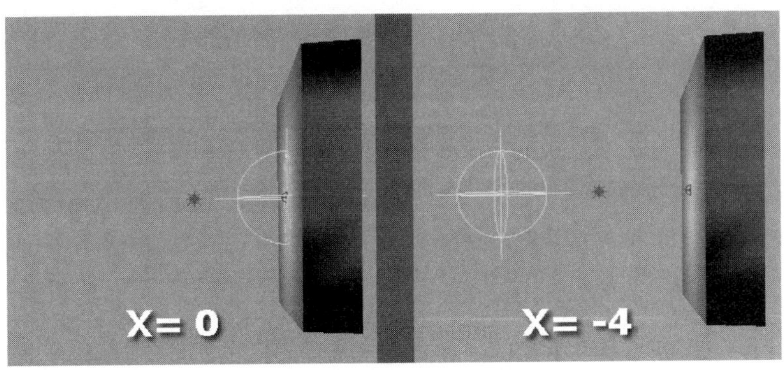

FIGURE 8.19A The bomb's new position yields a much different blast pattern.

ON THE DVD

Tick through the Timeslider manually. Notice that the explosion happens a few frames later, and the pieces now have a different trajectory. The explosion seems to overtake the entire object. The slab pieces leave an arc-like pattern. They are thrust outward by the leading edge of the blast wave, as seen in Figure 8.19b. We can change many parameters to adjust the blast. Save your work. Let's start with the same file again. Load the scene bomb_burst3.mb, which can be found on the companion DVD in the Chapter 8 folder.

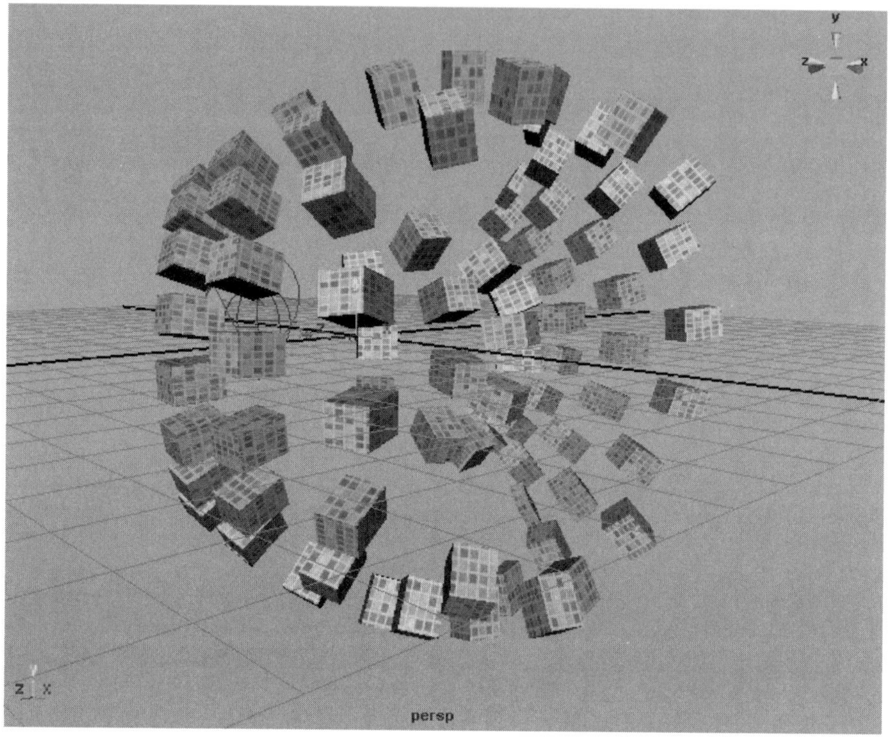

FIGURE 8.19B A render of the new BombLocator1 node shows a completely different blast pattern.

Let's continue. Select the BombLocator1 node from the Outliner window. Choose the Explosive1 tab in the Attribute window. Adjust the magnitude, size, and velocity sliders to the parameters in Figure 8.20a.

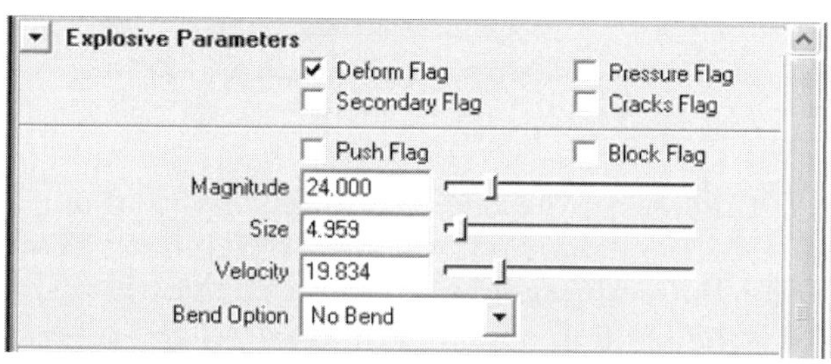

FIGURE 8.20A Altering explosive parameters can change the look of your destruction.

Tick through the simulation manually. The explosion blasts only a portion of the wall away this time. Cutting down the size, magnitude, and velocity of the blast limits the damage done and makes for a more interesting explosion, as witnessed in Figure 8.20b.

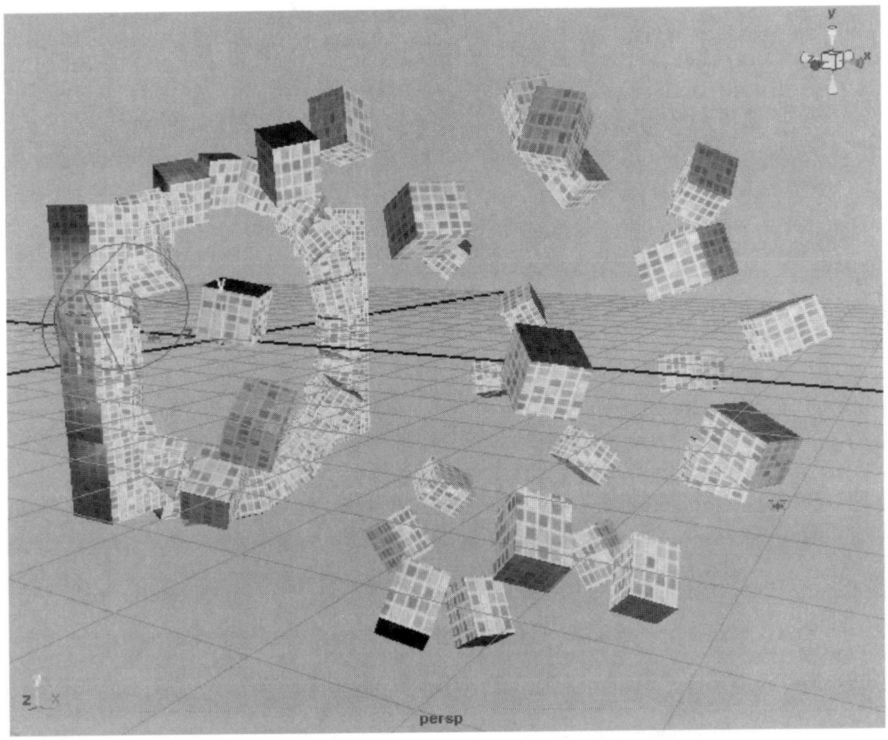

FIGURE 8.20B The blast pattern is now visibly different with the new parameter changes.

TCreating a Blast

Blast Code simulates a blast wave rather successfully. It is possible to craft a blast's energy to suit any situation. Once you get more sophisticated with Blast Code, it will be possible to graphically adjust the blast wave shape, noise, and other parameters. There are also provisions for toggling a shock wave event on or off. Blast and shock waves can readily be seen in the old atomic bomb footage of the 1950s.

Adjusting the Fracture Size U and Fracture Size V sliders under the Slabs tab of the BLayer1 attributes allows you to change the amount and size of the slabs (see Figure 8.21 and Figure 8.22).

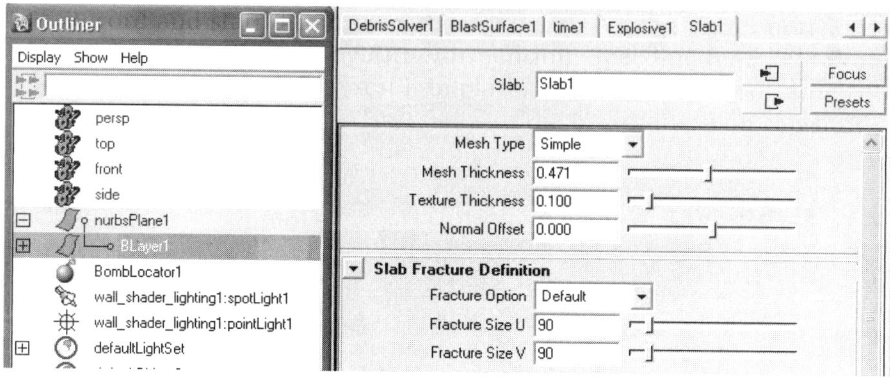

FIGURE 8.21 Altering slab thickness and fracture size changes the look of the blast debris.

FIGURE 8.22 Slab shrapnel becomes smaller and more plentiful by adjusting Fracture Size.

ON THE DVD

We encourage you to play with these parameters to get a feel for what is possible. Try moving the bomb to different positions and adjusting blast parameters. You may also want to try animating the position of the bomb over time to get even more interesting results. Save your work. The scene to this point has been saved as bomb_burst4.mb, which can be found on the companion DVD in the Chapter 8 folder.

Blast Code is capable of more than explosions. It's also able to produce far more realistic effects. Let's take a look at how we can add a new level of realism and open up all kinds of interesting new possibilities.

Creating Cracks

ON THE DVD

In a real-world situation, walls are not made of individually indestructible blocks. It can get old quickly when everything explodes into nice, even, and uniform bricks. Blast Code has some remarkable ways of roughing up those virtual explosions. Load the scene bomb_burst5.mb, which can be found on the companion DVD-ROM in the Chapter 8 folder. Select BLayer1 in the Outliner window. In the Attributes window choose the Slab1 tab. We are going to change a few parameters in the Slab Fracture Definition section. Change the default Fracture Option to Fracture Map. Since Fracture Map has been selected, we must provide Blast Code with a map. In the Fracture Map parameter, select the default procedural mountain texture. See Figures 8.23 and 8.24 for reference.

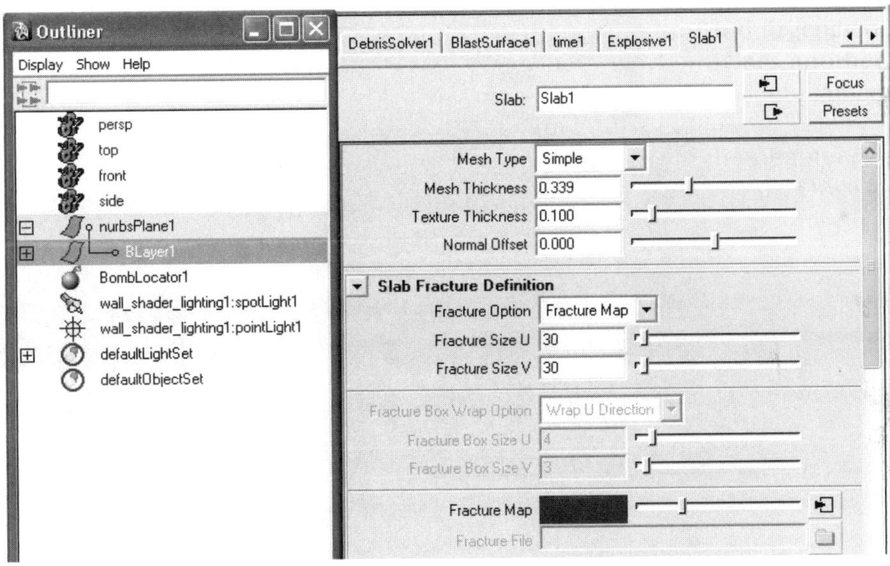

FIGURE 8.23 Selecting a Fracture Map yields much more realistic debris.

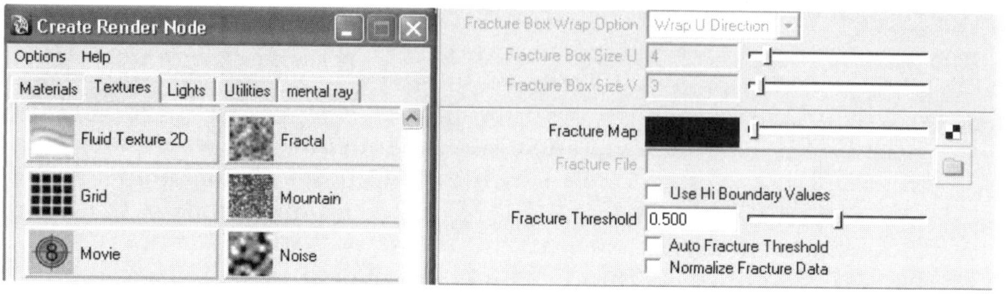

FIGURE 8.24 Assigning the standard Maya Mountain procedural texture creates great cracks.

Tick through the simulation now. You will see that our blocky rubble has had a much needed reality upgrade. At frame 5 the wall should look similar to Figure 8.25.

FIGURE 8.25 The Mountain texture as Fracture Map does a better job of making jagged debris.

The Fracture map can get a boost from an adjustment of the Fracture Size U and Fracture Size V sliders under the Slabs tab of the BLayer1 attributes. These sliders allow you to change the amount and size of the slabs (see Figure 8.26 and Figure 8.27).

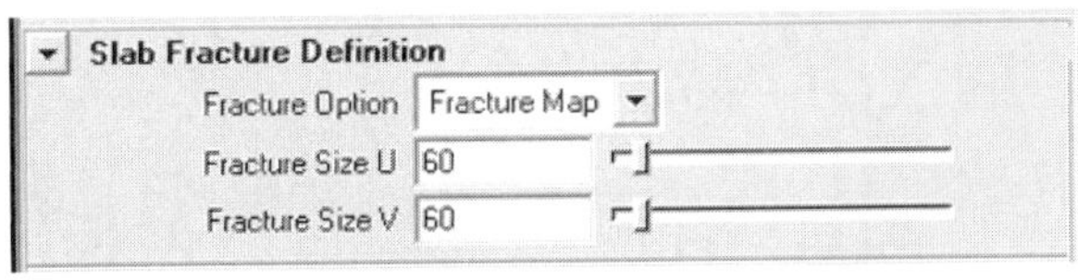

FIGURE 8.26 Altering slab thickness and fracture size changes the look of the blast debris.

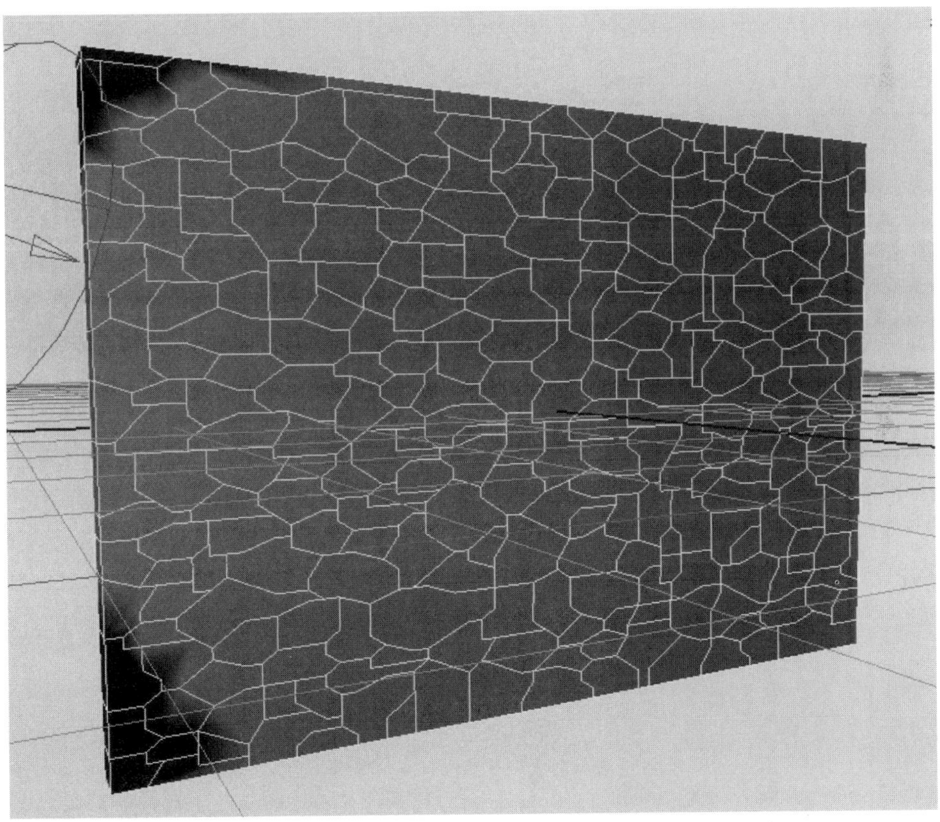

FIGURE 8.27 Slab pieces become smaller and more plentiful by adjusting fracture size.

Another fracture option is available that allows the use of a hand-drawn or otherwise generated fracture file that carves your damaged debris in the shape of the map. We have found a 1024 × 1024 pixel black and white 8 bit GIF to work remarkably well. Figure 8.28 and Figure 8.29 show a hand-drawn Photoshop logo and the resultant rendered frame.

FIGURE 8.28 A Photoshop 8 bit GIF used as a fracture file.

FIGURE 8.29 A rendered frame of the animation using logo_cracks.gif as a fracture file.

ON THE DVD

Save your work. The binary for Figure 8.27 and Maya binaries for Figure 8.29 and other creative examples using fracture files are located on the companion DVD-ROM in the Chapter 8 folder. These include red_bricks.mb and puzzle.mb and touch on some interesting concepts worth further investigation.

ON THE DVD

Another interesting effect that can be achieved with crack files and maps is the growing of cracks over time. Load the scene file growing_cracks.mb located on the companion DVD in the Chapter 8 folder. This file uses a textured map plane as a control surface. The slabs should have a standard hand-drawn crack map applied to them. This file can be found on the DVD as cracks.gif and can be directed to the Slabs tab of the BLayer1 node. Notice that the Fracture Option is set to File and can be seen in Figure 8.30a.

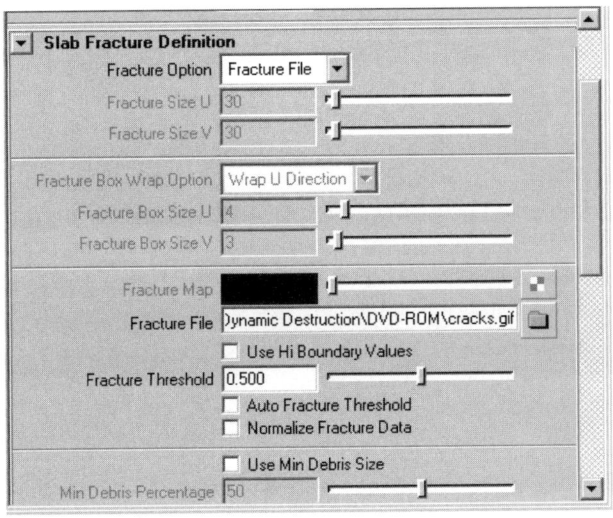

FIGURE 8.30A The Fracture Option is set to file and is directed to the hand-drawn file cracks.gif on the DVD-ROM.

This is the standard explosion scenario we have been using to this point. When loaded and toggled to frame 15, the scene should look like Figure 8.30b.

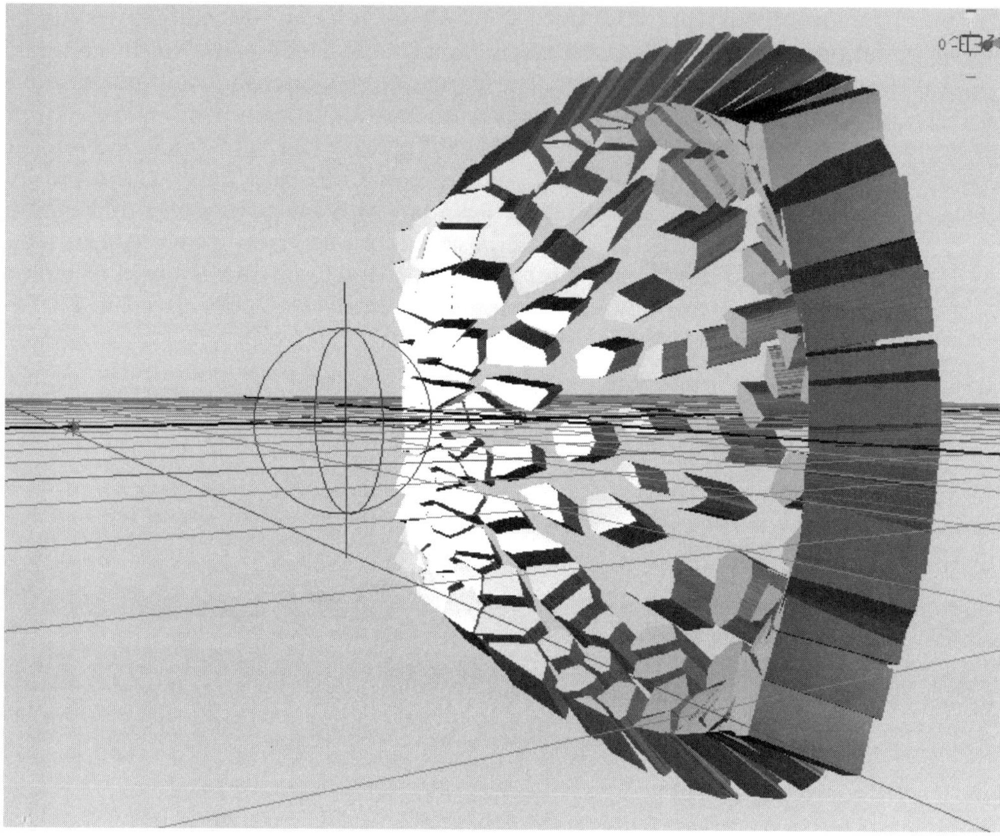

FIGURE 8.30B Scene file growing_cracks.mb at frame 15.

A particularly cool effect is to have a surface crack over time without it actually exploding to pieces. The cracks emanate from a center point and grow ever wider. This is a fairly easy procedure. Select the BLayer1 node in the Outline window. Under the Slab1 tab, two changes need to be made in the Simple Mesh section. Change the attributes as shown in Figure 8.31.

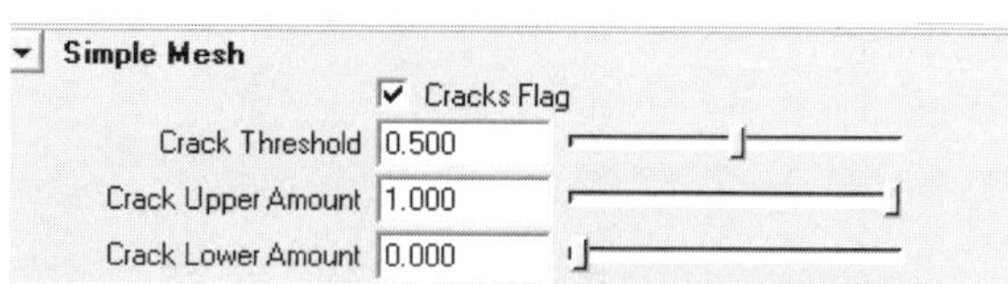

FIGURE 8.31 The Cracks Flag toggled on and Crack Upper Amount set to 1.0.

The next thing we must do is change the way the Explosive1 node affects the wall. Follow the changes made to the scene file in Figure 8.32 under the Explosive1 tab. Notice that the Deform Flag is toggled off and the Cracks Flag is toggled on. Additionally, among the Magnitude, Size, and Velocity parameters being tuned, the Blast Wave graph has been altered. Give yourself 100 to 200 frames in the Timeslider and run the simulation. Change all these parameters as shown.

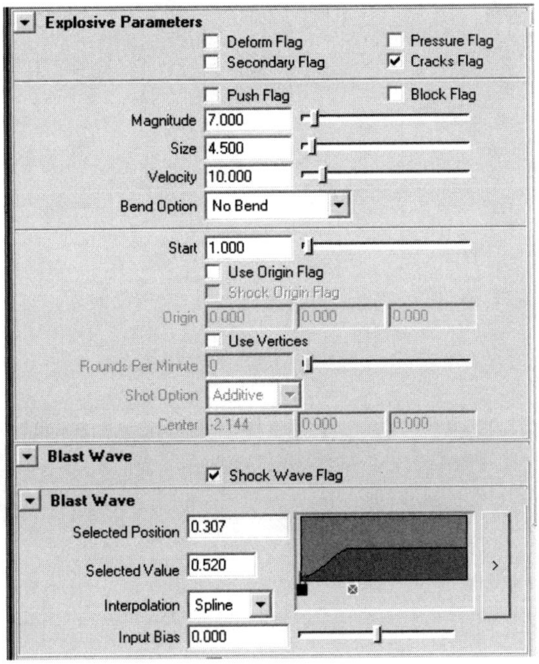

FIGURE 8.32 Multiple changes to the scene under the Explosive1 tab result in cracking.

Notice that the slabs are no longer deformed by the explosion. The cracking emanates from the central location and grows from that point outward. Figure 8.33 shows a rendered frame of the ice cracks heading from the center toward the outer edges of the slab ice wall.

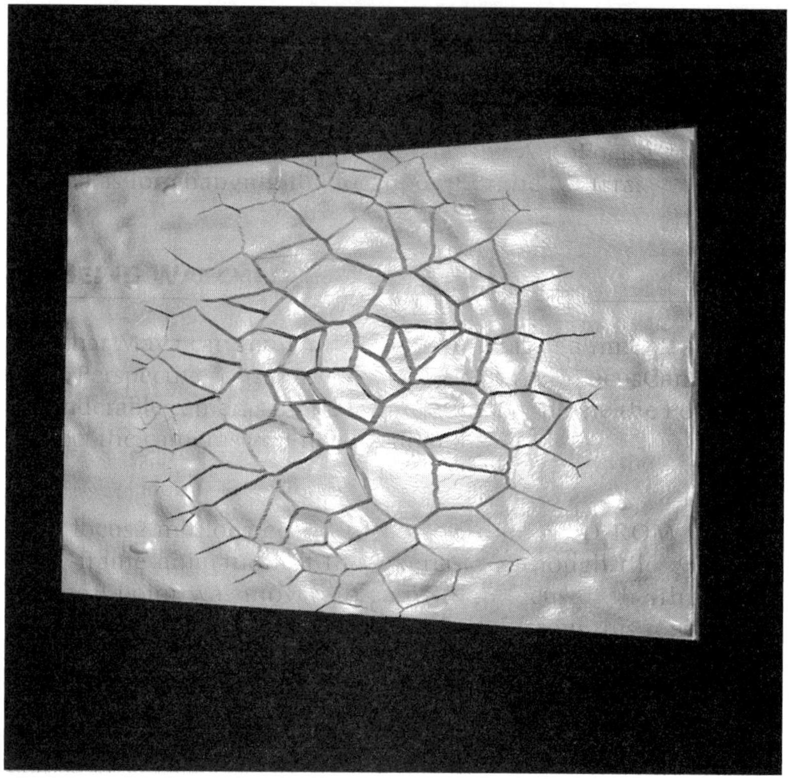

FIGURE 8.33 Rendered frame of creeping cracks in motion.

ON THE DVD

Save your scene. This completed scene file creeping_cracks2.mb can be found on the companion DVD-ROM in the Chapter 8 folder. For further study and investigation, we have also included a scene file called lava_flow3.mb and rendered QuickTime movie lava_flow3.mov that expands on the creeping cracks lesson.

COLLISION, GRAVITY, AND SECONDARY DEBRIS

ON THE DVD

The next step in the quest for a little more realism is to add some dynamic forces and create some secondary debris. Load the aforementioned red_bricks.mb scene file located on the companion DVD in the Chapter 8 folder. We will start with this as the basis for adding our forces. If you tick through the simulation, you will see what has now become our standard wall explosion. The bricks are thrust as individuals by the explosive force. They will continue on their paths indefinitely. Let's start by adding a ground plane to the scene. Create a polygon plane with the parameters listed in Figure 8.34a. Shade it any way you like. This will serve as a landing place for our bricks. Both brick wall and ground plane can be seen in Figure 8.34b.

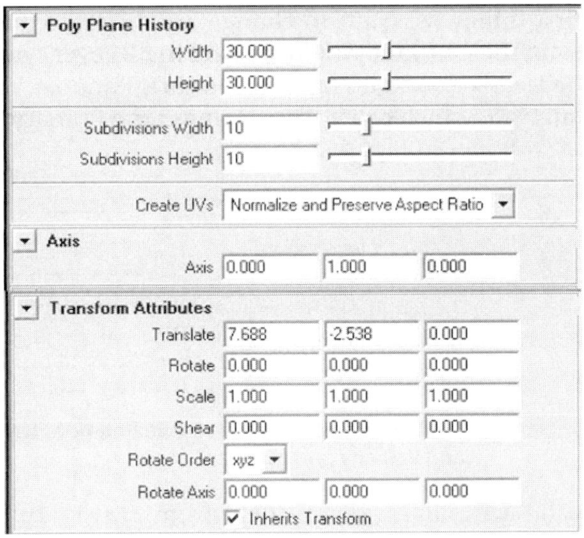

FIGURE 8.34A The plane will act as a collision obstacle for the exploding bricks. The new impact plane should have a position and dimensions similar to these.

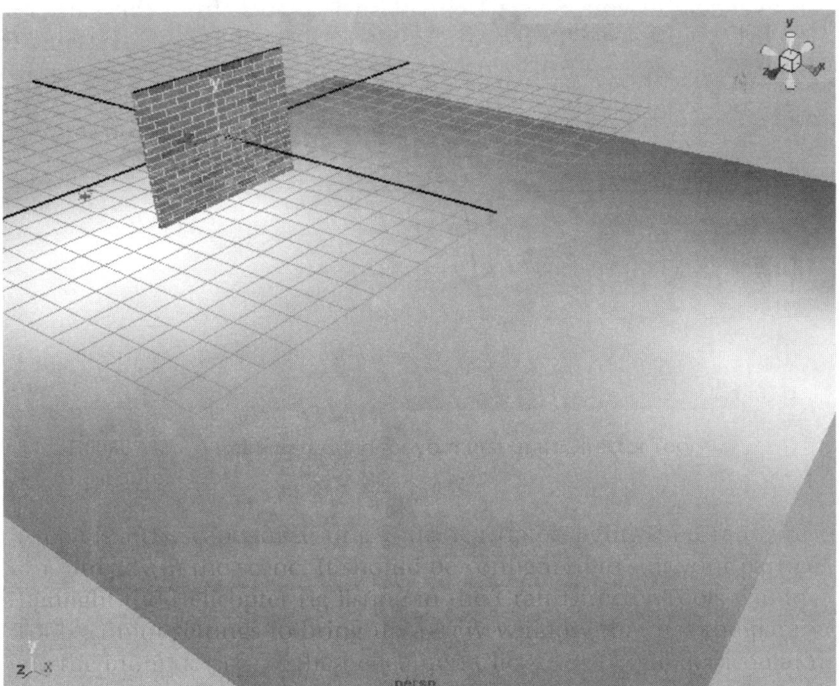

FIGURE 8.34B Brick wall and ground plane positioned for best view of impending explosion.

The first things we want to change are the trajectory, velocity, and rotation of our bricks. In the Outliner window select the BLayer1 node. In the Attributes Editor change the Debris Random Trajectory, Debris Random Velocity, and Debris Random Rotation all to .5, which can be found under the Primary Debris Attributes under the Slab1 tab, as shown in Figure 8.35.

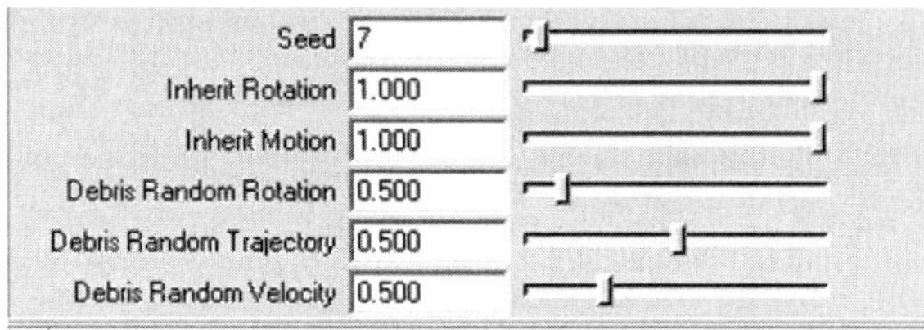

FIGURE 8.35 Setting for random Rotation, Trajectory, and Velocity parameters.

Let's add a standard gravity field from Maya's Dynamics menu, by selecting Fields > Gravity. Make sure that everything is unselected, since you don't want to attach it to anything specific yet. With this complete, open up the Blast window as before. Under the Particle tab are individual lists of the particles, collisions, and fields in the scene. Clicking on Update List ensures that the current list of scene elements is available to you. Select DebrisParticleShape1 from the Particles list and gravityField1 from the Fields list, as shown in Figure 8.36. Click the Attach Field button. The Bricks are now affected by the gravity field. Next we must tell Maya that a collision will occur between the bricks and the ground plane. Select the recently created polygon plane and click the New Collision button under the Particle tab, also shown in Figure 8.36.

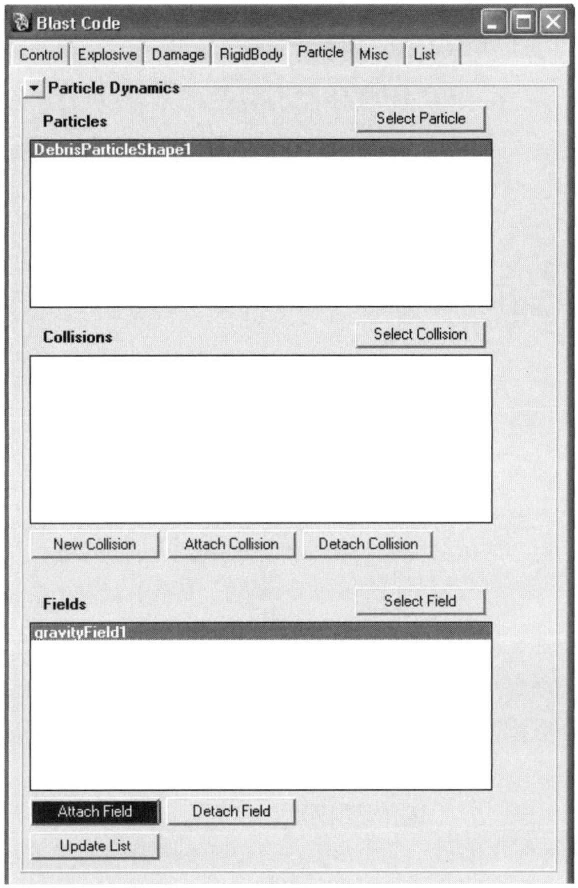

FIGURE 8.36 Attaching the gravity field to the bricks.

UPDATE OFTEN

When entering the various tabs under the Blast window in Blast Code, it is always a good idea to click the Update List or Update Attribute button if they are available. The various lists of elements that Blast Code is keeping track of does not refresh in real time, so it's a good habit to adopt to click these buttons upon entering a tab.

The plane is now listed as a particle collider and shows up in the Collisions list as pPlaneShape1. Select DebrisParticleShape1 from the Particles list and pPlaneShape1 from the Collisions List. Click the Attach Collision button (see Figure 8.37a). The bricks and ground plane now interact with each other.

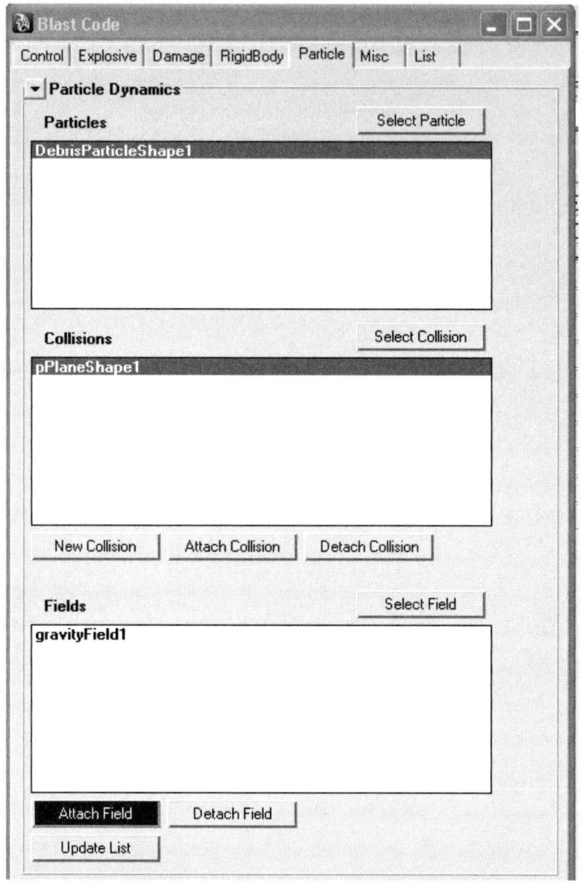

FIGURE 8.37A Assigning the collision of the bricks to the ground plane.

ON THE DVD

Save the scene. The scene file up to this point is located on the companion DVD-ROM in the Chapter 8 folder. It is called gravity_bricks.mb. Run the simulation. You may want to give yourself plenty of frames to have it play out. The results are devastating and a little unclear, but you can see in Figure 8.37b that some of the bricks are now landing on the ground plane.

FIGURE 8.37B Running the simulation shows that the bricks are now colliding with the ground plane.

A few adjustments will make for a better-looking animation. Select the BLayer1 node in the Outliner window. In the Attributes menu under the Explosive tab set the Magnitude, Size, and Velocity parameters to those shown in Figure 8.38. Let's also move the position of the explosive force. Under the BombLocator1 tab, set the position parameters to those of Figure 8.39. Running the simulation should have a much more effective result and should look similar to Figure 8.40.

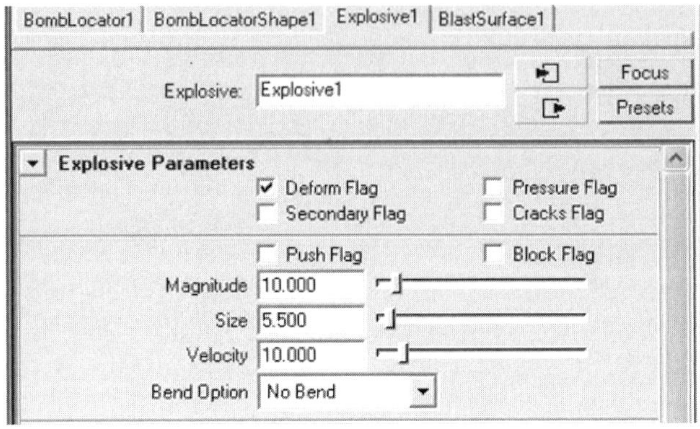

FIGURE 8.38 Adjusting the explosive's Magnitude, Size, and Velocity.

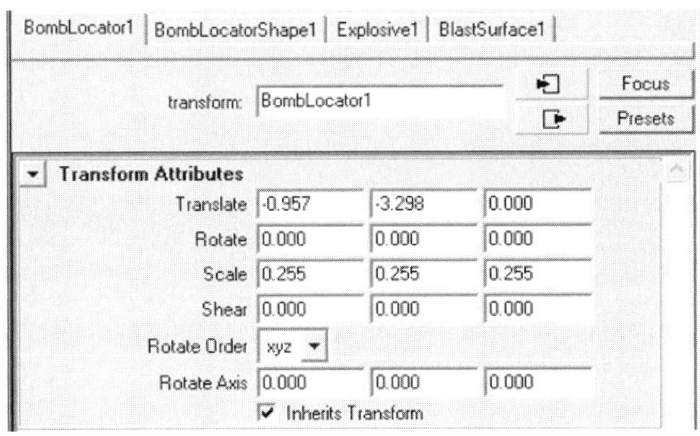

FIGURE 8.39 Repositioning the explosive for a more skyward thrust.

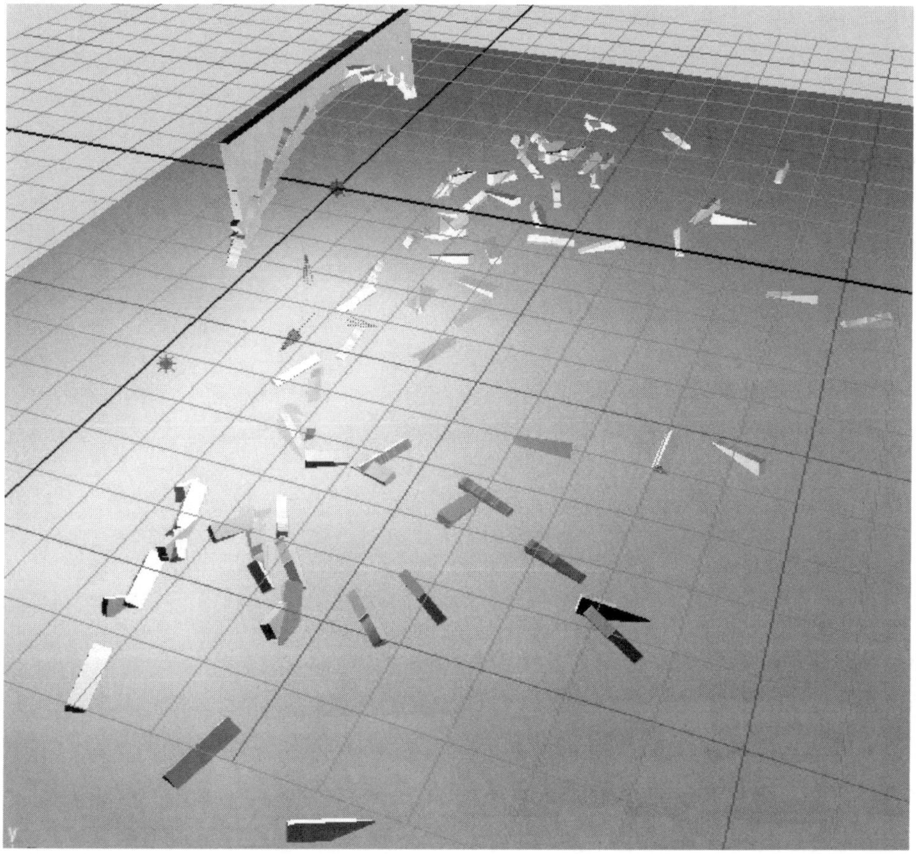

FIGURE 8.40 With the adjustments, the ground plane collides more successfully with the bricks.

ON THE DVD

If you had any trouble following to this point, this scene file is saved as gravity_bricks2.mb on the DVD in the Chapter 8 folder. One final interesting step will round off this little simulation nicely. Blast Code can generate what is called *secondary debris*. This is quite easy to do and really adds that much-needed second layer of flying fragments. Select the BLayer1 node in the Outliner window and go to the Attributes window. Under the Slab1 tab is a section called Secondary Debris Attributes. Set the attributes as shown in Figure 8.41. Don't forget to toggle the Secondary Flag on.

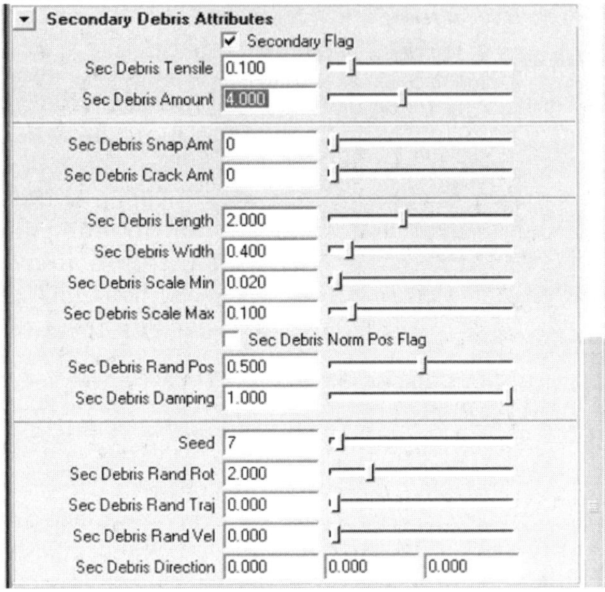

FIGURE 8.41 The Secondary Flag on and attributes set as the first step toward added realism.

With that accomplished, let's turn our attention to the Explosive1 tab in the Attributes window. The Secondary Flag must be selected here as well. This is shown in Figure 8.42.

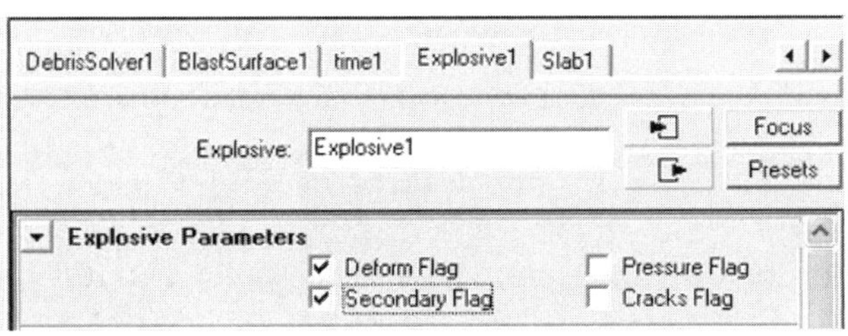

FIGURE 8.42 The Secondary Flag toggled on under the Explosive1 tab.

Set the Timeslider to about 120 frames and run the simulation. Stop it at around frame 40. You will notice that secondary debris has indeed been generated. It is new geometry in the scene and currently has no shader associated with it. Drag and drop the red brick shader, associated with the rest of the wall, on it as well. Rewind the simulation to the beginning and rerun it. Set the Timeslider to 200 frames. Also, select the ground plane and toggle it invisible. It won't affect the collisions, but it will make the fragments easier to see. Run the simulation to frame 120. Figure 8.43 shows the secondary debris animation at frame 120.

FIGURE 8.43 With the ground plane made invisible, you can clearly see the advantage to using secondary debris for creating added realism.

ON THE DVD

A rendered QuickTime movie located on the companion DVD-ROM in the Chapter 8 folder is entitled secondary_debris.mov. If you run the movie, you will notice the secondary debris. It adds quite a bit to the overall scene. There is a problem, however. About two seconds into the animation, the bricks are adjusting to their final resting place. The secondary debris continues to pour continuously for the duration. This can be alleviated by animating the Secondary Debris Amount attribute, as shown in Figure 8.41. Bringing the secondary debris amount to zero between frame 30 and 60 will eliminate the problem as the generation of secondary debris tapers off to nothing. Run the simulation to frame 120. Figure 8.44 shows the secondary debris animation at frame 120.

FIGURE 8.44 The secondary debris now has a limited lifespan and new debris is no longer generated.

ON THE DVD

The rendered QuickTime movie located on the companion DVD in the Chapter 8 folder is entitled secondary_debris2.mov. If you run this movie, you will notice that the secondary debris now stops at a more realistic time. It does not continue to flow long after the blast wave has past.

ON THE DVD

The power of Blast Code's Kiloton and Megaton are waiting to be tapped. We have barely scratched the surface of what they can do. Blast Code provides a logical workflow to carry out complex destruction scenarios with relative ease. This software could easily be the focus of a specialty career. Check the companion DVD in the Chapter 8 folder for some additional scenes and textures for further investigation. There are other visual effects arenas to investigate, however. Let's move on to the next chapter.

CHAPTER

9 MISCELLANEOUS TOOLS

In This Chapter

- Introduction
- Wire
- SmartDuplicate
- Stitching with Seamour

This leather Maya ball assembled with five-sided patches displays a variety of stitching examples created with Seamour.
Image courtesy of Matthias F. Richter (ticket01.com)

INTRODUCTION

This is a fun chapter because it covers some plugins that are harder to put into a collective group. They might be considered modeling or organizational or even animation. They certainly fit a small but interesting niche, and if the need arises can cut down production time. These plugins come from commercial software companies, and while some are minimally priced, some of these plugins are free.

WIRE

Ticket01 is an interesting company, in that they have managed to be successful by producing fun but helpful plugins. A few of their plugins have made it into the miscellaneous category, and we will cover them here. Wire is a potent tool for creating wires along curves. This tool can be used creatively to produce thick cables, thin wires, ropes, and the crazy abstractness that can only come from the imagination. Part of Wire's power lies within its ease of use. Let's create some wire-like forms.

Installing Wire is simple. Executing the installer program is easy and is no fuss. After installation, make sure the plugin is loaded and recognized by Maya. This can be done by going to the top of the screen in the Maya menu and selecting Window > Setting/Preferences > Plug-in Manager. Make sure that both the Loaded and Auto load boxes are selected next to the Wire.mll as seen in Figure 9.1. Wire works by creating objects based on one or two arbitrary curves that you draw for it. This is cool because it makes guiding a wire or rope model less tedious.

ON THE DVD

Let's start by drawing a single simple curve in the Y direction. Your curve can be quite curvy if you like. Figure 9.2 shows what your curve might look like. Alternatively, you can load the wire_1.mb scene on the companion DVD in the Chapter 9 folder and follow along.

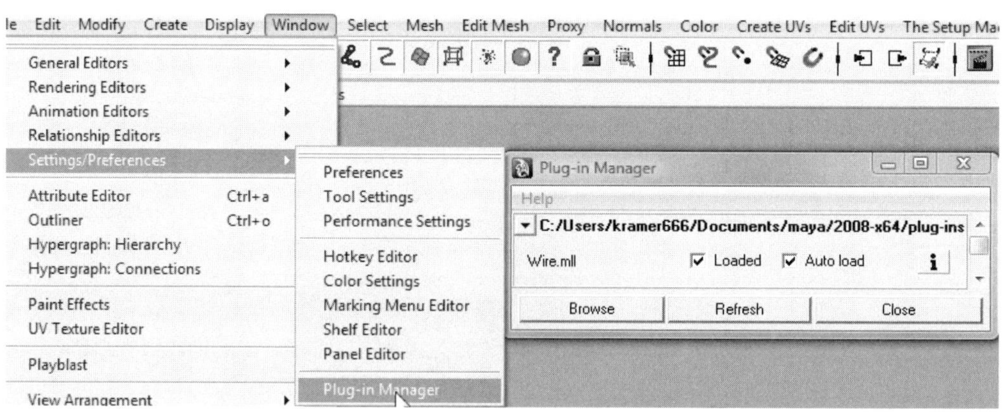

FIGURE 9.1 Selection of the Plug-in Manager and listing of the Wire plugin.

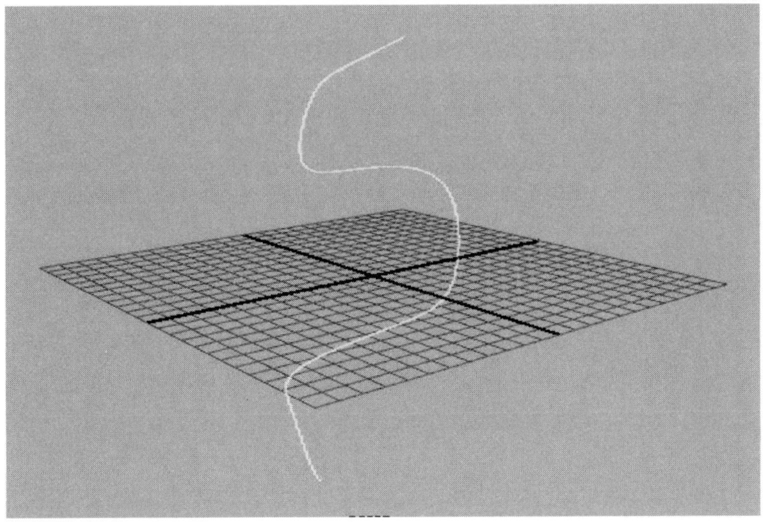

FIGURE 9.2 The guide curve used by Wire.

If the plugin has been loaded correctly, there will be a Ticket menu with the Maya menus. With the curve highlighted, select Ticket > Wire > Create Wire. This creates the actual wire curve based on the highlighted curve. It should look similar to Figure 9.3.

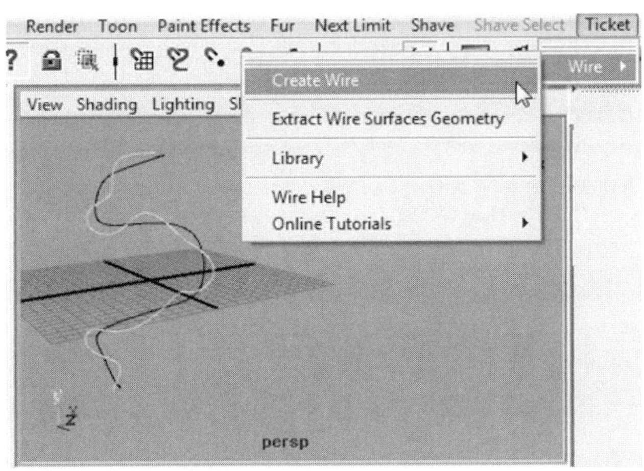

FIGURE 9.3 The wire curve formed from the user-created curve.

From this wire, we can begin to fashion the geometry that will make up the wire model. Select the wireNode1 node from the Outliner window and bring up the Attribute Editor. Figure 9.4 shows the Wire tab in the Attribute Editor of wireNode1. Defining a wire model is very intuitive and interactive.

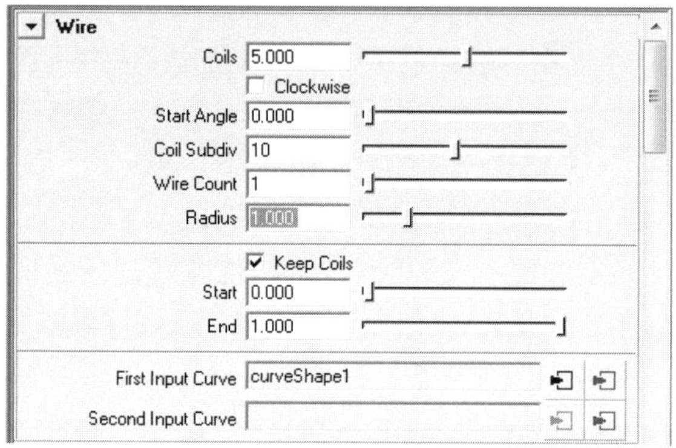

FIGURE 9.4 The wireNode1 Attribute Editor is used to define the wire.

It is easy to see changes made to the curve when you alter the parameters. If you test the slider gadgets, you can see how the wire will start to take shape. The following parameters are most notable.

- **Coils:** The number of times the wire wraps around the guide curve
- **Coil Subdiv:** Sets the number of segments per coil
- **Wire Count:** The total number of entwined wires that will make the final model
- **Radius:** Sets the radius of the coils or how tightly they wrap around the guide curve
- **First Input Curve:** The guide curve
- **Second Input Curve:** An optional secondary curve that can be used to define the wire

When you're finished, set the Wire parameters back to those shown in Figure 9.4. We now need to create a profile curve to extrude along the wire path we have created, using the following steps.

1. At the top of the screen, in the Maya menus, select Create > NURBS Primitives > Circle.
   The circle should have a Radius of 1.0 with 8 sections. This circle will be extruded to create our wire surface.
2. Open the wireNode1 Attribute Editor and find the Wire Extrusion tab shown in Figure 9.5.

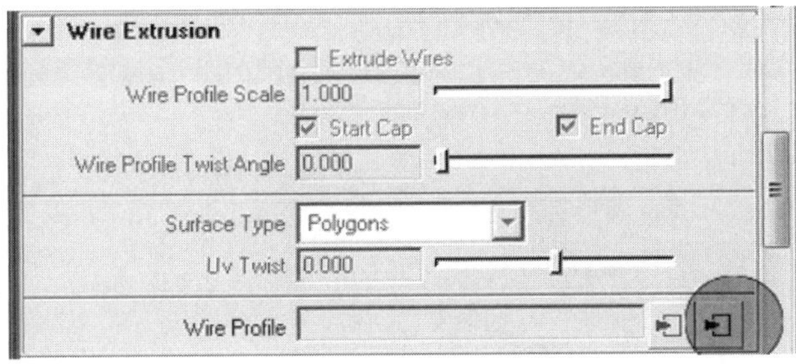

FIGURE 9.5 The Wire Extrusion tab in the Attribute Editor. Note the Wire Profile selection tab.

3. Click on the Browsing Selection box, as shown in Figure 9.5, and then immediately select the nurbsCircle1 node. The wireNode1 curve should turn pink when the nurbsCircle1 is selected.
4. Select the wireNode1 in the Outliner window and click on the Extrude Wires box in the Wire Extrusion window. Your freshly created wire geometry should look similar to Figure 9.6.

The Composition of a Wire

The wire geometry created can be made of polygons, combined polygons, NURBS, or subdivision surfaces. There is also an option to cap either end or both ends of the geometry created.

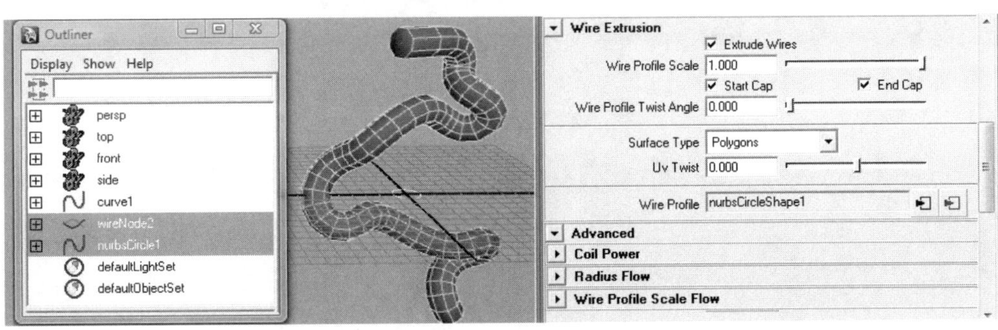

FIGURE 9.6 The Wire Extrusion tab and the wire geometry created by extruding nurbsCircle1.

What we have now is more of a tube than a wire. A few adjustments in the Attribute Editor will change that significantly. Follow these steps to get a more wire-like object.

1. With wireNode1 selected, go to the Wire tab in the Attribute Editor. Change the wire count to eight. There are now eight wires, but the geometry intersects sloppily, as shown in Figure 9.7.

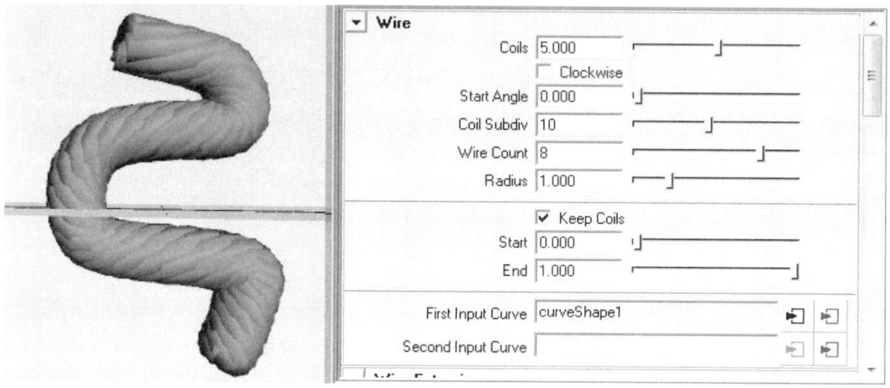

FIGURE 9.7 The addition of more wires makes the wire look more like a fat bulbous worm.

2. This can be changed by going to the Wire Extrusion tab of the wireNode1 Attribute Editor and changing the Wire Profile Scale. This is the NURBS circle we used to extrude into the wire. Changing this value to 0.275 yields a much more appealing eight-strand wire, as shown in Figure 9.8.

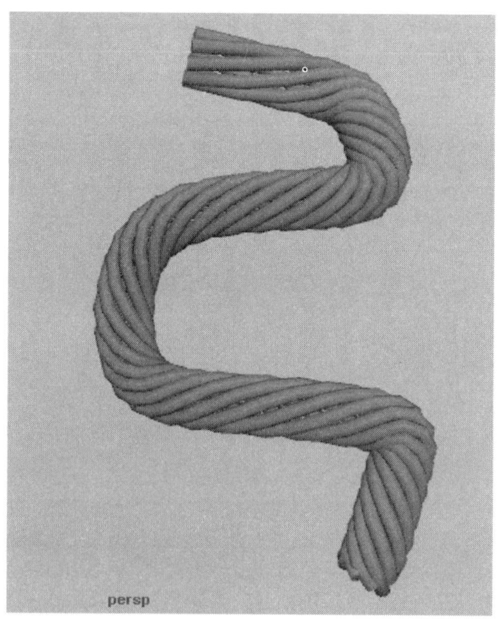

FIGURE 9.8 The wire model now looks more like a wire with eight strands.

3. Our model is shaping up, but the shape is a little kinked in spots. We can adjust the CVs of the original guide curve to give the wire a more attractive shape.
4. Select wireNode1 from the Outliner window and move to the Wire Extrusion tab. Toggle the Extrude Wires box off. This will make it easier to find and manipulate the CVs.
5. Select the curve1 guide wire in the Outliner window that was used to create the original wire. Press F9 to get into CV mode and manipulate the shape of the wire model to a more relaxed shape by moving the CVs of the guide curve, as shown in Figure 9.9.

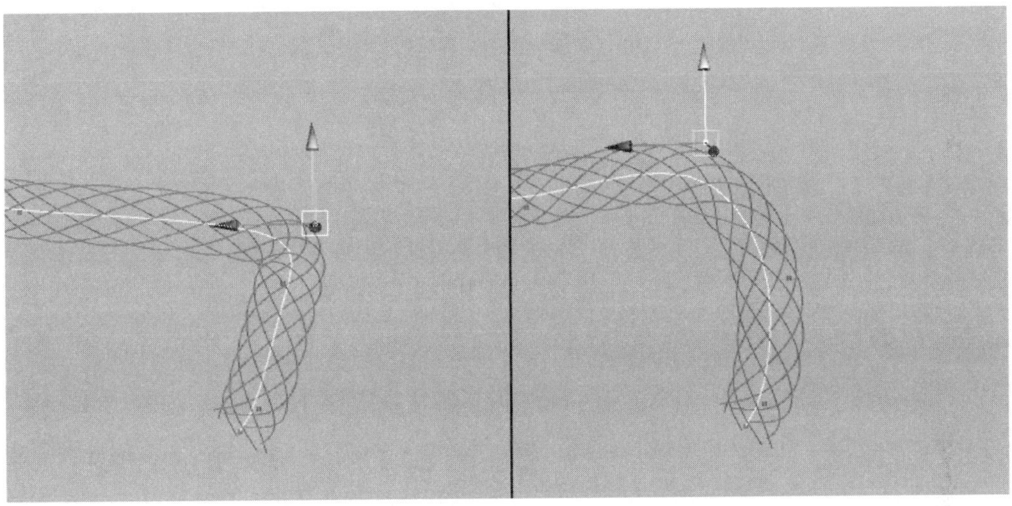

FIGURE 9.9 The guide curve CVs can alter the shape of the wire model with construction history.

6. Finally, for rendering purposes, the wire is a little blocky. The tessellation can be bumped up by changing the Coil Subdiv of wireNode1 in the Attribute Editor under the Wire tab. Changing the Coil Subdiv value to 30 produces a much smoother model, as shown in Figure 9.10.

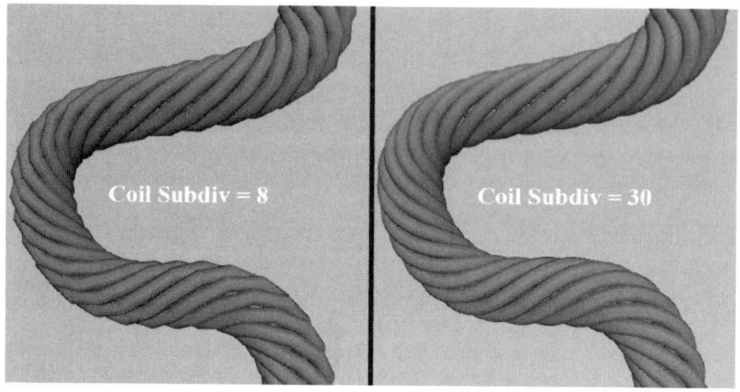

FIGURE 9.10 Higher Coil Subdiv values result in a smoother, more tessellated model.

ON THE DVD

You can get a much better perspective of the plugin by going back to the Wire tab in the Attribute window and toying with the slider gadgets again. Increasing the wire count, changing the radius, and adjusting the number of coils brings the interactive creation of a wire object into focus. Save your work. This scene, wire_2.mb, is on the companion DVD in the Chapter 9 folder.

ON THE DVD

Wires can be created across two guide curves instead of one. This can produce a more helix-like effect. Let's look at an example of this. Load wire_3 from the companion DVD in the Chapter 9 folder. Here we have two vertical curves and a circular profile curve. It is a similar procedure to making a wire with a single curve.

1. Select both vertical curves and create the wire by selecting Ticket > Wire > Create Wire, as shown in Figure 9.11.

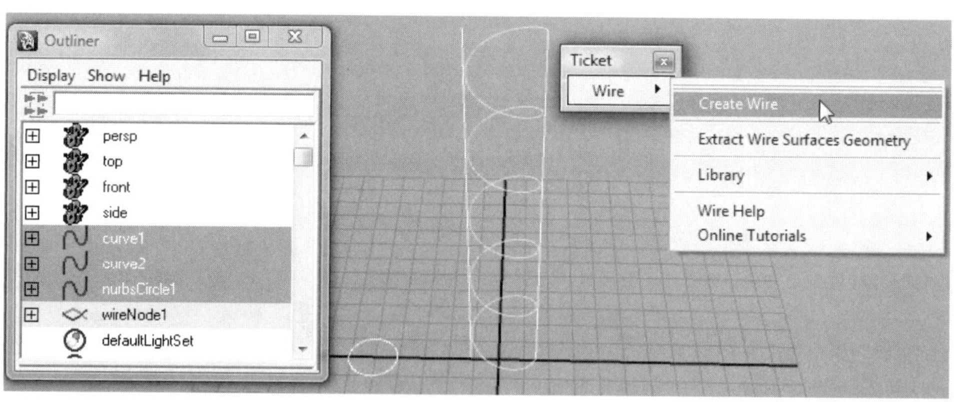

FIGURE 9.11 Two curves are used to generate the wire for this example.

2. Open the wireNode1 Attribute Editor and find the Wire Extrusion tab shown in Figure 9.5.

3. Click on the Browsing Selection box, as shown in Figure 9.5, and then select the nurbsCircle1 node. The wireNode1 curve should turn pink when you select nurbsCircle1.
4. Select wireNode1 in the Outliner window and click on the Extrude Wires box in the Wire Extrusion window. Your freshly created wire geometry should look similar to Figure 9.12.

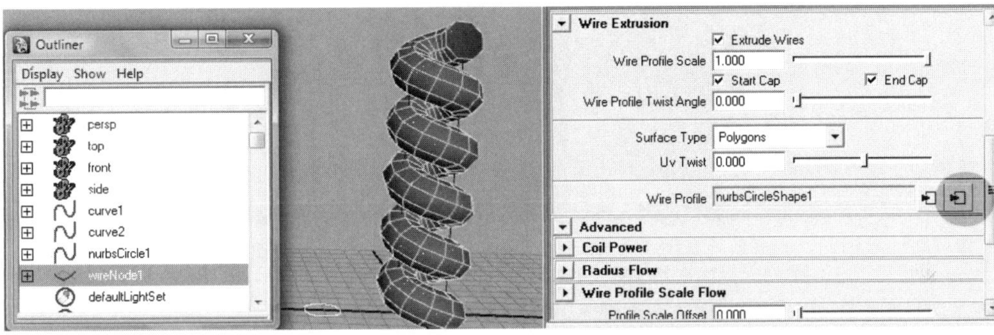

FIGURE 9.12 The circle profile produces a more spring- or helix-like shape using two guide curves.

CONSTRUCTION HISTORY, THE QUICKER FIXER-UPPER

Construction history can be very useful for getting the perfect model. Tweaking guide curve CVs or the profile curve CVs can have dramatic and helpful results. This is a very useful technique for fixing intersecting geometry but also aids in the creation of interesting freestyle shapes. Experimenting with oddly shaped profiles can bring surprising results.

Let's make a few more changes to the model and exploit some of the other features of the plugin.

1. Under the Wire Extrusion tab in the wireNode1 Attribute Editor, change the Surface Type to NURBS and change the Wire Profile Scale to 0.65. The model should now look like Figure 9.13.

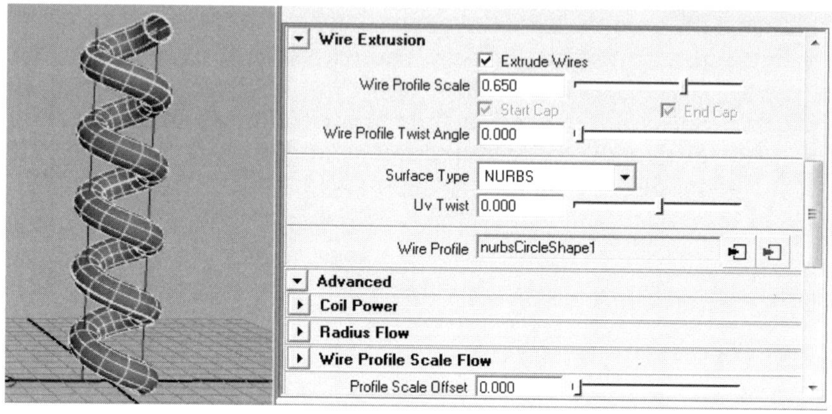

FIGURE 9.13 The smaller profile curve and change to the NURBS geometry.

2. Under the Wire Tab in the wireNode1 Attribute Editor, reduce the number of Coils to 2 and change the Wire Count to 3. The model should look like Figure 9.14.

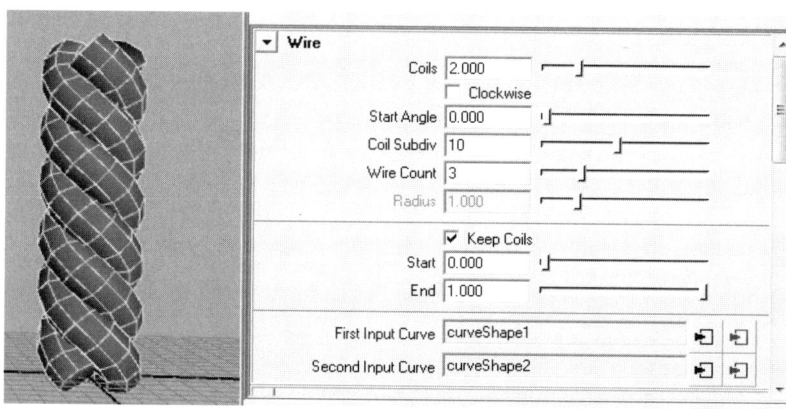

FIGURE 9.14 The Wire Count at 3 and the Coils at 2 make for a tighter, more crowded model.

3. There are myriad ways to alter the model. Select curve2 from the Outliner window and scale it in the X direction to 1.6. This is one of the original vertical guide curves.

4. Select the nurbsCircle1 curve from the Outliner window and rotate it 75 degrees on the X axis. This is the original profile curve. The model should now look like Figure 9.15.

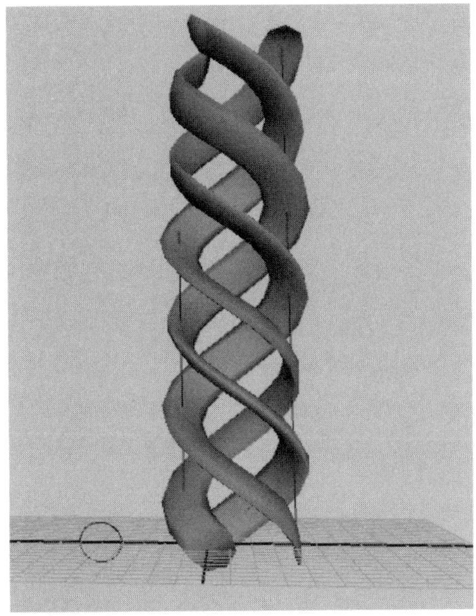

FIGURE 9.15 Using construction history can have a great influence on the final model.

5. Last, Wire Profile Scale Flow tab in the wireNode1 Attribute Editor allows you to change the scale of the profile curve over the length of the extrusion. Adding points to the curve can alter the scale for interesting effects. The simple scaling curve shown in Figure 9.16 yields a curvy pointed model.

ON THE DVD

Save your work. This scene can be found on the companion DVD in the Chapter 9 folder, as wire_4.mb, along with some bonus scenes.

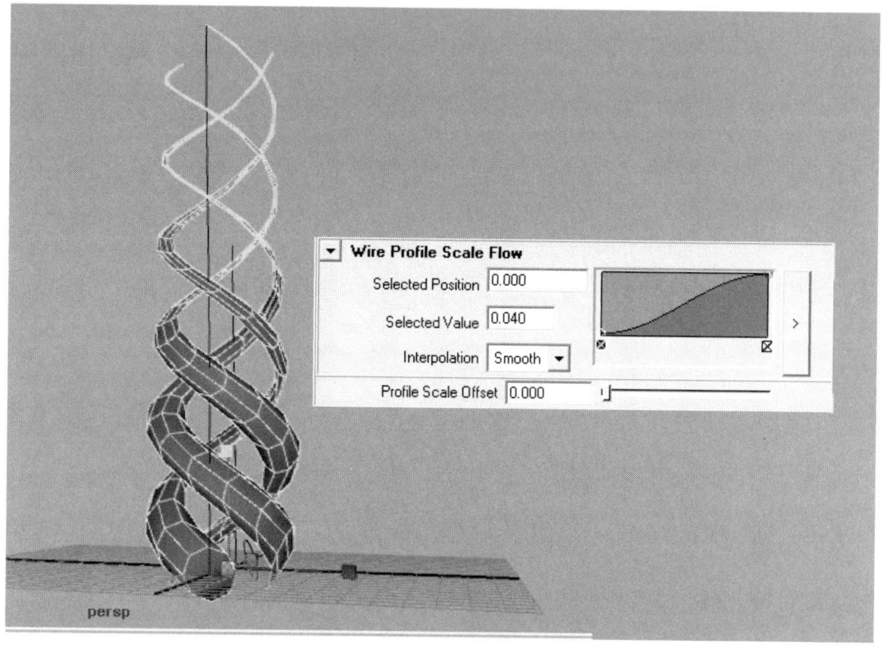

FIGURE 9.16 Using Wire Profile Scale Flow can change the profile scale over the extrusion.

ON THE DVD

A directory on the companion DVD in the Chapter 9 folder, called Wire_Images, has a few images of experiments with Wire. Figure 9.17 is an example of some of that experimentation. This image was created by drawing a single curve in a pretzel or knot-shaped pattern. The CVs of this curve were then manipulated by hand to create overlapping and underlapping of the curve where it crossed over itself. This manipulation essentially created a knot from the curve, but it can be quite a challenge. The curve was duplicated and slightly raised above the original curve in the Y direction. A wire was created from the two curves and a NURBS circle. The curves were then manipulated again to account for the intersection of the freshly created wire model. Construction history ensures that the model moves with the curves. This is a great way to fine-tune the model for a better and more interesting shape. The model was then shaded and rendered in mental ray to look like some sort of pulled and twisted hard candy confection.

FIGURE 9.17 Experimental images like this can be found on the DVD-ROM.

This is a really fascinating plugin that can save time if you need wires, cables, ropes, or the odd abstractions. Ticket01 has another nifty program for duplication. Let's look at the SmartDuplicate plugin for Maya.

SmartDuplicate

SmartDuplicate addresses the multistep process that had been required in Maya for duplicating objects on a curve. This plugin provides a neatly functioning alternative to the tedious Maya work-around. Installing SmartDuplicate is easy. Executing the installer program is hassle free.

After installation, make sure the plugin is loaded and recognized by Maya. This can be done by going to the top of the screen in the Maya menus and selecting Window > Setting/Preferences > Plug-in Manager. Make sure that both the Loaded and Auto load boxes are selected next to the SmartDuplicate.mll. If the plugin installation was successful, there will be a menu called Ticket. Let's learn about SmartDuplicate.

ON THE DVD

It's extremely easy to duplicate objects along a curve and animate them. Load the duplicate_1.mb scene on the companion DVD in the Chapter 9 folder. This is your basic closed curve, built flat on the XZ plane. Follow these steps to create a quick beaded necklace.

1. Create a NURBS sphere with the dimensions shown in Figure 9.18.
2. Next, go to the Ticket menu at the top of the screen. Select Ticket > SmartDuplicate > SmartDuplicate.

3. Select the curve and press Enter on the keyboard.
4. Select the newly created sphere and press Enter on the keyboard. This should duplicate the sphere on the curve at the default number.

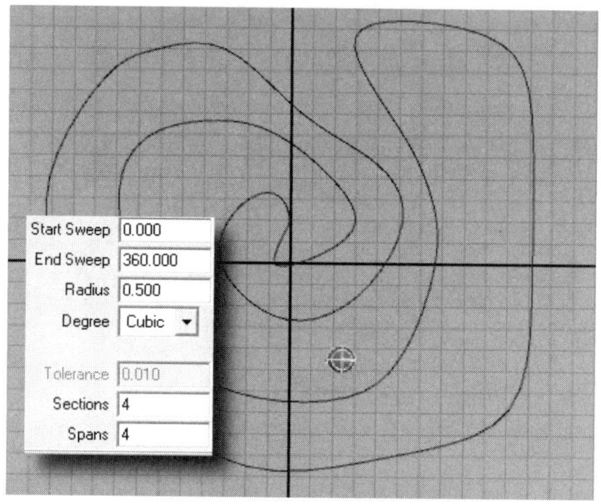

FIGURE 9.18 The loaded curve and the proper settings for the creation of a NURBS sphere.

5. These newly created spheres should be selected. If they are not, select them and go to the Attribute window. SmartDuplicate has created a node called smartDuplicate1, which includes the spheres. At the top of the Attribute window, each sphere in the node is listed separately. You have to click on the left arrow tab in the Attribute window to move to the smartDuplicate1 component. This is highlighted in Figure 9.19. Selecting the smartDuplicate1 attribute gives you access to the function of the SmartDuplicate plugin.

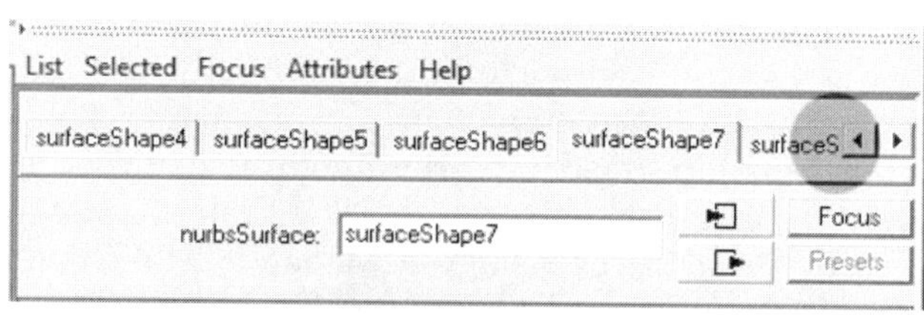

FIGURE 9.19 Clicking on the left arrow tab moves you over to the smartDuplicate1 component.

6. With the smartDuplicate1 component selected in the Attribute window, change the Duplicate attribute to 160. Wait. It may take a second or two, but a string of 160 spheres will be created along the curve, as shown in Figure 9.20.

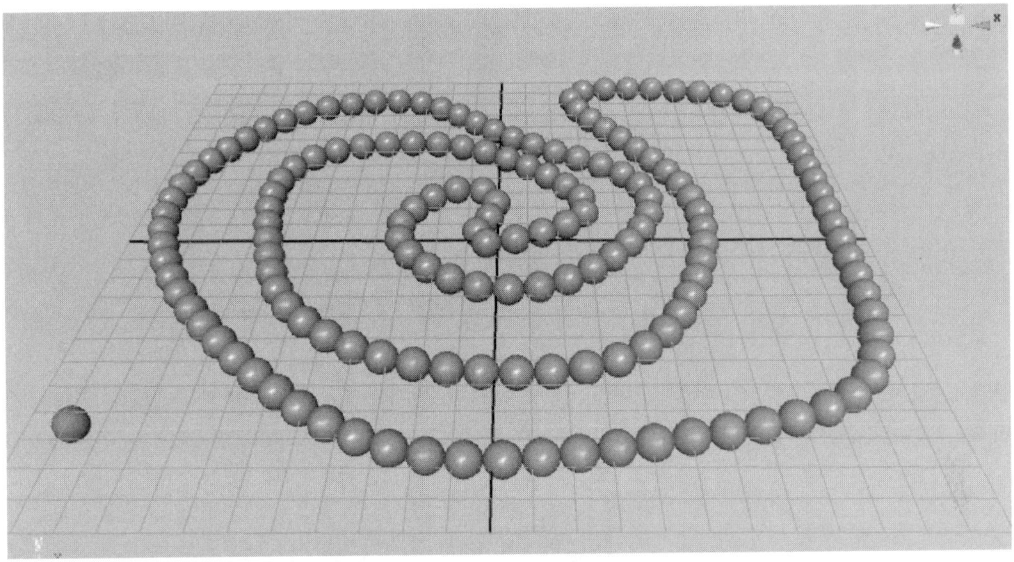

FIGURE 9.20 A string of 160 duplicate spheres evenly distributed on the curve like beads.

7. The start and end points for the dispersion of duplicates can be changed and animated. Change the Duplicates Start value to 40 and the Duplicates End to 120. This is shown in Figure 9.21.

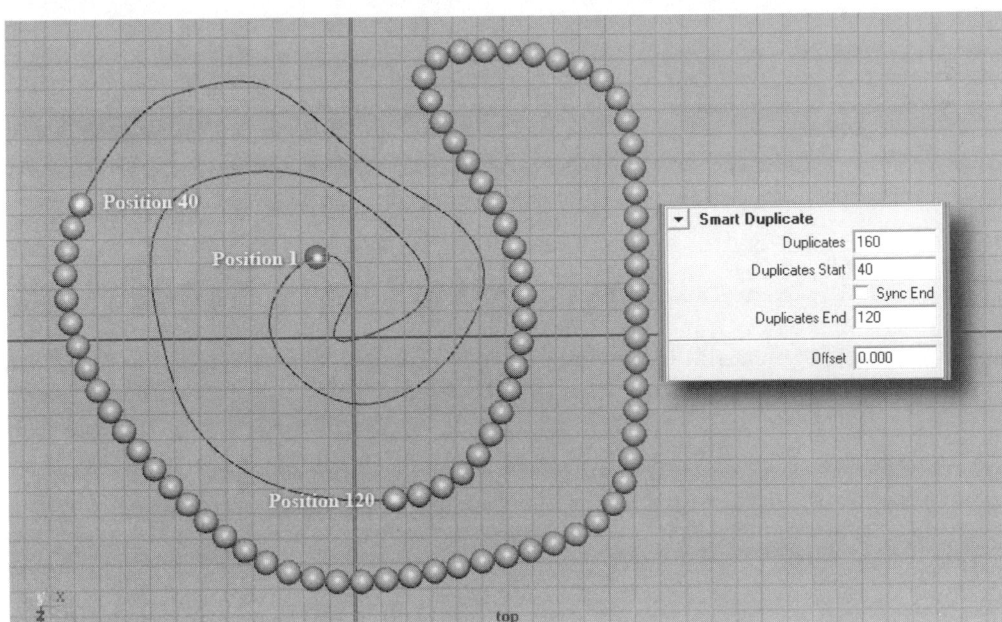

FIGURE 9.21 The start and end points of the dispersion of duplicates can be altered.

ON THE DVD

Most of the parameters of the smartDuplicate node can be animated. Save your work. This scene can be found on the companion DVD in the Chapter 9 folder as duplicate_2.mb.

ON THE DVD

Load duplicate 3 from the companion DVD as well. SmartDuplicate allows for the duplication of curves and animation, too. The scene has a single curve that spells out *Maya*, as shown in Figure 9.22. Notice that it also has a NURBS circle in the scene. We can duplicate that NURBS circle over the life of the *Maya* curve to create animated writing. Let's do that now.

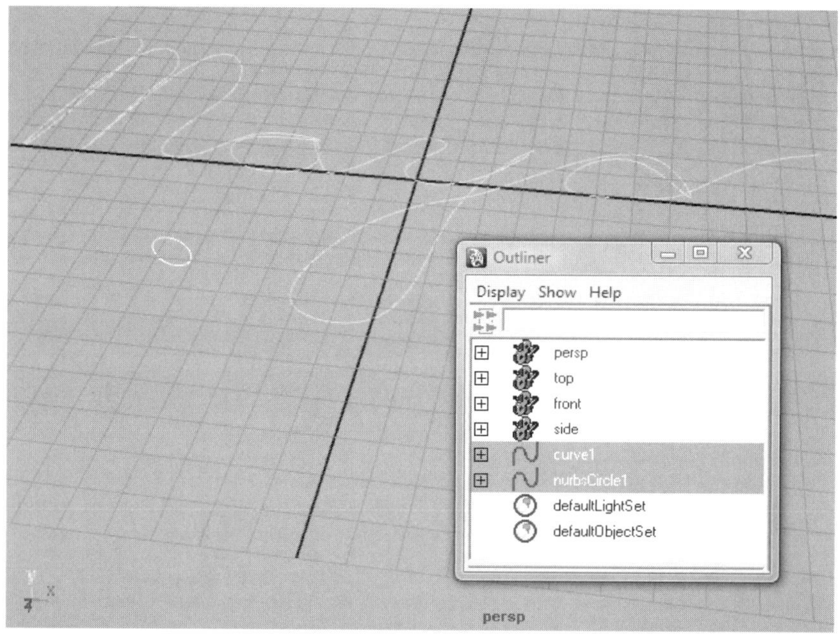

FIGURE 9.22 A curve spelling out Maya in script and a NURBS circle to duplicate across it.

1. In the Ticket menu, select Ticket > SmartDuplicate > SmartDuplicate.
2. Select the curve1 or *Maya* curve and press Enter on the keyboard.
3. Select the nurbsCircle1 node and press Enter on the keyboard. This should duplicate the sphere on the curve at the default value of 10.
4. We need to bump the number of duplicate NURBS circles up significantly. With the smartDuplicate1 component selected in the Attribute window, change the Duplicates attribute to 160. After a pause there will be 160 duplicate circles on the *Maya* curve dispersed evenly across its length. This is shown in Figure 9.23.

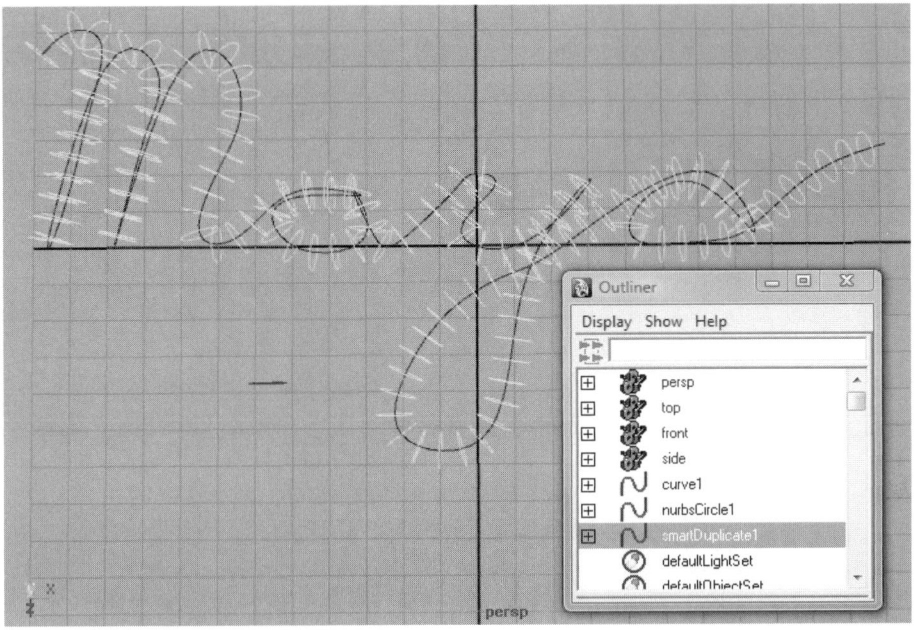

FIGURE 9.23 160 NURBS circle curves have been dispersed across the length of the *Maya* curve.

5. If the circles have not followed the path on the curve properly, make sure the Align to Guide box is checked. This can be found in the Attribute Editor of the smartDuplicate1 node. It is located in the Alignment tab.
6. With the smartDuplicate1 node selected, let's created a lofted surface over those 160 circles. Under the Surfaces menu, select Surfaces > Loft. The result should be similar to Figure 9.24. Notice the highlighted areas where the lofted surface is a little off.

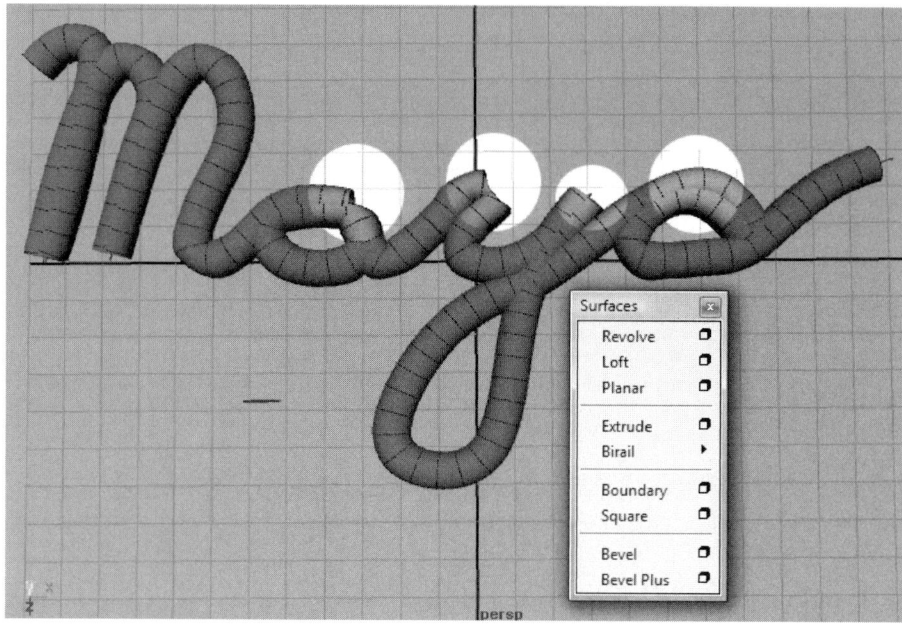

FIGURE 9.24 The lofted surface spells out *Maya*. Notice the highlighted geometry problems.

7. This can be corrected by adjusting the CVs of the guide curve. Select curve1 from the Outliner window and press the F9 key. This allows the edit of the CVs that make up this curve. By turning on X-Ray shading, it should be easier to select the more hidden CVs (see Figure 9.25).

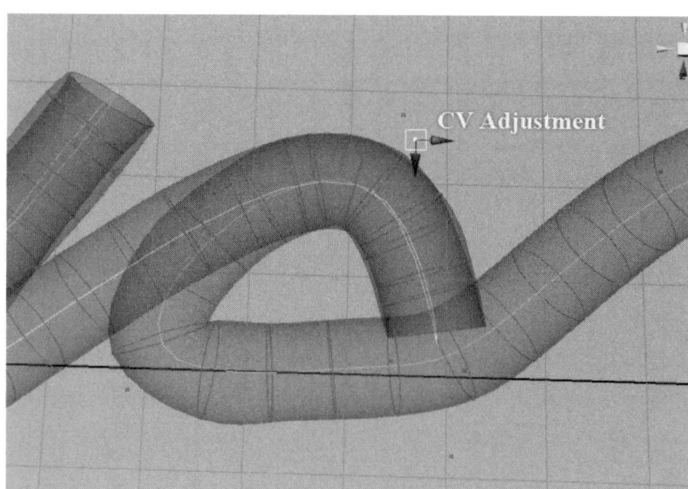

FIGURE 9.25 Adjustment of the guide curve CVs can usually tweak a better surface result.

8. We can animate a write-on by adjusting the Offset, located in the Smart Duplicate tab of the Attribute window. Animating a value from −1.0 to 0.0 over time creates the animated write-on from start to finish (see Figure 9.26).

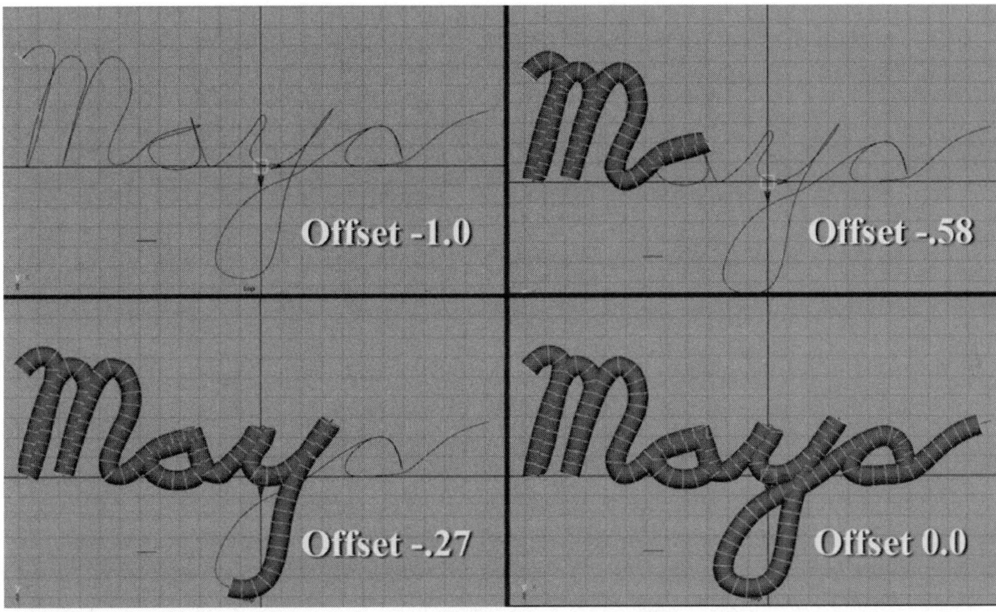

FIGURE 9.26 Four frames of the write-on animation at varying Offset values.

ON THE DVD

Save your work. There is a version of this animated write-on called duplicate_4.mb on the companion DVD in the Chapter 9 folder. Let's have one more quick example of how easy SmartDuplicate is to use before we move on. Load Bullets.mb from the companion DVD in the Chapter 9 folder. Let's duplicate the bullets over the curve1 node.

1. In the Ticket menu select Ticket > SmartDuplicate > SmartDuplicate.
2. Select the curve1 node from the Outliner window and press Enter on the keyboard.
3. Select the NURBS bullet and press Enter on the keyboard. This should duplicate the bullet model on the curve at the default value of 10. This result is shown in Figure 9.27.

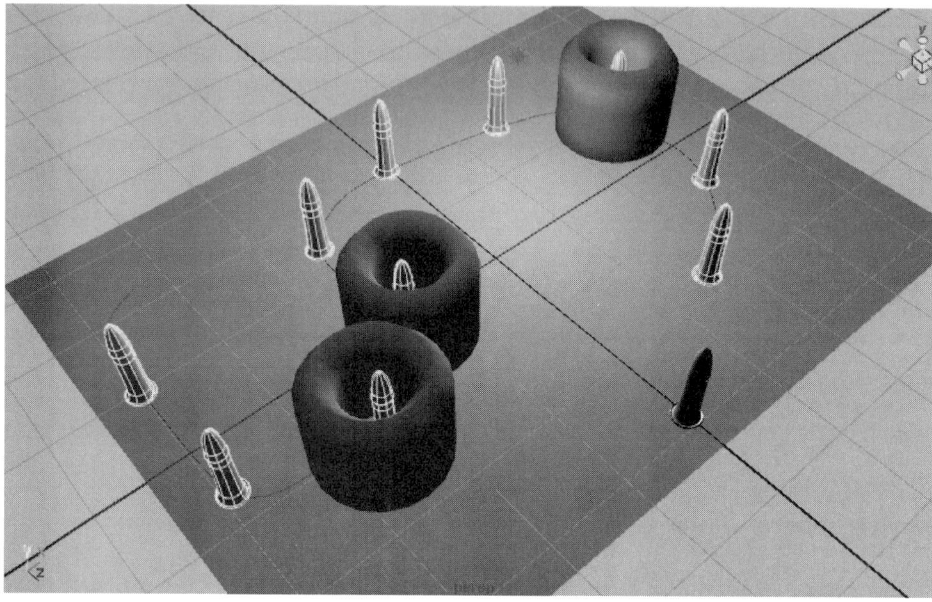

FIGURE 9.27 Ten duplicate bullet models are created on the curve.

4. Change the Duplicates attribute to 45. Now 45 duplicate bullets are evenly distributed over the curve's length, as shown in Figure 9.28.

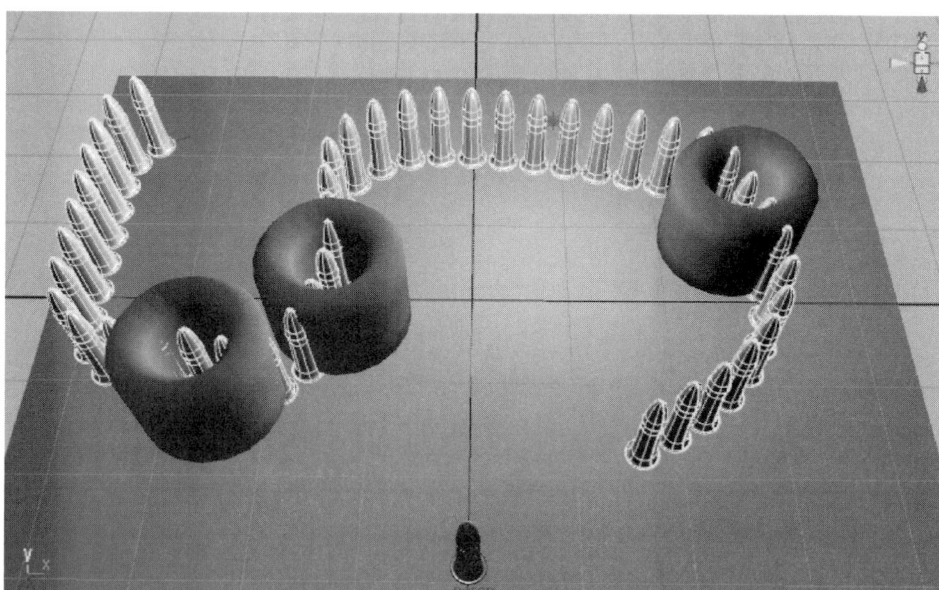

FIGURE 9.28 Here, 45 bullet models are uniformly distributed on the curve.

The obvious problem here is the barrel-shaped objects that are in the way of the bullets. This can be corrected by adjusting the CVs of the guide curve. Select curve1 from the Outliner window and press the F9 key. Editing the CVs that make up this curve, we can easily change the path of the curve to avoid the barrels. Turning on X-Ray shading will reveal any hidden CVs. Do this from the top orthogonal view to keep the curve on the XZ plane. Figure 9.29 shows how moving just a few CVs can change the path and avoid the obstacles.

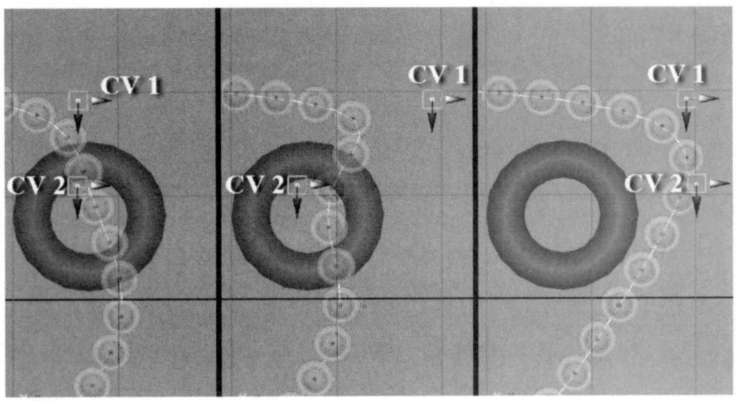

FIGURE 9.29 Simple changes in the guide curve's CVs can result in a newer and better distribution.

The barrels were there to demonstrate this concept and don't have any relevance in this image. Figure 9.30 shows an image without the barrels.

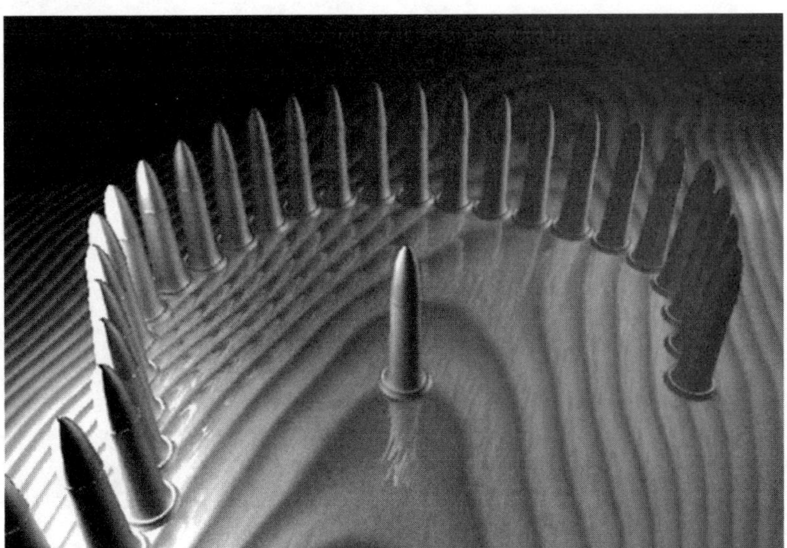

FIGURE 9.30 A shiny and adjustable row of bullets.

You can certainly save a lot of time with this plugin compared to a weak workaround. SmartDuplicate is handy and gets the job done. It is simple, powerful, and supports the duplication of multiple instances with different object types all at the same time. Let's look at another plugin from Ticket01 that has similar characteristics as Wire and SmartDuplicate but has a more narrow niche application. It's called Seamour.

STITCHING WITH SEAMOUR

Seamour, which may or may not be the combination of the words *seam* and *amour*, or a love affair with seams, creates stitching geometry. This plugin performs a tiresome function that you rarely see modeled but is a nifty addition to a model, giving it a new level of realism. Let's use Seamour to generate some stitchery.

ON THE DVD

On the companion DVD in the Chapter 9 folder is a scene called stitches_1.mb. The loaded file should look similar to Figure 9.31. A quick render will make it look like Figure 9.32. Installing Seamour is simple. Executing the installer program is easy and is no fuss. After installation, make sure the plugin is loaded and recognized by Maya. This can be done by going to the top of the screen in the Maya menus and selecting Window > Setting/Preferences > Plug-in Manager. Make sure that both the Loaded and Auto load boxes are selected next to Seamour.mll. There should now be a Ticket menu at the tope of the screen. If you have installed Wire and SmartDuplicate, they will be present in the Ticket menu as well.

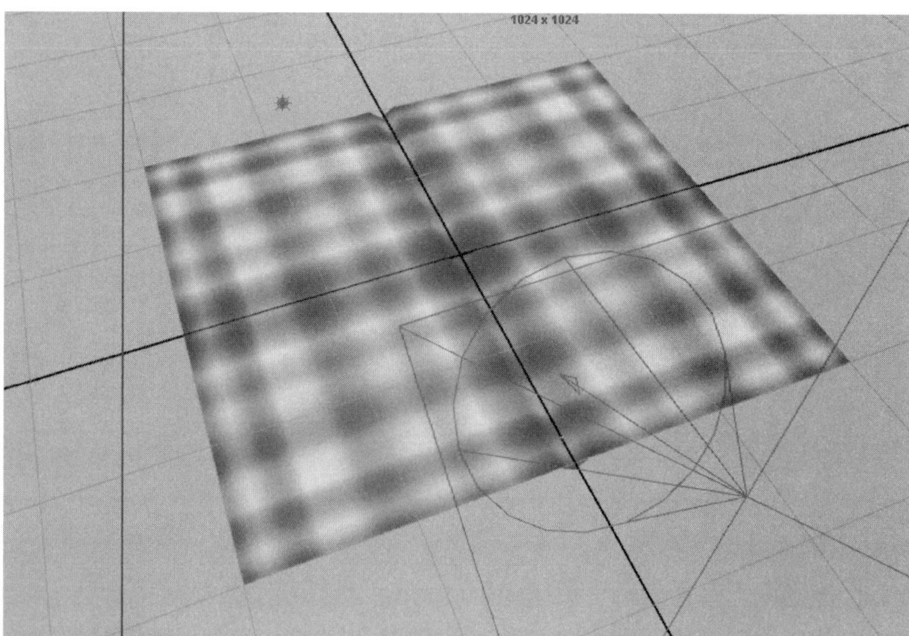

FIGURE 9.31 A mesh plane acts as a piece of cloth for stitching with Seamour.

FIGURE 9.32 A quick render of a plaid piece of cloth.

Seamour creates a shelf that is very helpful for accessing the tools. Your interface may not have the tool shelf open. This can be accomplished from the Maya menus. Select Display > UI Elements > Shelf, as shown in Figure 9.33. The Seamour shelf should appear.

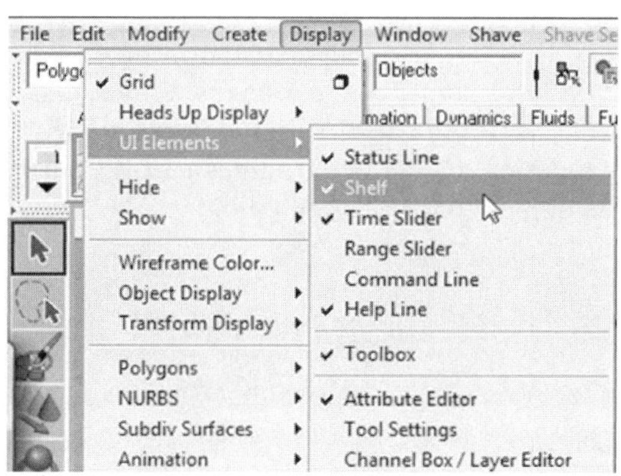

FIGURE 9.33 Turning the Maya Tool Shelf on in the Maya user interface.

Open the shelf to reveal the various Seamour tool icons, as shown in Figure 9.34.

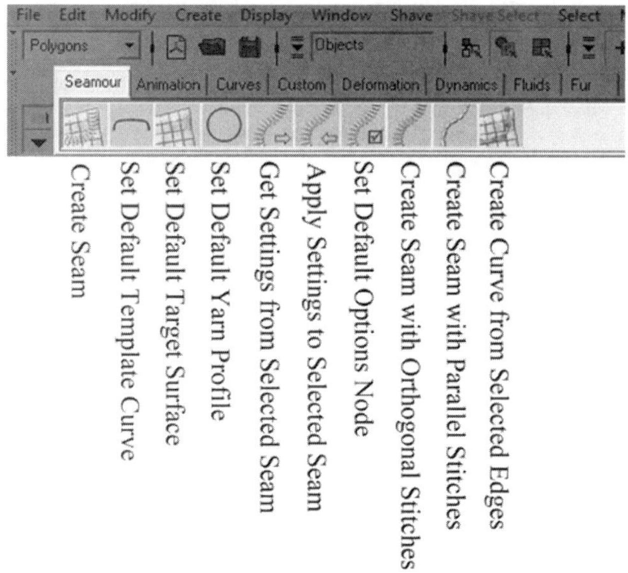

FIGURE 9.34 The Seamour icons with their functions listed below them.

Making a seam straight down the middle of our cloth is quite easy. It's best to do this in wireframe mode in the top orthogonal view. Follow these steps for a quick and easy seam.

1. We need to create a curve based on some of the edges of the polygonal cloth object. Select the polygonal edges of the mesh right down the center of the cloth, as shown in Figure 9.35. To do this, select the wireframe mesh and press the F10 key. Drag a selection box around the middle edges. If you accidentally select unneeded edges, which is fairly easy to do, you can deselect them by holding the Ctrl key down and drawing a selection box around the offending edges. Selected edges can be hard to see, as they are usually the Maya default light orange color.

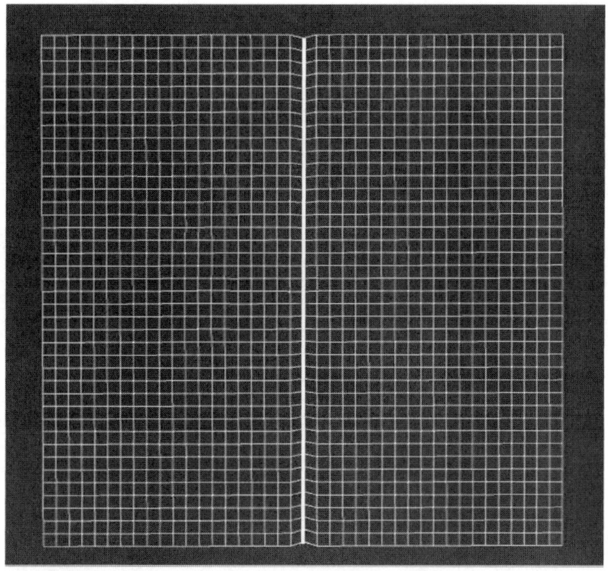

FIGURE 9.35 An exaggerated view of the edges needed to be selected to generate the edgeCurve.

2. The exaggerated edges selected and shown in Figure 9.35 must be made into a curve. This can be accomplished by clicking on the Create Curve from Selected Edges tool in the Seamour tool shelf (see Figure 9.34). The Outliner now lists a new curve node labeled edgeCurve, as shown in Figure 9.36.

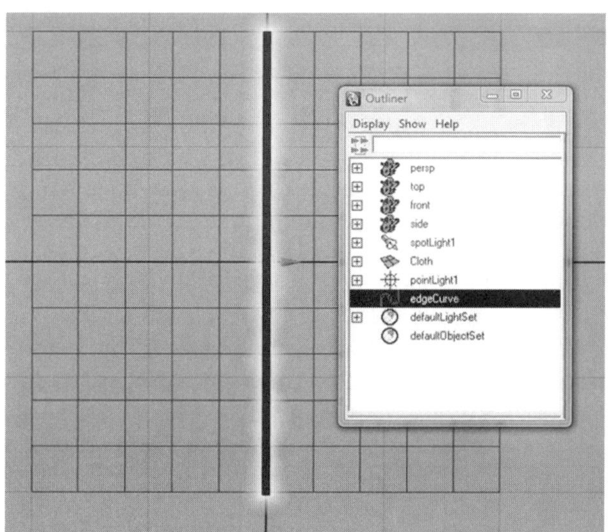

FIGURE 9.36 The dark line represents the edgeCurve generated and is listed in the Outliner.

3. For this example, we will create orthogonal stitching. These stitches are created by following the edge curve. This may be better viewed with smooth shading on and hardware texturing off. Select the edgeCurve node in the Outliner window and click on the Create Seam with Orthogonal Stitches icon in the Seamour tool shelf (this icon can be referenced in Figure 9.34). The direct results of this action are shown in Figure 9.37.

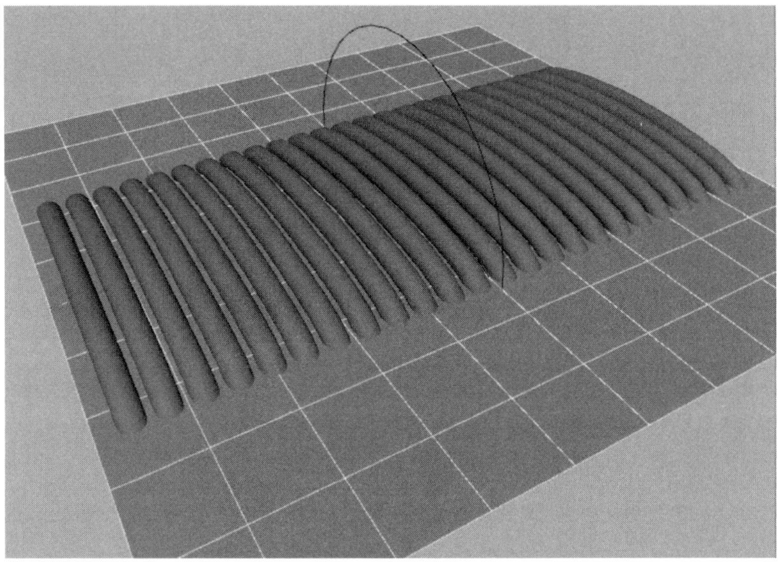

FIGURE 9.37 Oversized seams now appear on the edgeCurve.

4. A multitude of staple-shaped stitches have been replicated along the edgeCurve. They are currently too large and bulky for a realistic look. Let's adjust them. In the Outliner window, select the seam1 node that has been created. Load the Attribute Editor for the seam1 node.
5. Under the Yarn tab in the seam1 Attribute window, toggle the Relative Yarn scale box to off. This may make the seams jump in scale to unusable proportions. Set the Yarn Profile scale value to 0.025. This allows us to scale the profile of the yarn as we see fit. Also make sure that the Extrude Yarn toggle box is checked.
6. These stitches look quite large. Let's make them smaller. Under the Template tab in the seam1 Attribute window, change the Template Scale value to 0.15. The template is a staple-shaped curve that is generated by Seamour to give form to the individual stitches. Figure 9.38 shows how changing the Template Scale value alters the seams.

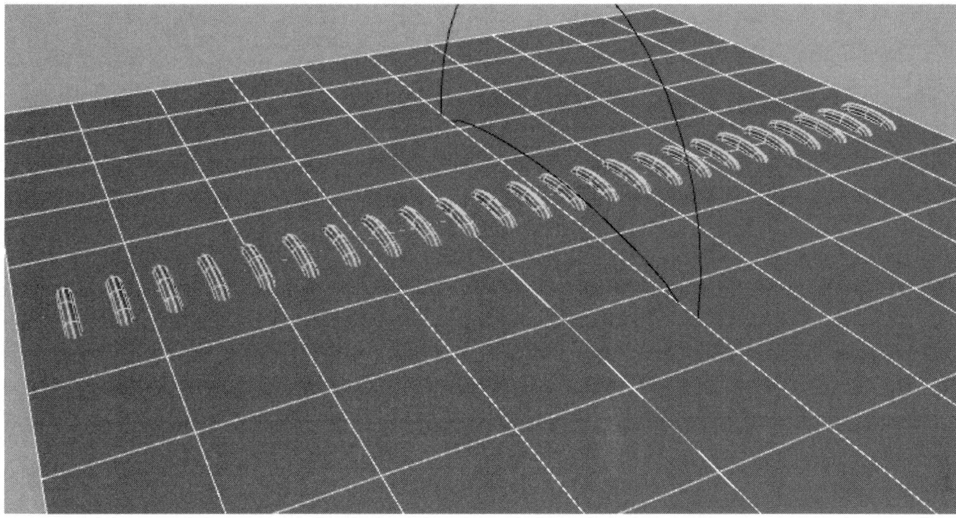

FIGURE 9.38 The seams start to take shape by scaling the template value down to size.

In Stitches

Seams in Seamour have a few basic components. The first is a user-designated or designed curve that can be made from polygon edges or that is drawn. The template defines the overall shape of the individual stitches, making them look similar to a staple. The yarn profile is the circular curve that is extruded over the template curve, creating the actual surface of each stitch. These components are tweaked in the Attribute Editor of the seam node to shape the stitching that suits your needs.

7. Let's create a few more stitches to tighten it up a bit. In the Seam tab of the Attribute menu, change the Stitches value to 70. This creates a tighter cluster of stitches plus an errant one. This is the first stitch in the series, so we can eliminate it by changing the value of Start with Stitch to 2 or, in other words, starting with the second stitch in the sequence.
8. The stitching looks a bit crowded. Let's bump the Yarn Profile to 0.09 and change the Template Scale to 0.084. Our stitchery should now look something like Figure 9.39.

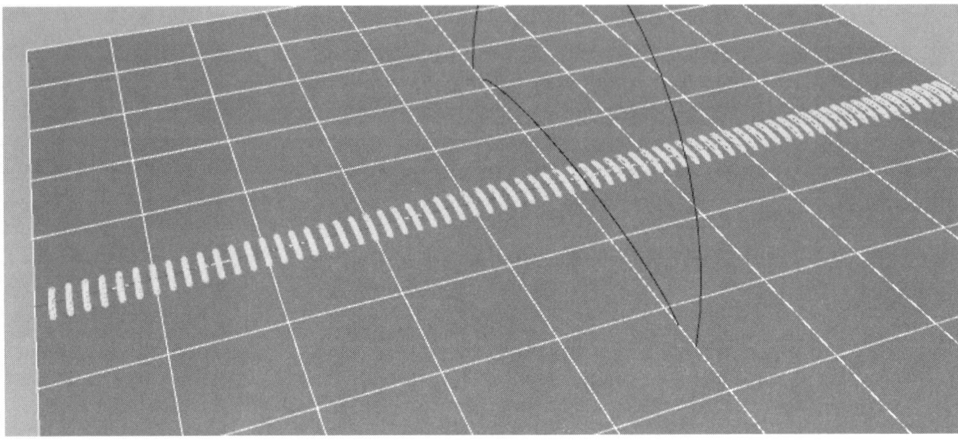

FIGURE 9.39 Readjusting scales and the number of stitches makes a better-looking seam.

9. Finally, a few shaders are included in this scene file. The tan shader labeled phongE1SG can be found in the Multilister. Drag this shader onto your stitching geometry and render it. The nice uniform stitching is fairly convincing, as shown in Figures 9.40 and 9.41.

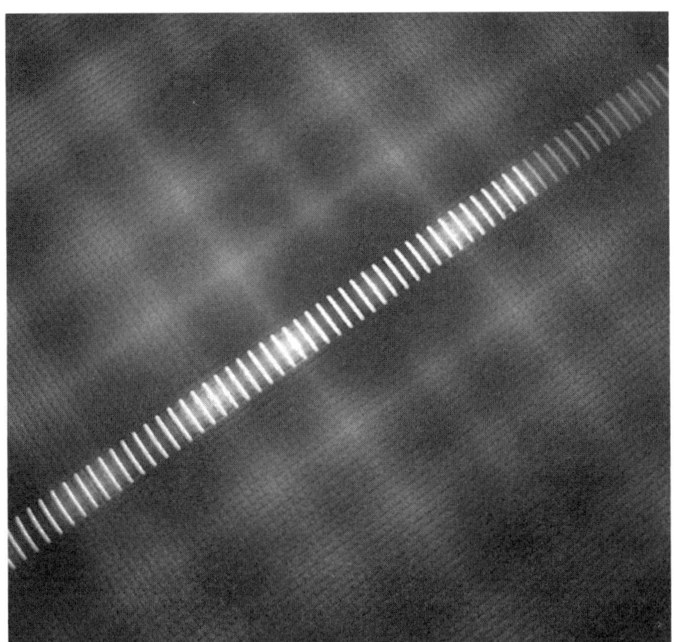

FIGURE 9.40 A render of the stitches as geometry.

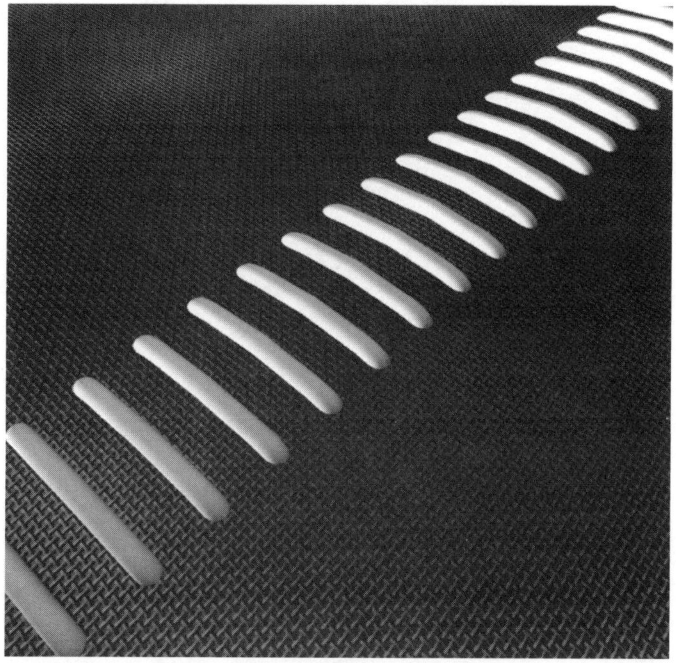

FIGURE 9.41 A closer look at the Seamour stitchery.

ON THE DVD

Save your work. This completed scene file, called stitches_2.mb, can be found on the companion DVD in the Chapter 9 folder.

Stitches don't have to be confined to the straight and narrow. Seamour can be used to do a more embroidered look. Let's see how to make a stitched and embroidered letter.

ON THE DVD

1. Load the scene file snakeskin_1.mb from the companion DVD in the Chapter 9 folder. The scene is composed of a 9 × 9 polygon ground plane and a simple curve that lies in the XZ plane. This is shown in Figure 9.42.

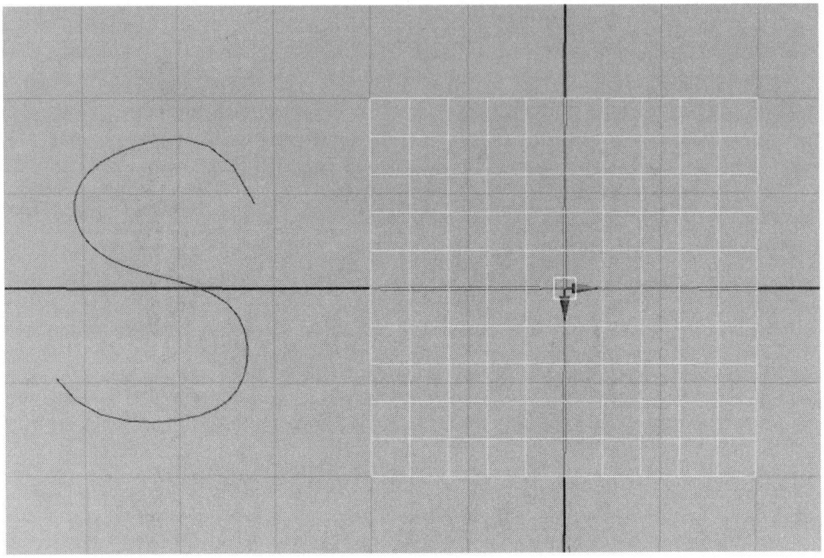

FIGURE 9.42 The Maya scene file contains both a plane and a curve in XZ space.

2. Unlike the previous example that had stitches that were far apart, too large, and excessively uniform, we will create a more embroidered look this time. Select curve2 from the Outliner window and translate it in the X direction to 0.0. Keep the other values as is. This will place the S curve squarely in the middle of the polygon plane (see Figure 9.43).

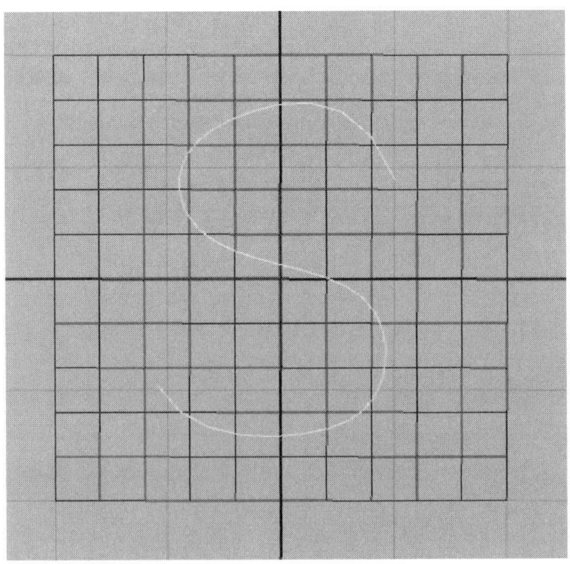

FIGURE 9.43 The S curve now rests squarely in the middle of the plane.

3. This is a slightly different approach than the previous example. With the S curve2 node selected in the Outliner window, click on the Create Seam with Orthogonal Stitches icon in the Seamour tool shelf (this icon can be referenced in Figure 9.34). This time a yarnProfile curve and stitch template curve appear in the scene without any extruded geometry. These nodes can be seen in the Outliner window and in Figure 9.44.

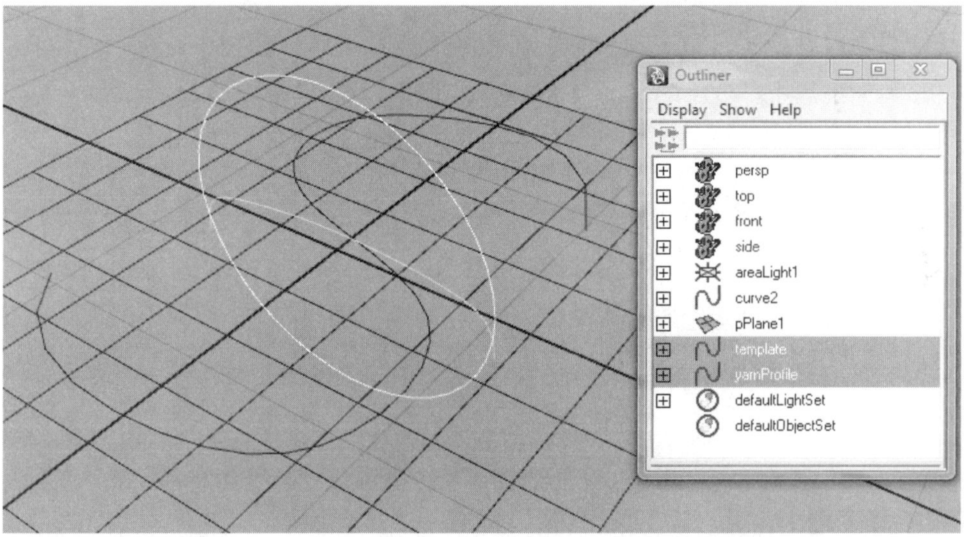

FIGURE 9.44 A yarnProfile curve and stitch template curve are visible in the scene.

4. Next, select the polygon plane and have your Attribute Editor open for the plane. Click on the Set Default Target Surface icon in the Seamour tool shelf. (This icon can be referenced in Figure 9.34.) This time nothing appears to happen, but the Attribute Editor has changed to show the seam default options.
5. Now select and highlight the S curve node. Click on the Create Seam with Orthogonal Stitches icon in the Seamour tool shelf. (This icon can be referenced in Figure 9.34.) This action introduces a seam1 node and begins to create the stitches on the S curve with the default values. In smooth shaded mode, the scene will look similar to Figure 9.45. Save your work.

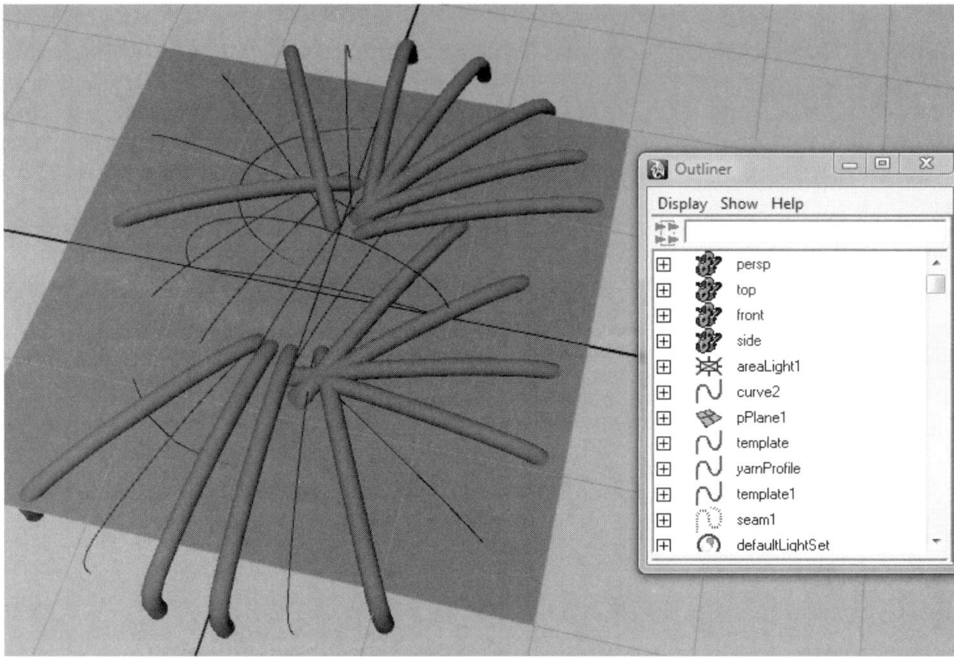

FIGURE 9.45 The stitching, although jumbled, begins to take form.

6. A few minute changes in the parameters of the seam1 node will make all the difference in the way your embroidery currently looks. Load the scene embroidery_2.mb if you got lost.

This is the work completed to this point. Follow these quick steps:

1. Select the seam1 node from the Outliner window. Under the Seam tab in the Attribute window, set the number of stitches to 400. If this burdens your system, you can create less. Also toggle Surface Clinging on and make sure Sync End to Count is checked. This ensures that whatever the number of stitches created, they will disperse evenly over the curve from beginning to end.
2. Under the Template tab, lower the Template scale value to 0.059. This shortens the stitches and makes the outline of the S curve prominent.
3. Under the Yarn tab, toggle the Relative Yarn Scale off and change the Template Scale value to a very low value of 0.009. This gives us very thin threads that are similar to embroidery thread.
4. Select the seam1 node and drop the tan *stringphong* shader that loaded with the scene. This can be found in the Multilister.
5. Rendering this scene now gives you a pretty good approximation of an embroidered stitch, as shown in Figure 9.46.

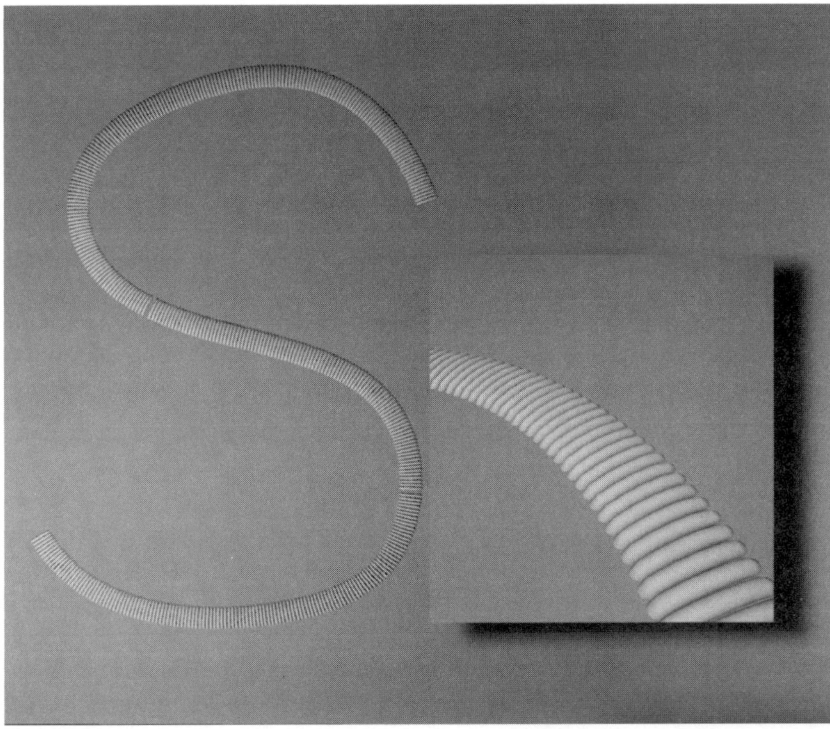

FIGURE 9.46 The first render makes it obvious that the stitches are taking form nicely.

ON THE DVD

The work thus far has been saved as embroidery_3.mb, and is available on the companion DVD in the Chapter 9 folder. There is only a quick tweak or two to make this scene more satisfying.

1. Select the seam1 node from the Outliner window. Under the Variation tab in the Attribute window, set both the Angle and Length to 1.0. to give variable random lengths to the stitches. Also, randomly skew the angle at which they rest on the curve.
2. Change the Random Seed value to change the randomness. Render it to see the results. Figure 9.47 shows a more haphazard distribution of stitches.

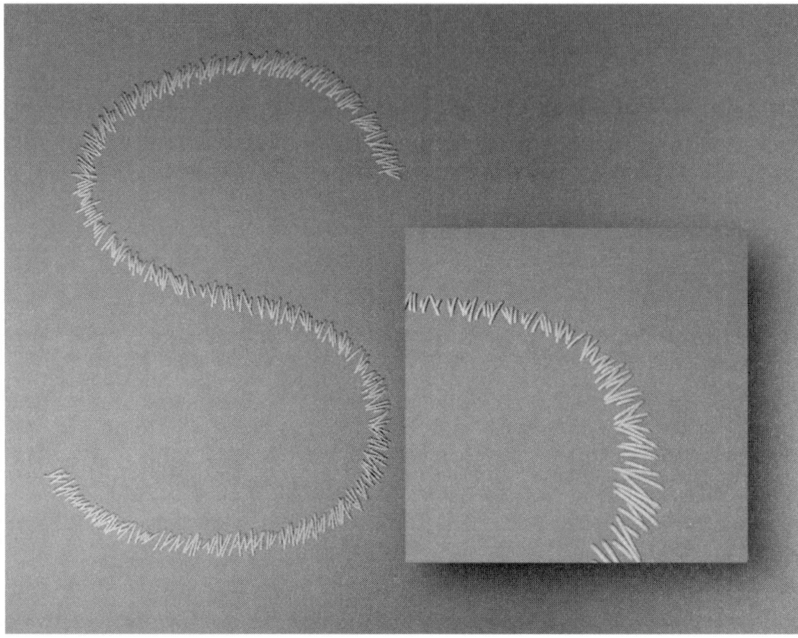

FIGURE 9.47 Randomization of stitch length and angle create a hand-embroidered look.

ON THE DVD

The final scene file with a lizard skin textured plane is saved on the companion DVD in the Chapter 9 folder as embroidery_4.mb. Figure 9.48 is a rendering of that file.

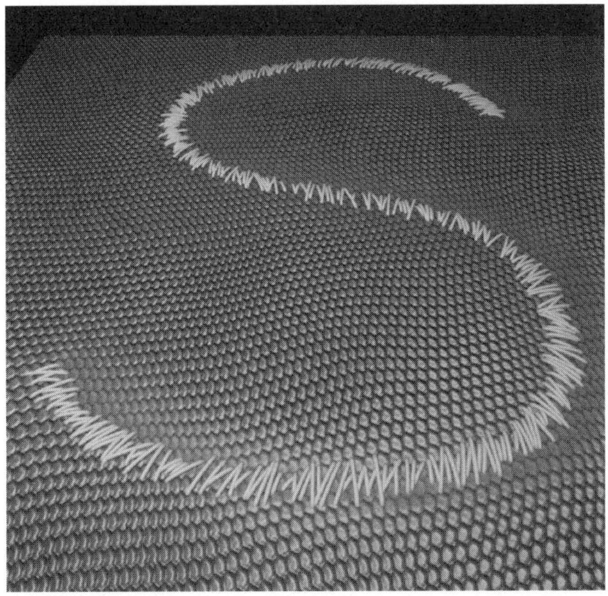

FIGURE 9.48 The final scene rendered with a lizard skin leather shader applied to the plane.

ON THE DVD

Additionally, there are bonus scene files on the companion DVD in the Chapter 9 folder. Snakeskin_2.mb uses a parallel stitch instead of an orthogonal stitch and fewer stitches than we had previously used. The technique for parallel stitching is the same as orthogonal stitching. We are simply using an alternative stitch type. A rendering of this file is shown in Figure 9.49.

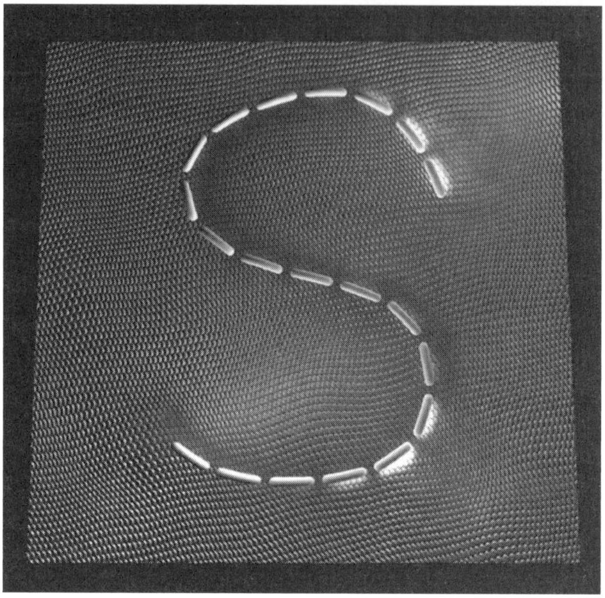

FIGURE 9.49 The snakeskin_2.mb scene file rendered with parallel stitching for a different look.

ON THE DVD

Finally, two more bonus scene files are on the companion DVD in the Chapter 9 folder. The files, baseball_PFX_Grass.mb and baseball_Shave_Grass.mb, are identical except for the grass. One has been done with Paint Effects, and the other has grass generated in Shave and a Haircut. If you still have Shave and a Haircut's trial active from Chapter 3, you can use the scene with the Shave and a Haircut grass. These files are just for study and show another use of Seamour. Figure 9.50 shows a rendering of the baseball scene with Shave and a Haircut grass.

FIGURE 9.50 A baseball with Seamour-generated stitching amid Shave and a Haircut grass.

ON THE DVD

These are just a few of the miscellaneous plugins available for Maya. There is a wealth of terrific freeware and shareware plugins on www.highend3d.com. A more direct link to the Maya-specific content is available on the DVD software link appendix. For now, it's time to head to our last chapter, which discusses cool stand-alone applications that can be very helpful when you integrate them into your Maya workflow.

CHAPTER

10

STAND-ALONE APPLICATIONS

In This Chapter

- Introduction
- Luxology's modo
- Nevercenter's Silo 2.0
- Pixologic's ZBrush 3.1
- Okino Computer Graphics's PolyTrans
- E-on Software's Vue 6 xStream

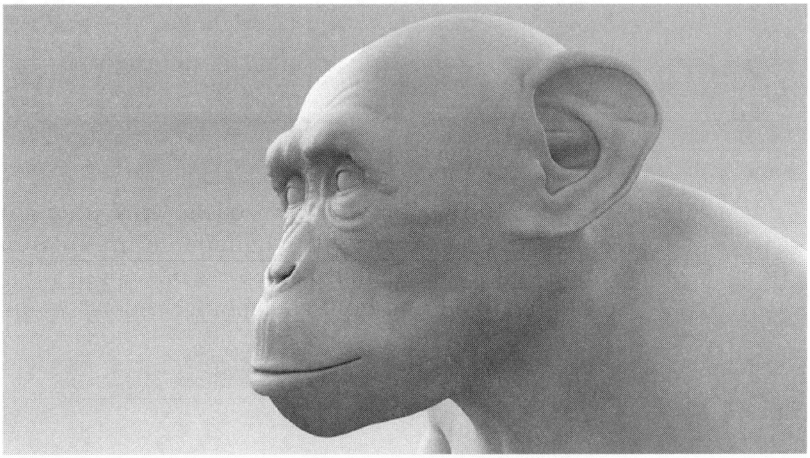

This bust of a chimp was created with ZBrush by Ty Shelton.
Image courtesy of www.tyshelton.com

INTRODUCTION

In Chapter 5, "Water, Waves, and Other Matter," we explored Next Limit's RealFlow, and although it is a stand-alone application, it had its own plugins for taking advantage of Maya. To review, a stand-alone program is a self-contained entity capable of being independent from other programs. Maya, XSI, Houdini, and Photoshop are all very capable stand-alone programs. In the case of a 3D animation program, you would expect a 3D animation stand-alone application to be able to model objects and scenes; color, texture, and light a scene; and allow the user to animate what he has created within this program. Just as a plugin is meant to enhance the functionality of its host application, stand-alones can also aid another stand-alone program. Many great artists are out there creating fantastic imagery, such as that seen in Figure 10.1, which was created in Luxology's modo. There are many alternate programs that are capable of producing cool 3D models in new ways, or have beautiful renderers with different approaches to creating the final image.

FIGURE 10.1 Sheep image created in Luxology modo.
Courtesy of Rodrigo Gelmi

The functions, techniques, and methodologies of other programs can help solve a problem, inspire the creative process differently, or create a look that may be difficult to achieve in Maya. Often, stand-alone programs have features that just can't be found in your primary application, and there are no plugins suitable for the task. Stand-alone applications can help bridge that gap and fill the void.

Just as RealFlow allows a wide assortment of 3D packages to use the proprietary data it generates via import plugins, so too can other stand-alone applications create content that is usable in Maya. The number-one priority is to finish a project with outstanding results. The production house that can see past the primary package to utilize the alternative functionality of another program is doing itself and the project's workflow a great service.

Programs can share data in many ways. File standards are a way of doing this. Good interoperability between programs is a matter of creating data generated in one program for use in another. While it is an amazing and unique tool, not many studios rely on Paint fx to create texture maps. It is more likely that texture maps are painted in a stand-alone program such as Adobe Photoshop, Corel Painter 10, Project Dogwaffle 1.2, or even Gimp 2.4. Most programs load and save TIF, JPG, and TARGA file formats. Maya is no exception. Most packages capable of 3D modeling can save their models in standard Maya readable formats such as OBJ and DXF.

Camera tracking data created in a program such as 2d3's Boujou 4.0 and The Pixel Farm's PFTrack 2.0 are often preferred over Maya Live. The ability to exchange data between various programs opens a project up to the tools of a wide and varied group of programs.

An increasingly popular standard for information exchange between applications emerged from Autodesk's Motionbuilder. The FBX open standard is being adopted by many other companies as the ideal solution for data exchange between programs. The FBX (.fbx) format allows the widest exchange of 3D information available. Motion, NURBS, polygons, cameras, lighting information, materials, skeletons, and even deformations can now be stored in a single file format. The long list of 3D applications supporting the FBX format is growing, thereby making the movement of data from one application in your pipeline to the next a much easier task.

In Support of FBX

The FBX format is growing ever more popular due to its flexibility. Here is a short list of companies supporting the standard: DAZ Productions, EI Technology Group, Eovia, eyeon Software, Luxology, MAXON, NaturalMotion, NewTek, NXN, Okino, QEDSoft, REALVIZ, Softimage, and Strata. You can discover more about the FBX standard at http://usa.autodesk.com/adsk/servlet/index?siteID=123112&id=6839916.

The use of other applications for film and television may rely on data generated from another source and used in conjunction with Maya. In this chapter, we will briefly explore a few stand-alone software packages that are being used in the professional animation and visual fx community. These programs are becoming popular alternative tools for a production pipeline. These programs provide unique features and an ability to provide something that may not be easily achievable by a production's primary package.

DEFINING WORKFLOW

The word *workflow* gets bandied about a great deal, so it's a good idea to know what it is. In terms of working with a 3D application, the workflow is the way in which you approach and then execute the steps necessary to complete a project. You can't put the cart before the horse, and you can't animate what isn't modeled. The workflow is a set of steps to reach the end goal. There are levels to a workflow. One person's creative process may not be the same as another's. Maya is open to a multitude of ways of accomplishing something. As individual artists, we all have a personal workflow. Working within the production pipeline, we may or may not be asked to work in a new way. As part of a larger project, the production pipeline dictates the workflow for consistency.

Here are a few programs that have excellent qualities worth investigating.

LUXOLOGY'S MODO

Modo 301 (www.luxology.com; modo™ Luxology LLC) is a complete 3D solution and continues to be a very user-friendly application for the computer artist. It is available for the PC and the Mac. Modo is winning fans and awards for its ease of use and the brilliant imagery that it generates. It incorporates next-generation technologies into a finely integrated package. The modo interface sports the increasingly popular gray and orange motif shown in Figure 10.2.

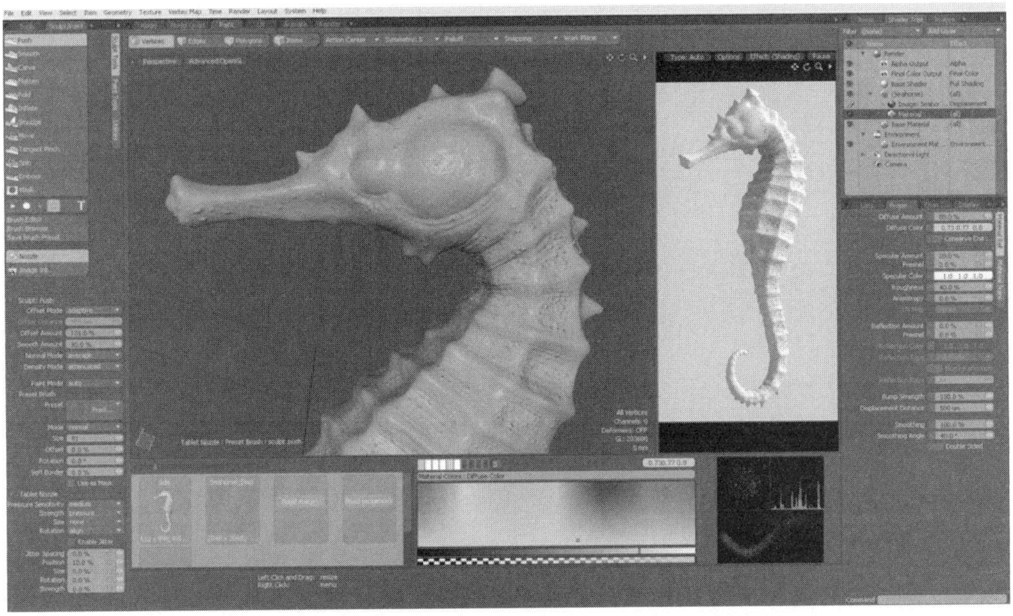

FIGURE 10.2 The modo interface is efficient. Navigation can be set to mimic that of Maya's.

It is very easy for the artist to adapt modo to his personal workflow. There are provisions to adapt modo to your own style and access the tools you need the most, and it is a logical process. It is easy to see the advantage for the artist in the thoughtful programming. Since modo is a complete package, it sports many areas of interest in 3D modeling and animation that make it increasingly popular. Here is the short list of features that make modo worthwhile.

Modo's modeler is gaining a reputation as one of the most advanced polygon and subdivision surface modelers around. It is very easy to get into a modeling comfort zone with modo. Considering modo's lineage, the modeling tools have the distinct feel of years of user feedback. It is equally adept at precision design and organic modeling. Many little touches, such as the snapping tools, make it fun to work with. You can snap points to other geometry or on a grid, and there are little niceties such as ghosted guides that allow you to snap horizontally, vertically, or at 90-degree intervals. You can snap any vertex, edge, or polygon center to any other. It is easy to bevel objects for finishing touches. The thickening tool is an amazing and addictive tool for adding thicknesses to flat surfaces (see Figure 10.3 and Figure 10.4).

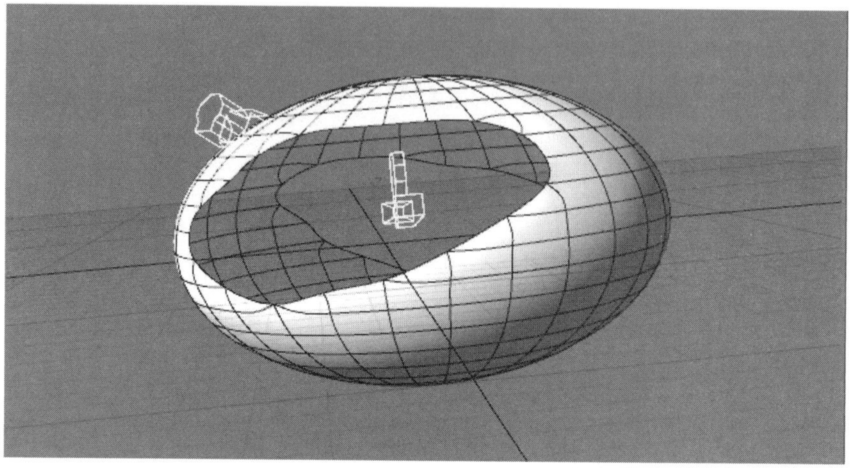

FIGURE 10.3 A Sub D sphere with two holes as a single surface.

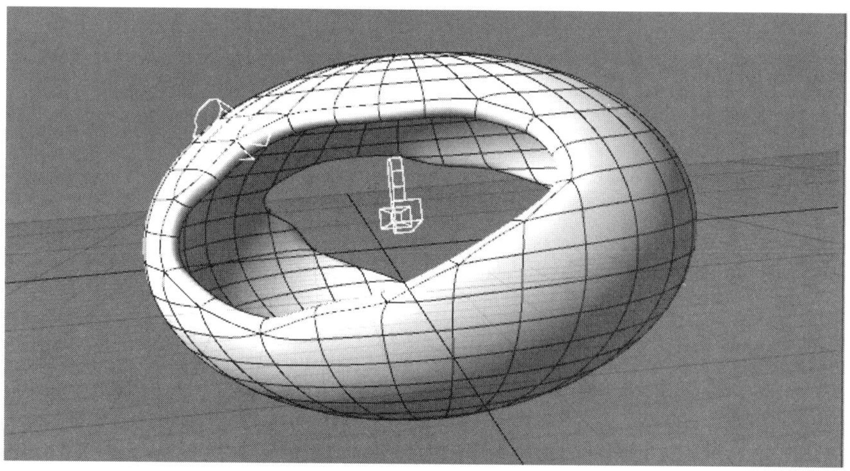

FIGURE 10.4 The sphere's surface is fortified with modo's Thicken tool.

Another neat feature is Mesh Paint, which, among other things, allows you to paint geometry on a surface. This could be used to paint hairs on a head, light post poles on a street, or even a fleet of Utah teapots in orbit, as shown in Figure 10.5.

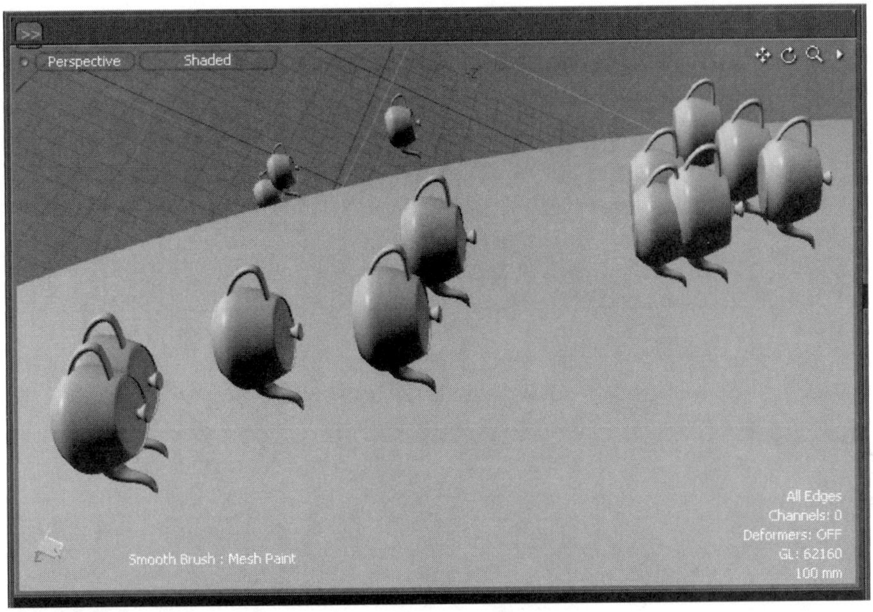

FIGURE 10.5 The Utah teapot painted as mesh instances on a spherical surface.

Modo's painting abilities are not confined to painting meshes. The program provides a full 3D paint system for texturing models. Modo can also sculpt a mesh by painting deformation into the geometry. This is an integrated part of modo and is similar to other stand-alone products, such as Autodesk's Mudbox and Pixologic's ZBrush, which we will look at later in this chapter. The image-based deformation allows you to deform geometry based on an image. Modo also can create true vector-based displacement. A 3D model can become a brush, which can be used to displace a surface. This vector-based displacement can displace a surface in a way that grayscale height information cannot. Street signs, pushpins, mushrooms, and even an ear can grow as a displacement from another surface.

Taken singly, any number of modo's abilities is invaluable. Many users have taken to using it solely for its UV editing tools. Gaining the best possible texture maps for a model usually requires UV editing. Modo does a very good job of doing a large part of the work for you. Often, the Unwrap tool is all that is needed, as shown in Figure 10.6.

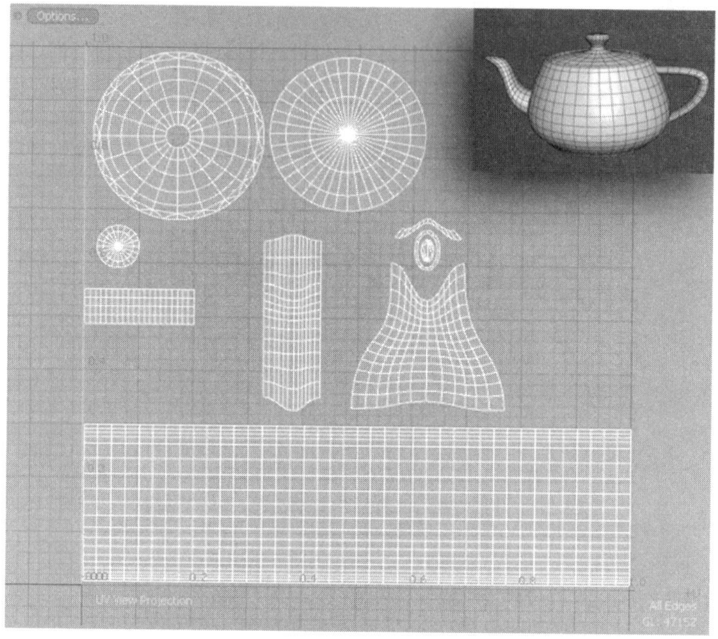

FIGURE 10.6 The Utah teapot model unwrapped using modo's excellent UV editing tools.

Difficulties in UV modeling, such as holes and overlapping geometry, are handled simply. A major feature of the UV toolset is its ability to adapt to topology changes after you have created a UV map or Blendshape. There is no lost work after changes are made.

THE PEOPLE BEHIND THE PRODUCT

The computer graphics community is ever expanding, but it's still a small world. It's always interesting to see the contributions people have made to the field. Luxology stands on the experienced foundation of prior successes in the CG field. The three founders of Luxology—Allen Hastings, Stuart Ferguson, and Brad Peebler—are names that may be very familiar to you. Allen Hastings was the creator of Videoscape 3D, which eventually he turned into LightWave 3D. Mr. Hastings is the chief scientist at Luxology. Modeler, the modeling component of LightWave 3D, was programmed by Stuart Ferguson, who now holds the chief technology officer post at Luxology. Brad Peebler, who became a LightWave 3D guru and vice president of 3D at NewTek, is Luxology's president. There is an astounding amount of experience behind modo, making it a growing application in a 3D artist's toolkit.

All the amazing tools of modo aside, a large portion of the appeal of modo is its renderer. Modo's renderer uses physically-based lighting to create accurately-lit scenes. The renderer alone is worth investigating in modo 301. It is a fast raytracer. Similar to the appeal of fryrender and Maxwell Render, modo is fast becoming a favorite of architecture firms that want to have photo-realistic images to present to clients. It's a huge plus to display photo-like images of buildings that have not even broken ground (see Figure 10.7). The renderer produces very accurate lighting models that include some upper-level rendering considerations such as blurry reflections, indirect caustics, fresnel reflections, subsurface scattering with transparency absorption, and photometric lighting. Although modo is driven by much of the same physics as fryrender and Maxwell Render, it doesn't look the same. Modo seems like a much more familiar interface. It feels somehow less scientific. Modo supports global illumination, and its rock solid animation is flicker-free for all kinds of visualization.

FIGURE 10.7 Modo excels at global illumination, which is great for architectural stills and visualizations.
Courtesy of Ahmed Alizera

Modo is multithreaded, can render across a network, and is licensed for up to 50 Mac or PC workstations, which is certainly a substantial render farm for the price. Modo has animation capabilities, but that is not its strong point. This is why many users go back and forth between modo and Maya. Major production studios developing games and visual fx for film and television are doing just that. Modo is also becoming very popular for package and product design (see Figure 10.8).

FIGURE 10.8 Modo is becoming popular for product and package design.
Courtesy of Andy Brown

The FBX file format makes it fairly simple to exchange data between modo and your Maya pipeline. Although some of the workflow paradigms are different from Maya, they are fun and functional, and the learning curve is quite easy. Those who are familiar with NewTek's LightWave and modeler will find it familiar. There are preferences in modo for Maya-style navigation. This goes a long way to helping your workflow in modo. The preferences can be accessed in modo via the System menu listing at the top of the modo Screen. Selecting System > Preferences in modo brings up the modo Preferences window. Within the Preferences window are the various preference settings for modo. Select Input > Remapping from the left side of the window. This brings up the Remapping parameters. On the right-hand side of the preferences window is the Mouse Input Presets. Selecting this presents several navigation options. Select Maya (see Figure 10.9).

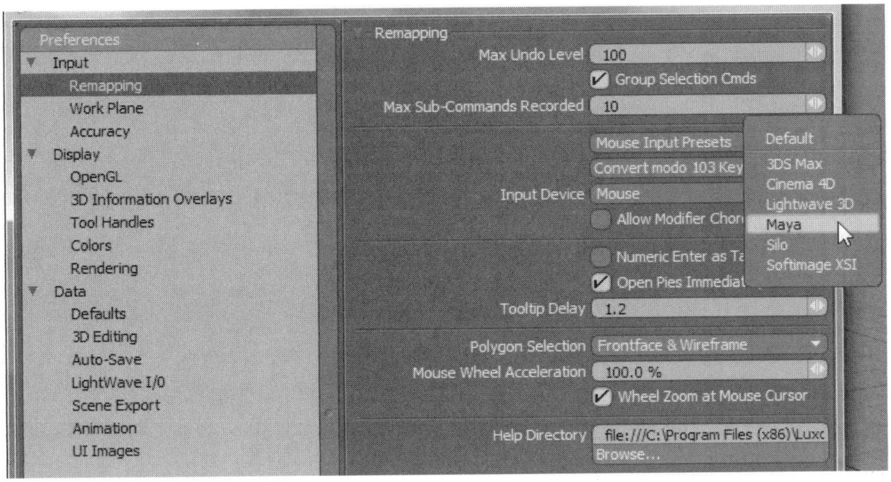

FIGURE 10.9 Familiar Maya navigation can be achieved via a preference selection in modo.

For die-hard Maya users, modo uses pie menus or, more familiar to the Maya user, marking menus. Modo utilizes Maya-style marking menus that can be configured for personal workflow use (see Figure 10.10).

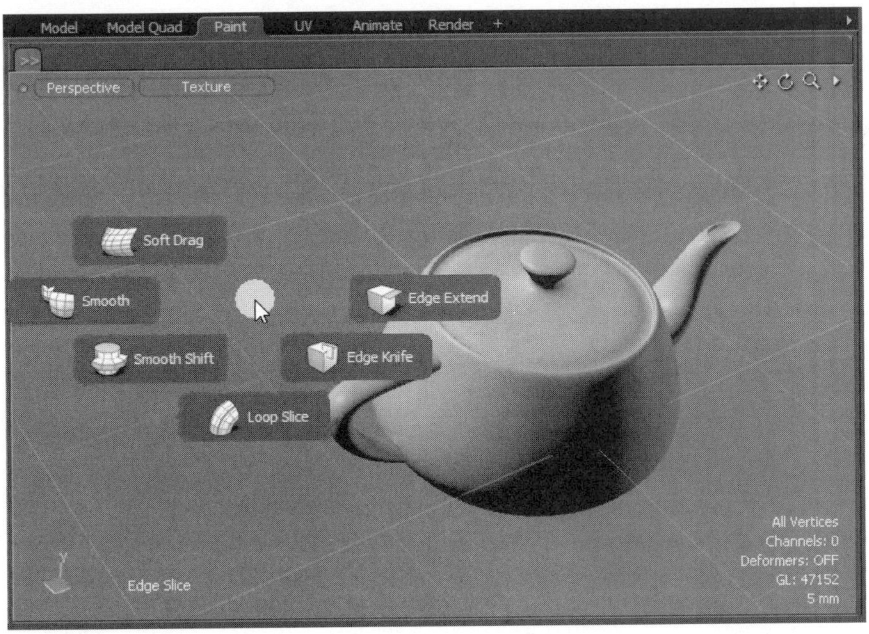

FIGURE 10.10 Modo sports user-configurable Maya-style marking menus called *pie menus*.

Modo is in the pipeline of many major production houses. That alone should make modo worthy of investigation as a tool in your Maya workflow. A few other tools are worth researching. One of them, Silo 2.0, is listed in the mapping configuration of modo shown in Figure 10.9. Silo 2.0 is gaining popularity among the Maya crowd. Let's take a brief look at Silo 2.0.

NEVERCENTER'S SILO 2.0

Although Maya is a terrific modeler, some artists are always looking for a new way of creating images. Often, they discover a workflow in some other program that strikes a chord with them. They take this new workflow to work, and it winds up being adopted by others. Silo is one of those programs. Silo is not a be-all and end-all program. It is a focused subdivision surface and polygon modeler that is becoming a favorite tool for creating organic shapes, as well as hard-edged surfaces. It's attractive for its inexpensive cost, able toolset, and ease of use. Let's look at some of Silo's tools and why it is being used in top studios in conjunction with Maya.

Silo is very easy to use. It sports the default gray background and is very clean (see Figure 10.11).

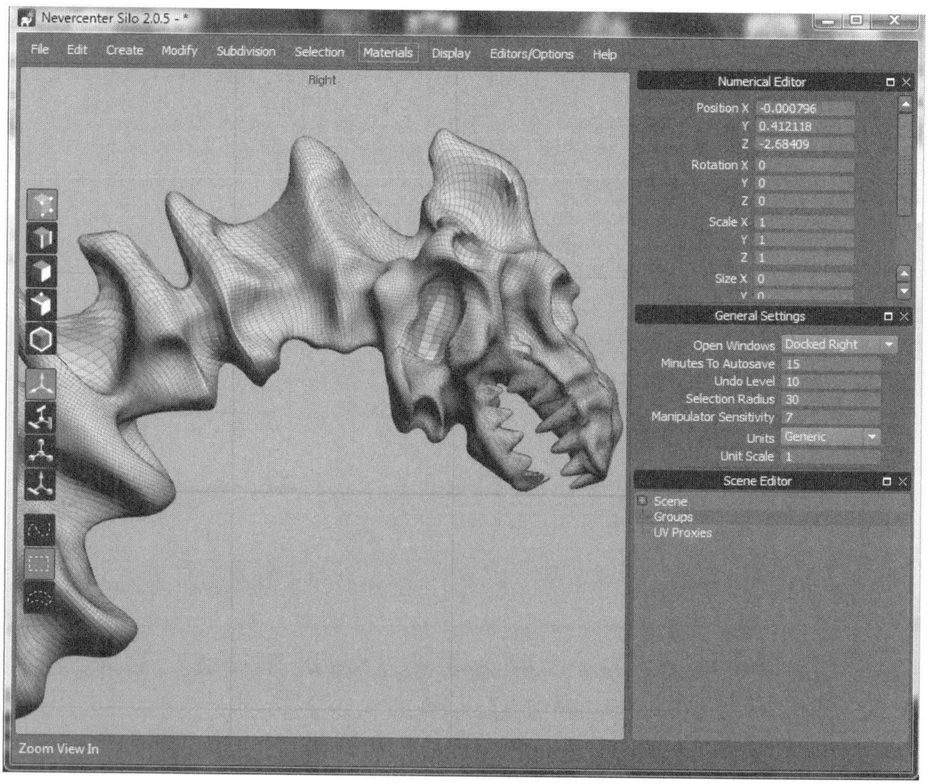

FIGURE 10.11 The Silo 2.0 interface by default mimics the navigation in Maya.

A great deal of development has gone into this version of Silo, making user configurability a priority. It is easy to configure Silo to your own workflow. Interface colors and buttons, mouse control, and keyboard shortcuts all can be changed to suit. By default, Silo navigates via a three-button mouse in the same way you navigate in Maya. Some users upload their own creative interface customizations, including Maya button sets to feel more at home. You can make the Silo interface clutter free or loaded with all your personal tool favorites at your disposal right on the screen. Silo is also open to plugin development. There already exists a Maya plugin for importing and exporting Silo ASCII and binary files. The biggest appeal of Silo is how efficient it is as a modeler. It is a very fast and powerful modeler. The workflow has been designed to be predictable while keeping mouse clicks to a minimum. Those mouse clicks can add up to lost productivity. It is quite easy to change from polygons to multiple levels of subdivision. The various components are easily selectable by Lasso, Area, or Paint selection modes. The Paint selection mode is as simple as moving the mouse over the components as if you were painting them.

Tweak is one of the niceties of Silo that makes it a pleasure to model with. By pressing Ctrl-LMB, you can interactively mold your model just by tweaking the vertices, edges, and faces of the model in 3D space. Tweak can select these components without even changing modes. Simply moving your mouse pointer over a component and engaging the Tweak command allows you to manipulate that component. It is a very interactive and intuitive way of adjusting a model.

Silo has some interesting and unique tools that can be very valuable. One of these tools is the Topology tool. This distinctive gizmo allows the user to create geometry by drawing on the surface of existing geometry. Figure 10.12 shows a simple subdivision sphere.

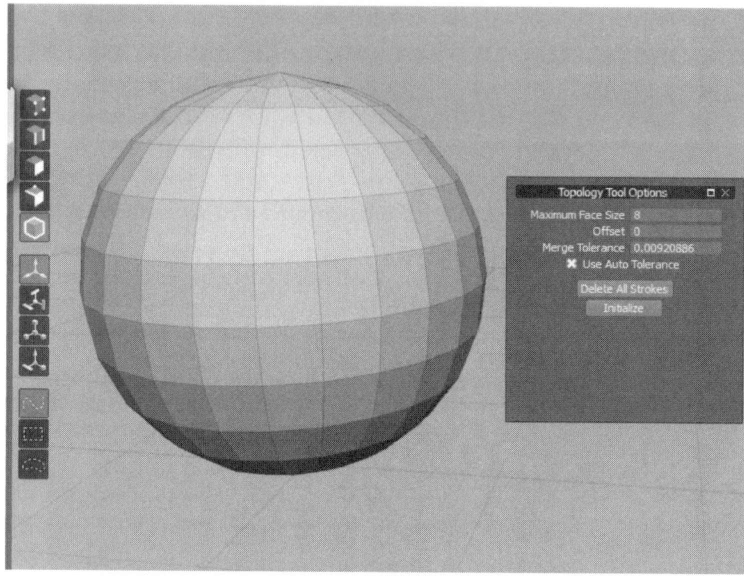

FIGURE 10.12 New surfaces can be created by drawing on a simple surface such as this one.

Pressing Ctrl-T engages the Topology tool, which allows you to draw on the surface of an object. By creating a pattern that describes a new surface, such as that in Figure 10.13, a distinct and separate surface can be made.

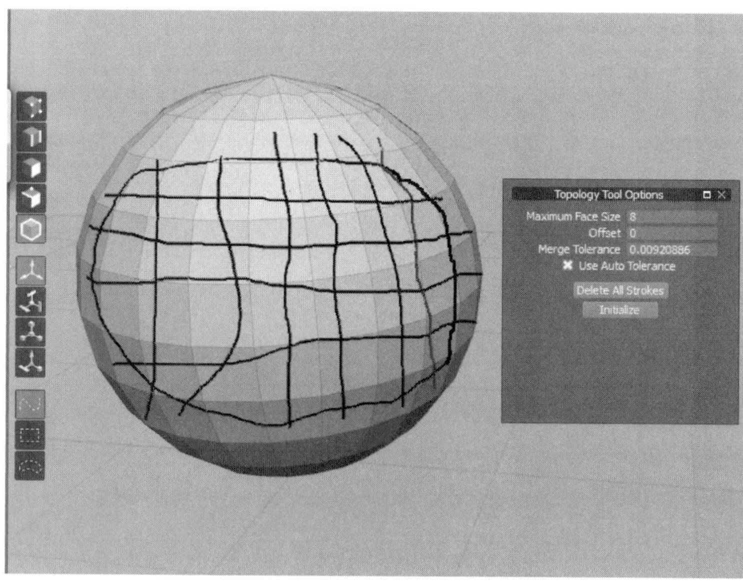

FIGURE 10.13 Guide curves drawn on the surface of the sphere can be used to create a new surface.

The strokes can be saved with the model in Silo's proprietary format. They can easily be undone one by one, in the order that they were painted. This is similar to drawing a curve on a surface in Maya. Once you have drawn your guide boundaries, simply press the Enter key. Figure 10.14 shows the newly created surface subdivided and offset from the surface in which it was created.

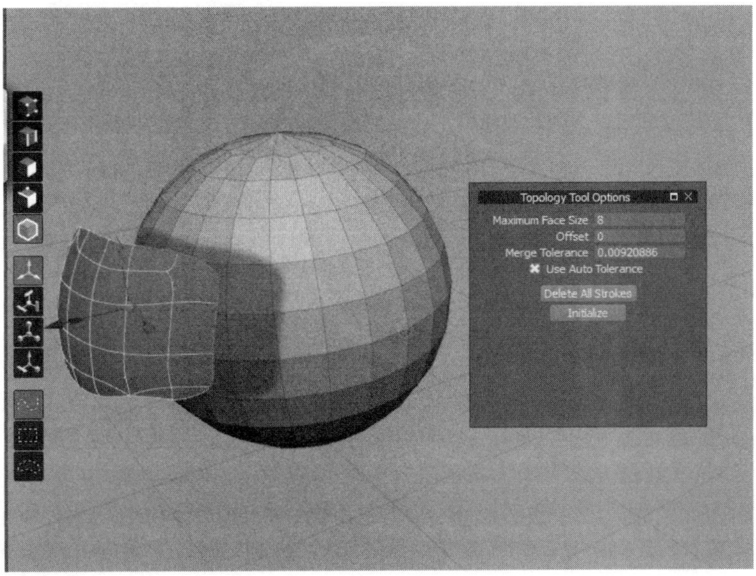

FIGURE 10.14 A new subdivided surface is determined by lines drawn on the surface of the sphere.

This tool is handy for making clothing on a character and cleaning up the topology of a model. A neat feature is the ability to draw the guide curves over several surfaces. This could be used to create a skin across multiple surfaces, such as the membrane between the arm and torso of a bat, form draping such as a tarp, or a cool shrink-wrap effect. Figure 10.15, Figure 10.16, and Figure 10.17 show three stages of creating a tarp-like covering over a sphere and a cube.

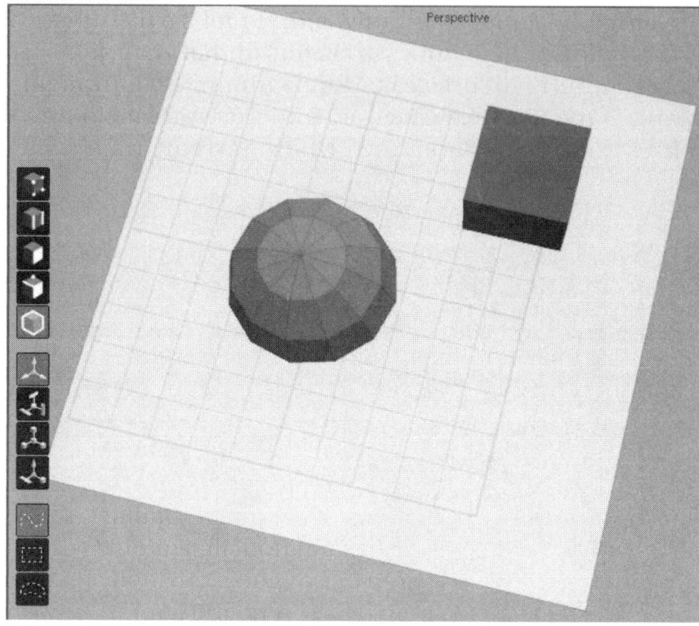

FIGURE 10.15 A sphere, cube, and plane object can be used to create a new surface.

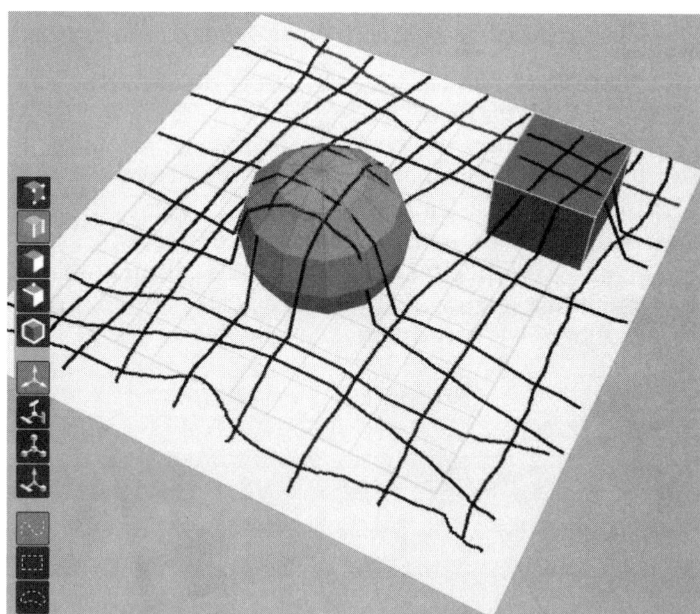

FIGURE 10.16 The Topology tool can be used to create a drape or tarp over multiple objects. Lines drawn across the separate objects can be used to generate a new surface.

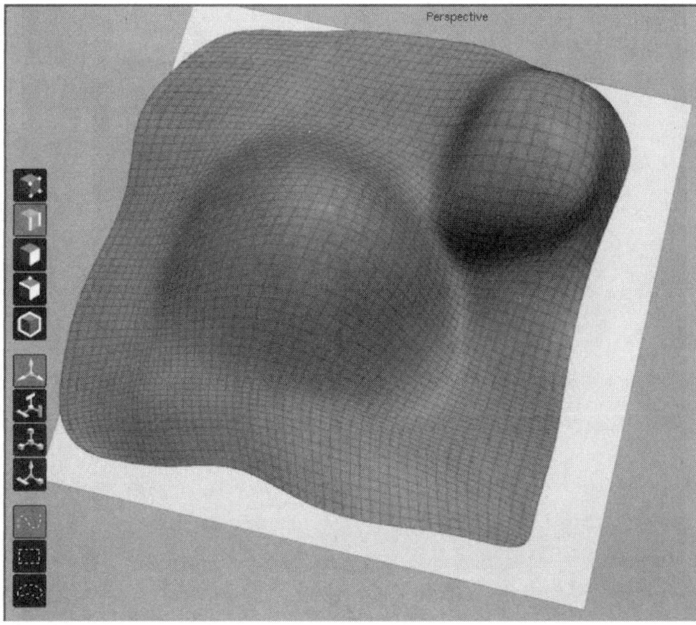

FIGURE 10.17 A new surface is generated and conforms to the lines drawn by the Topology tool across the sphere, cube, and plane surfaces.

Silo 2.0 has many great features that help the user build a model from scratch to a finely detailed and complete model. It's a very popular tool with the capability to sculpt geometry with a brush. This is similar to the same function in modo, Mudbox, ZBrush, and even Maya. The surface of an object can be molded and sculpted using a standard or custom brush. While Silo 2.0 does not contain the power of ZBrush, it does afford you a nice set of tools for doing real-time brush sculpting. The Brush Editor, shown in Figure 10.18, shares many characteristics with the Maya paint standard. Custom-created grayscale maps created in any paint program such as Photoshop can be used as brushes.

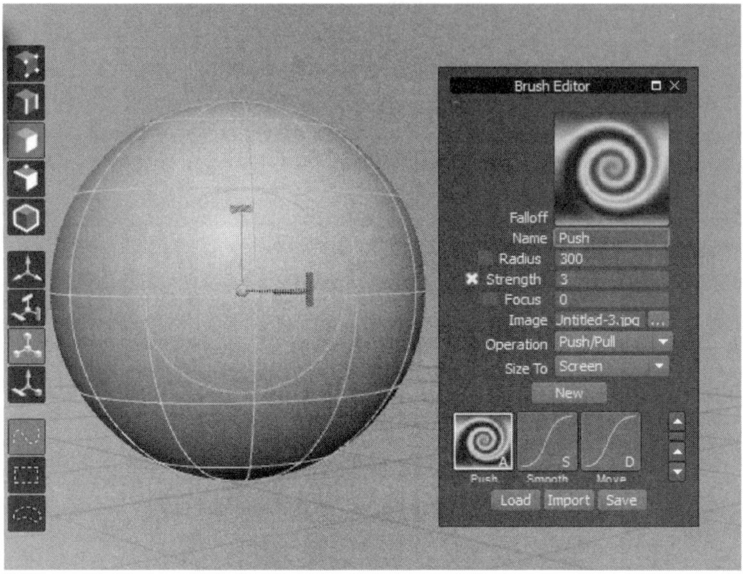

FIGURE 10.18 Silo 2.0's Brush Editor is very similar to that in Maya.

It is easy to convert the freshly-sculpted model to polygons with UVs for import into Maya via OBJ or export the displacement map. Figure 10.19 shows the subdivided sphere molded using a 512 × 512 grayscale image created in Photoshop.

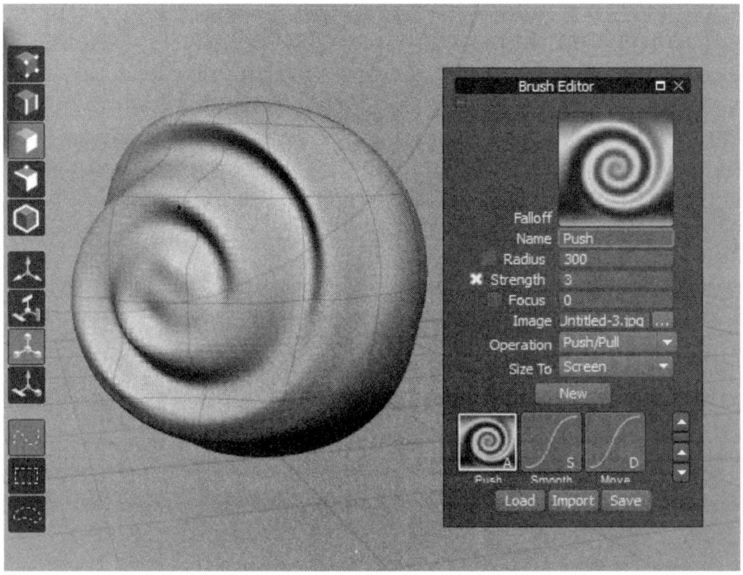

FIGURE 10.19 A custom Photoshop brush is used to fashion the sphere into a new form.

It's easy to see why Silo 2.0 is becoming a tool of choice for many Maya users. Its broad range of subdivision modeling tools is exemplary, and it has an easy learning curve. If you are accustomed to using a variety of tools to complete a project, then, for the price, Silo 2.0 really can't be beat. It could easily become a very welcome modeling tool in your Maya arsenal.

PIXOLOGIC'S ZBRUSH 3.1

We have briefly mentioned ZBrush 3.1 in this chapter, but it deserves its own section here. ZBrush from Pixologic is one of those rare programs that is so creative and useful it's a wonder how you did without it. Quick organic models can be created with little effort. Figure 10.20 shows a scary little worm creature that you would be hard pressed to create by other means.

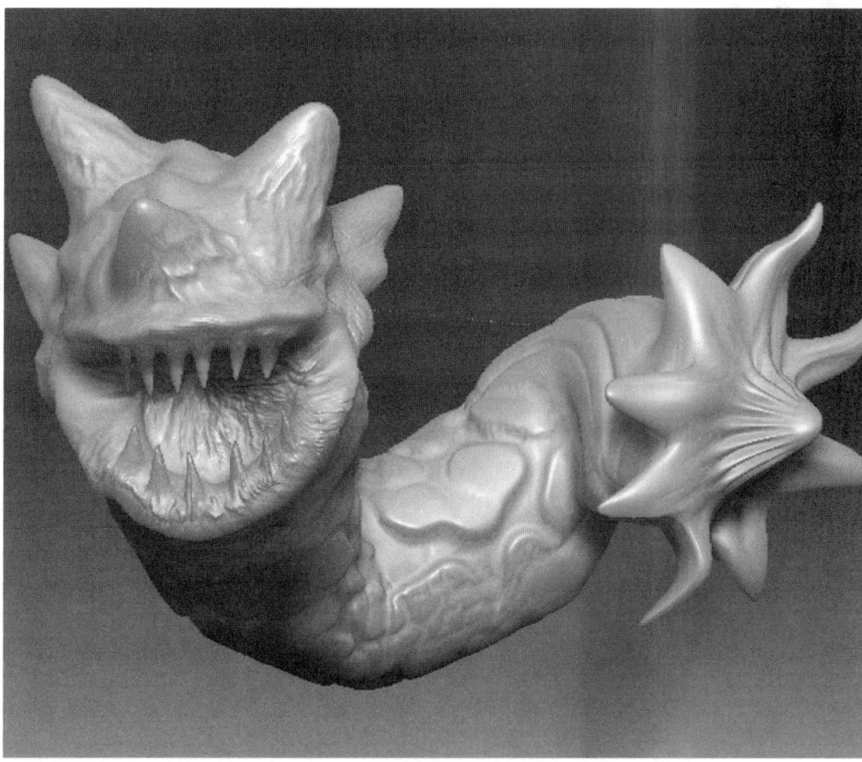

FIGURE 10.20 ZBrush 3.1 makes it easy to create a creature such as this in mere minutes.

ZBrush enables you to sculpt geometry in a very intuitive way. Molding a model into shape is much like real-world sculpting. It is a very hands-on approach that is easy to learn. Many noncomputer artists have taken to ZBrush because it does not let its technology get in the way of the artist's imagination and talent. Pixar hired many traditional animators who truly understood animation at its most basic level. The technology was removed from the rigs, enabling the animators, who understood anticipation, exaggeration, timing, and secondary animation in 2D cel animation, to translate those features to the 3D animation world. ZBrush invites an untapped but technically challenged class of talented artists to create in a whole new way.

ZBrush is much more than just a modeling program. In its meager beginnings, it was a 2.5D paint system relying on z-depth information to generate amazing, lushly textured 2D images. It has come full circle since then and has been developed to take advantage of the fully realized 3D world. ZBrush is a 3D paint and texturing system as well. Models built in ZBrush can be painted and textured in the application, producing unprecedented finished models. On its face, ZBrush is easy to use, but that ease belies very advanced technology. The deeper functions of ZBrush do make the learning curve a bit steeper, but it is well worth the effort. ZBrush is not a toy; it employs professional tools in a sophisticated application for visual effects and gaming. ZBrush's unique approach to modeling can create high-resolution models approaching a billion polygons. Highly-detailed models can be achieved, as shown in Figure 10.21.

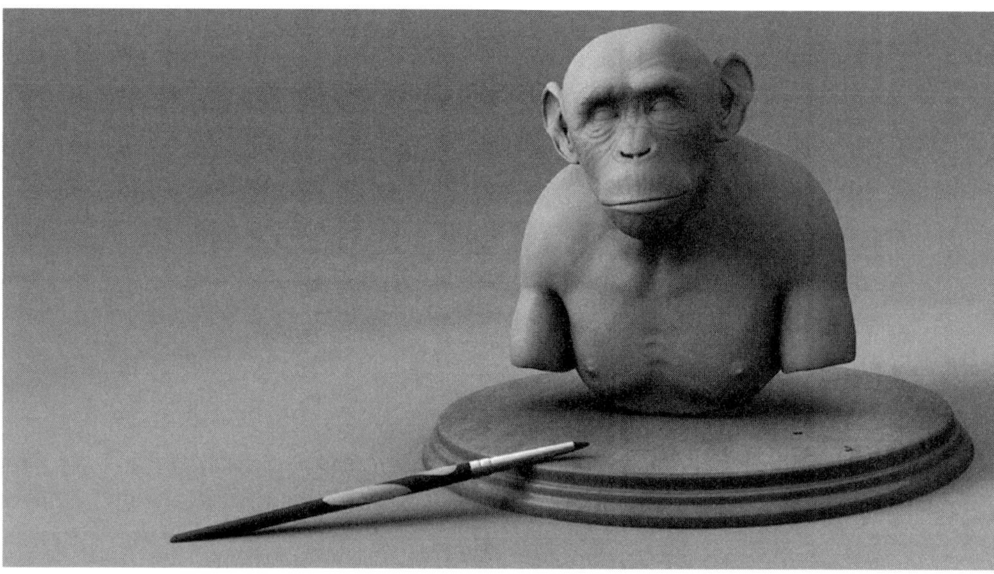

FIGURE 10.21 This bust of a chimp was created with ZBrush by Ty Shelton.
Image courtesy of www.tyshelton.com

ZBrush's features include the following:

- **HD Geometry:** ZBrush gets the most out of your computer's memory. It would have been nearly impossible to produce these kinds of models without it. HD geometry allows you to divide a model into a billion polygons so the system can evaluate only the polygons visible on-screen. This allows you to zoom in to a model, producing very fine details.
- **Matcap:** This feature lets you borrow color, lighting, and texture from another source, such as a photograph, and apply it to your 3D model. This capability lends itself to creating beautiful and realistic images. It is like a hyperactive version of the Clone Stamp Tool in Photoshop. Artists are taking ZBrush to new heights in digital painting and illustration.
- **Transpose:** ZBrush has new tools for posing a model. No sophisticated rigging is required, and it is no more difficult than posing an armature.
- **Speed:** All of this power and sophistication works without delay or lag time. A modest computer system can take advantage of ZBrush's full feature set. ZBrush can take full advantage of the additional functions of a pressure-sensitive pen and tablet.
- **ZSpheres:** This technology allows you to generate new geometry by adding and arranging spheres. This may remind you of meatballs, but is an order of magnitude more sophisticated and useable. The resulting mesh can be toggled, and adjustments, additions, and subtractions to these ZSpheres can build the base geometry for a more complex model. It is very efficient and easy to use.
- **Brushes:** ZBrush has a wide array of useful brushes. New ones can be created through a paint program such as Photoshop by creating alphas. Gravity can be applied to models via brushes simulating wind, gravity, and other forces.
- **Mesh extraction:** Existing geometry can be used to further detail your model. Multiple button models can be applied to a lapel or bullets added to a belt with ease.
- **Local subdivision:** Geometry can be subdivided where needed and doesn't have to be applied to the entire model. This allows you to add fine detail where necessary without making the whole model heavy.

ZBrush is not an animation program, and while it renders quite nicely, the bulk of your work may eventually head to another application, such as Maya. The workflow can be tricky. While we won't go into great detail here, we can examine on the surface how to get a detailed model into Maya. Complex images can be very polygon heavy, which can make it extremely impractical in Maya. Figure 10.22 shows a fairly complex model buckling under the weight of too many polygons. The split screen shows a model created in ZBrush and exported as a polygon mesh. The mesh for all its heavy polygon distribution still does not have enough polygons to correctly represent the surface modeled in ZBrush. The polygon mesh should be even tighter than represented here. For the purposes of this image, the polygons were reduced to be visible.

FIGURE 10.22 This split screen shows a 3D model in both wireframe and flat-shaded mode. The heavy distribution of polygons is still not enough to create the complicated surface that is required.

Creating a highly detailed but useable model in Maya requires displacement maps. A plugin for ZBrush that is available in the V3.1 update helps in the creation of displacement maps. The simplified process of creating a displacement map in ZBrush and utilizing it in Maya follows and is intended to show a simplified version of the workflow steps necessary in concept only. To take advantage of displacements in Maya, a more detailed investigation of the process can be found at the book's Web site at www.bigheadedkitty.com/zbrush.

To create a detailed displacement map from ZBrush, we must have a model. Figure 10.23 shows a smiling goblin head created in ZBrush. This model is the lower-count model we will use in Maya. The displacement map will have a profound effect on this low-count poly mesh. The detail will be evident without the burdensome heavy polygon count that would be necessary to reproduce a detailed model if a displacement map were not used.

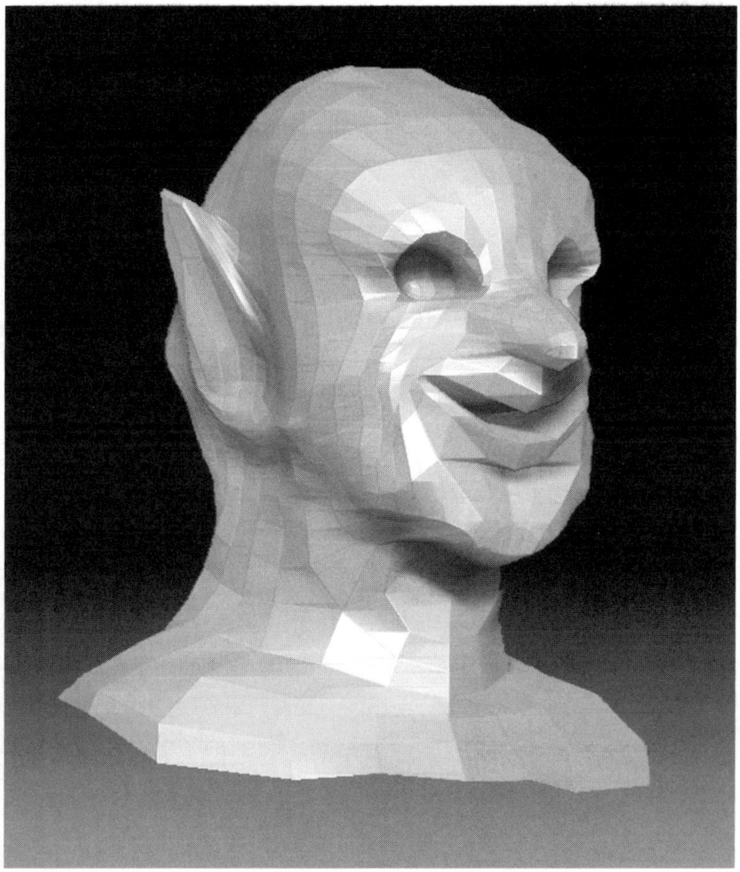

FIGURE 10.23 This reasonable low-poly-count model created and shown here in ZBrush will be the base model to displace inside of Maya.

The low-poly-count model is subdivided several times in ZBrush. This produces a mesh that is far more conducive to detail. ZBrush uses techniques for handling heavy poly meshes with ease. These meshes would otherwise be detrimental to a computer system's resources. The subdivided goblin model is shown in Figure 10.24.

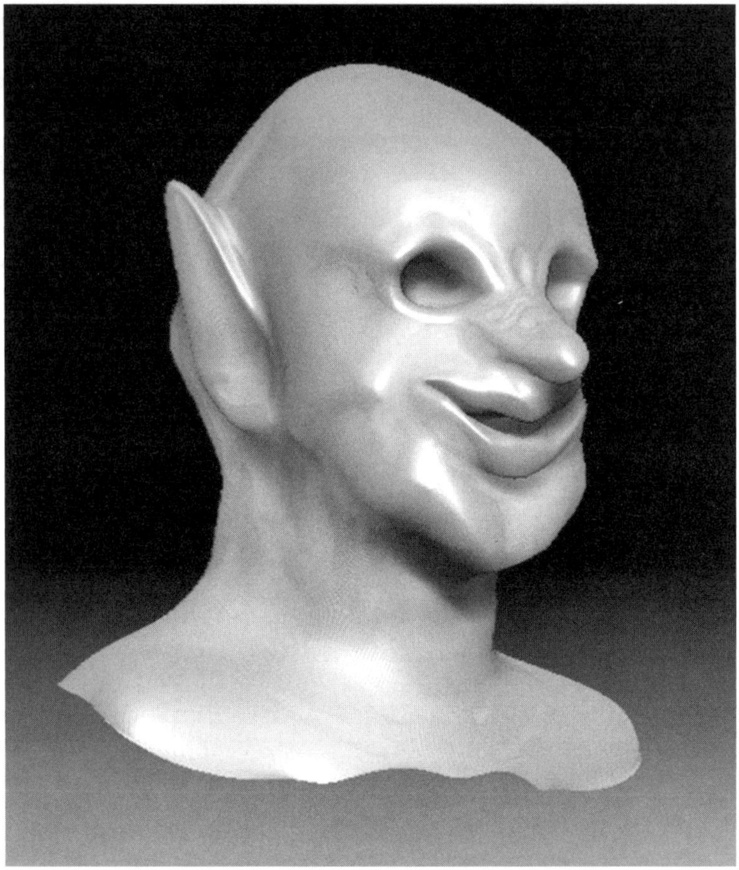

FIGURE 10.24 The low-count-poly model has been subdivided several levels to give it enough resolution to add fine detail.

The model now detailed in ZBrush has much finer 3D detail, as shown in Figure 10.25. This model could be exported as a 3D model as is. The resulting mesh, previously shown in Figure 10.22, would be cumbersome.

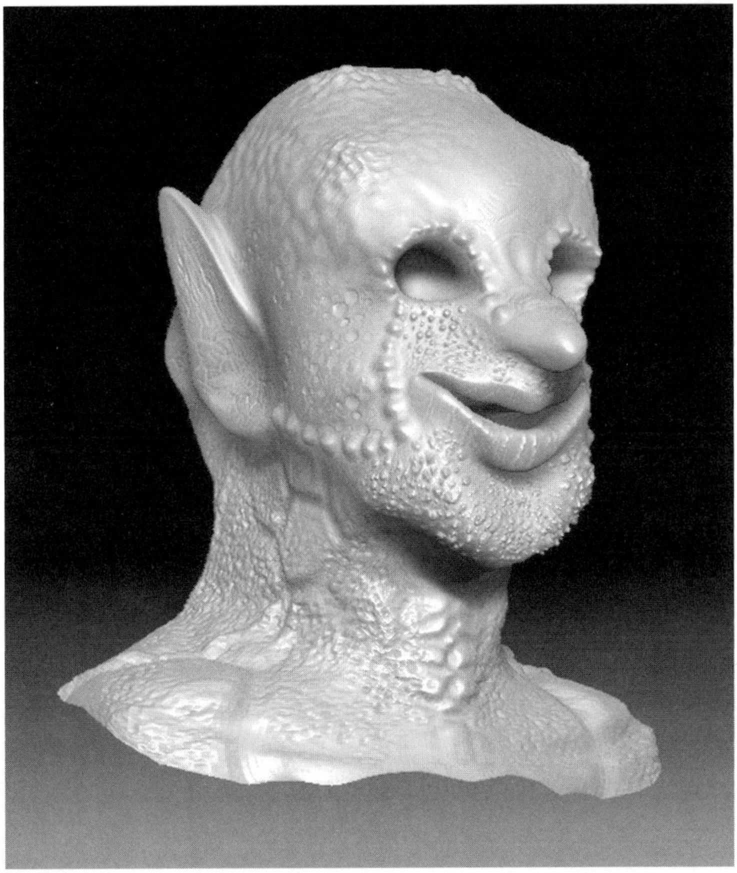

FIGURE 10.25 The subdivided mesh has been detailed in ZBrush and internally has created substantially more polygons for this model.

The model can now be used to generate a displacement map or maps. This is done through a plugin. The interfaces for the Displacement Exporter 3 are shown in Figure 10.26 and Figure 10.27. Note that there is no standardization for displacement maps, and each 3D application and renderer handles this in a different manner. To account for these idiosyncrasies and to accommodate the widest array of external programs, a code is entered into the plugin's interface. This code tells the Displacement Exporter 3 specifics of the displacement map that are required for the package for which you are creating the map.

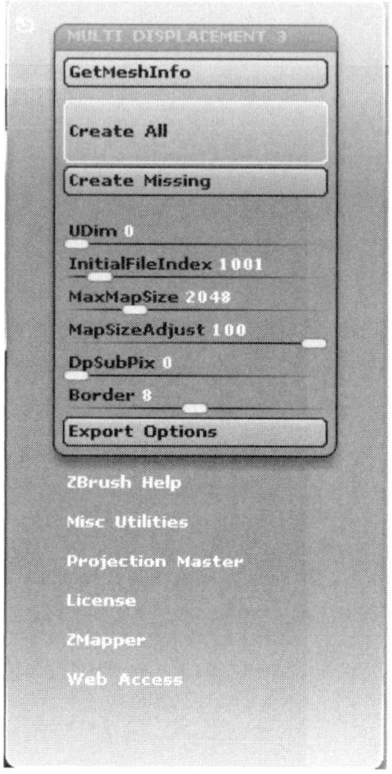

FIGURE 10.26 Part of the Displacement Exporter 3 plugin allows you to import more generic parameters of the displacement map you want to export.

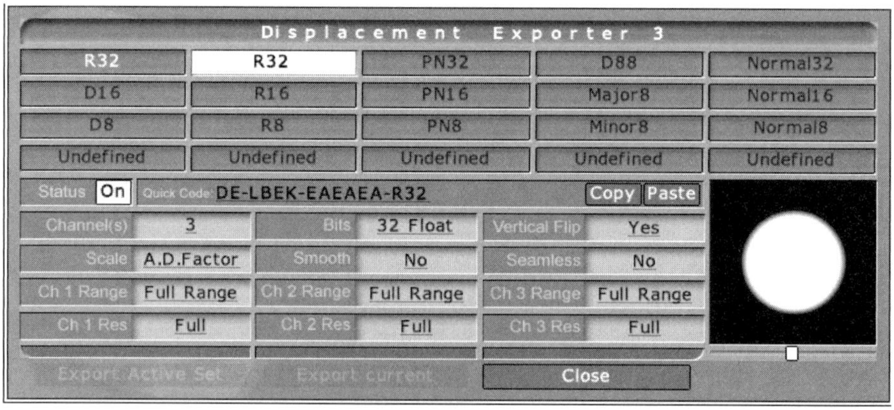

FIGURE 10.27 More specific information is set in this interface for the package for which you are creating the displacement map. The codes to generate a displacement map for Maya will be different from those of a displacement map for CINEMA 4D. More detailed information can be found at www.zbrushcentral.com.

The resultant displacement map will resemble Figure 10.28. Displacement maps tend to be very washed out, but the grayscale information within is key to the proper displacement of your object. Each of the square patches on the displacement map corresponds to the displacement on that particular portion of your model.

FIGURE 10.28 The displacement map generated from the model with the ZBrush Displacement Exporter 3 plugin is ready for import into Maya.

The low-poly-count version of the model has now been exported from ZBrush as an OBJ. The model can now be loaded into Maya and have the displacement map applied to gain the detail of the detailed version of the model created in ZBrush. Figure 10.29 shows the low-resolution version of the model now imported into the Maya interface.

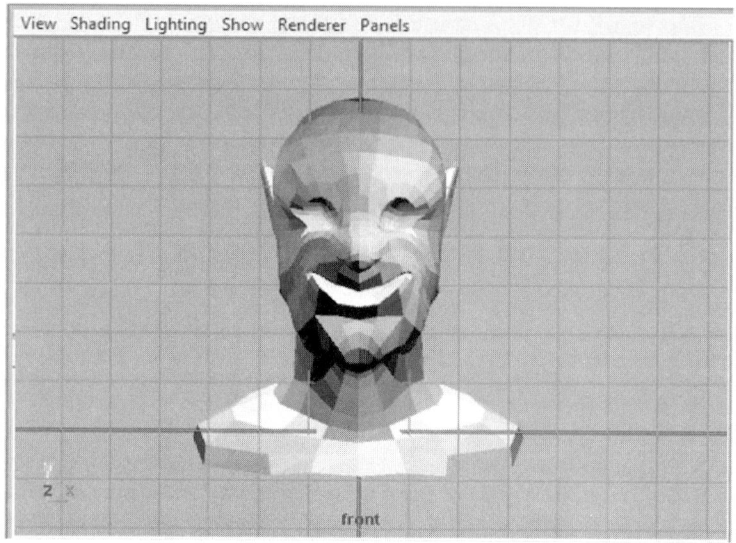

FIGURE 10.29 The low-poly-count version of the model that was exported as an OBJ from ZBrush is imported into Maya for displacement.

Displacements are best suited for renderers that utilize micro-poly displacement. This technique renders additional polygons as needed. Without micro-poly displacement, the low-poly base mesh would suffer from the detail generated by the displacement map, or the mesh would have to be subdivided further to account for the detail. In Maya, the mental ray renderer optimizes displacement efficiently by using micro-poly displacement to calculate the additional micro polygons. Figure 10.30 shows the Maya image of the low-poly-based mesh rendered with the ZBrush displacement map and rendered in mental ray.

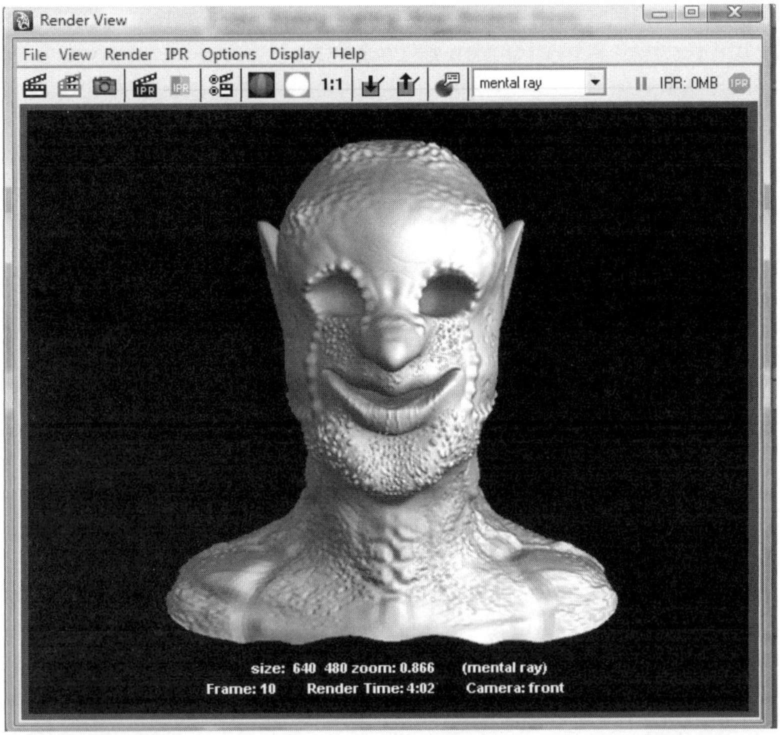

FIGURE 10.30 The base mesh rendered in Maya with the mental ray renderer utilizes micro-poly displacement to give great detail to the low-poly-count base mesh.

Pixologic has a thriving support system with thousands of very talented users. New macros and other goodies are always becoming available for use in your ZBrush work. As software packages go, Pixologic has done a very good job of fostering a creative and helpful environment for its users. You can check out this community at www.zbrushcentral.com. ZBrush is very open, so many interesting and sophisticated plugins have been developed free of charge.

Okino Computer Graphics' PolyTrans

Earlier in this chapter, we discussed the FBX file format and its growing acceptance in the 3D application community. It's still is a long way from universal harmony with all 3D programs. PolyTrans, from Okino Computer Graphics, is a 3D data translator and conversion program that hopes to quell the disparity among 3D application scene information. PolyTrans has been around for a long time and has built a reputation as a leader in the field. PolyTrans shares its marketplace between the world of CAD (computer-aided design) and DCC (animation and digital content creation). Okino specializes in data conversion pipelines encompassing most of the major animation packages, as well as many you have probably never heard of before. The list of data types that it converts is impressive. Whether you're converting scene files between Maya and 3D Studio Max, or from DirectX to DFX, PolyTrans does the job. PolyTrans converts data types such as materials, hierarchy, UV sets, lighting, cameras, NURBS, skeletons, skinning, and animation to alternate formats. It also converts 2D image data. Some data types can't translate from one format to the next, whether directly or indirectly. This can usually be attributed to a data type not being native to both packages. For instance, you can't translate NURBS to a package that doesn't support NURBS. You can find a definitive list of file formats and data types at http://www.okino.com/conv/filefrmt.htm?0.

Okino's user list is even more impressive than its translation abilities. Companies from Pixel Liberation Front to Pixar, and from ILM to Weta Digital, all use translation software from Okino in their pipelines. This Web site shows a notable yet incomplete list of clients: http://www.okino.com/conv/users.htm?0#brochure. As Maya users, it pays to look into PolyTrans. It could very well save you time, money, and aggravation. It could easily become one of those programs you don't know how you did without. In addition to the PolyTrans stand-alone program, certain 3D applications are supported with PolyTrans plugins. Maya and 3D Studio Max each have special PolyTrans plugins that are integrated into their respective interfaces. Maya and Studio Max scenes can't be translated in the stand-alone version of PolyTrans. Almost every element of a Maya scene can be translated to a host of other 3D platforms. An amazing feat is the ability to convert Studio Max files to other formats. Converting data from 3D Studio Max has always been a difficult proposition, in part because 3D Studio Max has always been so proprietary. The .3ds format is a 3d Studio file scene format. 3D Studio Max is the little brother to 3D Studio and became its successor. The two programs are often confused with each other, so the .3ds and .max formats are confused with each other as well. The .max format of 3D Studio Max is proprietary and quite dissimilar to the .3ds format of the old 3D Studio. Many programs read and write .3ds files, as it became an industry standard. This isn't so for .max files.

What does this mean for Maya users? In short, there are ever growing contingents of Max users out there. 3D Max is a terrific program. There is a reason they are both under the Autodesk banner today. Max users can become and are a viable part of a Maya production pipeline.

The "mirror twin," as it is called, is the PolyTrans workflow that translates data bidirectionally from Maya and 3D Max and vice versa. Mirror twin is the name given to this specific process by Okino. This is quite an accomplishment. Conversion between the two requires the PolyTrans for Maya and the PolyTrans for 3D Studio Max plugins. Both Maya and 3D Studio Max are required as well, as these plugins run as part of their respective host's applications. The scene shown in Figure 10.31 was constructed in Maya. A female form under a waterfall displaces the water. The body was exported to Next Limit's RealFlow, where the fluid dynamics of the waterfall and body were calculated into a waterfall mesh. The resulting RealFlow mesh data was imported back into Maya.

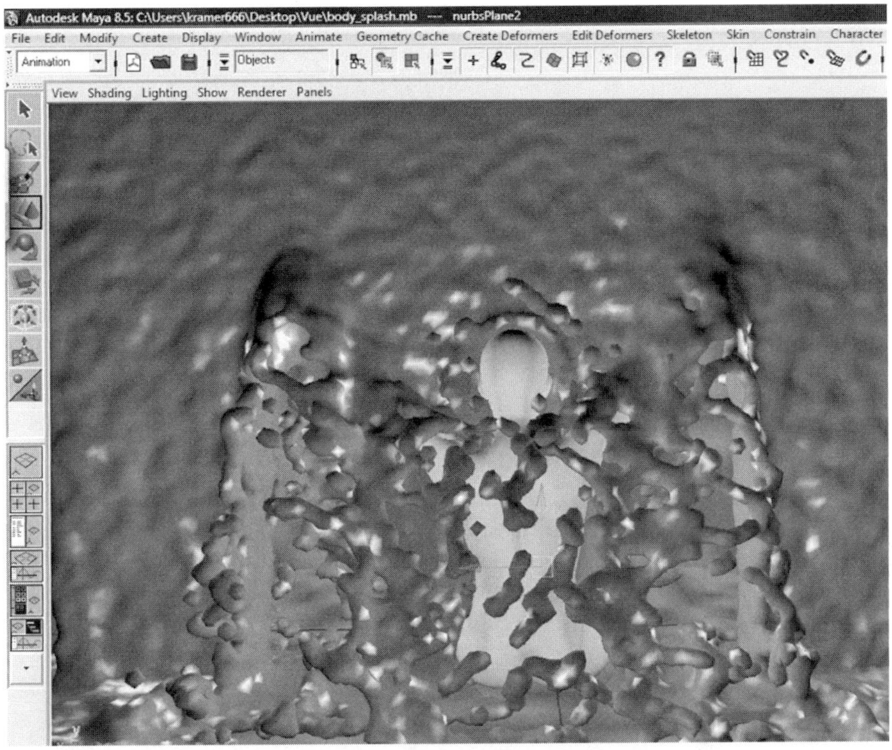

FIGURE 10.31 RealFlow was used to generate a dynamic mesh fluid simulation between a female form and a waterfall. It was then imported back into Maya.

Conversion between Maya and 3D Studio Max is done via a common and proprietary Okino format called a .bdf (bidirectional format) file. The Maya scene file is exported from the PolyTrans for Maya plugin. It is exported as Okino .bdf format. Figure 10.32 shows a close-up of the PolyTrans for Maya plugin interface within Maya. At the top of the list is the Okino .bdf file format. Figure 10.33 shows the plugin interface and the scene file to be converted.

FIGURE 10.32 A close-up view of the PolyTrans for Maya plugin. The plugin is a Maya integrated version of the stand-alone PolyTrans application.

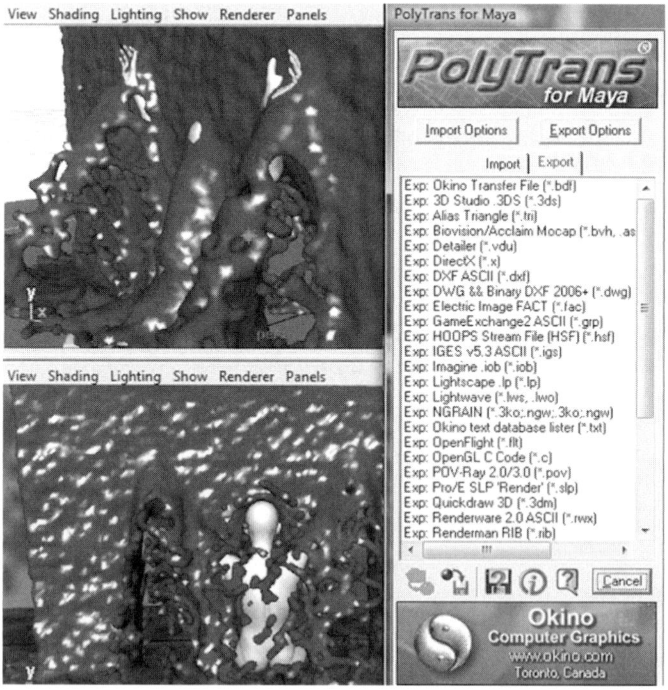

FIGURE 10.33 Multiple perspectives of the waterfall scene within Maya and the PolyTrans for Maya plugin in action.

Once the Maya scene has been exported as a PolyTrans .bdf format, it can be imported into 3D Studio Max using the PolyTrans for 3ds Max plugin. A close-up of this plugin's interface is shown in Figure 10.34, and Figure 10.35 shows the Maya scene residing quite comfortably inside 3D Studio Max V9. Figure 10.36 shows the converted scene file in the 3D Studio Max interface, just as it was in Maya, as previously shown in Figure 10.31.

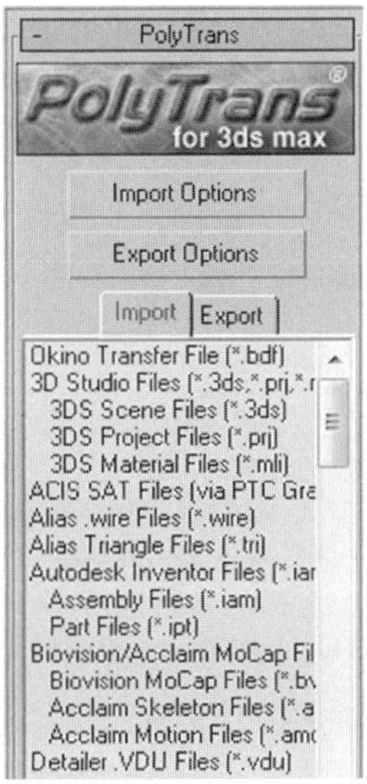

FIGURE 10.34 A close-up view of the PolyTrans for 3ds Max plugin. Note the Okino PolyTrans .bdf format at the top of the format list.

FIGURE 10.35 The Maya scene as it now appears in the interface of 3D Studio Max V9 after it was imported via the Okino PolyTrans .bdf file format exchange exported from Maya via the PolyTrans for Maya plugin.

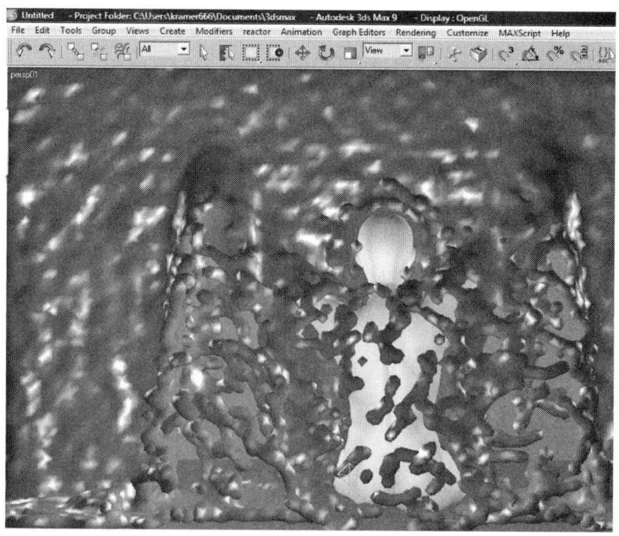

FIGURE 10.36 The Maya scene converted through PolyTrans for Maya as a .bdf file is imported into 3D Studio Max V9 with the PolyTrans for 3ds Max plugin.

The scenes look identical. The render of this scene file is now successfully rendered in 3ds Max's mental ray renderer and is shown in Figure10.37. After some minor tweaking, it is virtually identical to its counterpart rendering in Maya's mental ray.

FIGURE 10.37 The scene transferred from Maya to 3ds Max and rendered in mental ray.

The capability to exchange data between packages makes the workflow of a project flexible, diversified, and more viable. It opens up a greater world of possibilities in creativity, as well as the practicality of finding enough qualified people for the task at hand. It is comforting to know that parsing work among software applications such as Maya and 3D Studio Max is now a reliable and consistent task, thanks to PolyTrans.

We have limited this short chapter to an inspirational conversion between Maya and 3ds Max. PolyTrans is capable of the file conversions of many formats. This brings us near the closing of our book with a look at one last stand-alone application, utilizing it for something other than the functions for which it is widely known.

E-ON SOFTWARE'S VUE 6 XSTREAM

We want to quickly mention Vue 6 xStream from e-on software. For photo-realistic environments with natural terrain and lush vegetation, there is no program better than e-on software's Vue line. Figure 10.38 shows a realistic beach scene created in Vue.

FIGURE 10.38 A beach scene rendered in Vue 6 exploits the software's environment creation tools.
"Seychelles" by Raffy Raffy courtesy of e-on software

Vue, which is currently at version 6, offers a series of products with increasing degrees of complexity, sophistication, and pricing. They range from the quick and easy, click and render, Vue 6 Easel to sophisticated tools for world building in Vue 6 xStream, complete with dynamic winds, a powerful renderer, and integration with your favorite package. Vue 6 xStream is the top of e-on's product line. It can be integrated into your production pipeline alongside 3ds Max, LightWave, CINEMA 4D, Softimage XSI, and Maya. The integration into Maya comes in the form of a plugin. It allows you to render scenes in Maya or mental ray for Maya renderer. It is a viable solution for the creation of amazing scenery directly in your Maya work. The imagery produced with Vue is very realistic. Industrial Light and Magic has incorporated Vue into their film work. If you are not familiar with e-on and their Vue products, you can check out their demo reel at www.e-onsoftware.com/products/vue/vue_6_xstream/.

Here is a short list of the features that make Vue 6 an impressive software package for generating very natural real-world scenery.

- **EcoSystem Painter:** This tool allows you to interactively paint ecosystems over single or multiple surfaces. Entire lush ecosystems complete with trees, smaller plants, and rocks can be painted with the mouse. The use of a pressure-sensitive tablet allows you to control parameters and features based on pressure. Single instances of objects, such as trees, can be dropped right on the terrain. E-on's proprietary technology called *SolidGrowth* can be used to create plant instances distinctive from their neighbors.
- **Material Editor:** A robust material editor allows you to create just about any look imaginable. Materials can range from as simple as texture maps to multi-layered shaders that respond to environmental changes such as altitude. Other features include animatable materials and micro-poly displacement.
- **Plant Editor:** This amazing editor allows you to change pre-existing plant models from a library or create new plants never seen before. Plants can be animated with wind interaction, and the individual plant parameters can be animated to create plant growth from seed to full-grown plant. Other parameters can be animated to create seasonal changes and decay. Plants can also be rendered as billboards or 2D placards on flat geometry.
- **Atmosphere Engine:** Atmospheres are a large part of an environment and require sophistication to pass as real. Atmospheres in Vue can be of a volumetric nature or spectral. Spectral atmospheres are very accurate and realistic simulation models that generate atmospheres based on real-world light. These models take into account weather conditions, dust, and other particulates in concert with direct and ambient light. The atmosphere engine also takes into account sun features and angle of view. E-on also makes a plugin that uses the atmosphere engine to generate environments in a variety of packages, including Maya. This plugin called *Ozone* works within Maya to generate volumetric, spectral, and environment mapping. Ozone also allows you to save presets and has a library of atmospheres to pool from. Figure 10.39 shows a spectral atmosphere rendered in Maya with the Ozone plugin.

FIGURE 10.39 A beautiful sky rendered in Maya with e-on software's Ozone 3 plugin.

While Vue 6 xStream allows you to integrate Vue into Maya and utilize it as the Maya native renderer, we have taken some scenes created in Maya into Vue 6 xStream itself. The renderer is highly regarded. It is often used to render nonenvironment scenes. With all the superior features of a world-class renderer such as GI, subsurface scattering, micro-poly displacement, and even post-render effects, it can easily stand on its own merits. While using PolyTrans, we took scene files created in Maya directly into Vue 6 xStream. Figure 10.40 shows a scene with dice interacting with splashes of water in the Maya interface. As with the woman and the waterfall scene, the interaction of the dice and water were done in Next Limit's RealFlow and then imported back into Maya. The scene was then converted to .3ds files using PolyTrans.

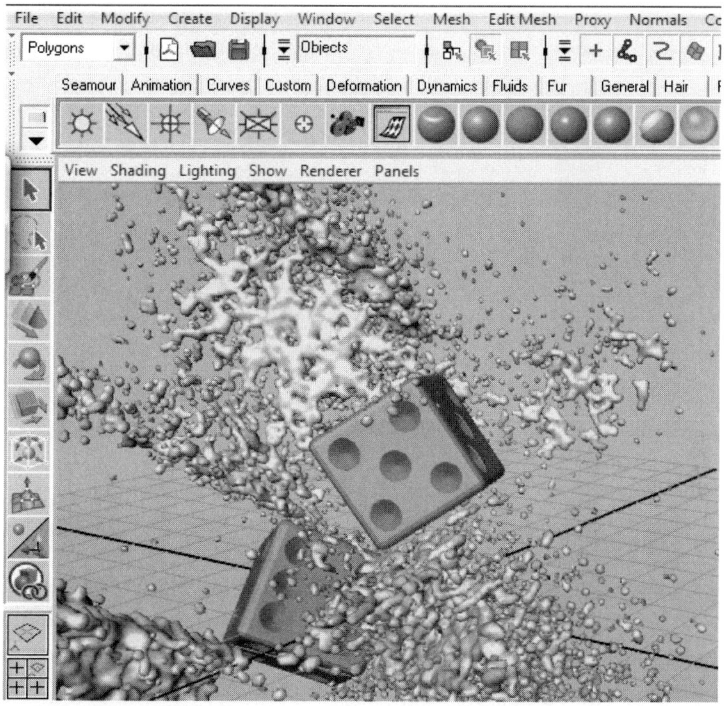

FIGURE 10.40 An image of dice modeled in Maya and incorporated into a fluid simulation in Next Limit's RealFlow was converted with PolyTrans into .3ds files.

The .3ds files were then imported into Vue 6 xStream. Figure 10.41 shows the Maya-created files inside the Vue interface.

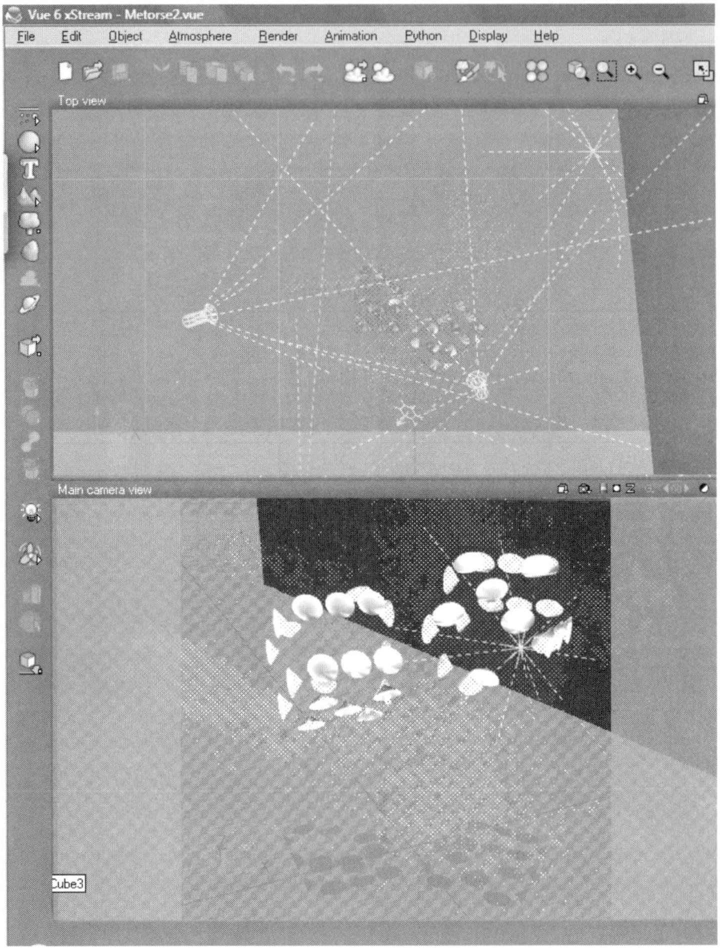

FIGURE 10.41 The Maya dice scene is now residing within the Vue 6 xStream interface, awaiting shaders and rendering.

Once the dice and water splashes from RealFlow were imported back into Maya, the idea was to take advantage of the terrific rendering qualities of the Vue renderer. Appropriate materials were created for the dice, ground and wall planes, and water splashes. The image was then rendered in Vue with caustics and global illumination. Figure 10.42 shows the Maya scene in Vue 6. The following render is shown in Figure 10.43.

FIGURE 10.42 The Maya-constructed dice scene imported into Vue 6 is shaded with the help of the Vue 6 Materials Editor. Thick, transparent, low-refraction red glass was used for the dice, and the splashes were given a water shader.

FIGURE 10.43 The final render of the Maya-originated dice scene in Vue 6 xStream's renderer. The global illumination and caustic reflections of the dice and water make for a realistic image.

The Vue 6 renderer creates very beautiful renders and stands up to the best renderers, including those covered in Chapter 4. Figure 10.44, Figure 10.45, and Figure 10.46 are all scene files that were built in Maya and exported to Vue 6. Further Vue 6 imagery can be seen at e-on's Web site at www.e-onsoftware.com/showcase/.

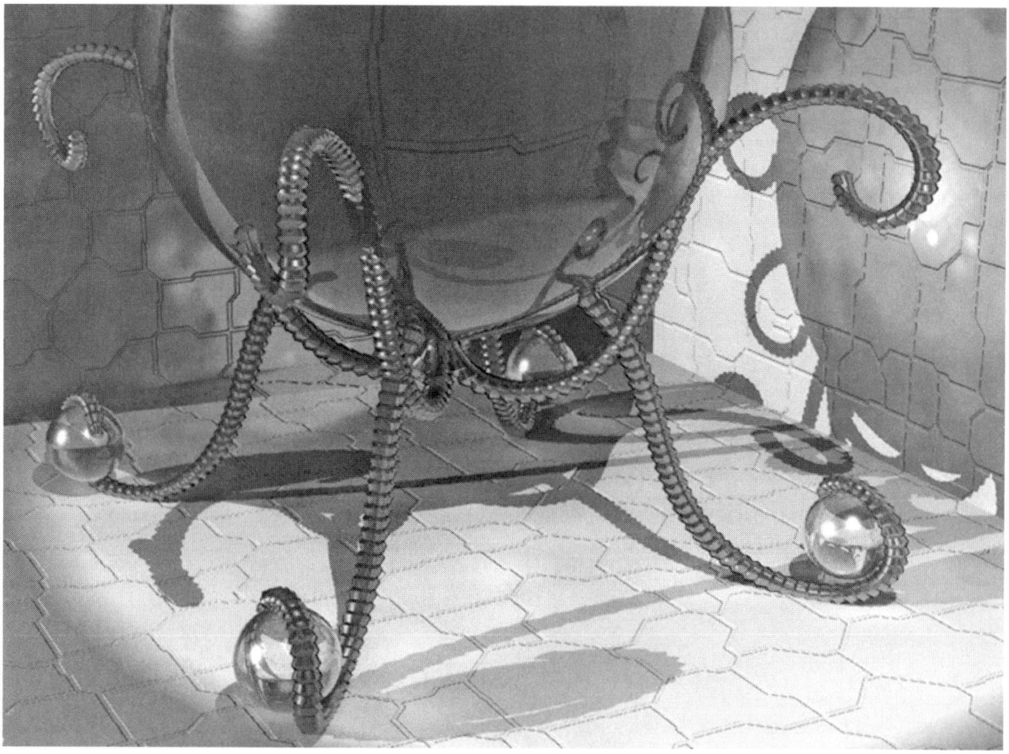

FIGURE 10.44 An image modeled in Maya and rendered in Vue 6 with caustics and global illumination.

FIGURE 10.45 This abstract form modeled in Maya and exported via PolyTrans as a .obj is shaded, lit, and rendered in Vue 6 with global illumination.

FIGURE 10.46 This familiar image modeled with Maya and RealFlow and previously shown rendered in mental ray with 3D Studio Max in Figure 10.37 is resuscitated for reshading and rendering in Vue 6.

This concludes our look at stand-alone programs. It also concludes this concise look at Maya plugin technology. This book is meant to introduce readers to software they might not have been aware of or known was possible. We looked at some high-end and sophisticated plugins to solve a variety of problems that face Maya artists and productions. While we did not delve into any one plugin too intensely, we hope you have gained a new appreciation for what is available and how it can be used.

The book has an accompanying Web site at www.bigheadedkitty.com. The Web site is a resource for questions, updates, and other general information about this book and Maya plugins in general. Please make sure to check there from time to time.

APPENDIX

A

CHAPTER AND RELATED LINKS

This appendix has links to the software covered in this book. Additionally, there are links to other software that may be of interest to Maya users. This appendix also includes some interesting CG-related links. This file may also be found on the book's Web site at http://www.bigheadedkitty.com/links/.

CHAPTER BREAKDOWN

Chapter 2 Cloth Simulation and Modeling

Syflex http://www.syflex.biz

Chapter 3 Hair and Fur

Shave and a Haircut http://www.joealter.com

Chapter 4 Color, Texture, Lighting, and Rendering

mental ray http://www.mentalimages.com/2_1_0_mentalray/index.html
Turtle 4.1 http://www.illuminatelabs.com/
finalRender Stage-2 http://www.cebas.com/products/products.php?UD=10-7888-35-788&PID=52
Maxwell Render http://www.maxwellrender.com
RenderMan for Maya https://renderman.pixar.com/products/tools/rfm_web infopage.html
Gelato 2.1 with Mango Plugin http://www.nvidia.com/object/gz_tutorials
GeoUV Texture Mapper http://www.geometricinformatics.com/products.php#geouv
MayaMan 2.0 http://www.animallogic.com/
3Delight http://www.3delight.com/en/index.php/home
Algorithmic Arts: Expressive Effects http://www.algorithmic.com/efx.html

Chapter 5 Water, Waves, and Other Matter

RealFlow http://www.realflow.com
Glu3D http://3daliens.com/glu3D/index.htm
One Picture Ltd: HyperMatter 2.0 Maya 5.x and 6.0 http://www.hypermatter.co.uk/products1.html
XFlow http://www.nextlimit.com/xflow/php
Digital Nature Tools http://www.digitalnaturetools.com/products/maya/dnt.htm

Chapter 6 Characters

Anzovin: The Setup Machine 2 http://www.anzovin.com/TSM2Maya/
Reiss Studio: BodyStudio v2.7 http://www.reiss-studio.com/trade/productview/55/3/
Advanced Skeleton Pro http://www.animationstudios.com.au/
cMuscleSystem http://www.cometdigital.com/
cSmartBlend http://www.cometdigital.com/
Muscle TK (Muscle Skinning System for Maya) http://www.cgtoolkit.net/muscletk.htm
Quidam 2 http://www.n-sided.com
Autodesk: MotionBuilder http://usa.autodesk.com/adsk/servlet/index?id=6837710&siteID=123112
endorphin http://www.naturalmotion.com/index.htm
Lifemode Interactive http://www.lifemi.com/products/
AI.implant http://www.ai-implant.com/
Creature Creator http://www.fxrsoft.com/default.asp?page=products/creaturecreator/mayadescription.html

Chapter 7 A Host of Helpers

Craft Director Tools http:/www.craftanimations.com

Chapter 8 Dynamic Destruction

Kiloton and Megaton http://www.blastcode.com

Chapter 9 Miscellaneous Tools

Wire http://cms.ticket01.com/
SmartDuplicate http://cms.ticket01.com/
Seamour http://cms.ticket01.com/
Xfrog http://www.xfrog.com
natFX http://www.bionatics.com/
Stroika http://www.kolektiv.com/products.php?PRODUCT_VIEW=Software
Animo http://www.animo.com/
Royal Render http://www.royalrender.de/
Muster 5.31 http://www.vvertex.com/
Qube! Render Farm Management http://www.pipelinefx.com/
MEL Studio Pro http://www.greymatter.com/p178146
2d3: boujou http://www.2d3.com/
famous3D http://famous3d.com/3d/products/index.html

Interactive Storyboard http://www.animationstudios.com.au/
digitalRaster: NEX v1.0 http://www.draster.com/
T-Splines http://www.tsplines.com/maya/
Right Hemisphere http://www.righthemisphere.com/
Zaxwerks http://www.zaxwerks.com/
Simplygon http://www.donyalabs.com/simplygon.asp

Chapter 10 Stand-Alone Applications

ZBrush http://www.pixologic.com
PolyTrans 4.3 for Maya http://www.okino.com/conv/pt4maya.htm
modo http://www.luxology.com
Vue 6 xStream http://www.e-onsoftware.com
Silo 2.0 http://nevercenter.com
Massive Prime http://www.massivesoftware.com/products/prime/
Massive Jet http://www.massivesoftware.com/products/jet/
Agent Libraries http://www.massivesoftware.com/products/agentlibrary/
Mudbox http://www.mudbox3d.com
PROVIDE3D http://www.provide3d.com/

Excellent Resources

Big Headed Kitty http://www.bigheadedkitty.com
Highend 3D http://www.highend3d.com
http://www.highend3d.com/maya/downloads/plugins/
Deathfall http://www.deathfall.com
CGSociety http://www.cgsociety.org/
3d Creative http://www.3dcreativemag.com
CGArena http://www.cgarena.com
ZBrushCentral http://www.zbrushcentral.com
CGIndia http://www.cgindia.org/
CG Focus http://www.cgfocus.com/

APPENDIX

B

PLUGINS COMPATIBILITY CHART

This appendix has version and compatibility information for the software covered in this book. This file may also be found on the book Web site at http://www.bigheadedkitty.com/versions/.

Chapter	**Plugin**	**Maya Compatibility**	**OS**
2	Syflex Cloth	Maya 8.0/8.5/2008	32/64 Bit Linux 32/64 Bit Windows OSX
3	Joe Alter Shave and a Haircut	Maya 8.0/8.5.1/2008	32/64 Bit Linux 32/64 Bit Windows OSX
4	Pixar RenderMan for Maya	Maya versions 7.0/ 8.5. Maya 8.0 is not supported. Intel Mac supported on Maya 8.5 and 2008	32 Bit Windows OSX
	Next Limit Maxwell Render	Maya 7.0/ 8.0/8.5/2008	32/64 Bit Linux 32/64 Bit Windows OSX
	Feversoft fryrender	Maya 8.0/8.5/2008	32/64 Bit Windows
	Animal Logic MayaMan	Maya 8.0/8.5/2008	32/64 Bit Linux 32/64 Bit Windows
	dna research 3Delight	Maya 8.0/8.5/2008	32/64 Bit Linux 32/64 Bit Windows OSX
5	Next Limit RealFlow	Maya 4.0 thru 2008	32/64 Bit Linux 32/64 Bit Windows OSX

CHAPTER	PLUGIN	MAYA COMPATIBILITY	OS
6	Anzovin Studio The Setup Machine 2	Maya 5.0/.6.0/6.5	32 Bit Windows
		Maya 7.0/8.0	32 Bit Windows OSX
		Maya 8.5/2005	32/64 Bit Windows
7	Craft Director Tools v. 8.1.7	Maya 7.0/ 8.0/8.5/2008	32 Bit Windows
		Maya 8.0/8.5/2008	64 Bit Windows
8	Blast Code Megaton and Kiloton	Maya 7.0/ 8.0/8.5/2008	32 Bit Windows
		Maya 8.0/8.5/2008	32 Bit Linux
		Maya 6.0/6.5/ 7.0/8.0/8.5, or 2008	OSX
9	ticket01 Wire	Maya 7.0/ 8.0/8.5/2008	32 Bit Windows
		Maya 8.0/8.5/2008	64 Bit Windows 32/64 Bit Linux
		Maya 8.5/2008	OSX
	ticket01 SmartDuplicate	Maya 7.0/ 8.0/8.5/2008	32 Bit Windows
		Maya 8.0/8.5/2008	64 Bit Windows 32/64 Bit Linux
		Maya 8.5/2008	OSX

Chapter	Plugin	Maya Compatibility	OS
9 (continued)	ticket01 Seamour	Maya 7.0/ 8.0/8.5	32 Bit Windows
		Maya 8.0/8.5	64 Bit Windows
		Maya 8.0/8.5	32/64 Bit Linux
		Maya 8.5	OSX
10	Luxology modo	Stand-Alone Program	32 Bit Windows OSX
	Nevercenter Silo	Stand-Alone Program	32 Bit Windows OSX
	Pixologic ZBrush	Stand-Alone Program	32 Bit Windows OSX
	Okino Computer Graphics PolyTrans for Maya	Maya 6.0/6.5/ 7.0/8.0/8.5, Plugin requires the most recent stand-alone PolyTrans or NuGraf base package.	32 Bit Windows
	E-on Software Vue 6 xStream	Stand-Alone Program	32/64 Bit Windows OSX

INDEX

D

E

F

G

H

I

T

U

License Agreement/Notice of Limited Warranty

By opening the sealed disc container in this book, you agree to the following terms and conditions. If, upon reading the following license agreement and notice of limited warranty, you cannot agree to the terms and conditions set forth, return the unused book with unopened disc to the place where you purchased it for a refund.

License:

The enclosed software is copyrighted by the copyright holder(s) indicated on the software disc. You are licensed to copy the software onto a single computer for use by a single user and to a backup disc. You may not reproduce, make copies, or distribute copies or rent or lease the software in whole or in part, except with written permission of the copyright holder(s). You may transfer the enclosed disc only together with this license, and only if you destroy all other copies of the software and the transferee agrees to the terms of the license. You may not decompile, reverse assemble, or reverse engineer the software.

Notice of Limited Warranty:

The enclosed disc is warranted by Course Technology to be free of physical defects in materials and workmanship for a period of sixty (60) days from end user's purchase of the book/disc combination. During the sixty-day term of the limited warranty, Course Technology will provide a replacement disc upon the return of a defective disc.

Limited Liability:

THE SOLE REMEDY FOR BREACH OF THIS LIMITED WARRANTY SHALL CONSIST ENTIRELY OF REPLACEMENT OF THE DEFECTIVE DISC. IN NO EVENT SHALL COURSE TECHNOLOGY OR THE AUTHOR BE LIABLE FOR ANY OTHER DAMAGES, INCLUDING LOSS OR CORRUPTION OF DATA, CHANGES IN THE FUNCTIONAL CHARACTERISTICS OF THE HARDWARE OR OPERATING SYSTEM, DELETERIOUS INTERACTION WITH OTHER SOFTWARE, OR ANY OTHER SPECIAL, INCIDENTAL, OR CONSEQUENTIAL DAMAGES THAT MAY ARISE, EVEN IF COURSE TECHNOLOGY AND/OR THE AUTHOR HAS PREVIOUSLY BEEN NOTIFIED THAT THE POSSIBILITY OF SUCH DAMAGES EXISTS.

Disclaimer of Warranties:

COURSE TECHNOLOGY AND THE AUTHOR SPECIFICALLY DISCLAIM ANY AND ALL OTHER WARRANTIES, EITHER EXPRESS OR IMPLIED, INCLUDING WARRANTIES OF MERCHANTABILITY, SUITABILITY TO A PARTICULAR TASK OR PURPOSE, OR FREEDOM FROM ERRORS. SOME STATES DO NOT ALLOW FOR EXCLUSION OF IMPLIED WARRANTIES OR LIMITATION OF INCIDENTAL OR CONSEQUENTIAL DAMAGES, SO THESE LIMITATIONS MIGHT NOT APPLY TO YOU.

Other:

This Agreement is governed by the laws of the State of Massachusetts without regard to choice of law principles. The United Convention of Contracts for the International Sale of Goods is specifically disclaimed. This Agreement constitutes the entire agreement between you and Course Technology regarding use of the software.